Essential Britten

John Bridcut is a documentary film-maker for British television. His enthusiasm for English music has been lifelong, and
his feature-length films, *Britten's Children* (2004), *The Passions
of Vaughan Williams* (2008) and *Elgar: The Man Behind the Mask*
(2010), have won awards. His most recent composer-portraits
have been *The Prince and the Composer* (2011), in which HRH
The Prince of Wales explored the life and music of Hubert
Parry, and *Delius: Composer, Lover, Enigma* (2012). Other film
subjects have included Prince Charles, Rudolf Nureyev, Roald
Dahl, Hillary Clinton, Mstislav Rostropovich and the Queen.
His book *Britten's Children* was published in 2006.

Essential Britten

A POCKET GUIDE FOR THE BRITTEN CENTENARY

John Bridcut

faber and faber

First published in 2010
by Faber and Faber Limited
The Bindery, 51 Hatton Garden
London EC1N 8HN
This edition first published in 2012

Typeset by Faber and Faber Limited
Printed in England by CPI Bookmarque, Croydon

On Receiving the First Aspen Award is published by Faber Music in
association with Faber and Faber
© Benjamin Britten, 1964
This edition © The Britten–Pears Foundation, 2012

A CIP record for this book
is available from the British Library

ISBN 978-0-571-29073-4

10 9 8 7 6 5 4 3 2

In memory of my beloved parents
Phoebe and Jack

Contents

Foreword

How reassuring and exciting it is when a compendium of fact, an assemblage of the details of a life and its works, can throw up a character, who seems to walk into the room fully-formed. No one can turn to John Bridcut's meticulous account of Benjamin Britten the musician – at first perhaps only in search of a mere date of composition or first performance – without being drawn on, and feeling that the man is there, finishing a string quartet in his head before starting to write it down, plunging into a cold bath before a morning's work, turning to the piano to produce 'the shimmer of sound like the shudder of electricity'. He is alive in these pages.

The man who was, in Leonard's Bernstein's words, 'at odds with the world', was simultaneously an adornment of his age whose reputation ebbed and flowed in the course of too short a life but who is now unchallenged in the pantheon of the great musicians of his century. At his centenary, in 2013, that achievement will be recognised and confirmed. Everything is here – the works, the tastes and opinions, the nerves and shyness and cold moments, the fast cars and the friendships, the loves. Bridcut has done a service by insisting that the facts – the first joy of a pocketbook – mustn't be left untouched by his own enthusiasm and deep feeling for the music, which gleams on every page. He is right to let that emotion lighten his task. I for one did want to know whether he thinks that *The Turn of the Screw* is a better opera than *Peter Grimes*, if only to disagree.

Anyone who has journeyed with Britten, or is starting out on that adventure, will want this book as a friendly guide along the way. Invaluable in its organisation of the story of an extraordinary life in music, it is also a reminder, laid out in all its simplicity, of how much is owed by all of us to Britten.

No one who turns these pages will leave without wanting to listen to something again, perhaps a piece that has been long-forgotten. Then you remember how, when he has you in his grip, he never lets go.

James Naughtie

August 2012

On Receiving the First Aspen Award

*Benjamin Britten defined the role of the composer in the eloquent accept-
ance speech he gave after receiving the Robert O. Anderson Aspen Award
in Colorado in August 1964. The creator of the* War Requiem *two years
earlier was chosen ahead of 100 artists, scholars, writers, poets, philosophers
and statesmen as 'the individual anywhere in the world judged to have made
the greatest contribution to the advancement of the humanities'. I remember
exploring this speech a few years later in a General Studies class at school,
and being struck by how unusual and stimulating it was. Britten's prize
amounted to more than £140,000 (tax-free) in today's money.*

I Ladies and Gentlemen, when last May your Chairman and your
President told me they wished to travel the 5,000 miles from Aspen to
Aldeburgh to have a talk with me, they hinted that it had something
to do with an Aspen Award for Services to the Humanities – an award
of very considerable importance and size. I imagined that they felt
I might advise them on a suitable recipient, and I began to consider
what I should say. Who would be suitable for such an honour? What
kind of person? Doctor? Priest? A social worker? A politician? Well,
. . . ! An Artist? Yes, possibly (that, I imagined, could be the reason
that Mr Anderson and Professor Eurich thought I might be the person to help them). So I ran through the names of the great figures
working in the Arts among us today. It was a fascinating problem;
rather like one's school-time game of ideal cricket elevens, or slightly
more recently, ideal casts for operas – but I certainly won't tell which
of our great poets, painters, or composers came to the top of my list.

Mr Anderson and Professor Eurich paid their visit to my home in
Aldeburgh. It was a charming and courteous visit, but it was also a
knock-out. It had not occurred to me, frankly, that it was I who was
to be the recipient of this magnificent award, and I was stunned. I am
afraid my friends must have felt I was a tongue-tied host. But I simply
could not imagine why *I* had been chosen for this very great honour.
I read again the simple and moving citation. The key-word seemed
to be 'humanities'. I went to the dictionary to look up its meaning; I
found *Humanity*: 'the quality of being human' (well, that applied to me
all right). But I found that the plural had a special meaning: 'Learning or literature concerned with human culture, as grammar, rhetoric,

poetry and especially the ancient Latin and Greek Classics'. (Here I really had no claims since I cannot properly spell even in my own language, and when I set Latin I have terrible trouble over the quantities – besides you can all hear how far removed I am from rhetoric.) *Humanitarian* was an entry close beside these, and I supposed I might have some claim here, but I was daunted by the definition: 'One who goes to excess in his human principles (in 1855 often contemptuous or hostile)'. I read on, quickly. *Humanist*: 'One versed in Humanities', and I was back where I started. But perhaps after all the clue was in the word 'human', and I began to feel that I might have a small claim.

II I certainly write music for human beings – directly and deliberately. I consider their voices, the range, the power, the subtlety and the colour potentialities of them. I consider the instruments they play – their most expressive and suitable individual sonorities, and where I may be said to have invented an instrument (such as the Slung Mugs of *Noye's Fludde*) I have borne in mind the pleasure the young performers will have in playing it. I also take note of the *human* circumstances of music, of its environment and conventions; for instance, I try to write dramatically effective music for the theatre – I certainly don't think opera is better for not being effective on the stage (some people think that effectiveness *must* be superficial). And then the best music to listen to in a great Gothic church is the polyphony which was written for it, and was calculated for its resonance: this was my approach in the *War Requiem* – I calculated it for a big, reverberant acoustic and that is where it sounds best. I believe, you see, in *occasional music*, although I admit there are some occasions which can intimidate one – I do not envy Purcell writing his *Ode to Celebrate King James's Return to London from Newmarket*. On the other hand almost every piece I have ever written has been composed with a certain occasion in mind, and usually for definite performers, and certainly always *human* ones.

III You may ask perhaps: how far can a composer go in thus considering the demands of people, of humanity? At many times in history the artist has made a conscious effort to speak with the voice of the people. Beethoven certainly tried, in works as different as the *Battle of Vittoria* and the Ninth Symphony, to utter the sentiments of a whole community. From the beginning of Christianity there have been musicians who have wanted and tried to be the servants of the Church, and to express the devotion and convictions of Christians, as such. Recently, we have had the example of Shostakovich, who set out in his 'Leningrad' Symphony to present a monument to his fellow citizens, an explicit expression for them of their own endurance and heroism. At a very different level, one finds composers such as Johann Strauss and George Gershwin aiming at providing people – the people – with the best dance music and songs which they were capable of making. And I can find nothing wrong with the objectives – declared or implicit – of these men; nothing wrong with offering to my fellow-men music which may inspire them or comfort them, which may touch them or entertain them, even educate them – directly and with intention. On the contrary, it is the composer's duty, as a member of society, to speak to or for his fellow human beings.

When I am asked to compose a work for an occasion, great or small, I want to know in some detail the conditions of the place where it will be performed, the size and acoustics, what instruments or singers will be available and suitable, the kind of people who will hear it, and what language they will understand – and even sometimes the age of the listeners and performers. For it is futile to offer children music by which they are bored, or which makes them feel inadequate or frustrated, which may set them against music for ever; and it is insulting to address anyone in a language which they do not understand. The text of my *War Requiem* was perfectly in place in Coventry Cathedral – the Owen poems in the vernacular, and the words of the Requiem Mass familiar to everyone – but it would have been pointless in Cairo or Peking.

During the act of composition one is continually referring back to the conditions of performance – as I have said, the acoustics and the forces available, the techniques of the instruments and the voices – such questions occupy one's attention continuously, and certainly affect the stuff of the music, and in my experience are not only a restriction, but a challenge, an inspiration. Music does not exist in a vacuum, it does not exist until it is performed, and performance imposes conditions. It is the easiest thing in the world to write a piece virtually or totally impossible to perform – but oddly enough that is not what I prefer to do; I prefer to study the conditions of performance and shape my music to them.

IV   Where does one stop, then, in answering people's demands? It seems that there is no clearly defined Halt sign on this road. The only brake which one can apply is that of one's own private and personal conscience; when that speaks clearly, one must halt; and it can speak for musical or non-musical reasons. In the last six months I have been several times asked to write a work as a memorial to the late President Kennedy. On each occasion I have refused – not because in any way I was out of sympathy with such an idea; on the contrary, I was

horrified and deeply moved by the tragic death of a very remarkable
man. But for me I do not feel the time is ripe; I cannot yet stand back
and see it clear. I should have to wait very much longer to do anything
like justice to this great theme. But had I in fact agreed to undertake a
limited commission, my artistic conscience would certainly have told
me in what direction I could go, and when I should have to stop.

There are many dangers which hedge round the unfortunate composer: pressure groups which demand true proletarian music, snobs
who demand the latest *avant-garde* tricks; critics who are already trying to document today for tomorrow, to be the first to find the correct
pigeon-hole definition. These people are dangerous – not because they
are necessarily of any importance in themselves, but because they may
make the composer, above all the young composer, self-conscious, and
instead of writing his own music, music which springs naturally from
his gift and personality, he may be frightened into writing pretentious
nonsense or deliberate obscurity. He may find himself writing more
and more for machines, in conditions dictated by machines, and not
by humanity: or of course he may end by creating grandiose clap-trap
when his real talent is for dance tunes or children's piano pieces. Finding one's place in society as a composer is not a straightforward job. It
is not helped by the attitude towards the composer in some societies.
My own, for instance, has for years treated the musician as a curiosity
to be barely tolerated. At a tennis party in my youth I was asked what
I was going to do when I grew up – what job I was aiming at. 'I am
going to be a composer', I said. 'Yes, but what else?' was the answer.
The average Briton thought, and still thinks, of the Arts as suspect and
expensive luxuries. The Manchester councillor who boasted he had
never been to a concert and didn't intend to go is no very rare bird
in England. By Act of Parliament, each local authority in England is
empowered to spend a sixpenny rate on the Arts. In fact it seems that
few of them spend more than one twentieth of this – a sign of no very
great enthusiasm! Until such a condition is changed, musicians will
continue to feel 'out of step' in our semi-Welfare State.

But if we in England have to face a considerable indifference, in
other countries conditions can have other, equally awkward effects.
In totalitarian regimes, we know that great official pressure is used to
bring the artist into line and make him conform to the State's ideol-
ogy. In the richer capitalist countries, money and snobbishness combine to demand the latest, newest manifestations, which I am told go
by the name in this country of 'Foundation Music'.

V   The *ideal* conditions for an artist or musician will never be found outside the *ideal* society, and when shall we see that? But I think I can tell you some of the things which any artist demands from any society. He demands that his art shall be accepted as an essential part of human activity, and human expression; and that he shall be accepted as a genuine practitioner of that art and consequently of value to the community; reasonably, he demands from society a secure living and a pension when he has worked long enough; this is a basis for society to offer a musician, a modest basis. In actual fact there are very few musicians in my country who will get a pension after forty years' work in an orchestra or in an opera house. This must be changed; we must at least be treated as civil servants. Once we have a material status, we can accept the responsibility of answering society's demands on us. And society should and will demand from us the utmost of our skill and gift in the full range of music-making. (Here we come back to 'occasional' music.) There should be special music made and played for all sorts of occasions: football matches, receptions, elections (why not?) and even presentations of awards! I would have been delighted to have been greeted with a special piece composed for today! It might have turned out to be another piece as good as the cantata Bach wrote for the Municipal Election at Mühlhausen, or the Galliard that Dowland wrote as a compliment to the Earl of Essex! Some of the greatest pieces of music in our possession were written for special occasions, grave or gay. But we shouldn't worry too much about the so-called 'permanent' value of our occasional music. A lot of it cannot make much sense after its first performance, and it is quite a good thing to please people, even if only for today. That is what we should aim at – pleasing people today as seriously as we can, and letting the future look after itself. Bach wrote his *St Matthew Passion* for performance on one day of the year only – the day which in the Christian Church was the culmination of the year, to which the year's worship was leading. It is one of the unhappiest results of the march of science and commerce that this unique work, at the turn of a switch, is at the mercy of any loud roomful of cocktail drinkers – to be listened to or switched off at will, without ceremony or occasion.

VI   The wording of your Institute's Constitution implies an effort to present the Arts as a counter-balance to Science in today's life. And though I am sure you do not imagine that there is not a lot of science, knowledge and skill in the art of making music (in the calculation of sound qualities and colours, the knowledge of the technique of instruments and voices, the balance of forms, the creation of moods,

and in the development of ideas), I would like to think you are suggesting that what is important in the Arts is *not* the scientific part, the
analysable part of music, but the something which emerges from it
but transcends it, which cannot be analysed because it is not *in* it, but
of it. It is the quality which cannot be acquired by simply the exercise
of a technique or a system: it is something to do with personality, with
gift, with spirit. I quite simply call it – magic: a quality which would
appear to be by no means unacknowledged by scientists, and which I
value more than any other part of music.

It is arguable that the richest and most productive eighteen months
in our music history is the time when Beethoven had just died, when
the other nineteenth-century giants, Wagner, Verdi and Brahms
had not begun; I mean the period in which Franz Schubert wrote
his *Winterreise*, the C Major Symphony, his last three piano sonatas,
the C major String Quintet, as well as a dozen other glorious pieces.
The very creation of these works in that space of time seems hardly
credible; but the standard of inspiration, of magic, is miraculous and
past all explanation. Though I have worked very hard at the *Winterreise* the last five years, every time I come back to it I am amazed not
only by the extraordinary mastery of it – for Schubert knew exactly
what he was doing (make no mistake about that), and he had thought
profoundly about it – but by the renewal of the magic: each time, the
mystery remains.

This magic comes only with the sounding of the music, with the
turning of the written note into sound – and it only comes (or comes
most intensely) when the listener is one with the composer, either as a
performer himself, or as a listener in active sympathy. Simply to read a
score in one's armchair is not enough for evoking this quality. Indeed,
this magic can be said to consist of just the music which is *not* in the
score. Sometimes one can be quite daunted when one opens the *Winterreise* – there seems to be nothing on the page. One must not exagger-
ate – the shape of the music in Schubert is clearly visible. What *cannot*
be indicated on the printed page are the innumerable small variants
of rhythm and phrasing which make up the performer's contribution.
In the *Winterreise*, it was not possible for Schubert to indicate exactly
the length of rests and pauses, or the colour of the singer's voice or the
clarity or smoothness of consonants. This is the responsibility of each
individual performer, and at each performance he will make modifica-
tions. The composer expects him to; he would be foolish if he did not.
For a musical experience needs three human beings at least. It requires
a composer, a performer, and a listener; and unless these three take part
together there is no musical experience. The experience will be that

much more intense and rewarding if the circumstances correspond to what the composer intended: if the *St. Matthew Passion* is performed on Good Friday in a church, to a congregation of Christians; if the *Winterreise* is performed in a room, or in a small hall of truly intimate character to a circle of friends; if *Don Giovanni* is played to an audience which understands the text and appreciates the musical allusions. The further one departs from these circumstances, the less true and more diluted is the experience likely to be.

One must face the fact today that the vast majority of musical performances take place as far away from the original as it is possible to imagine: I do not mean simply *Falstaff* being given in Tokyo, or the Mozart Requiem in Madras. I mean of course that such works *can* be audible in any corner of the globe, at any moment of the day or night, through a loudspeaker, without question of suitability or comprehensibility. Anyone, anywhere, at any time, can listen to the B minor Mass upon one condition only – that they possess a machine. No qualification is required of any sort – faith, virtue, education, experience, age. Music is now free for all. If I say the loudspeaker is the principal enemy of music, I don't mean that I am not grateful to it as a means of education or study, or as an evoker of memories. But it is not part of true musical *experience*. Regarded as such it is simply a substitute, and dangerous because deluding. Music demands more from a listener than simply the possession of a tape-machine or a transistor radio. It demands some preparation, some effort, a journey to a special place, saving up for a ticket, some homework on the programme perhaps, some clarification of the ears and sharpening of the instincts. It demands as much effort on the listener's part as the other two corners of the triangle, this holy triangle of composer, performer and listener.

VII Ladies and Gentlemen, this award is the latest of the kindnesses for which I am indebted to your country. I first came to the United States twenty-five years ago, at the time when I was a discouraged young composer – muddled, fed-up and looking for work, longing to be used. I was most generously treated here, by old and new friends, and to all of these I can never be sufficiently grateful. Their kindness was past description; I shall never forget it. But the thing I am *most* grateful to your country for is this: it was in California, in the unhappy summer of 1941, that, coming across a copy of the *Poetical Works of George Crabbe* in a Los Angeles bookshop, I first read his poem, *Peter Grimes*; and, at this same time, reading a most perceptive and revealing article about it by E. M. Forster, I suddenly realised where I belonged and what I lacked. I had become without roots, and when I got back to England six months later I was ready to put them down. I have lived since then in the same small corner of East Anglia, near where I was born. And I find as I get older that working becomes more and more difficult away from that home. Of course, I plot and plan my music when I am away on tour, and I get great stimulus and excitement from visiting other countries; with a congenial partner I like giving concerts, and in the last years we have travelled as far as Vancouver and Tokyo, Moscow and Java; I like making new friends, meeting new audiences, hearing new music. But I belong at home – there – in Aldeburgh. I have tried to bring music *to* it in the shape of our local Festival; and all the music I write comes *from* it. I believe in roots, in associations, in backgrounds, in personal relationships. I want my music to be of use to people, to please them, to 'enhance their lives' (to use Berenson's phrase). I do not write for posterity – in any case, the outlook for that is somewhat uncertain. I write music, now, in Aldeburgh, for people living there, and further afield, indeed for anyone who cares to play it or listen to it. But my music now has its roots, in where I live and work. And I only came to realise that in California in 1941.

VIII People have already asked me what I am going to do with your money; I have even been told in the post and in the press exactly how I ought to dispose of it. I shall of course pay no attention to these suggestions, however well- or ill-intentioned. The last prize I was given went straight away to the Aldeburgh Festival, the musical project I have most at heart. It would not surprise me if a considerable part of the Aspen Award went in that direction; I have not really decided. But one thing I know I want to do; I should like to give an annual Aspen Prize for a British composition. The conditions would change each year; one year it might be for a work for young voices and a school orchestra, another year for the celebration of a national event or centenary, another time a work for an instrument whose repertory is small; but in any case for specific or general usefulness. And the Jury would be instructed to choose only that work which was a pleasure to perform and inspiriting to listen to. In this way I would try to express my interpretation of the intention behind the Aspen Institute, and to express my warmest thanks, my most humble thanks, for the honour which you have awarded me today.

PART ONE
The status of Britten

I

The Britten Top Ten

The name of Benjamin Britten as a composer has made its indelible mark. Thanks to its alliteration, it trips off the tongue. Thanks to his surname, he cannot escape a national identity.

During his lifetime, his partnership with the similarly alliterated singer, Peter Pears (pronounced like the Lords, not the fruit), brought him further attention. Although they never spoke of it, most people knew then that they were an item.

The music of Britten was so distinctive that it sustained two parodies on the stage. As part of their early-1950s revue, *Airs on a Shoestring*, Michael Flanders and Donald Swann devised a 'Guide to Britten', which poked affectionate fun at about a dozen Britten works. They were warned it was a bit highbrow for provincial audiences, but in the event it went down well and everybody 'got' it – which showed how far the forty-year-old composer had penetrated public consciousness.

Eight years later, Dudley Moore was rather crueller in the way he mimicked Pears's voice and Britten's music in 'Little Miss Britten', a sketch for the satirical revue *Beyond the Fringe*. Moore's acute musical ear was near the knuckle in the way he adapted the nursery rhyme 'Little Miss Muffet' into a very Brittenish setting. Just like the prime minister of the time, Harold Macmillan, who turned up one evening to watch himself being lampooned, Britten went to see it and was not amused. He would not have been amused. But even this mockery was a compliment. It is hard to imagine a skit about any other contemporary composer having traction with a general audience.

Since his death in 1976, Britten's music has avoided the eclipse that so often afflicts composers posthumously. Many contemporary composers have been influenced by his ideas

and techniques, and his reputation is greater today, at the time
of his centenary, than it was for the last decade of his life. In
compiling a list of the pieces most popular with the public at
large, I have avoided those, like the *War Requiem* and *Death in
Venice*, that many may know *of*, rather than know. This is my
estimate of how the Britten Top Ten currently stands, with
the number of currently available recordings in brackets, as a
ready reckoner.

1 *The Young Person's Guide to the Orchestra* (25)
2 *Four Sea Interludes* from *Peter Grimes* (18)
3 *A Ceremony of Carols* (23)
4 *Simple Symphony* (18)
5 *Serenade* for tenor, horn and strings (15)
6 *Soirées Musicales* (4)
7 'The Foggy, Foggy Dew' (8)
8 *A Hymn to the Virgin* (35)
9 'The Salley Gardens' (16)
10 *Tell me the Truth about Love* (3)

It's not a bad list at all. It contains four or five indisputable
masterpieces. But it covers only the first half of Britten's composing life, and includes nothing sung in his fifteen operatic
works. It cannot therefore represent the full measure of his
music.

But it's a good starting-point.

My journey through Britten

My own journey to Britten began when I was about eleven, when we sang at school the ingenious four-part canon 'Old Abram Brown' from his 'kids' songs' (as he called them), *Friday Afternoons*. Soon after came Britten's *Jubilate in C*, then the exhilarating choral setting of *Psalm 150* for children, and 'As Dew in Aprille' from *A Ceremony of Carols*.

At secondary school, I enjoyed hearing the string orchestra play his *Simple Symphony*, and moved on to take part in the whole of *A Ceremony of Carols* in the arrangement for women's and men's voices with piano – though the original version for trebles and harp is far superior. Then came his wonderful miniature for men's voices, *The Ballad of Little Musgrave and Lady Barnard*, a tale of love, treachery and revenge, told in its limited range for three-part choir and piano with great poignancy and drama. Before I left school, I learnt (and loved) 'The Choirmaster's Burial' for the singing competition, from his Hardy settings *Winter Words*.

I was lucky enough to work with Britten just after leaving school, when as a member of the London Symphony Chorus I took part in his recording of Elgar's *The Dream of Gerontius*. I remember him arriving for his first rehearsal with us at Cecil Sharp House in London, when he greeted our chorus master Arthur Oldham with a kiss on both cheeks. (It was only later that I realised Arthur had been his protégé twenty years earlier in Aldeburgh.) Then we travelled to Suffolk for the recording sessions at Snape Maltings over several blissful hot days in the summer of 1971.

It was my first visit to Aldeburgh. The place was so sleepy that you could lie down in the middle of the High Street at about nine o'clock on a Saturday morning without mishap – and I proved the point by doing just that. We stayed in dormitory accommodation just up the coast at Thorpe-ness, and earned our Britten brownie points by bathing before breakfast in the cold North Sea. The recording in the freshly rebuilt Maltings was a thrill – we could find out what this great man had to say about Elgar (a combination that then seemed bizarre, though now I no longer think so), and also experience the electricity and efficiency of his conducting, and hear his precise, deep voice. I only wish I had recorded every precious moment in my memory. The Decca producer had the choir removed for all the solo singing (by Peter Pears, Yvonne Minton and John Shirley-Quirk), until we plucked up courage to ask Britten if we could remain in our seats – to which he graciously agreed. When I bought the boxed set of LPs the following year, I barely dared touch the sacred discs – and they remain a treasured possession even now.

My first experience of Britten opera was not the great *Peter Grimes*, which launched his operatic career, or his children's piece *Noye's Fludde*, but the black-and-white televised performance of *Billy Budd*, with Peter Glossop in the title role. I was absorbed, rather than overwhelmed, by it, but sufficiently to ensure I didn't miss the premiere of his television opera *Owen Wingrave* a few years later. I felt then, rather as I do now, little sympathy for the young pacifist, Owen, being bullied by his military family, and remain unconvinced by this opera as a piece of drama. Only on my third attempt was I really drawn into the operatic canon, and by a surprising route. It was later that year (1971) that I took part in what was apparently the first student performance of *Curlew River*. Its exploration of a mother's grief, through strange oriental sonorities threaded with plainsong, has gripped me ever since.

While at university I also encountered the *Nocturne*, his breathtaking evocation of night and dreams, and took part in his perfect schoolboy miniature *A Hymn to the Virgin*, as well as his ebullient choral work (too seldom performed today) *Spring Symphony*, which the London Symphony Chorus sang for his sixtieth birthday concert at the Royal Albert Hall.

Britten was too ill to attend, but sent us an encouraging telegram, which the conductor André Previn read out at the final rehearsal.

Two years later I went to the Aldeburgh Festival for the first time, where I particularly remember a bizarre recital of songs by the eccentric composer Lord Berners, interspersed with poetry by Ronald Firbank. Pears performed with a scarlet handkerchief in his breast pocket, and I could see Britten chuckling from his wheelchair in the Jubilee Hall box.

Shortly afterwards, bitten by Britten but not yet smitten, I ventured to see his newest opera, *Death in Venice*. It was towards the end of the first run at Covent Garden, but I found it tough going, and it was only many years later that I warmed to the extraordinary symphonic poem it actually is. But, having failed with his final opera, I turned on the advice of a friend to Britten's first success. She urged me to wangle myself a ticket to see the Royal Opera's sold-out new production of *Peter Grimes*, sung by Jon Vickers and Heather Harper. I queued for a standing-room ticket, stood (like many in Mayor Swallow's courtroom) for the ten-minute inquest into the death of Grimes's apprentice, which forms the Prologue to the opera, and then, during the first Sea Interlude, glided gratefully into an empty space in the front row of the stalls circle (one of the best seats in the house) where, uninterrupted by any latecomer, I was held – trapped for the full three acts – by the power and stagecraft of this astounding score. With the crowd thrust towards us at the start of the manhunt, shouting 'Peter Grimes!' as they all teetered on the very lip of the stage, about to tumble into the orchestra pit, it was terrifying but magnificent, and one of the most exciting evenings of my life.

Grimes took me captive. Since then I have never been released from the Britten spell. When I heard the news of his death on the car radio and the accompanying extract from the *Serenade* for tenor, horn and strings, I felt deeply moved. It was, for me as for so many, a personal as well as a national bereavement, even though I never knew him.

So, if you have yet to embark on a journey round Britten and his music, I would offer the following three dozen stopping-points (in alphabetical order) on the route-map to its heart. I believe each of them is indispensable.

Albert Herring
Antiphon
The Ballad of Little Musgrave and Lady Barnard
Billy Budd
A Birthday Hansel
A Boy was Born
Canticle II: Abraham and Isaac
Canticle III: Still Falls the Rain
Cello Suite no. 3
A Ceremony of Carols
Curlew River
Death in Venice
Four Sea Interludes and Passacaglia from *Peter Grimes*
Hymn to Saint Cecilia
A Hymn to the Virgin
Les Illuminations
A Midsummer Night's Dream
Missa Brevis
Nocturne
Noye's Fludde
Our Hunting Fathers
Paul Bunyan
Peter Grimes
Rejoice in the Lamb
Serenade for tenor, horn and strings
Seven Sonnets of Michelangelo
Sinfonia da Requiem
Spring Symphony
String Quartets nos. 1–3
The Turn of the Screw
Variations on a Theme of Frank Bridge
Violin Concerto

War Requiem
Winter Words
The Young Person's Guide to the Orchestra

I also couldn't be without some of the popular songs he so artfully arranged: 'The Foggy, Foggy Dew', 'O Waly, Waly', 'Oliver Cromwell', 'The Plough Boy' and 'The Salley Gardens'.

As someone who never particularly enjoys short journeys, I'm glad this journey is a long one. It's full of discoveries and surprises as each new generation of performers finds its own way into the music. Britten himself made so many definitive recordings that for a while he inhibited alternative ideas. Tenors often thought they had to sound like Peter Pears. But, just as no parliament can bind its successors, no composer can bind his or her performers. Britten's music needs no such protection anyway, and we are the richer for that.

3
The things they said about Britten

Britten drew plenty of fire for being (a) clever, (b) successful and (c) homosexual. Not everyone was as mischievous or ungrateful as those who called *Billy Budd* 'Twilight of the Sods' (supposedly the conductor Thomas Beecham, who was never short of a bon mot), or 'The Buggers' Opera' (reputedly Britten's prickly composer colleague, William Walton).

But some were.

THEODOR ADORNO
German musicologist 1903–69

A taste for bad taste, a simplicity founded in ignorance, immaturity that fancies itself clear minded, and a lack of technical capacity [faults he said were shared with Stravinsky and Shostakovich]. (1949)

W. H. AUDEN
British poet 1907–73

I think you are the white hope of music. (1942)

Wherever you go you are and probably always will be surrounded by people who adore you, nurse you and praise everything you do. But beware. You see, Bengy dear, you are always tempted to make things too easy for yourself in this way, i.e. to build yourself a warm nest of love by playing the lovable talented little boy. If you are really to develop to your full stature, you will have, I think, to suffer, and make others suffer. (1942)

JANET BAKER
British mezzo-soprano 1933–

To be with him was a bit like being with the Queen: in those circumstances you're never quite natural. I suppose it's almost like the sensation of being in love. Something happens to time, and one seems to be living in a highly volatile present. Nothing matters except the other person, and the moments you spend with them. (1981)

From those who worked with him he demanded absolute loyalty. The commitment had to be complete. If anybody fell below his high standards, they were asking for trouble. (1981)

BEVERLEY BAXTER
Canadian-born theatre critic and Conservative MP 1891–1964

(on *Gloriana*)
For minutes at a time – minutes piled upon minutes – it was as clamorous and ugly as hammers striking steel rails. (1953)

LENNOX BERKELEY
British composer 1903–89

(on hearing Britten play the first act of *Peter Grimes* on the piano in 1944)
Though greatly excited, I was not astonished, because I knew already that he was capable of something like this, and was expecting it.

LEONARD BERNSTEIN
American composer and conductor 1918–90

You are among the few composers whose work I cherish, in the most personal way. (1973)

Ben Britten was a man at odds with the world. It's strange, because on the surface Britten's music would seem to be decorative, positive, charming, but it's so much more than that. When you hear Britten's music, if you really *hear* it, not just listen to it superficially, you become aware of something very dark. There are gears that are grinding and not quite meshing, and they make a great pain. (1980)

R. V. BRITTEN
Father 1877–1934

Oh! Ben, my boy, what does it feel like to hear your own creation? Didn't you want to get up and shout – It's mine! It's mine! (1933)

ERIC CROZIER
Producer of Britten's operas 1914–94

From the first bar he was on top of his form, like a trained athlete beginning a race, nervously intense, poised, determined to succeed, and revelling in his mastery – and at such times he radiated a kind of magnetism that inspired everyone who played or sang with him. (1966)

I have been puzzled and astonished to see how much he has altered and how ugly he has become. His neck is thicker, his features coarser, and when his face is in repose his expression seems to be largely compounded of arrogance, impatience and hostility. (1966)

JOHN DRUMMOND
Television producer and arts administrator 1934–2006

Eventually Britten agreed to be interviewed [for a film about the singer Kathleen Ferrier] on condition that neither Nancy Evans, Ferrier's closest friend, nor Evans's husband, the librettist Eric Crozier, appeared in the programme. In a way typical of how things were at Aldeburgh. The proposal to exclude him and his wife was preposterous, and one I found it very hard to accept. (2000)

I never had any difficulty with Pears, right up to the end of his life, but with Britten I always felt I was walking on eggshells. It made for uncomfortable meetings. (2000)

QUEEN ELIZABETH THE QUEEN MOTHER
1900–2002

The record of *Les Illuminations* has arrived, and Ruth [Lady Fermoy] & I have played it several times, & listened with the greatest joy. There is no sound here [the Castle of Mey in northern Scotland] except the shushing of the sea & the crying of the seabirds, & this music is exactly right for the atmosphere here of sea & sky & silence. I find it extraordinarily moving. (1970)

OSIAN ELLIS
British harpist 1928–

Ben *liked* his players. He knew them by their names. He would remember your wife's name, even your kid's name – which is very unusual for a conductor. He was the one conductor who made you play your best – you couldn't do enough for him. I don't know another conductor who does that for you. (1991)

DIETRICH FISCHER-DIESKAU
German baritone 1925–

(on taking part in the premiere of Britten's *War Requiem*)
I was completely undone; I did not know where to hide my face. Dead friends and past suffering arose in my mind. (1989)

(on Britten's 1972 performance of Schumann's *Scenes from Goethe's Faust*, the year before his heart operation)
The applause kept swelling and would not die down. I can still see Ben, tottering slightly during and after the performance.

It made him seem like a tall tree shaken by the wind. His 'wonderful' at the end was almost inaudible. He seemed like someone who makes a religious profession in a delirium. Blissful and exhausted, he held out the score to the public in honour of Schumann. (1989)

Ben found it difficult to deal with the world. Though he was careful never to let anyone see that side of him, darkness reigned all the more frequently in his music, speaking of the shadow side of life. (1989)

E. M. FORSTER
British novelist 1879–1970

I am rather a fierce old man at the moment, and he is rather a spoilt boy, and certainly a busy one. (1950)

ALAN GARNER
British novelist 1934–

(on writing his novel *Elidor*)
I found myself playing the *War Requiem* in the frequent periods of floor-walking and breast-beating, and at the end of each playing I usually saw the answer to the problem. I should say that I am musically illiterate: my response is always limited to the emotional. I turned up the volume, wept, and then wrote. (1965)

JOHN GIELGUD
British actor and producer 1904–2000

(on producing Britten's *A Midsummer Night's Dream*)
I do hope we have done some credit to your beautiful work, which I love more and more. (1961)

COLIN GRAHAM
British opera producer 1931–2007

He was besotted by youth – he just worshipped youth and tried to maintain it in himself, in his own life, until the day he died. (2003)

WALTER GREATOREX
Britten's music master 1877–1949

So this is the little boy who likes Stravinsky! (1928)

JOYCE GRENFELL
British comedienne 1910–79

Of course Ben B is famous for hot weather friendships that cool in a trice and out goes whoever is the victim. But let's hope it's different this time. Why not? (1960)

(on singing to Britten a song she had written about the Aldeburgh Festival)
I sang it well and the reaction was so extraordinary that I was quite flummoxed. Ben ran to me and embraced me, weeping! He was *very* touched and moved. It was very dear and *entirely* unexpected. (1967)

PETER HALL
British theatre director 1930–

There is something thoughtful about him – like a precise headmaster who is going to stand no nonsense. But he has infinite charm and a great sense of humour. He has a reputation for gathering a court around him so that he can play the wilful emperor. But he is already a living legend. (1972)

VICTOR HELY-HUTCHINSON
British composer, BBC music executive 1901–47

I do wholeheartedly subscribe to the general opinion that Mr
Britten is the most interesting new arrival since Walton, and I
feel we should watch his work very carefully. (1933)

DAVID HEMMINGS
British actor, formerly boy soprano 1941–2003

You couldn't have had a better father, or a better friend.
I loved him dearly, I really did – I absolutely adored him. I
didn't fancy him, I wouldn't have gone to b . . . – well, I *did* go
to bed with him, but I didn't go to bed with him in *that* way.
(2003)

ROBIN HOLLOWAY
British composer 1943–

This music has the power to connect the avant-garde with the
lost paradise of tonality. (1977)

IMOGEN HOLST
British composer and conductor 1907–84

Your music seems to me the only reliable thing that is happening today in a world where everything else goes wrong all
the time. (1943)

He was looking *so* beautiful that my heart turned over so that
it was thumping when he embraced me, but I explained that
I'd run down the hill too fast. (1953)

We fought over the last glass [of claret]: I thought I'd won
because I poured mine into his glass when he was in the kitch-
en, but as soon as I turned aside he poured it back into mine. I
said: 'Do you *always* have to win?' and he said 'Well, I get very
cross if I don't.' (1953)

FRANK HOWES
British music critic on The Times 1891–1974

Mr Britten is still pursuing his old problem of seeing how much indigestible material he can dissolve in music. (1947)

JOHN IRELAND
British composer 1879–1962

This [*The Turn of the Screw*] contains the most remarkable and original music I have ever heard from the pen of a British composer. What he has accomplished in sound by the use of only 13 instruments was, to me, inexplicable; almost miraculous. This is not to say I liked the music, but it is gripping, vital, and often terrifying. I now am (perhaps reluctantly) compelled to regard Britten as possessing ten times the musical talent, intuition and ability of all other living British composers put together. (1954)

CHRISTOPHER ISHERWOOD
British novelist and playwright 1904–86

Well, have we convinced Ben he's queer, or haven't we? (1937)

I remember Ben as pale, boyish, indefatigable, scribbling music on his lap, then hurrying to the piano to play it. (1977)

(on visiting Britten in summer 1976)
I knew Ben was ill, but I didn't know how ill he was. He was so moved at seeing us again that he could hardly trust himself to speak. The others left us, and Ben and I sat in a room together, not speaking, just holding hands. (1977)

HANS KELLER
Austrian musicologist and critic 1919–85

Mozart and Britten are the only two composers I know who

strongly and widely attract people who do not understand them. (1952)

I personally would not hesitate to call Britten the greatest composer alive. (1963 – when Stravinsky and Shostakovich were still living)

CONSTANT LAMBERT
British composer 1905–1951

No composer of today has greater fluency or greater natural gifts. For that very reason the temptation to fritter these gifts away must be very great. (1938)

ANITA LASKER-WALLFISCH
German cellist and concentration camp survivor 1925–

(on the recital given at Bergen-Belsen by Menuhin and Britten)
Both soloist and accompanist were dressed in simple attire bordering on the slovenly, which matched the surroundings perfectly. It goes without saying that Menuhin played fault-lessly; he is, after all, Yehudi Menuhin. As for the accompa-nist, I can only say that I cannot imagine anything done more beautifully. He was completely unobtrusive and yet I found myself transfixed by him sitting there as if he wouldn't say boo to a goose – but playing to perfection. (1945)

ELISABETH LUTYENS
British composer 1906–83

B. Britten is, to me, a brilliant journalist able to produce an instant effect at first hearing, understandable to all. Each repeated hearing yields *less* – or so I find. (1973)

BB's operas are bad, for me, because they are superficial and the product of a talented schoolboy. There is no real thought of a man. (1973)

CHARLES MACKERRAS
Australian conductor 1925–2010

The greatest musician I have ever worked with. (2003)

Although we all revered Ben's musicianship and loved him as a man in many ways, we were slightly amused by the homosexuality. (2003)

Although *Grimes* is the work that changed the face of British opera, *The Turn of the Screw* is the ultimate masterpiece. (2009)

YEHUDI MENUHIN
American-born violinist and conductor 1916–1999

Ben was quicksilver, all nerve and movement. (1985)

OLIVIER MESSIAEN
French composer and organist 1908–92

(on the diatonic nature of *Peter Grimes*)
Something very brave in its own way for its time . . . A masterpiece.

GERALD MOORE
British pianist 1899–1987

Since the presiding genius there [at the Aldeburgh Festival] is the greatest accompanist in the world there is no call for my services. (1962)

ARVO PÄRT
Estonian composer 1935–

Why did the date of Benjamin Britten's death touch such a chord in me? Inexplicable feelings of guilt, more than that even, arose in me. I had just discovered Britten for myself. Just before his death I began to appreciate the unusual purity of his music. And besides, for a long time I had wanted to meet Britten personally – and now it would not come to that. (1984)

PETER PEARS
British tenor and Britten's partner, 1910–86

He could make lighter sounds than anyone else I can recall; he was anxious to imitate the timbre of early pianos rather than emphasising that of a modern Steinway. In the Schubert cycles he knew precisely what colour he wanted to project, and he managed to do it because of the speed with which his brain could communicate with the tips of his fingers. (1981)

Ben was no bohemian. He adhered to a regular life, beginning with a cold bath in the morning, to whose delights he introduced me. In domestic matters he was somewhat at a loss. He could make a cup of tea, boil an egg and wash up, but not much more. If he made his bed, he usually made a mess of it. (1981)

He was low church, and therefore inclined to be puritanical. (1981)

MSTISLAV ROSTROPOVICH
Russian cellist and conductor 1927–2007

(on first rehearsing Britten's Cello Sonata with the composer) After four or five very large whiskies we finally sat down and played through the sonata. We played like pigs, but we were so happy. (1977)

WULFF SCHERCHEN
Son of German conductor, Hermann Scherchen 1921–

Your friendship I have never been able to forget. It is an aching void of longing for the most intimate acquaintanceship I have ever known. Remember that when I lost you I lost half of myself, for you were my first friend, & the hours we spent together were and are the happiest and best of my life. (1941)

PETER SHAFFER
British playwright 1926–

(on the *War Requiem*)
The most impressive and moving piece of sacred music ever
to be composed in this country. (1962)

DMITRI SHOSTAKOVICH
Russian composer 1906–75

You great composer, I little composer.

EDITH SITWELL
British poet and critic 1887–1964

(on the First String Quartet)
It is still exploding in my head with a blinding light followed
by new ideas, points of view, even new vision. I'm not sure
that Britten hasn't been, spiritually, where Coleridge went
before he wrote *The Ancient Mariner* – to those polar regions.
Only Britten saw it, I think, from a freezing height, like a bird
– very, very high up. And Coleridge saw it from the sea. (1943)

(on Britten's setting of her poem 'Still Falls the Rain' in
Canticle III)
During the performance, I felt as if I were dead – killed in the
raid – yet with all my powers of feeling still alive. Most terrible and most moving – the appalling loneliness, for all that
it was a communal experience one was alone, each being was
alone, with space and eternity and the terror of death, and
then God. (1955)

(on the *War Requiem*)
The greatest work that has emerged from the grief, the
horror, and yet the pride and faith, of our time. What a wonderful work it is! [...] I am not a person who ever really cries.
Tears remain at the back of my eyes. On this occasion, the
tears were blood. (1962)

IGOR STRAVINSKY
Russian composer 1882–1971

We listened for a whole week here to Auntie Britten and
Uncle Pears. Britten himself makes a very nice impression and
has a huge success with the audience. (1949)

(on the tepid reception of his own piece *Abraham and Isaac*)
What can you do? Not everybody can have Benjamin Britten's
success with the critics. (1964)

The tide of applause virtually packaged along with the *War
Requiem* is so loud and the Battle-of-Britten sentiment is
so thick that these phenomena, and the national inferiority
feelings in music they expose, are at least as absorbing a subject of investigation as the music. Behold the critics as they
vie in abasement before the wonder of native-born genius.
(1966)

'The drums of Time' sings the baritone and 'boom, boom,
boom' go the obedient timpani. (1966)

MICHAEL TIPPETT
British composer 1905–98

Britten has been for me the most purely musical person I have
ever met and I have ever known. It always seemed to me that
music sprang out of his fingers when he played the piano, as it
did out of his mind when he composed. (1976)

RALPH VAUGHAN WILLIAMS
British composer 1872–1958

(on Britten's folksong arrangements)
The tune's the thing with which we'll catch the conscience
of the composer. Do these settings spring from a love of the
tune? Then, whatever our personal reaction may be, we must
respect them. (1943)

I do not propose after a single hearing to appraise the work or the music of *Gloriana*. The important thing to my mind, at the moment, is that, so far as I know, for the first time in history the Sovereign has commanded an opera by a composer from these islands for a great occasion. Those who cavil at the public expense involved should realise what such a gesture means to the prestige of our own music. (1953)

GALINA VISHNEVSKAYA
Russian soprano 1926–

(on her performance with Peter Pears of the *Romeo and Juliet* love duet by Tchaikovsky)
The way Ben played the long prelude could not be called piano playing at all – it was a unique, unparalleled moment. Standing on stage, I was listening with such rapture that I missed my entrance. The ensuing silence brought me to, but at first I didn't realise where I was or what I was supposed to do. Ben waited for a moment as if nothing had happened, then repeated the last bars of the prelude. (1984)

How often I ran my hand through his wiry hair! He would purr with pleasure, and say that in a past incarnation he must have been a horse. (1984)

(after Britten's heart operation)
At dinner – sitting to his left, as always – I heard with horror the heavy, hollow beating of his heart, and saw the pronounced throbbing of his shirt on the left side of his chest. (1984)

SUSANA WALTON
William Walton's Argentinian wife 1926–2010

(on the wedding of Britten's friends Marion Stein and the Earl of Harewood)
When Ben Britten, who had composed the wedding anthem, and Peter Pears, who had sung it, appeared dressed as choir-boys in white surplices over red cassocks, we burst into giggles

and were silenced only by a severe reprimand from John Piper
and his wife in the next pew. (1988)

WILLIAM WALTON
British composer 1902–83

In the last years your music has come to mean more & more
to me – it shines out as a beacon in a chaotic & barren musical world, & I am sure it does for thousands of others. (1963)

(on reports that Britten had been offered the music director's
post at the Royal Opera House)
There are enough buggers in the place already. It's time it was
stopped. (1951)

4

Britten online

Googling composers' names is rather fun. It gives a rough pecking order, providing you remember that the more common surnames may have many non-musical entries. The scores shift day by day, so they offer mere snapshots. My latest one shows Handel yielding 47.1 million results, Bach 37.5m, Verdi 31.1m, Mozart 28.6m, Beethoven 17.2m and Schubert 12.0m.

Britten is not in this stratosphere. But he does score 3.4 million, ahead of Stravinsky (2.8m), Schoenberg (1.9m), Vaughan Williams (1.5m) and Tippett (1.4m), all of which I suspect would bring a smile to his face. But he might be displeased to find himself in the shadow of Elgar (3.9m) and Sibelius (4.3m, though a quarter of that can be attributed to the software brand name). He is also well behind Mahler (5.3m) and Debussy (4.1m), but ahead of Shostakovich (1.9m). Tippett's haul reminded me that the Britten total could include results for the road haulage company Tibbett & Britten, the name of which has always amused me, but in fact they amount to only some 25,000, so Britten's position is unaffected.

For individual Britten works, most of which have distinctive titles, Google provides a rough interest-level almost thirty-five years after Britten's death. *A Ceremony of Carols* is comfortably in front, with *The Young Person's Guide* a clear second. The leading opera is, surprisingly, *The Rape of Lucretia*, well ahead of *Peter Grimes*. The appearance of all three string quartets may be unreliable because of their unspecific titles, although I have tightened the search in these instances. It is intriguing, though not unexpected, that the schoolboy miniature *A Hymn to the Virgin* scores so highly.

| 1 | *A Ceremony of Carols* | 546,000 |
| 2 | *The Young Person's Guide to the Orchestra* | 400,000 |

3	*The Rape of Lucretia*	157,000
4	*Rejoice in the Lamb*	151,000
5	String Quartet no. 2	149,000
6	String Quartet no. 3	144,000
7	*Variations on a Theme of Frank Bridge*	113,800
8	*A Hymn to the Virgin*	113,000
9=	*Hymn to St Cecilia*	110,000
9=	*Serenade* for tenor, horn & strings	110,000
11	String Quartet no. 1	109,000
12	*Peter Grimes*	107,000
13	*Lachrymae*	96,500
14	*Let's Make an Opera!*	74,200
15	*War Requiem*	68,900
16	*A Midsummer Night's Dream*	65,400
17	Violin Concerto	62,400
18	*Billy Budd*	49,700
19	*Tell me the Truth about Love*	43,900
20	*The Turn of the Screw*	45,400
21	*Gloriana*	40,700
22	*Seven Sonnets of Michelangelo*	39,500
23	*Nocturne*	30,500
24	*Simple Symphony*	30,100
25	*Death in Venice*	30,000

A spot-check on Spotify (www.spotify.com), the website where people have sampled particular movements for free, reveals that the most popular Britten track is 'Frolicsome Finale' from *Simple Symphony*, followed by the other three movements. Also at the top of the list are 'Dawn' and 'Moonlight' from the *Four Sea Interludes* from *Peter Grimes*. Then comes the opening of the *War Requiem*, the cabaret song *Tell me the Truth about Love*, and *The Young Person's Guide to the Orchestra*. But, on the day I checked, most popular of all (except 'Frolicsome Finale') were three separate recordings of Arvo Pärt's *Cantus in memoriam Benjamin Britten*.

On YouTube, the playlist results show a tight race between Bach and Mozart (15,400 each) and Beethoven and Chopin

(15,300). Close behind are Wagner, Verdi, Schubert and Handel (14,700). Britten scores 4,560, chasing Elgar (4,640) and Stravinsky (5,610), but comfortably in front of Schoenberg (3,090), Vaughan Williams (2,400) and Tippett (1,000).

But that's enough figures.

Round Britten Quiz I

ANSWERS ON PAGE 410

1 When was Britten prosecuted, and for what?
2 For which country did Britten compose a national anthem?
3 In respect of what was the fourteen-year-old Britten described as 'tall and inclined to be clumsy, but very hard-working'?
4 How many continents did Britten visit in his life?
5 What contribution did Britten make to capturing Robinson Crusoe in London during the war?
6 Who or what was 'Seizer'?

5
The things Britten said about them

Britten was not a man to mince his words. He kept a daily diary from 1928 to 1938, from the ages of fourteen to twenty-four, and it is peppered with brutally arrogant judgements of composers, singers, players and conductors. The one musician who could do no wrong was his mentor, the composer Frank Bridge.

Later in life he did concede that he had been somewhat 'violent' in his opinions, and he became both more generous and much more diplomatic as the years went by. But he never fully curbed the roughness of his tongue.

W. H. AUDEN
British poet 1907–73

He is the most charming, most vital genius & important person I know. (1936)

Auden was a powerful, revolutionary person. He was very much anti-bourgeois and that appealed. He also had some lively, slightly dotty ideas about music. He played the piano reasonably well, and was a great one for singing unlikely words to Anglican chants. (1963)

He was such a large personality, a whirlwind one, if you like, and I was swept away by his poetry. He was incredibly intelligent, very, very vocal; he talked marvellously well, he was very engaging and sympathetic and deeply interested in people. (1964)

J. S. BACH
German composer 1685–1750

The *Matthew Passion* written for a small group of young singers (half of them boys) in a smallish Gothic church – how can we recapture its original edgy resonance across the spaces of the damp (acoustically) Festival Hall, with a large chorus, mature & expressive soloists (half of them women) – to say nothing of the pitch having crept up nearly a tone, and with a paying audience rather than a worshipping congregation? (1963)

THE BEATLES
1960s British pop group

I think they're charming creatures; I don't happen to like their music very much, but that's just me. But if a person likes the Beatles, it doesn't by any means preclude their love of Beethoven. (1965)

Everything I read about the Beatles gives me pleasure. They have a wit and they have a directness – a freshness of approach which gives me a great pleasure, and I think they're also frightfully funny. (1968)

THOMAS BEECHAM
British conductor 1879–1961

That irresponsible man. (1937)

LUDWIG VAN BEETHOVEN
German composer 1770–1827

Beethoven is still first [in his list of composers], and I think always will be. Bach or Brahms comes next, I don't know which! (1928)

(on *Fidelio*)
This is a very deep religious & exhilarating experience.
Well as I know the incredible music, I did not realise what a
tremendous dramatic thrill it was. (1937)

Only yesterday I was listening to the *Coriolanus* Overture by
Beethoven. What a marvellous beginning, and how well the
development in sequence is carried out! But what galled me
was the crudity of the sound; the orchestral sounds seem often
so haphazard. (1963)

(on Piano Sonata no. 32 in C minor, op. 111)
The sound of the variations was so grotesque I just couldn't
see what they were all about. (1963)

ALBAN BERG
Austrian composer 1885–1935

I alternated between mad irritation at the ridiculous excess-
es of it [the opera *Wozzeck*], with the ludicrous, hideous &
impossible vocal writing, and being moved to tears by the
incredible haunting beauty of lots of bits of it. (1948)

ADRIAN BOULT
British conductor 1889–1983

Terrible execrable conductor. (1931)

(on his rehearsal of Britten's *Our Hunting Fathers*)
He doesn't really grasp the work – tho' he is marvellously
painstaking. (1937)

JOHANNES BRAHMS
German composer 1833–97

It's not bad Brahms I mind, it's good Brahms I can't stand.

FRANK BRIDGE
British composer 1879–1941

If anything happened to my musical father, I don't know what I should do. (1936)

Not only did he keep my nose to the grindstone, but he criticised my work relentlessly, and I, who had thought that I was already on the verge of immortality, saw my illusions shattered and I felt I was very small fry. (1946)

At about eighteen or nineteen, I began to rebel. When Bridge played questionable chords across the room at me and asked if that was what I meant, I would retort, 'Yes it is'. He'd grunt back, 'Well it oughtn't to be.' (1963)

WINSTON CHURCHILL
British prime minister 1874–1965

Mr Churchill's high living at Potsdam is an offence that stinks to high heaven. It is a political indecency – a moral crime. It is in this wrecked, beaten, hungry country that the United Nations leaders have met. And the first news we get is that they are gorging themselves on turkeys, hams, fresh eggs, juicy steaks, melons, strawberries, wines and whiskies. All around is the stricken enemy people, hungry and facing greater hunger. (1945)

AARON COPLAND
American composer 1900–90

As important and vital a composer as any living. (1940)

HARRIET COHEN
British pianist 1895–1967

She talks more unadulterated drivel than anyone I've ever met. (1937)

FREDERICK DELIUS
British composer 1862–1934

Perhaps the piece of music that brings tears most easily to the eyes of an expatriate Englishman is *On Hearing the First Cuckoo in Spring*. (1941)

EDWARD ELGAR
British composer 1857–1934

I am absolutely incapable of enjoying Elgar for more than two minutes. (1931)

Certainly the best way to make me like Elgar is to listen to him after Vaughan Willliams. (1935)

For the Fallen has always seemed to me to have in its opening bars a personal tenderness and grief, in the grotesque march an agony of distortion, and in the final sequences a ring of genuine splendour. (1969)

KATHLEEN FERRIER
British contralto 1912–53

I was impressed immediately by the nobility and beauty of her presence, and by the warmth and deep range of her voice. (1954)

There are many beautiful performances of hers recorded for our delight, but it is my own special selfish grief that none of my own music is among them – music that she sang with her own inimitable warmth, simplicity and devoted care, as indeed she sang everything – as if it were the most important in the world. (1954 – two Ferrier recordings of Britten have since been discovered and issued.)

DIETRICH FISCHER-DIESKAU
German baritone 1925–

I'm scared of Dieter. He's the school bully! (1970s)

KIRSTEN FLAGSTAD
Norwegian soprano 1895–1962

(on her performance as Isolde)
She certainly is a wonder – marvellously accurate – scarcely a semiquaver wrong ever & a great voice with a tremendous variety of tone. (1936)

E. M. FORSTER
British novelist 1879–1970

There is no doubt that E. M. Forster is our most musical novelist. (1969)

WALTER GREATOREX
British composer and Britten's music master 1877–1949

How ever the man got the job here I cannot imagine. His ideas of rhythm, logic, tone, or the music are absolutely lacking in sanity. (1930)

JOHN IRELAND
British composer and Britten's composition teacher 1879–1962

(on Ireland's choral work, *These Things Shall Be*)
All that pretentious tub-thumping, puking sentimentality and really flagrant dishonesty (to say nothing of the gross incompetence of it). (1937)

He nursed me very gently through a very, very difficult musical adolescence. (1957)

A composer of strong personal gifts and real single-mindedness of purpose. (1959)

ZOLTÁN KODÁLY
Hungarian composer 1882–1967

There can be no composer of our century who has done more for the musical life of his country than Zoltán Kodály. (1965)

(on the folk-songs collected by Kodály and arranged for children's voices)
They are of an originality, simplicity yet richness, which is startling. We can all learn from these, from their beauty of sound, freshness, their *multum in parvo*. (1967)

ERNST KRENEK
Austrian atonal composer 1900–91

The acme of pedantic dullness. (1935)

GUSTAV MAHLER
Austrian composer and conductor 1860–1911

(on the final movement of *Das Lied von der Erde*)
It is cruel that music should be so beautiful. It has the beauty of loneliness & of pain: of strength and freedom. The beauty of disappointment & never-satisfied love. The cruel beauty of nature, and everlasting beauty of monotony. I cannot understand it – it passes over me like a tidal wave – and that matters not a jot either, because it goes on for ever, even if it is never performed again – that final chord is printed on the atmosphere. (1937)

Emotionally, Mahler can be rather remote from me, but I love and admire his 'ear' for sound. (1963)

LAURITZ MELCHIOR
Danish operatic tenor 1890–1973

Melchior is simply superb. What a voice! The subtlety of his movements is incredible. (1933)

WOLFGANG AMADEUS MOZART
Austrian composer 1756–91

(on *The Marriage of Figaro*)
What gaiety and brilliance, what passion and tension, what characterisation, what construction. (1952)

(on Symphony no. 40 in G minor)
I feel that it is one of the most tragic and tense pieces which has ever been written. (1960)

The most controlled of composers, who can express the most turbulent feelings in the most unruffled way. (1962)

(on *Idomeneo*)
It is a really astounding piece, and every moment of it is red hot with excitement. (1969)

WILFRED OWEN
British poet 1893–1918

Owen is to me by far our greatest war poet, and one of the most original and touching poets of this century. (1963)

PETER PEARS
British tenor and Britten's partner 1910–86

(on his performance of the 'Agnus Dei' in Britten's *War Requiem*)
I think it's marvellous singing, absolutely marvellous . . . It's aiming at something so rare, and so special and so pure. (1963)

I was attracted, even in those early days, by his voice, which seemed to me to emanate from a personality, and not, like many other voices, to be a manufactured affair, super-imposed. (1967)

Pears has always possessed the all-important gift of being able to *phrase* music, of singing a series of notes in such a way that they make *sense*. (1967)

SAMUEL PEPYS
English MP and diarist 1633–1703

Last night I dreamt a most sensible dream imagining myself with him at a Ball as young Monmouth with Lady Castle-maine, and discussing, most distinctly, Bach, but adding 'then of course, he's not alive yet'. (1935)

GIACOMO PUCCINI
Italian composer 1858–1924

What makes Puccini a greater composer of operas than (in my humble opinion) a great *composer* is that he knows how long it takes a person to cross the room. (1950)

HENRY PURCELL
English composer 1659–95

There seems to be nothing this composer cannot do. (1945)

I recall a critic once asking me from whom I had learned to set English poetry to music. I told him Purcell; he was amazed. I suppose he expected me to say folk music and Vaughan Williams. (1963)

MSTISLAV ROSTROPOVICH
Russian cellist 1927–2007

Rostropovich freed one of my inhibitions. He's such a gloriously uninhibited musician himself, with this enormous feeling of generosity you get from the best Russian players. I'd heard about him, and rather unwillingly listened on the wireless. I immediately realised this was a new way of playing the cello, in fact almost a new, vital way of playing music. He took the bull by the horns and asked me to write a piece for him, which was my Cello Sonata, written 'on condition he came to Aldeburgh'! (1964)

ARTUR SCHNABEL
Austrian pianist 1882–1951

The greatest pianist I ever heard. (1952)

ARNOLD SCHOENBERG
Austrian composer 1874–1951

I mourn the death of Schoenberg. Every serious composer today has felt the effect of his courage, single-mindedness and determination, and has profited by the clarity of his teaching. (1951)

Not what you'd call a *magic* composer. (1953)

People in this country who thought Schoenberg was mad until recently have suddenly swung the other way and they think it's all wonderful. Neither estimation is honest. (1963)

FRANZ SCHUBERT
Austrian composer 1797–1828

The *Winterreise* is not for a great auditorium; but for those who like intimate song recitals there is no work which is more loved than this highly personal, introspective, & devastatingly pessimistic, document. (1963)

It is arguable that the richest and most productive eighteen months in our musical history is the time when Beethoven had just died, when the other 19th-century giants, Wagner, Verdi and Brahms had not begun; I mean the period in which

Franz Schubert wrote his *Winterreise*, the C major Symphony, his last three piano sonatas, the C major String Quintet, as well as a dozen other glorious pieces. The standard of inspiration, of magic, is miraculous and past all explanation. (1964)

My recent dream about meeting Schubert in Vienna blessed the following days in a way that I seldom remember in my life before. (1970)

WILLIAM SHAKESPEARE
English playwright and poet 1564–1616

I feel that everyone ought to set Shakespeare to music in order just to get to know the incredible beauty and intensity of these words. (1960)

DMITRI SHOSTAKOVICH
Russian composer 1906–75

(on the opera *Lady Macbeth of Mtsensk*)
The satire is biting & brilliant. The 'eminent English Renaissance' composers sniggering in the stalls was typical. There is more music in a page of *Macbeth* than in the whole of their 'elegant' output! (1936)

For years now, your work and life have been an example to me – of courage, integrity and human sympathy, and of wonderful invention and clear vision. I must say that there is no one composing to-day who has an equal influence on me. (1963)

When I was in Moscow he played Peter and me his two new string quartets. And I must say I was *shattered* by the tenth. I thought it was the most extraordinary piece of music – completely new for him, immensely simple, immensely direct, but quite, quite surprising and new, and much more for instance than the last two or three symphonies which I don't feel an awful lot of sympathy with. (1964)

I have been reading the scores of two of his finest Symphonies, the Fourth and the Fifth. I am amazed that the same man could write them both – the Fourth so prolific with ideas, with a tumultuous exuberance, amounting at times to wildness, but with always a musical heart to sustain it, and never an empty or pointless gesture – the Fifth, so controlled, so classical, neat even, in spite of its energy. It is the musical heart which links these two works together. (1966)

JEAN SIBELIUS
Finnish composer 1865–1957

I must confess that, for many, many years, the works of the Finnish master meant little to me. Then, by chance, hearing a performance of the Fourth Symphony, I became interested. I find his conception of sound extremely personal and original, and his musical thinking most stimulating. (1965)

RICHARD STRAUSS
German composer 1864–1949

(after receiving a score of *Der Rosenkavalier*)
I am impatient to see how the old magician makes his effects! There's a hell of a lot I can learn from him! (1943)

IGOR STRAVINSKY
Russian composer 1882–1971

(on *The Rake's Progress*)
I feel miserably disappointed that easily the greatest composer alive should have such an irresponsible & perverse view of opera. (1951)

Stravinsky, one of the greatest artistic figures of our time, has said some very silly things, and unless one is careful they are liable to prejudice one against his great music. (1962)

MICHAEL TIPPETT
British composer 1905–98

An *excellent* composer, and most delightful and intelligent man. (1942)

I wish your piano parts weren't so difficult! (1965)

ARTURO TOSCANINI
Italian conductor 1867–1957

Of course the crowd went mad, & of course they were right, he is a great man. (1935)

RALPH VAUGHAN WILLIAMS
British composer 1872–1958

He can be *imitated*, but he hasn't influenced. (1952)

We will miss him sadly – above all, his wonderful, uncompromising courage in fighting for all those things he believed in. (1958)

I was frankly suspicious of VW. My struggle all the time was to develop a consciously controlled professional technique. It was a struggle away from everything Vaughan Williams seemed to stand for. (1959)

The Fourth Symphony impressed me greatly. But Vaughan Williams was reported to have said of his own work, 'If that's modern music, all I can say is I don't like it.' This story, I must say, shocked me profoundly. In those days I was very violent in my opinions, very ready to have grievances. (1959)

GIUSEPPE VERDI
Italian composer 1813–1901

I am an arrogant and impatient listener; but in the case of a few composers, a very few, when I hear a work I do not like

I am convinced it is my own fault. Verdi is one of these composers. (1951)

Verdi has the gift, which only the very greatest have had: that
of writing a succession of the simplest harmonies in such a
way as to sound surprising and yet 'right'. (1951)

RICHARD WAGNER
German composer 1813–1883

He is the master of us all. (1933)

WILLIAM WALTON
British composer 1902–83

(on his First Symphony)
A great tragedy for English music. Last hope of W. gone now
– this is a conventional work, reactionary in the extreme &
dull & depressing. (1935)

He is so obviously the head-prefect of English music, whereas
I'm the promising young new boy. (1937)

(on his Viola Concerto)
A great turning-point in my musical life. You showed me the
way of being relaxed and fresh, and intensely personal. (1963)

ANTON WEBERN
Austrian composer 1883–1945

Peter Pears and I have performed some of Webern's songs.
We die a thousand deaths trying to get them exactly right and
it is still nearly impossible. (1963)

I'm not particularly attracted by Webern's music, though he
was clearly a master and a very brave man. To my taste he was
too limited a nature artistically on which to found a school.
(1963)

HENRY WOOD
British conductor 1869–1944

Wood is an absolute vandal. (1934)

Henry J. Wood is a public menace – & ought to be shot quickly, before he does much more murdering of classics ancient & modern. (1935)

Wood is really a marvel considering the amount he has to do. (1936)

6
Britten on screen

The amount of Britten material commercially available on DVD or Blu-Ray is at last expanding, and the impact of the 2013 centenary of his birth has encouraged that process.

In terms of documentary films, Tony Palmer's seminal programme for ITV's *The South Bank Show*, entitled *A Time There Was* (after the last song in Britten's Hardy cycle *Winter Words*), has only recently become available. It was first shown in 1980, with the full cooperation of Peter Pears, who spoke frankly for the first time about his relationship with Britten – memorably describing how he had died 'in my arms'. This film will always hold its place, because of the insights it offers from those who knew and worked closely with Britten.

Teresa Griffiths' 2002 film for Channel 4, *The Hidden Heart*, elaborates the Britten–Pears relationship, drawing particularly on the love letters they exchanged shortly before the end of their thirty-seven-year partnership.

My own film, *Britten's Children*, was shown by the BBC in 2004, and discusses Britten's music for and about children in the context of his friendships with adolescent boys. It features interviews with several of his erstwhile boy companions, most notably the actor David Hemmings (giving the last interview of his life), and the German schoolboy Wulff Scherchen, who spoke out for the first time about his intense relationship with Britten just before the Second World War. This film is planned for release on DVD shortly.

Decca has recently issued DVDs of four Britten operas, shown on BBC Television. These are available separately, or as a seven-disc set, with some folksongs and Mozart's *Idomeneo* thrown in. The ground-breaking performance of *Billy Budd* in 1966 was conducted by Charles Mackerras, directed by Basil Coleman, and starred Peter Glossop as Billy and

Peter Pears as Captain Vere. This encouraged Britten to
conduct a filmed performance of *Peter Grimes* in 1969 – the
last time Pears sang the role. Directed by Brian Large, it
also featured Heather Harper, Owen Brannigan and Bryan
Drake. This in turn led to Britten filming his 'opera for
television', *Owen Wingrave*, in 1971, again directed by Coleman, featuring Benjamin Luxon as Owen, Janet Baker as
Kate and Pears as Sir Philip Wingrave. By today's technical standards, both picture and sound in these historic films
have 'period flavour' – indeed, only *Wingrave* is in colour.
Back in 1963, there was also a television broadcast of Britten's reworked *The Beggar's Opera*, now issued on DVD. It
stars David Kelly, Janet Baker, Heather Harper and Bryan
Drake, and is conducted by Meredith Davies and directed
by Charles Rogers.

More recent opera DVD releases include:

Albert Herring (Graham-Hall, Johnson, Opie, Palmer, Rigby,
Glyndebourne Festival Opera/Haitink, directed by Peter
Hall), filmed 1985 (Warner Classics)

Billy Budd (Allen, Langridge, English National Opera/
Atherton, directed by Tim Albery), filmed 1988 – a gripping
realisation of this opera (Arthaus Musik)

Death in Venice (Tear, Opie, Chance, Glyndebourne Festival
Opera/Jenkins, directed by Reiner Moritz). This 1990 stage
performance transfers very unsubtly to the small screen: the
relationship between Aschenbach and Tadzio is very 'in-
your-face'.

Gloriana (Walker, Rolfe Johnson, English National Opera/
Elder, directed by Colin Graham), filmed 1984 (Arthaus
Musik)

Let's Make an Opera! (Palmer, Flowers, Milne, Richardson,
Graham Hall, Coull Quartet, City of Birmingham
Symphony Chorus/Halsey, directed by Petr Weigl), filmed
1996 (Arthaus Musik)

A Midsummer Night's Dream (Cotrubas, Bowman, Lott, Glyndebourne Festival Opera/Haitink, directed magically by Peter Hall), filmed 1981 (Kultur Films)

A Midsummer Night's Dream (Sala, Daniels, Gietz, Dazeley, Teatro del Liceu/Bicket, directed by Robert Carsen), filmed 2005 (Virgin Classics)

Owen Wingrave (Finley, Hill, Barstow, Hellekant, Berlin Symphony Orchestra/Nagano), filmed 2001 for Channel 4. The impressive updating by Margaret Williams of this problematic opera also includes the documentary *The Hidden Heart* (Arthaus Musik)

Peter Grimes (Langridge, Cairns, Opie, English National Opera/Atherton, directed by Tim Albery), filmed 1994 – a remarkable performance (Kultur Films)

Peter Grimes (Dean Griffey, Racette, Michaels-Moore, Metropolitan Opera/Runnicles, directed by Guy Halvorson), filmed 2008 (EMI)

Peter Grimes (Vickers, Harper, Bailey, Royal Opera House/Davis, directed by Elijah Moshinsky), filmed 1981 (Warner Classics)

The Rape of Lucretia (Rigby, Opie, Rolfe Johnson, English National Opera/Friend, directed by Graham Vick), filmed 1987 (Arthaus Musik)

The Turn of the Screw (Delunsch, Miller, McLaughlin, Mahler Chamber Orchestra/Harding, directed by Luc Bondy), filmed 2001 (Harmonia Mundi). There is also a BBC film from 2004, starring Mark Padmore and Lisa Milne, conducted by Richard Hickox, but the visual direction by Katie Mitchell is disappointing

Among other, non-operatic, DVD releases is his full-length ballet *The Prince of the Pagodas*, starring Darcey Bussell and Jonathan Cope in Kenneth MacMillan's Covent Garden production (Kultur Films), and several versions of *War Requiem*, including the film by Derek Jarman in which he illustrated the music with war newsreel, and added the voices of Nathaniel Parker, Tilda Swinton, Sean Bean and Laurence Olivier.

The Amadeus String Quartet was filmed playing each of the three Britten quartets. These were released on video separately, each with a companion piece by Schubert. They are available from Testament. Maxim Vengerov's masterclass at the Royal Academy of Music on the first movement of Britten's Violin Concerto is captured on a Masterclass Media Foundation DVD. There is also a valuable, and little-known, film from 1962 of Britten rehearsing a Canadian orchestra in his *Nocturne*, which they then perform with Pears in the solo role.

Britten's music has been used as incidental music in various feature films and television programmes. Ingmar Bergman used extracts from the Cello Suites in *Fanny and Alexander*, and Derek Jarman used the *Four Sea Interludes* from *Peter Grimes* in *The Angelic Conversation* in 1985. Frank Seitz's 1982 film *Doktor Faustus* features excerpts from *A Midsummer Night's Dream* and the *Cello Symphony*, while Leos Carax, in the 1986 film *Mauvais sang* (or *The Night is Young*) used *Simple Symphony* and *Variations on a Theme of Frank Bridge* – he used the latter again in *Les amants de Pont-Neuf* in 1991. On television, Ken Russell harnessed *Peter Grimes* and *The Young Person's Guide* to his film *Clouds of Glory: The Rime of the Ancient Mariner*; the *Corpus Christi Carol* was used in two Jeff Buckley programmes on French TV, *Fall in Light* and *Everybody Here Wants You*, as well as in Todd Louiso's film, *Love Liza*. The Spanish TV feature on Virginia Woolf for *Aleph, Lectures contades* featured *Les Illuminations* and the Cello Suites, while a BBC drama *No Night is Too Long* had extensive extracts from *Missa Brevis*.

7

The things Britten said about Britten

Even at school I can remember clearly the vocal and energetic surprise with which the other small boys caught me reading orchestral scores in bed. (1962)

I couldn't work alone. I can only work really because of the tradition that I am conscious of behind me.

Compared with Schubert or Mozart or the great ones, I write awfully little. (1961)

I do 99 per cent of my work *thinking* about it – walking, or in trains, aeroplanes, if it's not too bumpy, and in buses and cars and so forth. Then when the music is fixed in my head I go to the paper and work out more precisely the details. I don't use the piano except at the very end. (1956)

There is, unfortunately, a tendency in many quarters today to believe that brilliance of technique is a danger rather than a help. This is sheer nonsense. There has never been a composer worth his salt who has not had supreme technique. (1946)

I think I have all the technique to do anything. I must *be* more. (1944)

If I had been born in 1813 instead of 1913 I should have been a romantic, primarily concerned to express my personality in music. (1951)

I can't see any great defect in sweetness as long as it's not weakness. (1963)

Night and Silence, these are two of the things I cherish most. (1969)

I can find nothing wrong with offering to my fellow men

music which may inspire them or comfort them, which may touch them or entertain them, even educate them. (1964)

All of us spend far too much time worrying about whether a work is a shattering masterpiece. Let us not be so self-conscious. Maybe in thirty years' time very few works that are well-known today will still be played, but does that matter so much? (1966)

I would rather have my music used than write masterpieces which were not used. (1968)

I haven't yet achieved the simplicity I should like in my music, and I am enormously aware that I haven't yet come up to the technical standards [Frank] Bridge set me. (1963)

I always encourage my works to be sung, abroad, in the vernacular. Of course, something is lost, but not a great deal when you substitute the gibberish which can result from singers using languages they do not understand and cannot pronounce. (1960)

I like the piano very much as a background instrument, but I don't feel inclined to treat it as a melodic instrument. I find that it's limited in colour. I don't really like the sound of the modern piano. (1961)

It is a bit of a strain all this playing with experts. It isn't that I don't know what to do, but with so little time to practise, my fingers simply won't do what I want. I am gradually learning that one cannot do *everything* in this world. (1936)

I am the furthest removed from an ivory-tower composer that you can think of. (1969)

The whole of my life has been devoted to acts of creation, and I cannot take part in acts of destruction. (1942)

I wanted to have nothing to do with a military system that, to me, was part of Europe's decay. Mistakenly, as it turned out, I felt that Europe was finished. (1959)

I believe in letting an invader in and then setting him a good example. (1942)

I'm certainly a dedicated Christian, but I must confess I am influenced by the Bishop of Woolwich and [Dietrich] Bonhoeffer, and at the moment I do not find myself worshipping as regularly as perhaps I will later. (1963)

I know I am horribly intolerant in a youthful hot-headed way. (1937)

There was one very serious quarrel which I myself was involved with, with one of my closest friends in the [English Opera Group] company. And I can remember Kathleen [Ferrier] taking me aside one day and saying 'Look, do try and be nice'. And so I tried to be nice – and it worked. (1968)

(on *A Boy was Born*)
I can't help but like this work as I feel it is genuinely musical. (1935)

(on his Violin Concerto)
So far it is without question my best piece. It is rather serious, I'm afraid – but it's got some tunes in it! (1939)

(on 'Parade' in *Les Illuminations*)
It should be made to sound creepy, evil, dirty (apologies!), and really desperate. (1939)

(on his operetta *Paul Bunyan*)
Full of tunes that people even whistle! (1941)

(on being asked by an Australian music teacher why he had omitted the piano from his *Young Person's Guide to the Orchestra*)
The piano is not an orchestral instrument, but tell your students I'll include it in my 'Old Person's Guide to the Orchestra'. (1970)

(on his *Serenade* for tenor, horn and strings)
Not important stuff, but quite pleasant, I think. (1943)

(on the opening to his *Canticle II: Abraham and Isaac*)
That's worth a million dollars! (1952)

(on *The Turn of the Screw* and *Canticle III: Still Falls the Rain*)
I feel I am on the threshold of a new musical world. (1955)

(on *War Requiem*)
Some of my right-wing friends loathed it, 'though the music is superb, of course', they'd say. But that's neither here nor there to me. The message is what counts. (1963)

(on opera)
I have been fascinated by the most powerful medium of musical communication that I know. (1972)

So many of the great things of the world have come from the outsider, and that lone dog isn't always attractive. That is what I try to portray in *Peter Grimes*. (1967)

I want singers who can act. Mozart, Gluck and Verdi wanted the same thing. (1960)

Honours don't really touch one, but there are moments in one's depressions, when one feels one's work to be hopelessly inadequate (all too often!), that they *do* encourage. (1965)

I *must* get a better composer somehow – but how, but how? (1964)

(while gingerly walking on a hotel carpet with red lines in its pattern)
If I can get right up and down the corridor without touching the lines, it will mean that I am a composer. (1946)

(on being complimented on the boys' chorus in *Gloriana*)
It's because I'm still thirteen. (1953)

8

Britten in print

For twenty years the most comprehensive biography of Britten has been Humphrey Carpenter's brilliantly researched 680-page tome, *Benjamin Britten: A Biography*, published by Faber and Faber in 1992. It scores in the incomparable testimony gathered from Britten's closest associates. But it is weak in its musical analysis, obsessively centred on Britten's sexuality. Now Carpenter's supremacy is under threat from a new full-scale biography by the conductor and Britten scholar, Paul Kildea, written for the centenary. With fresh intuition and revelations, Kildea offers a contemporary take on the Britten phenomenon, unvarnished yet sympathetic. Another study is on its way from Neil Powell, who recently chronicled both the father-son relationship of Kingsley and Martin Amis, and the life of George Crabbe, who 'invented' Peter Grimes.

Shorter biographies worth seeking out are Michael Oliver's *Benjamin Britten* (Phaidon, 1996), which is full of original perceptions, Michael Kennedy's *Britten* (1981) in Dent's Master Musicians series (after thirty years, its well-thumbed contents have worn much better than its binding), and David Matthews's *Britten* (Haus Publishing, 2003), which has the revealing insights of a fellow composer.

The *magnum opus* of Britten scholarship is the multi-layered edition of his selected letters, which currently stands at five volumes, with one more to come. Britten's publisher at Faber Music, Donald Mitchell, began this project with the assistance of Philip Reed. The first two volumes, covering Britten's life up until 1945, were published in 1991, and set a new benchmark of knowledge in their footnotes, which sometimes run for pages at a time. As the further volumes emerged, Reed and Mervyn Cooke became the lead editors. The books are indispensable for anyone exploring Britten's life and music in depth, but their episodic nature is for most people inimical to a continuous read. The series is called *Letters from a Life*: volumes 1–3 are published by Faber & Faber, volumes 4 and 5 by Boydell Press, and they run to 3,598 pages so far!

An extensive and erudite selection of Britten's 1928–38 diaries has now been made by another Britten scholar, John Evans, and published as *Journeying Boy* by Faber & Faber (2009). This allows us a fascinating gaze (rather than glimpse) into Britten's daily life and concerns during his musical apprenticeship.

Reminiscences of thirty friends and associates are compiled in Alan Blyth's *Remembering Britten* (Hutchinson, 1981), though they are long on compliments and short on anecdotes. Beth Britten's memoir *My Brother Benjamin* (Kensal Press, 1986) is often unreliable on facts, but catches the family flavour. Imogen Holst's journal during Britten's composition of *Gloriana* is invaluable testimony from the coalface, and forms part of Christopher Grogan's fascinating study *Imogen Holst: A Life in Music* (Boydell Press, revised edition 2010). Peter Evans's *The Music of Benjamin Britten* (J. M. Dent, 1979) offers comprehensive analysis, but can be hard work for the layman. The economics of the music are deconstructed in Paul Kildea's *Selling Britten* (Oxford University Press, 2002), and his *Britten on Music* (OUP, 2003) provides an almost complete compendium of Britten's published judgments of his own and other people's.

With great gratitude I have drawn on information and ideas in all those books, which have been at my elbow throughout the preparation of this *Pocket Guide*. Other recommendations include:

Brett, Philip, *Music and Sexuality in Britten* (University of California Press, 2006)

Bridcut, John, *Britten's Children* (Faber and Faber, 2004)

Cooke, Mervyn (ed.), *The Cambridge Companion to Benjamin Britten* (Cambridge University Press, 1999)

Headington, Christopher, *Peter Pears: A Biography* (Faber and Faber, 1992)

Herbert, David (ed.), *The Operas of Benjamin Britten* (Hamish Hamilton, 1979)

Mitchell, Donald, *Britten & Auden in the Thirties* (Boydell Press, 1981)

Mitchell, Donald and John Evans, *Pictures from a Life: Benjamin Britten 1913–1976* (Faber and Faber, 1978)

Mitchell, Donald and Hans Keller (eds.), *Benjamin Britten: a Commentary on his Works from a Group of Specialists* (Rockliff, 1952)

Palmer, Christopher (ed.), *The Britten Companion* (Faber and Faber, 1984)

Round Britten Quiz II

ANSWERS ON PAGE 410

1 What was the most northerly city Britten visited?

2 When did Britten make his debut on BBC Television, and what was he doing?

3 How many and which works by Schoenberg did Britten perform in public?

4 What knocked Britten sideways at the age of ten?

5 What did Britten send the King's sister when she was ill?

6 Who walked in on Pears and Britten sitting up in a large double bed one morning, surrounded by papers, and was invited by Britten to 'come and join us – there's room for you too!'?

9

Britten the centenarian

Britten's mother was wrong when she lined her baby son up to be the fourth musical B, after Bach, Beethoven and Brahms. Much the more significant marker was the year of his birth – 1913, exactly one hundred years after Verdi and Wagner. It meant that one of the greatest operatic composers of the twentieth century would be indissolubly bound to the two greatest of the nineteenth. As it turned out, Britten was addicted to Wagner as a young man, and swallowed his operas whole, while he never stopped admiring, and learning from, the way Verdi wrote for both voice and stage. So they make a happy trio.

The musical world and the general media love anniversaries. But for figures on the margins of history this can be either a blessing or a curse. They can shine in solitary splendour in unaccustomed limelight, or they can be overshadowed by the giants who happen to share it with them. So Delius had plenty of room beside his fellow 2012 birthday boys, Debussy and Cage, but the tercentenaries of C. P. E. Bach and Gluck in 2014 may be swamped by the sesquicentenary of Richard Strauss.

In every year ending -13 or -63, Britten will always have to compete with the Verdi and Wagner celebrations. It gives precious little chance to Mascagni, Alkan or George Lloyd, and even Lutosławski must struggle. Forty years ago, most music buffs thought Britten was *passé*; the idea that he could look Verdi and Wagner in the eye, and stand his ground, would have been mere illusion. That's not how it looks today.

His centenary celebrations began early. The thirty-year research project *Letters from a Life*, which makes a judicious selection from some 80,000 letters in the Britten archive, was long ago designed to reach completion in 2013. The two new biographies of Britten have been timed for the anniversary, together with a fresh account of his life in pictures. Many of his juvenile manuscripts have been lined up for publication, while a complete Thematic Catalogue, numbering at least 1,200 works, is being made available online, along with more of his extensive personal archive. Aldeburgh Music and the Britten–Pears Young Artist Programme (formerly the Britten–Pears School for Advanced Musical Studies) are no longer seasonal organizations, but operate all year round. The Britten–Pears Foundation is building a new archive centre beside his old home in Aldeburgh. Jointly with the Royal Philharmonic Society (itself marking its bicentenary), it is honouring Britten's concern for living composers by the award of six major commissions of new music. During the centenary year, details of all Britten-related activities around the world are listed on www.britten100.org.

All this is quite apart from specific concert and recital series, opera festivals, and exhibitions to mark the centenary – with a place of honour for the Aldeburgh Festival itself, sixty-five years old in 2013. But Britten's music – his operatic canon in particular – has already been enjoying rude health. For the first seven months of 2012, the Operabase website listed thirty-two professional productions of ten different Britten operas in thirty-one cities around the world. Nineteen of these productions were new – six were of *Peter Grimes*, including one at La Scala. There were thirty-three performances in different countries of *The Turn of the Screw*. The Met in New York put on *Billy Budd*, Prague staged six performances of *Gloriana*, and Copenhagen and Los Angeles *Albert Herring*. This was before the centenary had even begun. It suggests remarkable confidence in Britten at the box office, and not just in the English-speaking world. Even the Royal Opera House in London has been planning a new production of *Gloriana* – its first since the ill-fated premiere in 1953.

It's no mean achievement for a composer who wanted his music to be 'useful, and to the living'.

PART TWO
The life of Britten

10

Britten year by year

Age 0, 1913–14

Edward Benjamin Britten is born in the Suffolk town of Lowestoft on 22 November 1913, six months after the notorious premiere of Stravinsky's *The Rite of Spring*. His parents, Edith Britten (*née* Hockey) and Robert Britten, a dentist, choose the biblical name Benjamin to indicate he would remain their youngest and last child. They already have three others: Barbara, Robert (Bobby) and Elizabeth (Beth), so Benjamin is the fourth B of the family. His ambitious mother soon envisages him as the fourth B on a larger stage, to follow Bach, Beethoven and Brahms – appropriately enough, since 22 November is also the feast-day of the patron saint of music, St Cecilia.

At two months, he is baptised in St John's Church, Lowestoft. At three months, he nearly dies of pneumonia, the first of many illnesses in his life. At eight months, the First World War begins.

Ages 1–2, 1914–16

Britten is called 'Dear' so frequently that he comes to believe it is his name. His earliest musical memory is of his mother singing him to sleep.

Age 3, 1916–17

Britten gets his first stage experience – as an elf in a domestic Christmas performance of *Cinderella*.

Bolsheviks take power in Russia after the October Revolution led by Lenin.

Age 4, 1917–18

Britten has his first piano lessons from his mother.

The poet Wilfred Owen writes 'Strange Meeting', which Britten was to set to music as the culmination of his *War Requiem* four decades later. Owen is killed in action seven days before the armistice ending the First World War.

Age 5, 1918–19

Britten, 'with madly curly hair and pink tights', plays Tom, the boy chimney sweep, in a local production of *The Water Babies* – thirty years before writing his own opera *The Little Sweep*.

He writes his earliest known composition: 'Do you no that my Daddy has gone to London today' (for two voices and piano).

Age 6, 1919–20

Britten writes his first stage work: a play, 'The Royal Falily' (*sic*), with a short musical interlude.

Age 7, 1920–1

Britten goes to his first school, Southolme, a short walk from his home, and begins piano lessons with Miss Ethel Astle.

Age 8, 1921–2

Britten passes his Associated Board piano examination at Elementary grade with honours in July, and his parents give him a book of Chopin Polonaises as a reward.

Age 9, 1922–3

Britten is given *A Dictionary of Musical Terms* for his birthday by his Uncle Willie. He writes a song, *Beware!*, which later becomes his earliest composition to be published. He starts viola lessons with Audrey Alston – a rare choice of instrument for one so young, who has not first taken up the violin. But it was also the instrument of Bach, Mozart, Beethoven, Mendelssohn, Dvořák, Vaughan Williams, Hindemith and Bridge. He joins South Lodge preparatory school in Lowestoft.

Age 10, 1923–4

Britten's parents give him Beethoven's thirty-two piano sonatas (edited by Liszt and arranged in order of difficulty) for his birthday. Miss Alston takes him to an orchestral concert in Norwich, where the composer Frank Bridge conducts his suite *The Sea*. Britten is 'knocked sideways'.

Age 11, 1924–5

Britten acquires his first orchestral miniature score: Beethoven's 'Eroica' Symphony. This is followed by Beethoven's 5th and 6th Symphonies, Stravinsky's *Firebird* Suite, and the Overture to Wagner's opera *Tannhäuser*. He also acquires the complete Chopin Waltzes and a vocal score of Elgar's *The Dream of Gerontius*.

Age 12, 1925–6

Britten's father sends the BBC the ninety-one-page full score of his son's *Ouverture Never Prepared* for orchestra. (It is not known how the BBC responded.) Benjamin collects the scores of Schubert's 'Unfinished' Symphony, the overtures to Mozart's operas *The Marriage of Figaro* and *The Magic Flute*, and to Wagner's *The Mastersingers of Nuremberg* and *Lohengrin*. Miss Astle gives him a different edition of the complete Beethoven piano sonatas. He passes his Advanced level Associated Board exam with honours.

Age 13, 1926–7

Britten becomes head boy of South Lodge school. He also writes his first symphony (in D minor): 117 pages of full score for a vast orchestra, including eight horns and an oboe

d'amore. At the Norwich Triennial Festival he meets Frank
Bridge, who looks over his recent compositions and offers
him lessons. Bridge also suggests piano lessons with Harold
Samuel in London.

Age 14, 1927–8

Britten leaves his prep school as Captain of Cricket and Victor
Ludorum. But he blots his copybook by turning his end-of-
term essay on 'Animals' into a polemic against hunting and
war: this was eight years before his orchestral song cycle *Our
Hunting Fathers*. During his last term he begins his *Quatre
chansons françaises* after studying Ravel's *Introduction and Allegro*
and Debussy's *Prélude à l'après-midi d'un faune*.

He joins the Norfolk public school, Gresham's, as a board-
er, where he opts out of the school cadet force. He has his first
experience of plainsong, which is chanted daily in chapel. He
continues to go to London for composition advice from Frank
Bridge, and to attend concerts with him.

Age 15, 1928–9

Britten has a letter about Beethoven's Cello Sonata in C published in the *Musical Times*. He plays viola in a school recital
of piano trios by Mozart and Brahms.

Age 16, 1929–30

Britten counts his sixteenth birthday as a 'red letter day' in his
life, because of his parents' present: a full score of Beethoven's
opera *Fidelio*.

His *Bagatelle* for piano trio is performed in his final year
at Gresham's School, with the director of music playing the
piano part. Wins scholarship to the Royal College of Music,
after an interview with the composers Ralph Vaughan Williams and John Ireland. Ireland becomes his composition
teacher, and Arthur Benjamin his piano teacher. Lives in digs
in Bayswater.

Age 17, 1930–1

Britten moves to Kensington to share a flat with his sister Beth. He joins the English Madrigal Choir with his elder sister Barbara.

Age 18, 1931–2

Britten plays piano trios with fellow RCM students Remo Lauricella (violin) and Bernard Richards (cello). He writes his opus 1, a *Sinfonietta* for ten instruments (wind and string quintets): his rehearsals for it at the RCM are bedevilled by irregular attendance by his fellow students. He also writes his first stage work, a ballet *Plymouth Town*.

Age 19, 1932–3

Britten meets Schoenberg after hearing his *Variations for Orchestra*. He writes his choral variations *A Boy Was Born*. The BBC broadcasts his music for the first time in February 1933 (the *Phantasy* string quintet).

Hitler comes to power in Germany. Britten sees the German film *Emil and the Detectives*, which greatly impresses him.

Age 20, 1933–4

Britten graduates from the Royal College of Music. His plans to study with the Austrian composer Alban Berg in Vienna are overruled by his mother, who says on RCM advice that Berg is 'not a good influence'.

He does visit Florence in April 1934 for the biennial festival of the International Society of Contemporary Music, where his *Phantasy* oboe quartet is played – his first overseas performance. He also meets the German conductor Hermann Scherchen and his teenage son, Wulff. This first trip abroad is interrupted by the death of his father from cancer. Later in the year he travels to Basel, Vienna, Munich and Paris on an extended tour with his mother. He sees fifteen operas in five weeks, including *Rigoletto*, *Aida*, *Falstaff*, *Die Fledermaus*, *Die Zauberflöte*, *Arabella*, *Salome*, *Carmen*, *Die Meistersinger* and *Götterdämmerung*.

During 1934, three leading British composers die: Holst, Delius and (on the day Britten's *A Boy was Born* is first broadcast) Elgar.

Age 21, 1934–5

Britten is restless. Since leaving the RCM in 1933, his career has been in the doldrums. He has wrestled ineffectively with pieces for string quartet, taken far too long to write his children's songs *Friday Afternoons*, and produced a few minor pieces of church and chamber music. For his one extended score, *Simple Symphony*, he 'dished up' musical ideas from his childhood – surprising for someone so young and apparently full of promise (and ideas). He has found no clear way to capitalise on *A Boy Was Born*, and resolves to keep practising the piano in case he needs to depend on performing rather than composing. He does use these fallow months to develop as a conductor (of an amateur orchestra in Suffolk) and to listen (voraciously and often impatiently) to all sorts of music on the wireless and gramophone.

Then, out of the blue, his life changes, on 27 April 1935 – his second 'red letter day'. He is approached by the new General Post Office Film Unit to write the music for a short documentary *The King's Stamp*. He overcomes his reluctance to tackle 'this God-forsaken subject', writes to precise timings, and is pleased with the result. He soon starts on another film *Coal Face*, which leads to more than two dozen film commissions over the next three years at the same time as writing substantial concert pieces at breakneck speed. The creative block has passed, and from now on the creative juices almost never dry up. Although he soon stops writing film scores, a cinematic technique peppers his work for the rest of his life. He also never forgets the discipline of writing to tight deadlines and low budgets.

Through his GPO work he meets the poet W. H. Auden. Their seven-year friendship will propel Britten's composing career. But he finds the intellectual brilliance of Auden, Christopher Isherwood and their circle intimidating, and admits to an 'overwhelming inferiority complex'. Auden urges him to put his homosexual longings into practice.

Britten develops a platonic friendship with Piers Dunkerley, a thirteen-year-old pupil at South Lodge, which was to last twenty-five years. He writes in his diary: 'I am lost without some children (of either sex) near me'.

Mussolini annexes part of Abyssinia after securing initial British and French assent in the Hoare–Laval pact.

Age 22, 1935–6

Britten is left largely indifferent by the year of three kings: George V (about whose death he 'can't feel any emotion'), Edward VIII ('a king with too much personality', but the abdication broadcast is 'deeply moving'), and George VI ('poor man masters his stutter well').

He feels 'infinitely better off' than a year before, earning his living as a composer 'with occasionally something to spare'. As well as his £5 a week from the GPO Film Unit, he signs up with the publisher Boosey & Hawkes, which guarantees him £3 a week in royalties. As a result he is on more than twice the national average wage.

Three months before the outbreak of the Spanish Civil War, he visits Barcelona and meets the composer Lennox Berkeley, who then joins him on holiday in Cornwall, and becomes attracted to him. After their collaboration on the film *Night Mail*, Auden devises the text for Britten's first orchestral song cycle *Our Hunting Fathers*. The premiere in Norwich is Britten's first fully professional conducting engagement. Members of the orchestra respond to his setting of 'Rats Away!' by running around in rehearsal as if chasing rats on the floor, and are chided by Vaughan Williams, who is taking part in the same concert.

Britten's third 'red letter day' is 11 November 1936, when
he 'discovers' Mozart. He is 'knocked flat' after seeing *The
Marriage of Figaro* at Covent Garden. 'It is without exception
the loveliest thing I have ever seen on any stage. This simple
beauty (expressing every emotion) is withering to any ambitions one might have – & yet it is good to have lived in a
world that could produce such perfection.' Two days later he
buys the miniature score, and then the whole opera on 78 rpm
records: he says the performance is still 'haunting me beyond
words' and is 'a land-mark in my history'.

Age 23, 1936–7

Britten and Beth both succumb to flu at New Year 1937: their
mother comes to London to look after them, but falls ill herself.
She develops pneumonia and dies of a heart attack – for which
he feels partly responsible. Although grief-stricken, he is liberated from her dominating influence, and finally from his childhood. He gets to know a young singer called Peter Pears, as a
result of the death of their mutual friend Peter Burra.

In May 1937 Britten is commissioned by the conductor
Boyd Neel to write a piece for strings for the Salzburg Festival.
Fired by the prospect of an international platform, and by the
idea of a tribute to his mentor, he dashes off in just five weeks
his ten brilliant *Variations on a Theme of Frank Bridge*, a twenty-
five-minute work that is one of his enduring achievements.

Age 24, 1937–8

Britten writes incidental music for a BBC religious programme
The Company of Heaven, including 'A thousand gleaming fires'
– his first piece for the tenor voice of Pears, then a member of
the BBC Singers. He performs his own Piano Concerto at the
Proms, conducted by Sir Henry Wood. The BBC broadcasts
it on radio and the infant television service.

Britten uses his mother's legacy to buy, and then convert,
The Old Mill at Snape – the first home of his own. He shares
it with Lennox Berkeley. He adopts a twelve-year-old Basque

boy, Andoni Barrutia, a refugee from the Spanish Civil War, but the arrangement fails after two weeks. The American composer Aaron Copland visits Britten in Suffolk. Britten resurrects his brief 1934 friendship with Wulff Scherchen, and they fall in love. Pears and Berkeley are also in love with Britten, but in neither case is it requited. He gives Beth away at her wedding to Kit Welford.

Hitler annexes Austria. Britten approves of Neville Chamberlain's efforts to avert war with Germany.

Age 25, 1938–9

Britten, as he turns twenty-five, describes himself as '*very* depressed' by the idea of his youth 'slipping away'.

In January 1939 Auden and Isherwood leave for New York. In April Britten and Pears follow them to North America, though their trip was initially intended to last only a few months. Britten perhaps sees it as a 'cooling-off period' in his relationship with Scherchen: he also feels disillusioned with the BBC (though it had been generous in championing a composer still in his early twenties). At Southampton, they are seen off by Frank Bridge, who gives Britten his viola as a 'bon voyage' present: they will never meet again.

Britten writes his Violin Concerto and a glittering 'fanfare' for piano and strings *Young Apollo*, which for the soloist (Britten himself) evokes the absent Scherchen. At the same time, Britten and Pears become lovers, the start of a partnership that will last thirty-seven years. They lodge with the Mayer family on Long Island, New York: Elizabeth Mayer becomes a surrogate mother to Britten. He writes the first of almost sixty arrangements of works by Henry Purcell across a period of thirty years.

The Second World War breaks out in September, which results in Britten and Pears remaining in the United States for a further two and a half years. The same month, he is commissioned by the Japanese government to write a work in honour of the Imperial House.

Age 26, 1939–40

Britten contracts a serious streptococcal illness in early 1940, which confines him to bed for six weeks. He then writes *Sinfonia da Requiem* for the Japanese government, which they reject a year before the attack on Pearl Harbor. In England Wulff Scherchen is interned as an enemy alien and transported to an internment camp in Canada: Britten's correspondence with him becomes sporadic and his feelings fade. He completes the first of many works dedicated to his partner Peter Pears: *Seven Sonnets of Michelangelo*, although the original motivation for them may have been Scherchen. Britten and Pears move to Brooklyn, New York, where they share a house with Auden and his friends, but find their bohemian lifestyle uncongenial.

Age 27, 1940–1

Britten's mentor Frank Bridge dies. Britten and Auden complete their high-school operetta *Paul Bunyan* (in effect, a musical), but its run at Columbia University is not well received by the New York critics. Britten and Pears perform four folksong arrangements, the first of well over a thousand such performances. Britten is appointed conductor of a semi-professional orchestra on Long Island, while Pears trains a local choral society.

They spend the summer with British friends near San Diego, and Britten chances on a volume of eighteenth-century poetry by the Suffolk cleric George Crabbe. While reading his poem 'The Borough' about a brutal fisherman called Peter Grimes, Britten realises 'in a flash' that he must write an opera on the subject, and also that he must somehow return to England. But there he has been criticised for his avoidance of military service, and 'having saved one's art and one's skin at the cost of failure to do one's duty'.

Age 28, 1941–2

Britten suffers writer's block while he and Pears spend several months waiting for a transatlantic passage home, though packed and ready to leave at twenty-four hours' notice. In December 1941 Japanese aircraft attack Pearl Harbor, and the United States enters the war. A month later Britten goes to Boston to hear his *Sinfonia da Requiem* conducted by Serge Koussevitzky, and is thrilled by the performance. Koussevitzky offers Britten a fee of $1,000 to write his projected opera about Peter Grimes.

In March 1942 Britten and Pears at last secure berths on a neutral Swedish freighter sailing across the Atlantic in convoy. The actual crossing takes twelve days, but initial slow progress up the eastern American seaboard extends the journey to five weeks. 'Scares apart', Britten said, 'that month at sea was one of the most enjoyable of my life'. He just 'couldn't stop the flow' of music, writing his *Ceremony of Carols* and an unaccompanied choral work *Hymn to St Cecilia* – his final, and perhaps most perfect, collaboration with Auden.

Soon after disembarking at Liverpool, he asks the left-wing author Montagu Slater to write the libretto for *Peter Grimes*. Two or three weeks later, Britten faces a tribunal to plead his conscientious objection to war service. He and Pears are allowed to continue their work as musicians. In September they give the premiere of Britten's *Seven Sonnets of Michelangelo* to acclaim, and the work is recorded immediately. But Britten finds public performances a strain on his nerves, 'rather like parading naked in public', and soon gives up performing as a piano soloist, apart from the occasional Mozart concerto when doubling as its conductor. He continues to accompany singers and occasionally to play chamber music.

Age 29, 1942–3

Britten spends several weeks in hospital with a severe attack of measles. But despite his illness, his reacquaintance with England prompts a period of prolific composition, lasting twelve years. While convalescing at The Old Mill, he writes his *Serenade* for Pears to sing with the horn-player Dennis Brain. He also writes a string orchestra piece and the cantata *Rejoice in the Lamb*, while continuing to plan *Peter Grimes*, although progress on the libretto is slow. He and Pears also give recitals all over the country. He meets his fellow composer Michael Tippett for the first time, and they become friends.

Age 30, 1943–4

Britten starts writing the music for *Peter Grimes* at the start of 1944. Pears's work as a principal tenor at Sadler's Wells Opera Company leads to an agreement that the company will stage the new opera in 1945. Koussevitzky, whose Tanglewood Festival is in abeyance because of the war, consents to this arrangement. Britten begins a lifelong recording relationship with Decca.

Age 31, 1944–5

Britten's fourth 'red letter day', 7 June 1945, secures his place in musical history, when his opera *Peter Grimes* opens at Sadler's Wells Theatre in London a month after the end of the war in Europe. It is universally acclaimed: the critics describe it as 'masterly', 'thrilling' and 'a work of genius'. Even the conductor on a no. 38 London bus which passes the theatre is heard to cry out to his passengers: 'Any more for Peter Grimes, the sadistic fisherman?' But, despite this success, tensions within the opera company convince Britten that he has no future at Sadler's Wells, and that in the austere post-war economic climate he must write opera on a smaller scale.

In July Britten persuades Yehudi Menuhin to take him as his accompanist (in place of Gerald Moore, who had been booked) on a recital tour of Germany. He is haunted by the experience of performing to the emaciated survivors of Belsen concentration camp and seeing a country in ruins. As soon as he returns home, he develops a high fever but writes his darkest song cycle *The Holy Sonnets of John Donne*. The same month, atomic bombs are dropped on Hiroshima and Nagasaki, and Japan surrenders.

Age 32, 1945–6

Britten writes his most famous piece for *Instruments of the Orchestra*, a film sponsored by the Ministry of Education. Based on a theme of Purcell, it becomes known in concert form as *The Young Person's Guide to the Orchestra*. At Glyndebourne he produces the first of his seven chamber operas, *The Rape of Lucretia*, which has mixed reviews and is then taken on tour round Britain to almost empty theatres. The result is a loss of £14,000, and the cancellation of plans for a long-term collaboration between Britten and Glyndebourne. Instead the English Opera Group is created, with Britten its leading light as both composer and conductor.

He travels to Tanglewood for the delayed American premiere of *Peter Grimes*, conducted by Leonard Bernstein.

Age 33, 1946–7

Britten conducts his new comic opera *Albert Herring* at Glyndebourne under the aegis of the new EOG. It is then taken on tour to the Netherlands and Switzerland, together with *The Rape of Lucretia*. During the journey, Pears, Eric Crozier and Britten hatch the idea of staging their own Aldeburgh Festival of Music & The Arts.

Lucretia is recorded in an abridged version by HMV – the first of his operas to be committed to disc. A month later, his *Donne Sonnets* are also recorded. *Peter Grimes* is given a new production at Covent Garden.

Britten moves from The Old Mill in Snape to a large house in Aldeburgh, 4 Crabbe Street.

Age 34, 1947–8

Britten writes *The Beggar's Opera*, a re-creation of the eighteenth-century confection of popular ballads of the time, but in his own musical voice. In New York the Metropolitan Opera stages a new production of *Peter Grimes*.

The first Aldeburgh Festival opens with the first performance of *Saint Nicolas*, written for Pears's old school, Lancing College, and includes three performances of *Albert Herring* conducted by Britten, chamber music by Schubert, Ravel, Bridge and Tippett, and lectures on poets and painters by E. M. Forster, Kenneth Clark and William Plomer.

Age 35, 1948–9

Britten becomes severely depressed, and is told by his doctor to take three months off work. When Pears takes him on holiday to Italy, he begins an affair with Venice which lasts for the rest of his life. His first of seven visits, in January 1949, revitalises him, and he embarks (with Eric Crozier as the librettist and producer) on a children's opera *The Little Sweep*, which forms part of an 'entertainment' for the second Aldeburgh Festival, *Let's Make an Opera!* He writes it in a fortnight.

Britten writes his *Spring Symphony*, his first large-scale piece for chorus and orchestra. Once again, Serge Koussevitzky, who has commissioned it, agrees to forgo the first performance, which is given in Holland in July 1949.

Britten and Pears embark on a major recital tour of the United States and Canada.

Age 36, 1949–50

Britten starts writing the music for *Billy Budd*, for which E. M. Forster and Eric Crozier have written the libretto. It's his first grand opera since *Peter Grimes*, but Sadler's Wells Opera turns down the chance of staging the premiere.

Britten is now the owner of two Rolls-Royces.

Age 37, 1950–1

Britten arranges (with Imogen Holst) a new performing version of Purcell's opera *Dido and Aeneas*, which the EOG perform as part of the Festival of Britain. He continues work on *Billy Budd*. For the first time in many years, he looks over the score of his first opera *Paul Bunyan* and decides, 'the whole thing embarrasses me hugely'.

Schoenberg dies in October 1951. Britten says, 'The world is a poorer place now this giant is no more.'

Age 38, 1951–2

Britten steps in to conduct the premiere of *Billy Budd* at Covent Garden when the intended conductor Josef Krips withdraws. He is encouraged by his friend Lord Harewood (cousin of the new Queen, Elizabeth II) to write a national opera, which is commissioned for the Coronation in 1953. Britten declines the post of Music Director at the Royal Opera House.

Professional jealousy results from the publication of a 400-page book of essays on Britten's music by eighteen musicians, critics and musicologists. It is seen by some as an excessive compliment to one so young.

Age 39, 1952–3

Britten's house on the Aldeburgh seafront is invaded by the sea in the damaging East Anglian weather of January 1953, and the reception of his Coronation opera *Gloriana* in June is also stormy. Its focus on the conflict between the public duty and private affections of Elizabeth I is criticised as inappropriate to the occasion. It is revived once the following year, but then disappears from view, to become the least successful of his operas since *Paul Bunyan*. Many years are to pass before it finds its feet.

Britten, appointed Companion of Honour at the Coronation, is one of several homosexuals in public life interviewed by the police, but no proceedings follow.

Age 40, 1953–4

Britten writes his chamber opera *The Turn of the Screw*, based on the Henry James ghost story which had first excited him

more than twenty years before. He is held up by an attack of
bursitis in his right arm. All recital and conducting work is
cancelled. The opera's central character of Miles requires a
treble voice: Britten's choice of David Hemmings, although
inspired dramatically, is potentially problematic, as he
develops an infatuation for the boy. The premiere in Venice
is a triumph.

Age 41, 1954-5

Britten records *The Turn of the Screw* – the first of his operas
to be committed to disc so soon after its premiere. He starts
work on a full-length ballet, *The Prince of the Pagodas*.

   After more than a decade of almost continuous work for the
stage, he and Pears set off in November 1955 on a five-month
world tour – intended as holiday, but interrupted by several
song recitals.

Age 42, 1955-6

Britten's world tour takes him and Pears from the Netherlands
to Yugoslavia and Turkey, before they fly to India, Ceylon,
Malaya, Thailand, Indonesia, Hong Kong and Japan. He is
profoundly affected by the gamelan music he experiences on
Bali and by the formulaic Noh play he attends in Japan. Both
are to become substantial influences on his own music, not
least on *The Prince of the Pagodas*, the longest orchestral score
he was ever to write. On his return home, he finds it difficult
to complete, and uncharacteristically misses his deadlines.

   Anglo-French troops take control of the Suez Canal, but
withdraw later under American and United Nations pressure.

Age 43, 1956-7

Britten's three-act ballet is finally performed at Covent Garden,
with choreography by John Cranko. He takes *The Turn of the
Screw* to Canada on an EOG tour: during the transatlantic voyage he embarks on his first opera for television, *Noye's Fludde*,

based on a medieval mystery play and intended for performance by children of varying musical ability from his local community. Television interest subsequently wanes, but Britten's does not.

The horn player, Dennis Brain, is killed in a car accident.

Age 44, 1957–8

Britten and Pears move house again: they swap their beach-side home for The Red House, a larger Aldeburgh property owned by the artist Mary Potter. It lies further inland, beside the golf course, and affords them greater privacy, 'away from the gaping faces and irritating publicity of that sea-front'.

Noye's Fludde is performed at the 1958 Aldeburgh Festival by Suffolk schoolchildren: some of the players and singers are only beginners.

Vaughan Williams dies in August 1958, and Britten writes to his widow, praising 'a very great man' of 'uncompromising courage'.

Age 45, 1958–9

Britten records *Peter Grimes*, one of the first operas to appear under the Decca label in stereo. The Jubilee Hall in Alde-burgh is expanded in size, and Britten plans to stage a new opera there in the 1960 Aldeburgh Festival. He and Pears themselves construct its libretto from Shakespeare's comedy, *A Midsummer Night's Dream*.

Age 46, 1959–60

Britten completes *A Midsummer Night's Dream*, and revises *Billy Budd* as an opera in two acts instead of four. He records the new version for the BBC.

At a London concert, Britten meets two Russian musicians who become important fixtures in the last fifteen years of his life: the composer Dmitri Shostakovich and the cellist Mstislav Rostropovich, for whom he immediately offers to write a sonata, the first of six Britten works for cello.

Age 47, 1960–1

Britten is commissioned to write a major choral work for the consecration of the new cathedral in Coventry, which is being built beside the bombed shell of the old. He decides to intersperse the Latin text of the Requiem Mass with the harrowing First World War poetry of Wilfred Owen.

He builds a swimming pool beside The Red House, to replace the sea that was only yards away from their home in Crabbe Street three years before.

Age 48, 1961–2

Britten's *War Requiem* is performed at Coventry, with three solo roles for a Briton, a German and a Russian. Both the work and the occasion speak powerfully of the folly of war at a time when the Cold War and nuclear nervousness are at their height – so much so that the Soviet authorities forbid the soprano Galina Vishnevskaya (Rostropovich's wife) to sing alongside a German (Dietrich Fischer-Dieskau) in the premiere. Heather Harper, the Irish soprano, takes her place.

Age 49, 1962–3

Britten and Pears take the first steps to convert a disused barn beside The Red House into a library of music, art and literature, to double as a rehearsal room. They record two of the greatest song cycles of the romantic repertoire: Schubert's *Die Winterreise* and Schumann's *Dichterliebe*. The Soviet authorities relent and allow Vishnevskaya to sing in the recording of *War Requiem*, which sells 200,000 copies in the first year, so great is its hold on public imagination. Britten travels to the Soviet Union to take part in a Festival of British Music.

Age 50, 1963–4

Britten's half-century is extensively celebrated. His actual birthday is marked by an hour-long programme of discussion and performances on the BBC's sole television channel, despite the news earlier in the evening of the assassination of President Kennedy in Dallas.

Britten devises a new type of chamber opera, *Curlew River*, the first of three 'church parables' based on the masked, ritualistic, all-male style of the Japanese Noh play he had seen eight years before in Tokyo. He invents the 'curlew-mark', a notation device to signify a gathering-point for performers required to play unsynchronised music without a conductor.

During a visit to Moscow, he is criticised at home for discussing the artistic tastes of 'the people' in an interview in *Pravda*.

Britten receives the first Aspen Award in Colorado, designed to recognise 'the individual anywhere in the world judged to have made the greatest contribution to the advancement of the humanities', and delivers a lecture about the role of the artist in the society of his time. There were more than a hundred other nominations.

Age 51, 1964–5

Britten is admitted to the select Order of Merit by personal choice of the Queen. On medical advice he takes a rest from performances and travels to India.

He and Pears visit Armenia as guests of the Union of Composers, where they stay with the Rostropoviches. During his visit he sets six poems of Pushkin (in hastily acquired Russian) for Galina Vishnevskaya to perform with her cellist husband as piano accompanist. On his return to England, he writes the first of three suites for solo cello, inspired by the example of J. S. Bach.

Thirty years after his music was first published by Boosey & Hawkes, Britten is instrumental in the launch of Faber Music, which publishes every new piece thereafter.

He starts to plan the conversion of a disused brewery building in Snape into a concert hall, to stage larger musical events in the Aldeburgh Festival.

Age 52, 1965–6

Britten invites the Rostropoviches to stay at The Red House over Christmas. He returns to the Soviet Union for the Russian premiere of the *War Requiem*.

Britten has an operation on his colon to relieve diverticulitis. He begins to revise and publish compositions of his childhood years. *Gloriana* is revived on the London stage for the first time since 1954.

Age 53, 1966–7

Britten and Pears spend Christmas and New Year in the Soviet Union with the Rostropoviches. They try to attend church on Christmas Day, but this proves impossible.

Homosexuality between consenting adults in private is made legal. The new Maltings concert hall at Snape is opened by the Queen. The Aldeburgh Festival is extended to three weeks in celebration.

Britten and Pears go on a lengthy recital tour in north and south America, after EOG performances of two of the Church Parables at Expo 67 in Montreal.

Age 54, 1967–8

Britten and Schubert are featured composers at the Edinburgh Festival. During it, Soviet forces invade Czechoslovakia, but Britten declines to sign letters of protest, for fear of jeopardising his friendships with Russian musicians and East–West cultural links.

Britten is admitted to hospital with the same heart disease that had ended Mahler's life, but manages to complete *The Prodigal Son*, his third 'parable for church performance'.

Age 55, 1968–9

Britten conducts a television film of *Peter Grimes* – the last time Pears sings the title role.

The new Maltings concert hall is destroyed by fire after the first night of the 1969 Aldeburgh Festival, which nonetheless proceeds without interruption. Britten vows to rebuild the hall within a year, and increases his recital schedule to raise funds.

Britten records *Introduction and Allegro*, the fifteen-minute piece for strings by Elgar, despite having said in his youth that he was 'absolutely incapable of enjoying Elgar for more than two minutes'.

Age 56, 1969–70

Britten conducts a strike-breaking performance of Bach's *Christmas Oratorio*. Under instructions from the Musicians' Union, the English Chamber Orchestra refuses to work with a non-union harpsichord player, Philip Ledger, so Britten rescores the work at the last minute for harpsichord and two organs. With Pears he spends two months on a recital tour of New Zealand and Australia, where he supervises EOG performances of the Church Parables in Adelaide. The twenty-third Aldeburgh Festival opens in the rebuilt Maltings. Britten conducts the first performance outside the USSR of Shostakovich's Fourteenth Symphony, of which he is the dedicatee.

Britten buys a cottage at Horham, twenty miles inland on the Suffolk–Norfolk border, as his composing retreat.

Age 57, 1970–1

Britten films his television opera *Owen Wingrave* for the BBC at the Maltings. It is transmitted in May 1971, and shown in twelve other countries within a week. He records Bach's *St John Passion* and Elgar's *The Dream of Gerontius*, and takes part in another festival of British music in the Soviet Union. He begins writing his final opera *Death in Venice*, based on Thomas Mann's story of a middle-aged artist's infatuation with a beautiful boy, under the shadow of death. Britten is told he needs major heart surgery, but he decides to delay this until the opera is complete.

Age 58, 1971–2

Britten revives a rarely-heard Schumann work, *Scenes from Goethe's Faust*. The ensuing recording is the last time he conducts an orchestra. The increasing strain on his heart requires him to take frequent rests during the sessions.

Age 59, 1972–3

Britten completes his composition sketch of *Death in Venice* in December 1972, and the full score in March. He then undergoes open heart surgery in May. He suffers a slight stroke during the six-hour operation, which is not fully successful. He is unable to attend the opera's premiere in June: in September he is given a private performance, and makes some adjustments. He cannot perform in public any more, and his ability to compose is restricted for more than a year.

Britten weeps when he hears of the death of his estranged friend W. H. Auden, whom he last met in 1953.

Age 60, 1973–4

Britten's sixtieth birthday prompts wide celebnrations, in which he plays little part owing to his ill health. He gains confidence in composing again through revising earlier works, and then writes his first new piece in July 1974 – a setting of a T. S. Eliot poem for tenor and harp.

He attends the recording of *Death in Venice* at the Maltings, conducted by Steuart Bedford.

Age 61, 1974–5

Britten writes his last two major works: the cantata *Phaedra* and his third string quartet, which includes themes from *Death in Venice*. His friend Dmitri Shostakovich dies, and the Rostropoviches leave the Soviet Union after a long period of official disapproval.

Age 62, 1975–6

Britten breaks down when he hears a BBC studio recording of his first opera *Paul Bunyan*, the first airing of the score for thirty-five years. It is then given its first British stage performance at the Aldeburgh Festival.

Britten becomes the first composer to be awarded a peerage, the honour that Elgar coveted in vain: he is now called Lord Britten of Aldeburgh. A short choral work for Suffolk schoolchildren, written in August, is Britten's last completed composition, but he begins work on a cantata *Praise We Great Men*.

The Amadeus Quartet visits The Red House to rehearse the third string quartet with its composer. Britten appears in public for the last time in October – an early party for the thirtieth Aldeburgh Festival the following June. A very salty kedgeree is served – one of his favourite 'nursery' foods – and Pears sings the Britten–Auden cabaret song *Tell me the Truth about Love* and Noël Coward's 'I'll see you again'.

Age 63, 1976

On 4 December, twelve days after his sixty-third birthday, Benjamin Britten dies at home, in the arms of Peter Pears. His death is the lead story on the BBC news. At his funeral the choir sings *A Hymn to the Virgin*, the anthem he had written at school when he was sixteen.

11

Britten's favourites

Most of Britten's mature works have a dedication. He liked to thank particular friends and colleagues in this way. Sometimes the dedications are to those who had commissioned the work, sometimes to those who would be its first performers. But on other occasions he was thanking particular friends or colleagues, sometimes with a musical portrait rather than a dedication. This list of dedications forms a gallery of his intimates – men, women and children – at various stages of his composing life.

Britten's men

ARTHUR BENJAMIN

Holiday Diary, op. 5 (1934)

'To Arthur Benjamin', the Australian composer who was his piano teacher at the Royal College of Music from 1930 to 1933. Soon after they met, he warned his pupil he wasn't built to be a piano soloist, which left the young Britten nervous: 'How I am going to make my pennies Heaven only knows.' Britten told him that *Holiday Diary* was 'my first real attempt (and probably last!) at piano writing' – which was almost true.

LENNOX BERKELEY

Piano Concerto, op. 13 (1938)

'To Lennox Berkeley', who may or may not have had a brief affair with Britten – probably not. They had met as fellow composers at a music festival in Barcelona in 1936, and holidayed together in Cornwall that summer. In 1938 he was

Britten's lodger at his new home in Snape, where he witnessed the gestation of this concerto. But Britten kept him at arm's length. 'In spite of his avowed sexual weakness for young men of my age and form [. . .] we have come to an agreement on that subject.' Berkeley later married, and asked Britten to be godfather to his son Michael.

JAMES BOWMAN

Canticle IV: Journey of the Magi, op. 86 (1971)

'To James, Peter and John', Messrs Bowman, Pears and Shirley-Quirk respectively, the three singers who gave the first performance with Britten at the piano. James Bowman, the pre-eminent counter-tenor of the time, had taken over the part of Oberon in *A Midsummer Night's Dream* from Alfred Deller, and later created the offstage role of Apollo in *Death in Venice*. He once affectionately described Britten and Pears as like a couple of respectable prep-school masters.

HENRY BOYS

Violin Concerto, op. 15 (1939)

'To Henry Boys', later teacher and critic, who was a contemporary of Britten at the Royal College of Music. Their friendship was sealed when Britten gave him a private play-through of his new choral work *A Boy was Born*, and Boys responded warmly. Shared musical enthusiasms included Mahler, particularly *Das Lied von der Erde*.

JULIAN BREAM

Nocturnal after John Dowland, op. 70 (1963)

'For Julian Bream', the premier British guitarist and lutenist. He made his debut at the 1952 Aldeburgh Festival at the age of nineteen, and soon after formed a recital partnership with Pears. Britten and Pears had often included Elizabethan lute songs in their recitals, arranged for voice and piano, but this stopped once Julian with his lute came on the scene. He inspired Britten to write for the guitar: first a set of folk-songs, then the cycle *Songs from the Chinese*, and finally this solo piece.

FRANK BRIDGE

Sinfonietta, op. 1 (1932)
'To Frank Bridge'

Variations on a Theme of Frank Bridge, op. 10 (1937)
'To F. B. A tribute with affection and admiration'
It was natural, but thoughtful, of Britten to dedicate what he considered his first 'mature' piece to the composer who had encouraged, stimulated and bullied him over his technique. Five years after the *Sinfonietta* came the famous set of variations for string orchestra, first performed at the Salzburg Festival, no less, and based on a string quartet theme by Bridge. Five further works of his were quoted in Britten's finale.

ROBERT BRITTEN (FATHER)

Five Walztes (1925)
'Composed by Edward Benjamin Britten Opus 3, 1925, and dedicated to My Father: R. V. Britten Esq'

Quatre chansons françaises (1928)
'To Mr and Mrs R. V. Britten on the twenty-seventh anniversary of their wedding, September 5th 1928'

A Boy was Born, op. 3 (1933)
'To my Father'

Sinfonia da Requiem, op. 20 (1940)
'In memory of my parents'
Mr Britten, the Lowestoft dentist, was a distant, formal father to his children (despite being four years younger than his wife), and had little direct influence on his son's musical

development. But he did send some of Benjamin's early work to the BBC, and encouraged his interest in sport. At the age of fourteen, the boy recorded in his diary a forecast made by his father, with the word 'REMEMBER' written above it: 'Daddy remarks, in the evening, that I will be a terrible one for love, and that when the time comes I will think that my love is different from any other and that it is *the* love.'

ROBERT BRITTEN (BROTHER)

Friday Afternoons, op. 7 (1934)

'To R. H. M. Britten and the boys of Clive House, Prestatyn, 1934'. Bobby and Benjie (seven years his junior) were not close, and had frequent arguments, though Britten was surprised at how sympathetic his elder brother was about his 'queerness'. By his mid-twenties Robert was running a preparatory school in North Wales: Britten wrote these songs for the boys' weekly singing practice. On a visit there, he annoyed Bobby by taking two boys for a long walk and disrupting their timetable. But Britten later said they were getting on much better, 'even tho' he is very much out of things, and considers me very "free"!!'

ANTONIO BROSA

Reveille (1937)

'For Toni Brosa', the Spanish violinist who formed a recital partnership with Britten in the 1930s. He gave the first complete performance of Britten's Violin Suite, along with Beethoven's Violin Sonata in G (which Britten found hard to rehearse because of 'such lovely playing'). *Reveille*, a short concert study for violin, was both thank-you letter and private joke. Brosa (unlike Britten) was known as a late riser – hence the piece's title and its tempo marking: *rubato e pigro* (elastic and lazy). Britten also wrote his Violin Concerto for him, 'the most accomplished, intelligent, natural & sweet-sounding violinist in the world!'

ROGER BURNEY

War Requiem, op. 66 (1962)

'In loving memory of Roger Burney, Sub-Lieutenant RNVR, Piers Dunkerley, Captain Royal Marines, David Gill, Ordinary Seaman, Royal Navy, Michael Halliday, Lieutenant RNZNVR'. Burney was a friend of Pears and a pacifist, but he changed his views after the Germans sank the *Athenia*, a British passenger liner, early in the Second World War. He then signed up for the Royal Naval Volunteer Reserve, which took him to New York. There he met up with Britten and Pears. Shortly afterwards, he served in a French submarine, which was sunk in February 1942, without survivors. He was twenty-two.

PETER BURRA

Mont Juic, op. 12 (1937)

'In memory of Peter Burra', the young writer on art, music and letters whom Britten first met in Barcelona in 1936, along with Lennox Berkeley. So when Britten and Berkeley jointly wrote this suite of Catalan dances as a souvenir, a dedication to Burra seemed only natural. By then Britten and Burra had developed a mutual attraction, which was cut short by Burra's death in an air crash. 'He was a darling of the 1st rank,' Britten wrote, and the time he spent helping to sort out his belongings (and perhaps destroying embarrassing papers) drew him closer to Burra's friend Peter Pears, who was doing the same.

ISADOR CAPLAN

Owen Wingrave, op. 85 (1970)

'To Joan and Isador Caplan'. The ground-breaking scheme to hand over a clutch of Britten's manuscripts to the nation in lieu of death duties, and then receive them back on permanent loan, was devised by Isador Caplan as Britten's solicitor. They first met during the war, when Caplan was living in the same building as Britten's friend Erwin Stein and his family. Later, Caplan was instrumental in setting up the Britten–Pears Library, and Britten appointed him an executor of his estate. He was a committed pacifist – hence the dedication of this anti-military opera to him and his wife.

ALBERTO CAVALCANTI

Soirées Musicales, op. 9 (1936)

'To M. Alberto Cavalcanti', the Brazilian film director and sound engineer who under John Grierson ran the GPO Film Unit. He it was who first hired Britten to write incidental music for a documentary, *The King's Stamp*. Britten had been nominated by Edward Clark of the BBC, who had in turn been 'pestered' by Frank Bridge, keen to give his protégé a break. When planning another film, *The Tocher*, Cavalcanti suggested that Britten should use tunes by Rossini. He did, and then turned some of them into this orchestral suite – so the dedication is another thank-you.

ALEXANDER CHUHALDIN

Young Apollo, op. 16 (1939)

'Dedicated to Alexander Chuhaldin', the Russian-born violinist and conductor whom Britten first met in Toronto, directing his Frank Bridge Variations on Canadian radio. Chuhaldin, said Britten, 'thinks I'm the cat's whiskers', and advanced his career by introducing him to Serge Koussevitzky. That led to the commission for *Peter Grimes*, with a substantial fee of a thousand dollars. Chuhaldin conducted the first performance of *Young Apollo*, with Britten as piano soloist, in August 1939. Britten played it once more, and then never again, which presumably left the dedicatee scratching his head.

STEPHEN CROWDY

'Alla valse', from *Alla quartetto serioso* (1933)

'To Stephen', evidently a friend of both Britten and his sister Beth. He pops up in Britten's diary at intervals between 1932 and 1937, usually when they were having a meal or seeing a film in London. He came to the first performance of *Three Divertimenti* in February 1936, no doubt because the second movement ('Waltz') was the final version of the 'Alla valse' that Britten had originally written for him.

ERIC CROZIER

Canticle I: My Beloved is Mine, op. 40 (1947)

Crozier worked for Sadler's Wells Opera during the war, and was the first producer of *Peter Grimes*. He then shifted his allegiance to Britten's English Opera Group, and became a close friend and collaborator, producing *The Rape of Lucretia* at Glyndebourne, writing librettos for him, and sharing his house for a while. He did the naval research for *Billy Budd* and assisted E. M. Forster with the libretto. He claimed that Britten had promised to dedicate this Canticle to him, but had changed his mind. In the early fifties, Crozier fell out of favour, and was deeply hurt: he wrote a tart memoir about the composer's strengths and weaknesses.

OSIAN ELLIS

Suite for Harp, op. 83 (1969)

'For Osian Ellis', the harpist of the English Opera Group, whose playing informed Britten's harp writing in *A Midsummer Night's Dream* and all three Church Parables. As principal harp of the London Symphony Orchestra, he took part in Britten's recording of the *War Requiem*. After the composer's heart operation, it was often Ellis who partnered Pears in recital, and Britten wrote songs for them both.

LEONARD ELMHIRST

Five Flower Songs, op. 47 (1950)

'To Leonard and Dorothy Elmhirst on the occasion of their twenty-fifth wedding anniversary – 3rd April 1950'. The Elmhirsts were staunch patrons of music at Dartington in Devon. Leonard was the son of a Yorkshire clergyman-farmer and landowner, who spent several years working on rural reconstruction projects in India under the influence of Rabindranath Tagore. He and Dorothy married in 1925, bought Dartington Hall, opened a school and set about rehabilitating the estate. Britten chose this floral tribute on account of their mutual interest in plants, and Dartington students first sang it on the lawn there, with Elmhirst listening from his study window.

DIETRICH FISCHER-DIESKAU

Songs and Proverbs of William Blake, op. 74 (1965)

'For Dieter: the past and the future' – the foremost German singer for whom, at Pears's suggestion, Britten wrote the baritone role in *War Requiem* in 1962. *Cantata Misericordium* was also written for them both, followed by this song cycle – Britten's only one specifically for baritone. Although he found Fischer-Dieskau intimidating – he once called him 'the school bully' – he would have assigned him the title role in his opera *King Lear*, had he ever written it.

E. M. FORSTER

Albert Herring, op. 39 (1947)

'Dedicated to E. M. Forster, in admiration', the novelist whom he had first met through Auden and Isherwood in 1937. It was the transcript of a Forster talk about the poet George Crabbe that eventually drew Britten home after three years in north America, and Forster was invited to lecture at the first Aldeburgh Festival. Britten sounded him out there about writing an opera libretto. The result was *Billy Budd* three years later. When the *Herring* score was published in 1948, Britten gave Forster a copy – 'a very humble tribute to a very great man'. Forster replied: 'It makes me feel a little strange! What are any of us doing with greatness? I do feel very proud, but proudest of your affection.'

ANTHONY GISHFORD

Folk Song Arrangements, vol. 4 (1957)

'To Anthony Gishford', the music publisher who worked closely with Britten at Boosey & Hawkes, and later at Faber Music. He became chairman of the English Opera Group, and in 1966 went on holiday with Britten in Morocco when the composer was convalescing after an operation.

LEON GOOSSENS

Phantasy, op. 2 (1932)

'To Leon Goossens', then principal oboe of the newly formed London Philharmonic Orchestra. He gave this work (for oboe and string trio) its first performance on the radio in 1933, when Britten pronounced that he did his part 'splendidly'. He played it again at the ISCM Festival in Florence in 1934.

PERCY GRAINGER

Suite on English Folk Tunes: 'A time there was . . . ', op. 90 (1974)

'Lovingly and reverently dedicated to the memory of Percy Grainger', the Australian-born composer, whose recompositions of folksong so impressed the nineteen-year-old Britten for their originality, 'knocking all the V[aughan] Williams and R. O. Morris arrangements into a cocked hat'. He and Pears included them in their recitals, and Britten recorded some of his 'masterly' orchestral and choral arrangements. They met when Grainger was an old man: he gave Britten one of his piano pieces, inscribed 'To Benjamin Britten in tonal fellow-ship from Percy Grainger'.

GEORGE, EARL OF HAREWOOD

A Wedding Anthem (Amo Ergo Sum), op. 46 (1949)

'For Marion and George, 29 September 1949'

Billy Budd, op. 50 (1951)

'To George and Marion, December 1951'

Britten got to know King George VI's nephew through his friend Marion Stein (daughter of Erwin), whom Harewood married in 1949. Britten often gave weddings a wide berth, but for the Harewoods' he wrote this anthem, and conducted the choir that sang it. He went on to dedicate *Billy Budd* to them: 'You have both been such very great friends, helpful in every way artistic and personal, and generous to a degree, that he really belongs to you', he wrote. Harewood devoted much of his career to opera management: he also updated Kobbé's famous *Complete Opera Book*. When the Harewoods divorced in 1967, Britten took Marion's side and severed contact with George.

RALPH HAWKES

Our Hunting Fathers, op. 8 (1936)

'Dedicated to Ralph Hawkes, Esq', a director of his new pub-lishers at the time, Boosey & Hawkes. He championed Britten loyally against some resistance on the firm's board, and felt vin-dicated by the later success of *Peter Grimes*. Britten once thanked him as 'Sponsor, Publisher, Agent, Maecenas – what you will', and said that no composer starting out could have been so for-tunate. It was only after Hawkes died in 1950 that Britten's relationship with Boosey & Hawkes began to deteriorate.

HANS WERNER HENZE

Children's Crusade, op. 82 (1969)

'To Hans Werner Henze', the German composer, who has lived most of his life in Italy. He was a protégé of Prince Ludwig of Hesse, who introduced him to Britten in the 1950s. Henze was one composer that Britten admired from the coming generation. He took comfort from the fact that Henze had modified his initially strict application of Schoenberg's serial technique of composition. Children's Crusade is a setting of a poem by Bertolt Brecht, whom Henze also set.

DEREK HILL

A Hymn of St Columba – Regis regum rectissimi (1962)

'For Derek Hill', the artist, who had asked him for a piece for the 1,400th anniversary of St Columba's missionary journey from Ireland to Iona. After its first performance in Holland in May 1963, a recording was played on the hillside in County Donegal where the saint was supposed to have preached. The wind rendered it almost inaudible.

WALTER HUSSEY

Rejoice in the Lamb, op. 30 (1943)

'For the Rev. Walter Hussey and the choir of St Matthew's Church, Northampton, on the occasion of the 50th anniversary of the consecration of their church, 21 September 1943'. Hussey used his position as parish priest in Northampton, and later on as Dean of Chichester, to sponsor the arts. He commissioned Bernstein's Chichester Psalms, pieces by Tippett and Walton, and art and sculpture from Henry Moore, Graham Sutherland and Marc Chagall. Rejoice in the Lamb and an organ prelude and fugue were Britten's contributions.

CHRISTOPHER ISHERWOOD

On This Island, op. 11 (1937)

'To Christopher Isherwood', the novelist and close friend of W. H. Auden. This dedication, at the height of Britten's association with both of them, is a reminder that Auden is absent from this gallery of intimates, even though the poems in this song cycle were his. A year later he and Isherwood dedicated their play *On the Frontier* to Britten, who had written its music. Isherwood gave Britten advice about his sexuality. They kept in touch in later years, although Isherwood's emigration to the USA in 1939 was permanent.

HANS KELLER

String Quartet no. 3, op. 94 (1975)

'To Hans Keller', the Austrian musicologist, who with Donald Mitchell edited the first critique of Britten's music in 1952. He became an argumentative friend, though not a close one, and translated several of Britten's librettos and texts. Keller had long pressed Britten for a third quartet, and argued that the essence of a string quartet was its four-part texture. Britten was perhaps making a debating point when he entitled two of this quartet's movements 'Duets' and 'Solo'.

CUTHBERT KELLY

Realisation of Purcell's *Saul and the Witch at Endor* (1945)

'To Cuthbert Kelly', who founded and directed the vocal sextet, the New English Singers, to which Peter Pears belonged in the 1930s. They specialised in Elizabethan madrigals and folksongs. Kelly was a man of strong opinions, who engaged Pears in discussions about language, literature and philosophy as well as singing technique.

LINCOLN KIRSTEIN

Matinées Musicales, op. 24 (1941)

'To Lincoln Kirstein', founder of the American Ballet Company, who was introduced to Britten by Auden. He requested these adaptations of Rossini, to complement Britten's earlier *Soirées Musicales* in a ballet he called *Divertimento*. It was choreographed by Balanchine, and first produced in Rio de Janeiro. Kirstein went on to convert the Frank Bridge Variations and *Les Illuminations* into ballets.

SERGE KOUSSEVITZKY

Spring Symphony, op. 44 (1949)

'For Serge Koussevitzky and the Boston Symphony Orchestra'. The conductor and music patron Koussevitzky commissioned *Peter Grimes* in 1942 for the Tanglewood Festival, but graciously agreed to it being staged first in London, on account of the war. Britten went to the American premiere in Tanglewood in 1946, whereupon Koussevitzky immediately asked for a symphony with voice – for another $1,000 fee. The result was *Spring Symphony*. Britten once again balked at a Tanglewood premiere, and asked if he would mind it being performed first in Holland. Koussevitzky said he most certainly did. But he later relented.

JAMES LAWRIE

The Beggar's Opera, op. 43 (1948)

'Dedicated to James Lawrie', a businessman and financier who was a founding director of the English Opera Group, and later became its chairman. He was also chairman of the National School of Opera, and managing director of the National Film Corporation.

PRINCE LUDWIG OF HESSE AND BY RHINE

Songs from the Chinese, op. 58 (1957)

'To Peg and Lu, from Ben, Peter [Pears] and Julian [Bream]'

Sechs Hölderlin-Fragmente, op. 61 (1958)

'Meinem Freund, dem Prinzen Ludwig von Hessen und bei Rhein, zum fünfzigsten Geburtstag'.

Prince Ludwig was a cousin of Queen Elizabeth II, and his elder brother was married to the Duke of Edinburgh's sister. He was an art historian and poet, and provided the German singing translation for many of Britten's librettos. In 1937 he married Margaret Campbell Geddes, and their home at Wolfsgarten near Darmstadt was a frequent retreat for Britten: he began *Death in Venice* there in 1971. As 'Lu and Peg', they were companions for Britten and Pears on their Far Eastern tour in 1956. The following year Britten's songs for voice and guitar were dedicated to them, and in 1958 Ludwig's fiftieth birthday was marked with Britten's Hölderlin songs.

GEORGE MALCOLM

Missa Brevis in D, op. 63 (1959)

'For George Malcolm and the boys of Westminster Cathedral Choir'. Malcolm, the conductor and harpsichordist, ran the music at the Roman Catholic cathedral, and this Mass was first performed shortly before he retired. Britten had been impressed by the bright 'continental' sound of his trebles, in contrast with the breathy 'cathedral hoot' then common in Anglican choirs.

RICHARD DE LA MARE

Tit for Tat (1928–31, revised 1968)

'For Dick de la Mare June 4th 1969', whose seventieth birthday this was. He was the son of the poet Walter de la Mare, whose poems Britten set in this collection as a teenager. He was chairman of Faber and Faber in the 1960s: when Britten wanted to leave Boosey & Hawkes, de la Mare set up Faber Music as the first new music publishers in Britain for forty years.

WILLIAM MAYER

'Little Sir William' (1940)

'To William Mayer', who as a German refugee became medical director of the Long Island Home in the USA. He and his wife Elizabeth provided Britten and Pears with a secure base during their stay in New York, giving them (in Britten's words) 'strength, and courage to see ourselves and to face what we saw'. They were both 'rocks who knew and loved the past, and yet were not daunted by the future'. Dr Mayer lived rather longer than his namesake in the folksong: he died at sixty-nine in 1956, a few months after Britten had an evening reunion with him in Germany.

NOEL MEWTON-WOOD

Canticle III: Still Falls the Rain, op. 55 (1954)

'To the memory of Noel Mewton-Wood', a young Australian pianist who had accompanied Pears when Britten was unavailable. After the death of his homosexual partner, Mewton-Wood committed suicide.

DONALD MITCHELL

The Burning Fiery Furnace, op. 77 (1966)

'To Donald and Kathleen Mitchell'. The musicologist Donald Mitchell has specialised in the music of Britten and Mahler. His first involvement with Britten came with his and Hans Keller's collection of essays, published in 1952. At the composer's suggestion, he helped found Faber Music in 1964, which published all Britten's music from then on, including the three Church Parables.

BOYD NEEL

Prelude and Fugue, op. 29 (1943)

'To Boyd Neel and his orchestra, on the occasion of their 10th birthday, 23 June 1943'. Boyd Neel was a medic and a naval officer before he founded his string orchestra, which specialised in baroque music. He directed the score Britten wrote for the feature film *Love from a Stranger*, and then commissioned the Frank Bridge Variations for his orchestra to play at the 1937 Salzburg Festival. The players marked their tenth anniversary in the middle of the war, so only eighteen of them could attend – which is why Britten scored his *Prelude and Fugue* for eighteen players. The orchestra was later renamed Philomusica of London.

IGNACY JAN PADEREWSKI

Mazurka Elegiaca, op. 23 no. 2 (1941)

'In memoriam I. J. Paderewski', the Polish pianist and composer, who became prime minister in 1919 for the first year of Poland's independent existence, and was a signatory to the Treaty of Versailles. To mark his death in 1941, several composers, including Bartók, Martin, Milhaud and Britten, were asked to contribute to a book of pieces for solo piano. In the telegram to Britten the request for 'two piano pieces' omitted the final 's', so his resulting *Mazurka Elegiaca* (for two pianos) was a misfit for the memorial volume, and had to be published separately.

PETER PEARS

'Being Beauteous' from *Les Illuminations*, op. 18 (1939)
'To P.N.L.P.'

Seven Sonnets of Michelangelo, op. 22 (1940)
'To Peter'

The Holy Sonnets of John Donne, op. 35 (1945)
'For Peter'

Canticle II: Abraham and Isaac, op. 51 (1952)
'For Kathleen Ferrier and Peter Pears'

'Second Lute Song of the Earl of Essex' from *Gloriana*, **op. 53 (1953)**
'For Peter Pears'

Canticle IV: Journey of the Magi, op. 86 (1971)
'To James, Peter and John'

Death in Venice, op. 88 (1973)
'To Peter'

Sacred and Profane, op. 91 (1975)
'For P.P. and the Wilbye Consort'

The tally of eight dedications is apt recognition for Britten's partner and muse of more than thirty-five years. They first became friends and a recital duo in 1937, though it took another two years for their relationship to blossom into what would now be regarded as a marriage. In all, Britten wrote thirteen operas with Pears's voice in mind, five choral works, three orchestral song cycles and eleven works for solo voice(s), not to mention numerous folksong arrangements. He outlived Britten by ten years.

JOHN PIPER

Winter Words, op. 52 (1953)
'To John and Myfanwy Piper', close collaborators in his operatic projects over almost thirty years. John Piper, as a painter and a designer, was in charge of the stage design of most of the operas from *The Rape of Lucretia* in 1946 to *Death in Venice* in 1973, as well as the ballet *The Prince of the Pagodas*. Britten felt the songs for *Winter Words*, written during and after the travails of *Gloriana*, were some of his most personal, so the dedication reflects his affection for the Pipers.

WILLIAM PLOMER

Canticle V: The Death of Saint Narcissus, op. 89 (1974)

'In loving memory of William Plomer', poet and novelist, who, after *Gloriana*, wrote the librettos for the three Church Parables. They were modelled on the Japanese Noh theatre, which, on Plomer's recommendation, Britten saw for himself in Japan. Plomer's death in 1973 upset him greatly, and led to this dedication of the first new piece written after his major heart surgery.

WILLIAM PRIMROSE

Lachrymae, op. 48 (1950)

'For William Primrose', the Scottish viola player whom he met in 1949 and immediately enlisted for a chamber recital at the Aldeburgh Festival, with the promise of a new work for the viola. Primrose said the recital would be 'a privilege without a viola piece from you, but with it my cup would indeed overflow!' Shortly before the concert, Primrose telephoned to find out how the piece was progressing. Britten was aghast, because he had forgotten all about it. Without pausing for breath he told Primrose it was 'in the post', and a day or two later it was!

STEPHEN REISS

A Midsummer Night's Dream, op. 64 (1960)

'Dedicated to Stephen Reiss', general manager of the Aldeburgh Festival for sixteen years. He extended the Jubilee Hall to accommodate a larger audience and a larger pit in opera performances, thereby facilitating the medium-sized orchestra Britten wanted for his Shakespeare opera. Reiss also oversaw the conversion of Snape Maltings into a concert hall. But his relationship with Britten deteriorated, and after a confrontation in 1971 Reiss resigned. Years before, they had briefly coincided at Gresham's School.

SVIATOSLAV RICHTER

Cadenzas to Mozart's Piano Concerto in E flat major, K482 (1966)

'For Slava Richter', the pianist who became another of his Russian intimates, after Shostakovich, Rostropovich and Vishnevskaya. Magical film footage of him and Britten playing Mozart's D major Sonata for two pianos captures the joy of their music-making.

ALEC ROBERTSON

Alleluia! for Alec's 80th Birthday (1971)

Alec Robertson was an expert on Gregorian chant working in the BBC's Gramophone Department, who supplied Britten with the plainsong 'Hodie Christus natus est', with which he opened and closed *A Ceremony of Carols*. This *Alleluia* took part of that chant, and worked it into a tiny three-part canon.

RAE ROBERTSON

Scottish Ballad, op. 26 (1941)

'For Ethel Bartlett and Rae Robertson', the married British piano duo, who were living in the USA at the same time as Britten and Pears. They invited them to stay in California during summer 1941, and Britten wrote the *Scottish Ballad* as a thank-you present. The work, for two pianos and orchestra, is built around several Scottish tunes, presumably in recognition of Robertson's origins.

MSTISLAV ROSTROPOVICH

Cello Sonata in C, op. 65 (1961)

'For Mstislav Rostropovich'

Symphony for Cello and Orchestra, op. 68 (1963)

'For Mstislav Rostropovich'

Suite for Cello op. 72 (1964)

'For Slava'

The Poet's Echo, op. 76 (1965)

'For Galya and Slava'

Second Suite for Cello, op. 80 (1967)

'For Slava'

Third Suite for Cello, op. 87 (1971)

'For Slava'

With these six dedications, Rostropovich was the most acknowledged of Britten's musical collaborators apart from Pears. From their first meeting in 1960, the Russian's sense of the absurd certainly appealed to the schoolboy in Britten. But his artistry on the cello fostered Britten's fresh enthusiasm for the instrument, and a consequent stream of new music. Their recording of Schubert's Arpeggione Sonata exemplifies their almost uncanny connection with each other.

PAUL SACHER

Tema Sacher (1976)

The conductor Paul Sacher founded the Basel Chamber Orchestra in 1926, and was a noted patron of contemporary music, commissioning Bartók's *Music for Strings* and many other works by composers such as Berio, Birtwistle, Carter and Stravinsky. In 1959 he asked Britten for a Basel piece to mark his old university's 500th anniversary, which resulted in *Cantata Academica*. For Sacher's seventieth birthday, Britten wrote a theme for cello, on which other composers such as Boulez, Dutilleux and Henze were supposed to write variations, but didn't.

EDWARD SACKVILLE-WEST

Serenade for tenor, horn and strings, op. 31 (1943)

'To E. S.-W.', writer, critic and BBC producer, who advised him on his selection of poems for the *Serenade*. Sackville-West was twelve years older than Britten, and became briefly infatuated with him. Later in 1943 Britten wrote an extensive score for Sackville-West's BBC radio drama based on Homer, *The Rescue*.

DICK SHEPPARD

Canticle I: My Beloved is Mine, op. 40 (1947)

'This Canticle was written for the Dick Sheppard Memorial Concert on 1 November 1947'. Canon Sheppard had died in 1937, a year after helping to found the Peace Pledge Union, which Britten, as a lifelong pacifist, backed from the start. He supported it financially for thirty years – despite its rejection of his 1937 *Pacifist March* because (according to Sheppard) it was 'not much liked by members'.

JOHN SHIRLEY-QUIRK

Canticle IV: Journey of the Magi, op. 86 (1971)

'To James, Peter and John', the trio for whom this Canticle was written, and who would take the principal parts in *Death in Venice* two years later. The seven roles assigned to Shirley-Quirk's bass-baritone in Britten's final opera reflected his regard for the singer's intelligence and versatility. He first sang for the composer in *Curlew River* and created the role of Spencer Coyle in *Owen Wingrave*.

DMITRI SHOSTAKOVICH

The Prodigal Son, op. 81 (1968)

'To Dmitri Shostakovich', the Russian composer whom he first met at a London concert in 1960. Their friendship deepened, and Britten visited the Soviet Union six times. This work was prompted by the sight of Rembrandt's Prodigal Son painting in Leningrad. Such was his respect for Shostakovich that he gave him a sneak preview of his unfinished score for *Death in Venice*.

MONTAGU SLATER

Temporal Variations [originally *Temporal Suite*] (1936)

'To Montagu Slater'

Ballad of Heroes, op. 14 (1939)

'To Montagu and Enid Slater', left-wing friends from before the war. As poet and playwright, Montagu worked for the GPO Film Unit, and Britten collaborated with him on *Coal Face* in 1935. He also wrote music for some of Slater's plays, in particular *Stay Down Miner* in May 1936. The *Temporal Suite* followed a few months later. On his return from the USA, Britten invited Slater to write the libretto for *Peter Grimes*, which was not a trouble-free collaboration. He also wrote the script for the film of *The Young Person's Guide to the Orchestra*.

ERWIN STEIN

Birthday Song for Erwin (1945)

The Rape of Lucretia, op. 37 (1946)

'Dedicated to Erwin Stein', Austrian critic, music publisher and one-time pupil of Schoenberg. Britten first met him in Vienna in 1934, but their friendship developed in London once Stein had fled Austria with his wife Sophie and daughter Marion after its annexation by Hitler. He joined Britten's publishers, Boosey & Hawkes, and was one of his closest musical confidants – indeed some saw him as a Svengali figure. *Birthday Song for Erwin* was written for his sixtieth birthday, and performed by Britten and Pears in the London flat they all shared in the 1940s.

MICHAEL TIPPETT

Curlew River, op. 71 (1964)

'To Michael Tippett, in friendship and admiration', who, despite being almost nine years older, made his mark as a composer only some years after Britten's rise to prominence. In their not unwary friendship, they shared a love of Purcell, a keen pacifism, and an unabashed homosexuality. Tippett dedicated his *Concerto for Orchestra* to Britten for his fiftieth birthday, and Britten responded with this dedication the following year.

WILLIAM TITLEY

Sonatina Romantica (1940)

'For Dr William B. Titley to play', a keen young amateur pianist. Titley was also superintendent of the Long Island Home, the psychiatric institution run by Dr William Mayer at Amityville, New York. The Mayers arranged for Britten and Pears to be billeted with the Titleys for a while, and after listening to Bill's endless attempts to master Weber's *Invitation to the Waltz* Britten wrote this *Sonatina* for him to play instead – a thank-you gift with an ulterior motive.

MAURICE VINDEN

Jubilate Deo in E flat and *Te Deum* in C (1934)

'Written for Maurice Vinden & the Choir of St Mark's, North Audley Street, London', where Britten regularly worshipped when he was first in London as a student. Britten praised its choristers for singing 'like angels' when rehearsing for the first performance of *A Boy was Born* in February 1934. Vinden was their choirmaster, and presumably conducted the first performances of these two canticles, though there is no record of either.

KIT WELFORD

'Seascape' from *On This Island*, op. 11 (1937)

'For Kit Welford', a keen amateur yachtsman who the following January became Britten's brother-in-law by marrying his sister Beth. This movement was probably composed in the Welford family home near Saxmundham, where Britten spent much of October 1937, awaiting the conversion of The Old Mill in Snape – for which the architect was Kit's father, Arthur Welford.

PAUL WITTGENSTEIN

Diversions, op. 21 (1940)

'For Paul Wittgenstein', the Austrian pianist (and brother of the philosopher Ludwig), who lost his right arm in the Great War. Remarkably, he maintained his concert career by commissioning piano works for the left hand alone, from composers such as Ravel, Korngold, Prokofiev and Richard Strauss. In 1940 he asked Britten for a concerto, for a fee of $700. Britten embarked on it without delay. Despite trying to interfere with the scoring and write his own cadenza ('the man really is an old sour puss', said Britten), the cantankerous Wittgenstein gave the premiere in early 1942, and made a further payment to Britten in 1950 to maintain his exclusive performance rights to the work.

RICHARD WOOD

The Ballad of Little Musgrave and Lady Barnard (1943)

'For Richard Wood and the musicians of Oflag VIIb – Germany, 1943'. Lieutenant Wood's sister Anne was a singer and a friend of Peter Pears. While a prisoner of war at Eichstätt, Wood organised an ambitious music festival of six events, from symphonic music to folk-dancing and jazz. He conducted a twenty-nine-piece orchestra in a Rossini overture, a Mozart flute concerto, some Elgar dances and a Schubert symphony. The *Ballad* was written for his prison-camp choir of some three dozen singers: they 'cordially disliked' it at first but warmed to it during the four performances they gave.

Britten's women

AUDREY ALSTON

Simple Symphony, op. 4 (1934)

'Dedicated to Audrey Alston (Mrs Lincolne Sutton)', who played a pivotal role in Britten's career. She was a friend of his mother, and first taught him the viola as a boy. She invited him along to some of the string quartet recitals she gave in Norwich, introduced him to Frank Bridge's music, and then to the man himself. With this dedication, the barely adult composer was paying his childhood dues.

JANET BAKER

Phaedra, op. 93 (1975)

'For Janet Baker', who had impressed Britten with her performance of the title part in *The Rape of Lucretia*, originally written for Kathleen Ferrier. She also created the unsympathetic role of Kate in *Owen Wingrave*, which she found difficult. At the end of his life he wrote this operatic cantata for her, and Baker was 'overwhelmed by its passion and feeling'. Working on it with Britten was 'awesome', she said. 'That moment is mine for ever.'

ETHEL BARTLETT

Scottish Ballad, op. 26 (1941)

'For Ethel Bartlett and Rae Robertson', the British husband-and-wife piano duo who gave the first performances of his *Introduction and Rondo alla Burlesca* and *Mazurka Elegiaca*, both in New York in 1941. They spent the summer in Escondido,

California, and invited Britten and Pears to stay with them for several months, during which Britten began the *Scottish Ballad*. Bartlett would have relished the heading 'Britten's women' (though perhaps not its plural form), since she fell hopelessly in love with him. His confusion at being propositioned by his hostess, seventeen years his senior, was compounded when her husband stepped in to encourage the idea. Britten decorously declined their suggestion.

MARY BEHREND

String Quartet no. 2 in C, op. 36 (1945)

'For Mrs. J. L. Behrend', who commissioned this quartet. With her husband 'Bow', she was a generous sponsor of the arts. During the war she commissioned a portrait of Britten and Pears from the artist Kenneth Green, which now hangs in the National Portrait Gallery. The Behrends gave financial support to the Aldeburgh Festival and English Opera Group. She died in her nineties in 1977, penniless.

JOY BOUGHTON

Six Metamorphoses after Ovid, op. 49 (1951)

'For Joy Boughton', the oboist, who was a regular with the English Opera Group orchestra. To give extra atmosphere for these six portraits of mythical figures, she gave the first performance in a punt on an artificial lake near Aldeburgh. The effect was marred only slightly when the manuscript blew into the water.

EDITH BRITTEN

Quatre chansons françaises (1928)

'To Mr and Mrs R. V. Britten on the twenty-seventh anniversary of their wedding, September 5th 1928'

The Birds (1934)

'For my Mother'

Sinfonia da Requiem, op. 20 (1940)

'In memory of my parents'

Edith Britten was an accomplished amateur singer and pianist. She had boundless faith in Benjamin's musical talent from his earliest years, taught him the rudiments of the piano, and arranged musical evenings at home at which he would perform. He was devoted to her, and grief-stricken (yet simultaneously liberated) by her sudden death in 1937. *The Birds* was performed at her funeral.

JOAN CAPLAN

Owen Wingrave, op. 85 (1970)

'To Joan and Isador Caplan', who first met in a London law firm before the war. Isador Caplan was a partner, and married Joan Bray, as she then was, in 1938. Their long friendship with Britten and Pears dates from the mid-1940s, when Isador became Britten's legal adviser.

ELIZABETH SPRAGUE COOLIDGE

String Quartet no. 1 in D, op. 25 (1941)

'To Mrs Elizabeth Sprague Coolidge', a celebrated American patron of music. They met after Frank Bridge had recommended Britten, and the old lady (she was over seventy-five) gave him a commission for a string quartet he had already been planning. She awarded him the Coolidge Medal for services to chamber music while he was writing it, and presented it to 'Benjy', as she called him, in front of an illustrious audience at the Library of Congress in Washington.

FIDELITY CRANBROOK

Cantata Misericordium, op. 69 (1963)

'To Fidelity Cranbrook', the feisty Countess of Cranbrook, who added lustre and clout to the Aldeburgh Festival by

serving as its chairman for its first thirty-five years, seeing off
some of the local and vocal opposition it provoked, and medi-
ating the fierce personal tensions within the organisation. She
continued to attend the Festival right up to her death in 2009
at the age of ninety-six.

JOAN CROSS

Realisations of Purcell's *Music for a While* and *Mad Bess* (1945)

'For Joan Cross'

Folk Song Arrangements, vol. 3 (1945–6)

'To Joan Cross'

Cross was a leading British soprano of the inter-war and post-
war years. As artistic director of Sadler's Wells Opera, she was
largely responsible for the company's decision to stage *Peter
Grimes* in 1945, in which she sang the part of Ellen Orford.
The Purcell arrangements followed that November. She
created several Britten operatic roles, notably the Queen in
Gloriana, and was a close, though not uncritical, colleague of
Britten in the English Opera Group.

QUEEN ELIZABETH II

Gloriana, op. 53 (1953)

'This work is dedicated by gracious permission to Her Majesty Queen Elizabeth II, in honour of whose Coronation
it was composed'. Britten's commission for *Gloriana* came
about through the Earl of Harewood, cousin of the Queen.
The first night at the Royal Opera House was rather a sticky
affair, with many in the top-drawer audience tut-tutting at
what they felt was an inappropriate exploration of Elizabeth
I's private life and old age.

QUEEN ELIZABETH THE QUEEN MOTHER

A Birthday Hansel, op. 92 (1975)

'These songs were written at the special wish of Her Majesty The Queen for her mother's seventy-fifth birthday, August 4th 1975'. The Queen Mother made occasional forays to the Aldeburgh Festival and became its Patron, and in turn Britten and Pears gave occasional recitals for her at Sandringham. This song cycle for voice and harp was a surprise present, and Britten attended a private performance of it in Norfolk for the Queen Mother, the Queen and Princess Margaret.

DOROTHY ELMHIRST

Five Flower Songs, op. 47 (1950)

'To Leonard and Dorothy Elmhirst on the occasion of their twenty-fifth wedding anniversary – 3rd April 1950'. One of the wealthiest women in America, Dorothy Whitney was a philanthropist and social activist. She met Elmhirst while he was at Cornell University, New York, and they were married in 1925. They established a rural community life project at Dartington Hall in Devon, where Dorothy fostered artistic ventures. She anonymously gave £2,000 to the English Opera Group at its launch in 1947, and provided further support three years later for its production of Purcell's *Dido and Aeneas*.

NANCY EVANS

A Charm of Lullabies, op. 41 (1947)

'For Nancy Evans', who as a leading mezzo-soprano had shared the title role with Kathleen Ferrier in *The Rape of Lucretia* the previous year, and created the role of Nancy in *Albert Herring* in 1947. (The duplication of the name was presumably no accident, as the libretto was written by her prospective husband, Eric Crozier.) Her regular performances

with the English Opera Group and at the Aldeburgh Festival
ended in 1955, when Crozier had lost favour with Britten.

KATHLEEN FERRIER

Canticle II: Abraham and Isaac, op. 51 (1952)

'For Kathleen Ferrier and Peter Pears' to sing with Britten at
the piano during a fund-raising recital tour. In the late 1940s
the Lancashire contralto took the musical world by storm
with her performances of Bach, Gluck and Mahler. She created the title role in Britten's *The Rape of Lucretia*, and sang in
the premiere of his *Spring Symphony*. Britten admired the way
Ferrier's voice communicated her warm and outgoing personality. She last performed the part of Isaac in this Canticle at
the 1952 Aldeburgh Festival, when she was already seriously
ill with cancer. It was one of Britten's abiding griefs that the
recording of this concert was inadvertently wiped by the BBC.

JUNE GORDON

'The Holly and the Ivy' (1957)

'For June Gordon and the Haddo House Choral Society,
1957'. June Gordon, Marchioness of Aberdeen and Temair,
pianist and conductor, was an almost exact contemporary
of Britten's, and a fellow graduate of the Royal College of
Music. In 1945 she started a Choral and Operatic Society at
her husband's ancestral home, Haddo House in Aberdeen-
shire, and went on to conduct numerous concert and opera
performances there. She died in 2009 at the age of ninety-five.

IMOGEN HOLST

Realisation of Purcell's *Three Divine Hymns* (1944–5)
'To Imogen Holst'

The Prince of the Pagodas, op. 57 (1956)
'To Imogen Holst and Ninette de Valois'

The Sycamore Tree (1930, revised 1967)

'For Imo'

Imogen Holst was Britten's music assistant, amanuensis even, in the 1950s and 60s, and his collaborator in the Aldeburgh Festival. She was the daughter of the composer Gustav Holst, and a substantial musician in her own right. The dedication of the Purcell arrangements came shortly after she first met Britten and Pears giving their wartime recitals. Ten years later she helped with the sheer physical labour of preparing the vocal and full scores of *Gloriana* and Britten's three-act ballet. This, he said, was really '*her* child', and he gave her the composition draft as a fiftieth birthday present.

NATALIE KOUSSEVITZKY

Peter Grimes, op. 33 (1945)

'For the Koussevitzky Music Foundation, dedicated to the memory of Natalie Koussevitzky', wife of the Russian-born conductor, Serge Koussevitzky. She was the daughter of a successful tea-merchant, and married Serge in Russia in the early twentieth century: they left after the Revolution. Natalie died in January 1942, the same month as the meeting between Britten and her husband which led to the commission of *Grimes*. Koussevitzky set up the Foundation in her memory, and required all its commissions to be dedicated to her.

TERTIA LIEBENTHAL

Who are these Children?, op. 84 (1969)

'To Tertia Liebenthal', who organised concerts at the National Gallery of Scotland in Edinburgh. She started them as a morale-boosting exercise in the war, and this set of songs by the Scottish poet William Soutar was designed to mark the 700th concert. She was eighty years old at the time of the dedication, but died before the first performance.

ALMA MAHLER

Nocturne, op. 60 (1958)

'To Alma Mahler', widow of the composer Gustav Mahler, whose music Britten had grown to love in the 1930s. He first met her in New York in 1942, when she was present at an early private performance of the Michelangelo Sonnets. He sent her a copy of the score 'with love', and they corresponded intermittently. She later told him she was '*always* your *admiring* friend, and your picture *always* stands in front of me'.

PRINCESS MARGARET OF HESSE AND BY RHINE

Songs from the Chinese, op. 58 (1957)

'To Peg and Lu, from Ben, Peter [Pears] and Julian [Bream]'. Margaret Campbell Geddes was the daughter of one of Lloyd George's cabinet ministers. She met Prince Ludwig of Hesse on holiday in Bavaria, and he arranged a diplomatic posting in London to be closer to her. Their marriage there in 1937 was struck by tragedy when Ludwig's elder brother and his family were killed in an air crash on the way to the wedding. Peg and Lu, as they were known, were introduced to Britten by Lord Harewood, and became close friends.

BEATA MAYER

'The Ash Grove' (1941)

'To Beata Mayer', daughter of William and Elizabeth Mayer, who opened their home to Britten and Pears during their time in New York from 1939 to 1942. Beata had trained as a nurse and cared for Britten during a serious illness in early 1940. The folksong 'The Ash Grove', published after Britten's return to England in 1942, was a touching choice, referring as it does to 'my dear one, the joy of my heart . . . Ah, then little thought I how soon we should part.' Beata was the same age as Britten, and her mother had hopes of them marrying.

ELIZABETH MAYER

'Interlude', no. 6 of *Les Illuminations*, op. 18 (1939)

'To E.M.'

Hymn to St Cecilia, op. 27 (1942)

'To Elizabeth Mayer'

Mayer lived on Long Island, New York, where her husband William was medical director of a psychiatric institution. Pears first met her on his American singing tour in 1937, and made contact again when he returned with Britten in 1939. She more or less adopted Britten and Pears into her family, and remained a close confidante for the rest of her life.

KATHLEEN MITCHELL

The Burning Fiery Furnace, op. 77 (1966)

'To Donald and Kathleen Mitchell', close friends of Britten during his later career. Shortly before he died, he was planning a Christmas opera for children, based on a mystery play, along the lines of *Noye's Fludde* almost two decades before. It was intended for Pimlico School in London, where Kathleen was headmistress.

CLYTIE MUNDY

'The Salley Gardens' (1940)

'To Clytie Mundy', the Australian singer who was Pears's teacher for two years in New York, at the time he first sang this folksong arrangement. He and Britten performed it more than any other. Clytie was also the name of the miniature dachshund they acquired in 1954.

MEG MUNDY

'O can ye sew cushions?' (1943)

'To Meg Mundy', daughter of Clytie and John Mundy, and

soprano. She was invited by Pears to join his new vocal quintet, the Elizabethan Singers, in New York in 1941.

URSULA NETTLESHIP

A Ceremony of Carols, op. 28 (1942)

'For Ursula Nettleship', a choral trainer who first met Britten
at her sister's Cornish retreat at Crantock. Britten spent two
summer holidays there. After their return from America in
1942, Britten and Pears had difficulty finding a London base,
and for two months Nettleship accommodated them in her
house in Cheyne Walk. *A Ceremony of Carols* was first performed during this Chelsea residency. She was later involved
with the Aldeburgh Festival, where she prepared some of the
choral performances.

MYFANWY PIPER

Winter Words, op. 52 (1953)

'To John and Myfanwy Piper'. Myfanwy Piper was perhaps
the most successful of Britten's opera librettists. Shortly after
Winter Words was completed, she began work on her masterly
adaptation of Henry James's story *The Turn of the Screw*, and
was later recalled by Britten for his second James opera *Owen
Wingrave*, and then *Death in Venice*.

MARY POTTER

Alpine Suite (1955)

'For Mary Potter', artist and close friend for almost twenty-
five years. While Britten lived on the Aldeburgh seafront,
she and her husband, the author Stephen Potter, lived inland
at The Red House, where Britten was frequently her tennis
partner. After her divorce, she accompanied Britten and Pears
on holiday to Zermatt, but was prevented from skiing by injury. So Britten wrote this suite for the three of them to play on
their recorders. In 1957 she and Britten swapped houses, and

later she moved to a studio he built for her in The Red House grounds. She paid her rent in paintings.

MARGARET RITCHIE

Realisation of Purcell's *The Blessed Virgin's Expostulation* (1944)

'For Margaret Ritchie' (also known as Mabel), who became a leading soprano in the English Opera Group, creating the roles of Lucia in *The Rape of Lucretia* and Miss Wordsworth in *Albert Herring*. She became concerned at Britten's casting of young boys in his operas, and asked Eric Crozier to use his influence with Britten to stop it.

ENID SLATER

Ballad of Heroes, op. 14 (1939)

'To Montagu and Enid Slater', who got to know Britten through his work with the GPO Film Unit in the mid-1930s. Enid was an accomplished photographer whose images of Britten before the war, often at The Old Mill in Snape, publicly defined his appearance and manner at that time. She became a confidante, whom Britten asked to keep an eye on his devoted young Cambridge friend Wulff Scherchen when he went to America in 1939.

CECILY SMITHWICK

The Oxen (1967)

'For Cecily Smithwick and the East Coker W. I.' Cecily Smithwick was the sister of Peter Pears and lived in Somerset. She requested a carol from Britten, and members of the Women's Institute were invited to suggest possible texts. One of these was Hardy's poem. The carol was first performed by the East Coker Women's Institute Choir in 1968 – on 28 January, somewhat incongruously.

SYLVIA SPENCER

The Grasshopper and *The Wasp* (1935, later published as *Two Insect Pieces*)

'For Sylvia Spencer', oboist, who had graduated from the Royal College of Music shortly before Britten arrived. She led an early performance of his *Phantasy* oboe quartet, and he wrote these pieces and played them through with her in April 1935, though it is unclear whether they ever performed them in public.

ROSAMUND STRODE

A Wealden Trio: The Song of the Women (1930, revised 1967)

'For Rosamund', who first met Britten at Dartington in 1948, as a founder member of the Purcell Singers. She sang the soprano solo in the first performance of Britten's student carol 'New Prince, New Pomp' at Aldeburgh in 1955, and worked there part-time before succeeding Imogen Holst as Britten's music assistant in 1964. He wrote to her at one point: 'Your simply incredible skills, loyalty, and understanding is something beyond my range, and I never cease to be grateful for and touched by it'.

MARION THORPE

A Wedding Anthem (Amo Ergo Sum), op. 46 (1949)

'For Marion and George, 29 September 1949'

Billy Budd, op. 50 (1951)

'To George and Marion, December 1951'

Fancie (1961)

'For M. H.'

The pianist Marion Stein was only twelve when she first met Britten at the premiere of *Ballad of Heroes* in 1939, shortly after her parents' arrival from Vienna. When the Steins' flat was destroyed by fire in 1944, they moved in with Britten and Pears in St John's Wood. Britten's friendship with her was lifelong, and readily extended to George Harewood when she married him in 1949, though his relationship with the latter did not survive their divorce in 1967. By then, Marion had co-founded the Leeds Piano Competition, for which Britten wrote a competition piece. She went on to marry the Liberal Party leader, Jeremy Thorpe, in 1973.

MILDRED TITLEY

'The Bonny Earl o' Moray' (1940)

'To Mildred Titley', the psychiatrist Dr Mildred Squire, who worked at the Long Island Home in Amityville, New York, where Britten and Pears were staying in 1940. She was married to the home's superintendent, Dr William Titley.

NINETTE DE VALOIS

The Prince of the Pagodas, op. 57 (1956)

'To Imogen Holst and Ninette de Valois', the great British ballerina and choreographer who co-founded what became the Royal Ballet. She was closely involved in preparing this full-length ballet with the choreographer John Cranko.

GALINA VISHNEVSKAYA

The Poet's Echo, op. 76 (1965)

'For Galya and Slava', the indomitable husband-and-wife partnership of post-war Russian music. Vishnevskaya was a soprano with the Bolshoi Opera when she married the cellist Mstislav (Slava) Rostropovich in 1955. Holidaying with the Rostropoviches in Armenia, Britten wrote these settings of Pushkin for his hosts to perform (Rostropovich also played the piano). Three years earlier Britten had written the soprano role in *War Requiem* for her, but she was unable to take part in the Coventry premiere because the Soviet authorities would not allow her to sing alongside a German (the baritone, Dietrich Fischer-Dieskau). They relented for the recording.

SOPHIE WYSS

Les Illuminations, op. 18 (1939)

'For Sophie Wyss', the Swiss soprano who was Britten's first muse. His settings of Auden poems, *On This Island*, were written for her, as was his revolutionary orchestral song cycle *Our Hunting Fathers*. Her performance at the Norwich premiere was 'excellent', Britten said. Although *Les Illuminations* later became associated with Peter Pears, the cycle was written for Wyss's soprano, and first performed and broadcast by her in wartime London.

Britten's children

FRANCIS BARTON

'Burlesque' from *Three Divertimenti for String Quartet*: *'Go play, boy, play'* (1936)

'To Francis Barton', a prep-school friend, for whom Britten always had a soft spot. These string quartet pieces evoked aspects of boyhood, which brought Francis to mind. Two years later Pears teased Britten about him: 'The flat looked as though you might have been entertaining someone – perhaps Francis? Or not yet? Tell me about it.' He added that Francis sounded 'just the sort of person I should hopelessly lose my heart to'. Barton became a major-general: late in life Britten told his sister that Francis 'meant a great deal to me in those very early days – his affection softened many blows'.

DAPHNE BLACK

'Daphne': *Poco andante grazioso*, no. 2 from *Three Character Pieces* for piano [originally *Three Pieces*] (1930)

This is a character study, rather than a dedication. Daphne Black was a Lowestoft friend, the daughter of one of Britten's tennis partners. She was still at school at this time.

DAVID BOYD

'Theme (What to do?)' from *Alla quartetto serioso: 'Go, play, boy, play'* (1933)

'To David B.', the nephew of Britten's next-door neighbours in Lowestoft, and the brother of John Boyd (see below). David was a regular companion for bathing, beach tea-parties, picnics, walking the dog, putting, playing badminton or football (not normally one of Britten's favourite pastimes, so he was specially favoured). When David was ill in bed, Britten took games round to him – 'a topping kid'.

JOHN BOYD

'John': *Poco allegro vivace*, no. 1 from *Three Character Pieces* for piano [originally *Three Pieces*] (1930)

This is a character study of the elder nephew of Britten's next-door neighbours. Like his brother David, he seemed to spend much of his time in Lowestoft, when not boarding at Seaford College in Sussex. Britten enjoyed the brothers' company in his late teens and early twenties.

ROGER DUNCAN

Noye's Fludde, op. 59 (1958)

'To my nephew and nieces, Sebastian, Sally and Roguey Welford, and my young friend Roger Duncan'. Roger was the closest of all Britten's boy companions, and one of the best-looking. His rather feckless father was the poet and playwright Ronald Duncan, librettist of *The Rape of Lucretia*. Roger is often described as Britten's godson, which he wasn't, but Britten did once ask Duncan senior if he could 'share' Roger with him, an offer that was accepted. Roger and Britten exchanged florid, loving letters all through the boy's schooldays, and Britten had him to stay for weeks at a time during the holidays. Both were keen sportsmen.

PIERS DUNKERLEY

War Requiem, op. 66 (1962)

'In loving memory of Roger Burney, Sub-Lieutenant RNVR, Piers Dunkerley, Captain Royal Marines, David Gill, Ordinary Seaman, Royal Navy, Michael Halliday, Lieutenant RNZNVR'. Piers Dunkerley is unique in the Britten entourage, because an infatuation that began when he was a handsome, cheeky schoolboy lasted into adulthood (when he was a handsome, teasing Marine), and became lifelong. But Dunkerley's life was short. He served in the Forces during and after the war, leaving in 1958 to become engaged. He found civilian life hard, and was hurt when Britten turned down his invitation to be his best man. Shortly before his wedding he committed suicide. Britten seems to have felt he was a casualty of war.

PETER FLOUD

Sketch no. 3 (unfinished) for string orchestra (1930)

This Sketch was a portrait of a kindred spirit at Gresham's. Floud was two years older than Britten, but they spent many hours 'gramophoning' together and playing chamber music. He introduced Britten to Proust, and they discussed the evils of the school cadet force and prefect system. Britten said Floud was 'one of the very few (about 4) boys who think in the school'; he was 'terribly sorry' when he left. They wrote long letters to each other, and later met occasionally in London for a meal or a concert.

GATHORNE, JULIET, SOPHIE, CHRISTINA, HUGH, JONATHAN AND SAMUEL GATHORNE-HARDY

The Little Sweep, op. 45 (1949)

'Affectionately dedicated to the real Gay, Juliet, Sophie, Tina, Hughie, Jonny and Sammy – the Gathorne-Hardys of Great Glemham, Suffolk' – the first five of these were the children, and the last two the nephews, of the Aldeburgh Festival chairman,

Fidelity, Countess of Cranbrook. The opera is set in Suffolk, featuring children with the same names, so the local audience would have got the in-joke. Jonny and Sammy both later reported that their friendship with Britten had been unusually close.

DAVID GILL

War Requiem, op. 66 (1962)

'In loving memory of Roger Burney, Sub-Lieutenant RNVR, Piers Dunkerley, Captain Royal Marines, David Gill, Ordinary Seaman, Royal Navy, Michael Halliday, Lieutenant RNZNVR'. David Gill was a cousin of Britten's boyhood friend in Lowestoft, Basil Reeve, and a chorister in St Paul's Cathedral choir in London. Britten got to know him in 1932–3, when David was eleven or twelve years old. Years later Britten was shocked to hear he'd been killed in the war: he told Gill's mother he'd been very fond of him, and that David had 'helped a great deal by singing over music I had written' – a reference to *A Boy Was Born*.

ARNOLD AND HUMPHREY GYDE

Folk Song Arrangements, vol. 2 (1942)

'To my young friends, Arnold and Humphrey Gyde', the two sons of the French Swiss soprano Sophie Wyss and her publisher husband Arnold Gyde. Britten wrote mostly for Wyss's voice before the war. When he came back from America in 1942, his new muse was Peter Pears. With these French folksongs, he signed off their association, and touchingly dedicated them to Humphrey, his six-year-old godson, and his elder brother Arnold. 'It gives me great pleasure to do this', Britten wrote, 'because I am so fond of them.'

JOHN HAHESSY

Corpus Christi Carol (1961)

'For John Hahessy', who had been head chorister at

Westminster Cathedral when *Missa Brevis* was first performed there. When his voice began to change, and he temporarily had an alto register, he made several recordings with Britten, including *Canticle II: Abraham and Isaac* and this carol, which is an adaptation of the fifth variation of *A Boy was Born*. Hahessy later became a professional tenor, with the name John Elwes.

MICHAEL HALLIDAY

'Variation I (On the see-saw)' from *Alla quartetto serioso: 'Go, play, boy, play'* (1933)

'To Michael'

War Requiem, op. 66 (1962)

'In loving memory of Roger Burney, Sub-Lieutenant RNVR, Piers Dunkerley, Captain Royal Marines, David Gill, Ordinary Seaman, Royal Navy, Michael Halliday, Lieutenant RNZNVR'. Halliday was one of Britten's contemporaries at South Lodge School, and 'rather an outsider until Ben took him in hand, and looked after him', as a mutual friend recalled. He was 'short, stocky, rather tough-looking and dour', very much a loner. The Variation's dedication is probably for Halliday, as Britten was in contact with him in London at this time, just after Halliday had joined the Merchant Navy. Britten heard in 1944 that he was missing in action – 'poor silly old dear that he was' – hence the *War Requiem* dedication.

GÁBOR AND ZOLTÁN JENEY

Gemini Variations, op. 73 (1965)

'For Zoltán and Gábor Jeney', the twin boys of thirteen he met in Budapest in 1964. Impressed by their pianistic and instrumental prowess (Zoltán's on the flute, Gábor's on the violin), he agreed to write them this 'quartet for two players', which required them each to change instruments several times. Britten later supported Gábor financially at the Royal College of Music.

LANCING COLLEGE

Saint Nicolas, op. 42 (1948)

'This Cantata was written for performance at the centenary celebrations of Lancing College, Sussex, on 24 July 1948'. The part of Nicolas was assigned to Peter Pears, who had attended the boys' public school from 1923 to 1928.

DAVID LAYTON

Sketch no. 1: 'D. Layton, *Poco presto*', later published as the first of *Two Portraits* (1930)

Alla Marcia (1933)

'To David Layton', one of Britten's closest friends at Gresham's School, and a fellow viola-player. They played tennis and cricket together, and both opted out of the school cadet force. On his last school day, Layton was one of the boys Britten said he was 'terribly sorry to leave': this Sketch was written shortly after. He also had Layton in mind for the wiry march he wrote for string quartet three years later. Britten visited his 'good-looking, aristocratic, acme of ideal manhood, friend David Layton' at Trinity College, Cambridge, in 1936.

LONDON BOY SINGERS

'King Herod and the Cock' (1962)

'For the London Boy Singers', a choir founded under Britten's patronage to perpetuate the training methods of George Malcolm after his retirement from Westminster Cathedral.

HUMPHREY, PAMELA, CAROLINE AND VIRGINIA
MAUD

The Young Person's Guide to the Orchestra, op. 34 (1945)

'This work is affectionately inscribed to the children of John and Jean Maud: Humphrey, Pamela, Caroline and Virginia,

for their edification and entertainment'. The pianist Jean
Maud often gave wartime recitals alongside Britten and Pears,
and her cello-playing son Humphrey became one of Britten's
boy companions after the war. *The Young Person's Guide* was
published in 1947, the year of Humphrey's thirteenth birthday – which is when the dedication was made. The first of
his three sisters, Pamela, had died some years before, and the
family were touched by Britten's inclusion of her here.

CHRISTOPHER MAYER

'Oliver Cromwell' (1940)

'To Christopher Mayer', son of William and Elizabeth Mayer,
with whom Britten and Pears lodged intermittently in New
York between 1939 and 1942. Christopher was still at school.
'Oliver Cromwell' is the last, shortest and most energetic folksong in the first collection Britten published after his return
to England in 1942.

OLD BUCKENHAM HALL

Psalm 150, op. 67 (1962)

'Written for the centenary celebrations of Old Buckenham
Hall School – formerly South Lodge School, Lowestoft – July
1962'. Britten had been at this prep school between 1923 and
1928.

BOBBY ROTHMAN

'The trees they grow so high' (1943)

'To Bobby Rothman', son of Britten's store-owning American friend, David Rothman. At thirteen Bobby was a Britten
favourite, and the delicacy of their relationship was revealed
indirectly by Elizabeth Mayer. She sent Pears a photograph
of Britten and Bobby, taken by the boy's father. But, said
Pears, she had 'tactfully' cut off half the picture – the half with
Bobby in it. Britten said he was too shy to tell Bobby about

this dedication, but the words of the folksong reminded him 'so much' of him. 'You've tied me to a boy', it says, 'when you know he is too young.' Of the seven folksongs in Britten's first collection, this was the only one Pears never recorded.

WULFF SCHERCHEN

'Antique', no. 3b of *Les Illuminations*, op. 18 (1939)

'To K. H. W. S.', Wolfgang Scherchen, known as 'Wulff'. He was the son of the German conductor Hermann Scherchen, and a boy of thirteen when Britten first met him in Florence in 1934. Their friendship developed four years later, perhaps a more intimate one than any other in Britten's life to date. He dedicated one movement of his Rimbaud song cycle to him – by which time Britten had moved to North America, still pining for his friend. He also made clear that his vision of Keats's 'dazzling Sun-god' in *Young Apollo* was inspired by Wulff.

MICHAEL TYLER

'Michael': *Poco presto e molto capriccioso*, no. 3 from *Three Character Pieces* for piano [originally *Three Pieces*] (1930)

Michael Tyler was a friend from Britten's teenage years. The piece quotes *Ragamuffin* (a piano piece by Britten's composition teacher, John Ireland), which may have prompted the naming of this character study.

VIENNA BOYS' CHOIR

The Golden Vanity, op. 78 (1966)

'Für die Wiener Sängerknaben', who had excited Britten's admiration since he was twenty. 'I have seldom heard such superb singing – rhythm, intonation, purest tone, & lovely taste,' he gushed. They impressed him again in 1964 in a performance of *War Requiem*, after which the boys asked him to write them a little opera. *The Golden Vanity* was the result.

SEBASTIAN, SALLY AND ROSEMARY WELFORD

Noye's Fludde, op. 59 (1958)

'To my nephew and nieces, Sebastian, Sally and Roguey Welford, and my young friend Roger Duncan'. The three children of Britten's sister Beth and her husband Dr Kit Welford were now nineteen, fifteen and thirteen. The Welfords lived in Suffolk, and for a time, during Britten's absence abroad, at his home in Snape, The Old Mill.

THE BOYS OF WESTMINSTER CATHEDRAL CHOIR

Missa Brevis in D, op. 63 (1959)

'For George Malcolm and the boys of Westminster Cathedral Choir'. Among the boys, whose bright, direct tone Britten so much admired, were his godson Michael Berkeley (son of Lennox) and John Hahessy, both of whom took part in the first performance at High Mass in July 1959 and in the subsequent recording. Britten had dropped in to the cathedral the previous January, at the suggestion of Peter Pears, and told the Master of the Music, George Malcolm, that the choir sang with 'a brilliance and authority which was staggering'.

Other dedicatees

ALDEBURGH MUSIC CLUB

Scherzo for recorder quartet (1954)

'To the Aldeburgh Music Club', members of which would sometimes congregate at Britten's house, where he and Pears would get out their recorders for informal music-making.

BASEL UNIVERSITY

Cantata Academica, Carmen Basiliense, op. 62 (1959)

'Composuit Universitati Basiliensi, sollemnia saecularia quinta celebranti, dedicavit Benjamin Britten MCMLX.'

Translated, this means: 'Benjamin Britten composed this piece and dedicated it to the University of Basel as it celebrates five solemn centuries'.

ENGLISH OPERA GROUP

The Turn of the Screw, op. 54 (1954)

'This opera was written for and is affectionately dedicated to those members of the English Opera Group who took part in the first performance'. Britten co-founded the English Opera Group in 1946, to produce operas by English composers and in the English language. Later it was managed by the Royal Opera. It was wound up in 1974 and briefly succeeded by English Music Theatre.

LEEDS FESTIVAL

National Anthem, arranged for chorus and orchestra (1961)

'For the Leeds Festival 1961', with which Britten was connected through George and Marion Harewood, who lived nearby. He had written the *Nocturne* for an earlier Festival.

ST GEORGE'S CHAPEL, WINDSOR

Jubilate Deo in C (1961)

'Written for St George's Chapel, Windsor, at the request of HRH The Duke of Edinburgh', as a companion piece for Britten's *Te Deum* in C of 1934.

ST MARK'S CHURCH, SWINDON

Festival Te Deum, op. 32 (1944)

'Written for the Centenary Festival of St Mark's, Swindon'

ST MATTHEW'S CHURCH, NORTHAMPTON

Prelude and Fugue on a Theme of Vittoria (1946)

'For St Matthew's Church, Northampton, St Matthew's Day, 1946'. The parish priest was the arts patron Walter Hussey.

ST MICHAEL'S COLLEGE, TENBURY WELLS

Antiphon, op. 56b (1956)

'For the centenary of St Michael's College, Tenbury', where the organist was Kenneth Beard. He conducted the premiere of Britten's anthem in the presence of the composer.

ST PETER MANCROFT, NORWICH

Hymn to St Peter, op. 56a (1955)

'Written for the Quincentenary of St Peter Mancroft, Norwich, 1955', where the organist was C. J. R. Coleman, who had been organist of St John's, Lowestoft when Britten was a boy.

WILBYE CONSORT

Sacred and Profane, op. 91 (1975)

'For P. P. and the Wilbye Consort', a group of six professionals founded by Pears in 1967 to sing Elizabethan and Jacobean madrigals. Pears directed the group and often sang along impromptu with the second tenor part.

Returning the compliment

One of the first musical dedications to Britten came in 1947 in the *Stabat Mater* by his friend Lennox Berkeley, who thereby repaid Britten's tribute to him nine years before in his Piano Concerto. Such a reciprocal gesture came rather faster from Shostakovich, who aptly chose his song cycle symphony (no. 14) for a Britten dedication in 1969, only

a year after Britten had ear-marked *The Prodigal Son* for
Shostakovich.

For Britten's fiftieth birthday in 1963, three young British
composers combined to write *Reflections on a Theme of Ben-*
jamin Britten. They took his teasing 'tema seriale' from his
Cantata Academica (which he'd written to prove to musicologists how the serial technique could be used in a tonal way),
and used it as the basis of a three-movement work for flute,
bassoon, horn, viola and harp. The opening 'Rondo' was by
Richard Rodney Bennett, the 'Intermezzo' by Nicholas Maw,
and the final 'Tarantella' by Malcolm Williamson.

Peter Maxwell Davies wrote his own birthday tribute,
a septet *In Nomine*. So did Tippett with his Concerto for
Orchestra. Walton followed a few years later with his orchestral *Improvisations on an Impromptu of Benjamin Britten*, which
developed a theme from Britten's Piano Concerto.

At the time of his sixtieth birthday, Thea Musgrave dedicated her opera *The Voice of Ariadne* to Britten, while after his
death came *Cantus in memoriam Benjamin Britten* for strings
and bell by Arvo Pärt, and Peter Racine Fricker's *Sinfonia* for
voices and wind.

12

Britten's prizes

Date	Age	Prize/Award
1927	13	Badminton prize, South Lodge School
1927	13	Winner of 'Throwing the Cricket Ball' contest, South Lodge (his record lasted several years)
1928	14	Victor Ludorum, South Lodge
1928	14	Music scholarship to Gresham's School, Holt
1930	16	Maths prize at Gresham's
1930	16	Wyndham Birch Prize, Gresham's
1930	16	Open Scholarship to Royal College of Music (£40 a year)
1930	16	Awarded School Certificate with 5 credits
1931	17	RCM Ernest Farrar Prize for composition
1932	18	RCM Cobbett Prize (13 guineas) for *Phantasy Quintet*
1932	18	RCM Sullivan Prize (£10) for *Sinfonietta*
1932	19	Awarded grant (£50) by Mendelssohn Scholarship committee
1933	19	Octavia Travelling Scholarship
1933	19	Further grant (£80) from Mendelssohn Scholarship committee
1933	19	RCM Ernest Farrar Prize (again)
1934	20	Associate of the Royal College of Music
1934	20	Winner of Old Boys' race at South Lodge
1934	21	Appointed Mendelssohn Scholar for six months, with an award of £100. He declines this because it was not for a full year (with an award of £300)
1941	27	Elizabeth Sprague Coolidge Medal from Library of Congress for 'eminent services to chamber music'. This is said to have been in recognition of the string quartet he deemed

to be his first, commissioned by the same Mrs
Coolidge, though Britten makes clear in a
letter that the prize was awarded before the
quartet had been completed, let alone heard

1951	37	Honorary Freeman of the Borough of Lowestoft
1953	39	Companion of Honour
1953	39	Membership, Swedish Academy of Music
1954	40	Honorary D.Mus., Queen's University, Belfast
1955	41	Honorary Membership, Belgian Royal Academy of Sciences, Letters and Arts
1955	41	Honorary Membership, Accademia Nazionale Cherubini di Musica, Lettere, Arti Figurative, Florence
1957	43	Honorary Membership of American Academy and the National Institute of Arts and Letters (limited to fifty citizens of foreign countries noted for outstanding contributions to the arts)
1957	43	Fellowship of the Royal College of Music
1957	43	Honorary Membership, Royal Academy of Music
1958	44	Honorary Membership, Accademia Nazionale di Santa Cecilia, Rome
1959	45	Honorary Membership, Akademie der Künste, Berlin, East Germany
1959	45	President, Society of Recorder Players
1959	45	Honorary D.Mus., University of Cambridge
1961	47	Hanseatic Goethe Prize, Hamburg (£2,225)
1961	47	Honorary D.Mus., University of Nottingham
1962	48	Honorary D.Mus., University of Hull
1962	48	Commander of the Royal Order of the Pole Star (Sweden)
1962	48	Honorary Membership, Akademie der Künste, Hamburg
1962	48	2nd Honorary Freeman of the Borough of Aldeburgh
1963	49	Honorary D.Mus., University of Oxford
1964	50	Aspen Award for 'the individual anywhere in the world judged to have made the greatest

contribution to the advancement of the humanities' (£10,750). The citation read: 'To Benjamin Britten, who, as a brilliant composer, performer, and interpreter through music of human feelings, moods, and thoughts, has truly inspired man to understand, clarify and appreciate more fully his own nature, purpose and destiny'

1964	50	Three Grammy Awards for *War Requiem*: best classical composition by a contemporary composer; best classical performance, choral; album of the year, classical
1964	51	Gold Medal of Royal Philharmonic Society
1964	51	Honorary D.Mus., University of London
1964	51	Hon D.Mus., University of Manchester
1965	51	Order of Merit
1965	51	Freedom of Worshipful Company of Musicians
1965	51	Honorary Membership, Serbian Academy of the Sciences and the Arts, Belgrade
1965	51	Honorary Fellowship, Magdalene College, Cambridge
1965	51	Honorary D.Mus., University of Leicester
1965	51	Wihuri Sibelius Prize, Helsinki (£8,900)
1967	53	Mahler Medal of the Bruckner and Mahler Society of America
1967	53	Honorary D.Mus., University of East Anglia
1968	54	Leonie Sonning Prize, Copenhagen (£3,075)
1968	54	Correspondent (Musical Section), Académie des Beaux-Arts, Paris
1972	58	Honorary Membership, Bayerischen Akademie der Schönen Künste, Munich
1974	60	Ernst von Siemens Award, West Germany (£14,050)
1974	61	Ravel Prize (£3,300), for 'recalling the scrupulous attention to detail, the search for beauty of expression, sonority and invention which characterise the music of Ravel'

1975	61	Honorary D.Mus., University of Warwick
1976	62	Mozart Medal
1976	62	Honorary D.Mus., University of Wales
1976	62	Life peerage (Baron Britten of Aldeburgh)
1976	62	1st Citation of Honour, McGill University, Montreal
1976	62	Foreign Associate, Académie des Beaux-Arts, Paris
1977	posth.	Mozart Medal, Mozartgemeinde, Vienna

Round Britten Quiz III

ANSWERS ON PAGE 410

1 Which of Britten's operas was inspired by William Blake?

2 What did Britten's headmaster tell him not to do, to protect his hands?

3 In which work does Britten use the Russian *Kontakion* for the dead?

4 Which 'very great man' did Britten, at the age of forty-four, say had been 'such a tremendous figure to me, all my musical life'?

5 What did Britten say was a disadvantage of living in Suffolk?

6 Which was the last piece that Britten conducted in public?

13

Britten's cars

Britten loved speed. He revelled in writing fast music, which he often marked 'Quick'. There was an alertness and liveliness that spoke of mental as well as physical energy. He found both when he was holding either a tennis racquet or a steering wheel.

He belonged to a generation that never took a driving test. That was introduced in June 1935 for people who had been driving for a year or less. But by then he was already twenty-one, and had been driving intermittently with his parents. He regarded the new test as too rigorous, with the result that people were clogging up public transport instead of getting out on the roads themselves!

He graduated to a car of his own (or, at least, one he shared with his sister Beth) on Saturday 30 May 1936, when they bought a second-hand Lagonda for just £6 (the equivalent of about £300 today). They found it at a garage in Hatch End, near Harrow, and decided to buy it 'as it seems in such good condition. Probably fool-hardy, but the offer is tempting.' Foolhardy indeed, as they came to discover.

Day one began well. They drove to Pinner and then to their mother's new home in Frinton, Essex. After the day's adventure, Britten judged that, considering it had cost so little, 'the car does amazingly well. True it is not the acme of comfort yet – still less with hood up – and cannot exceed 40 [mph] – but we go a long way round (Hatfield, Ware etc) and do 90 odd miles in 3¼ hrs.' The next day took the gilt off the gingerbread, as he discovered ('first catastrophe') that the car radiator had a large leak, which required an all-day visit (on a Sunday) to the local garage. But they collected it at about 6 p.m. and had a short drive along the seafront in wind and rain.

He spent the whole of the Monday morning 'playing about with car – cleaning, oiling, repairing etc. – a thing quite unbelievable for me before today!' But on Tuesday, while Britten continued work on his big new piece *Our Hunting Fathers*, Beth took the Lagonda back to their London flat on her own, a journey that took nearly five hours because of 'very bad brakes, filthy weather & on top of all that the ignition pin comes out & she spends 1 hour finding a garage & having it put right. So much for 2nd hand cars!'

On Thursday Beth telephoned to say she had had 'a smash in the Lagonda, & mucked up one wheel'. She'd had a disagreement with a London taxi – 'a very slight accident', as she later recalled, 'and we were both able to drive away, but the taxi driver was very nasty about it and called the police'. A court summons followed, which she only found after coming back from holiday: because she had not responded to it, she was had up for contempt of court and fined the then substantial sum of £10. Britten was with her in court, and had to fetch the money there and then to prevent his sister being taken into custody. Furthermore, because they only had third-party insurance they had to foot the bill for a damaged wheel. Britten commented that it took 'a lot of Beethoven sonatas' to cheer him up after that.

On Saturday Beth returned to Frinton with two friends. Her brother found the car 'a bit battered one side' but otherwise 'not much damaged' after its eventful first week in Britten hands. The second week was rather quieter, but ended in a long country drive towards Harwich with Beth, when he managed to run the car into a hedge while turning: 'very annoying as I've never done that sort of thing before'.

Early on Monday morning both his sisters set off to London, but thanks to engine trouble the journey took them four hours. 'Is it really worth it?' Britten asked ruefully. Then there were further problems with the headlights and a leaking roof. The Lagonda did make it to Cornwall for a Britten family holiday at Crantock in August, only to refuse to budge once she had got there. After some further repairs she was back on the Cornish lanes, only to run out of petrol. Then it was back to the garage for an 'overhaul' before the long journey home.

'It is always slow going', Britten commented, 'as she doesn't climb too rapidly, & as the brakes are practically non-existent we don't descend too rapidly'. In fact it was all so slow that he and Beth had to sleep out in the open on Salisbury Plain. Britten felt the car had done 'marvellously – no trouble at all', but he noted that 'she eats oil': six pints (and thirteen gallons of petrol) for 350 miles.

At Christmas 1936 the Lagonda was uncooperative once again. 'She's as obstinate as a mule', Britten wrote, '& it takes another car from the garage down the road, pulling her, to start her in the afternoon'. She did manage to take Britten and his sisters to Ipswich, but the return late-night journey was 'very tiresome', thanks to 'foul fog combined with skiddy roads, bad brakes & rotten lights'. Furthermore, the car was increasingly 'a bugger to start'. On one occasion Britten stopped to relieve himself behind a hedge, and when he tried to start the car again the starter knob came out in his hand. Her fate was sealed. In March the Lagonda was unceremoniously dumped.

Britten was undaunted, however, and two months later he and Beth bought a Lea-Francis saloon car, just after he had met Peter Pears for the first time, and was writing cabaret songs such as *Johnny* for the singer Hedli Anderson. 'We take the plunge', he said – 'probably mad.' At first he found it difficult to manage, but the next day they drove off to see an aunt in the Cotswolds. 'It runs splendidly', he said. They went on to Bath to impress another aunt – and to Painswick in Gloucestershire two days after. But then their triumphal procession came to such an abrupt halt that Britten missed writing up his diary for the first time in nine years. They had a collision while overtaking on the way home, with Britten at the wheel, and their five-day-old pride and joy was a write-off. It left Beth 'stiff and bruised', and Britten 'rather the worse for wear'. The police told him he would be charged with dangerous driving – a sharp blow to his competitive pride. 'Blast their eyes', Britten fumed. 'It's infuriating, because I know I was in the right.'

Two weeks later, the solicitors handling his defence took statements from Beth and Ben and drove them to 'the scene of the crime, and we re-enact the whole thing'. They saw 'the poor wrecked car' which hadn't been moved. He began to feel that the 'grinding ache' of the impending court case was putting him off his stride as he tried to write his Auden song cycle *On This Island* and the Frank Bridge Variations. In Burnham magistrates' court, near Slough, the evidence of eyewitnesses of the crash supported Britten, who was acquitted without having to give evidence. The other driver, 'the villain in the grey car', was convicted. But Britten was in no hurry to buy another car.

It was only after he had moved into The Old Mill at Snape that he felt he once again needed his own transport for 'tootling about the place'. He bought a second-hand Morris 8 in April 1938, in which he regularly ferried his new young friend Wulff Scherchen around.

But the bigger excitement came a year later, when his older friend and would-be lover Lennox Berkeley took delivery of an AC sports car in London. Berkeley was sharing The Old Mill with him, so they proudly drove to Suffolk together on 11 March 1939. It was a brand-new, hand-made 16-horsepower Sports Drophead Coupé, registration number FLA 633. Berkeley then had to go to Paris, which allowed Britten to exploit his talents as a boy racer – he even boasted he was handling the new car 'like a schoolboy'. He wrote to Berkeley:

> I have done all that is to be done re licence & registration card, & everything is going well with the car – I did 85 in her on Saturday just to show that the wheels were going round properly. But don't worry I'm very careful! It was on the Newmarket road which is nice & straight . . . It *is* grand to have such a car to drive! But it's useless to say thank-you! You can't say thank you for a car – or should I say the permission to drive one.

Although some of his friends believed the Acedes was a present from Berkeley, it is clear from this that Berkeley owned it but made it freely available to Britten – who took full advantage of his swanky new accoutrement to impress Berkeley's rival, Wulff Scherchen. A few feet of ciné film show them together at Snape, with Britten at the wheel, pleased as Punch. He thought nothing of driving from Snape to Bognor just to have lunch with Wulff and his mother in mid-April, and Scherchen remembers some scarily fast rides on the A23:

> He'd only demonstrated to me the previous day that if you stomped on the brakes the car didn't necessarily run straight. So I didn't really enjoy being driven at 90, but he thought it great fun – 'Brighton in twenty minutes instead of half an hour', you know, a real achievement!

It was a short-lived thrill. At the end of April Britten and Pears left the country for North America, an absence that was to last three years. The beloved AC had to stay behind.

At first Britten had no licence to drive in America. This didn't stop him racing up and down a deserted beach on Long Island for several hours in someone else's car when he was in a black depression during the winter of 1939–40. The following July he became a car owner again. His handsome fee from the Japanese for writing *Sinfonia da Requiem* was fortunately paid up front, before they'd decided to reject the work. By then Britten had spent it – partly on a 'cheap' nine-year-old green Ford, 'an old Jaloppy' as he called it. He paid $95 (around £1,150 in today's money). The two-seater wasn't quite in the AC class, but although the body was 'dilapidated' the engine was 'fine'. He said it was almost the only open car on Long Island, and 'we can touch 55 going downhill, if we hold on tight'.

In August 1940 he and Pears set off to the Berkshire Festival in Massachusetts, with the violinist Toni Brosa and his wife squeezed into a dickie seat in the back, and a trunk strapped on to the side. Pears wrote chattily to Beth that they were wearing all the clothes they were taking, to avoid having to pack them. They broke down on the way. 'It was hot, and you know how popular old green Fords are when they hold up a hundred Cadillacs – Ben almost died with shame. I went to get a breakdown van, the man was out, and of course when I finally brought him back in a van after 20 minutes, Ben had just managed to start the car.' The garage put the car to rights, but it broke down again the following day, before they finally reached Cape Cod. Then the two of them drove on to Owl's Head Inn, near Rockland in Maine. 'You can imagine what Ben's nerves were like driving for three hundred miles when you never knew when you might stop! We had to stop at every comfort station we passed!' After two weeks there, they drove back to Massachusetts, to join Auden on a farm. But they had electrical trouble on the way, and a flat tyre. 'Who would buy an old car?' Pears said: 'they are nothing but trouble and strife'. No wonder they didn't trust their Jalopy to take them coast-to-coast, to California and back, in summer 1941: instead Britten borrowed a Ford V8 from friends.

Back in England, just at the time he moved from The Old Mill into a large seafront house in Aldeburgh, he decided to replace his small red Morris with a large, second-hand Rolls-Royce convertible, a 1929 20/25 hp four-door tourer – a sign of his post-*Peter Grimes* prestige. It apparently provoked a rare fit of jealousy in his colleague Vaughan Williams, forty-two years his senior, who felt that, if Britten had a Rolls, he'd better buy one too.

It was in Britten's Rolls-Royce that the Aldeburgh Festival was conceived. When his operas *The Rape of Lucretia* and *Albert Herring* went on tour in Europe, most of the company travelled by train. But Britten took the Rolls. With Pears, the producer Eric Crozier and his partner, the mezzo-soprano Nancy Evans, he went by road and ferry to Amsterdam and later to Lucerne. (George Behrend, son of his friends Mary and 'Bow', was the chauffeur.) On the long journey they dreamt up the idea of starting a music festival in their home town.

Britten also impressed numerous young friends with the Rolls: there's a famous photograph of him with what looks like eleven teenaged passengers crammed in at Lancing

College, at the time of the premiere there of *Saint Nicolas* in 1948. Humphrey Maud, who used as a boy to steer it from the front passenger seat (without mishap), remembers it had a horn that sounded 'like a buffalo waiting to mate'.

It did indeed find a mate, in the shape of a younger Rolls-Royce convertible (a 1935 20/25 Tickford saloon, registration BXV 794) which Britten acquired several years later. It was intended to transport him and Pears to the recitals they gave all over the country, and the official certificate survives which gave Britten latitude from postwar fuel rationing because of this. But the Tickford Rolls was quite a gas-guzzler, managing barely twelve miles to the gallon, and prone to breakdowns, and after a few months Britten sold it on and replaced it with his third Rolls-Royce convertible, this time a Wraith built in 1938 (registration FLK 8). This was rather more reliable, and took Britten and Pears on a working holiday through France to Monaco, where they stayed for ten days before moving on to Salzburg. Britten kept the Wraith until 1960, but the original 1929 tourer soldiered on until 1964. He was evidently not entirely happy without a Rolls or two under his roof – a rare luxury in the life of this puritan, even parsimonious, man. 'It's really the only thing I spend on myself', he said.

He shared his passion for convertibles with many of his companions. David Hemmings remembered the excitement of being met off the train in 1954 by Britten and being driven to Crag House in an open-topped car, and Roger Duncan had fond memories of FLK 8. The Wraith was probably the motor in which Britten raced around the Suffolk lanes with his music assistant Imogen Holst. She found the experience 'absolutely *thrilling*': it felt 'just like flying', she said. But at other times she was relieved when someone else was driving. When Britten told her he'd 'nearly had a smash' near Ongar, she found her heart was 'beating furiously'. He did indeed have a minor accident around this time, but was unhurt. Maud and Duncan remember Britten swearing that it was fine to keep the hood of his Mercedes convertible (TLF 6) folded back in bad weather, because 'if you drove fast enough the rain would sweep up in a curve, and the passengers would not get wet'.

Britten tended to have one 'flash' car, and one that was more practical. So by 1957 he had a Jensen convertible (TXU 989) and a Morris (VRT 532), replaced respectively by the Mercedes and a Standard Vanguard (YRT 453). Then came an Alvis convertible (861 PBJ) which impressed Rostropovich and Stephen Terry, his Puck in *A Midsummer Night's Dream*. It was 'a wonderful, beautiful car, extraordinarily luxurious – walnut and leather'. Its partner was a new Morris (FRT 4C) – replaced in 1965 by a Rover 2000 (CRT 429C).

14

Britten at home

Britten was based at twenty-two different addresses at various times in his life, including his various London *pieds-à-terre*. But only five of them (all in Suffolk) would he ever have called 'home'.

Blue plaques have been erected on his birthplace in Lowestoft, on the block of flats in Cromwell Road, Kensington, where he lived with his sister in the 1930s, on The Old Mill in Snape (commemorating the writing of *Peter Grimes* there) and on his beachside house in Crabbe Street, Aldeburgh. The Red House remains the focus of Britten scholarship through the Britten–Pears Library which is housed there, just as the Snape Maltings remains both one of our premier concert halls and the centre for contemporary music-making by aspiring professionals, as originally envisaged in the Britten–Pears School.

Aldeburgh Parish Church has a handsome Britten window in the north wall, designed by John Piper to represent his three Church Parables, and his grave outside lies next to those of Peter Pears and Imogen Holst, with the simple inscription: 'BENJAMIN BRITTEN 1913–1976'. Only Churchill's is briefer. Aldeburgh also boasts a memorial on the foreshore – a Maggi Hambling sculpture of two giant scallop shells in stainless steel, on which words from *Peter Grimes* are inscribed: 'I hear those voices that will not be drowned'. But its design has upset some local residents.

The Benjamin Britten High School opened in 1979 on the outskirts of Lowestoft and now specialises in maths and computer studies, while a Britten boarding house at his old school Gresham's in Norfolk was opened in 1992. Another *alma mater*, the Royal College of Music in Kensington, has a Britten Theatre, in which his chamber operas are frequently produced.

1913–30   21 Kirkley Cliff Road, Lowestoft, Suffolk:
          Britten is born in the family home above his father's
          dental surgery.

1930–1   51 Prince's Square, Bayswater, London W2:
          'rather a nice place, but rather full of old ladies'.

1931–3   Burleigh House, 173 Cromwell Road, Kensington,
          London SW5:
          shares flat with his sister Beth.

1933–5   21 Kirkley Cliff Road:
          returns to family home after leaving RCM.

1935–6   Flat 2, West Cottage Green, West End Green,
          London NW6:
          shares 'pleasant, tho' cold, flat in West Hampstead'
          with Beth.

1936–7   559 Finchley Road, London NW3:
          shares with Beth.

1937–8   38 Upper Park Road, London NW3:
          rents a room.

1937–8   Peasenhall Hall, Saxmundham, Suffolk:
          lives with the Welfords (parents of his future
          brother-in-law) while building work proceeds on
          The Old Mill.

1938–9   The Old Mill, Snape, Suffolk:
          moves into his own home on 9 April, after sub-
          stantial conversion work since his purchase in
          August 1937. 'Once I am through with domestic
          worries, I shall enjoy it a lot. At the moment I am
          having crisis after crisis – sacking this person, con-
          soling that, being in fact bread-winner & house-
          wife combined – not pleasant, definitely.' Shares
          with Lennox Berkeley.

1938–9   43 Nevern Square, Earl's Court, London SW5:
          shares with Peter Pears when in London.

1939   67 Hallam Street, London W1:
          shares with Pears.

1939–40   Long Island Home, Amityville, Long Island, New
          York, USA:

lodges with Pears at the home of William and
Elizabeth Mayer.

1940–1   7 Middagh Street, Brooklyn Heights, New York:
Britten and Pears share a house with Auden and
others.

1941–2   Long Island Home, Amityville:
returns to the Mayers.

1942–7   The Old Mill, Snape:
returns to his own home (which Berkeley, then
Beth and her family, have been using during the
war) on the exact fourth anniversary of his initial
move there.

1942–3   104a Cheyne Walk, Chelsea, London SW10:
lodges with Pears at Ursula Nettleship's house.
'5.12.42 to 31.1.43: 8 weeks at £1 a week each.
Light and heat: £2, telephone £9. Total £27.'

1943–6   45a St John's Wood High Street, London NW8:
Erwin, Sophie and Marion Stein share this home from
1944 after the destruction of their own flat by fire.

1946–9   3 Oxford Square, Paddington, London W2

1947–57   Crag House, 4 Crabbe Street, Aldeburgh, Suffolk

1949–53   22 Melbury Road, London W14:
home of Erwin and Marion Stein.

1953–8   5 Chester Gate, London NW1:
Britten and Pears live on one side of Regent's Park
in 'a sweet little house that Peter is slowly doing up
with exquisite taste', while Ralph and Ursula
Vaughan Williams live on the other.

1957–76   The Red House, Golf Lane, Aldeburgh:
formerly owned by the artist Mary Potter, who
moves into 4 Crabbe Street in a house-swap.

1958–65   59 Marlborough Place, St John's Wood, London
NW8

1965–70   99 Offord Road, Islington, London N1

1970–6   8 Halliford Street, London N1:
after his 1973 heart operation, Britten is only rarely
in London.

1970–6   Chapel House, Horham, Suffolk:
          this cottage becomes Britten's composing retreat,
          because The Red House is constantly busy and
          noisy from low-flying American military aircraft.
          But the bedroom at the top of the stairs in The Red
          House is where Britten dies.

Britten was not exactly someone who could look after himself.
He needed mothering all his life, whether it was by his own
mother, his sisters, Elizabeth Mayer, Peter Pears, or (for many
years in Aldeburgh) his housekeeper, Nellie Hudson.

He did at least give it a try himself, when he moved into the
West Hampstead flat with Beth in November 1935. He went
shopping for fixtures and fittings with enthusiasm, and was
excited enough to spend time staining the floors and laying
carpets. He even mended the electric fire. The flat was looking 'definitely good now': Barbara came for dinner, and 'we
have a fine home-cooked meal' (cooked, one suspects, by Barbara). But after a week he was bemoaning the time taken up
by household jobs. There was no time, he said, 'for anything
except waking up, bed-making etc.' before having to go out.
'Perhaps when our incomes are larger we'll be able to afford
help in this line.'

Hey presto, the very next day a Mrs Traynor came at 6 p.m.
for three and a half hours to clean and cook dinner, which
she did every three or four days from then on. But it was not
enough. Beth sometimes held the fort, but when she was
out, Britten's diary recorded that he got a meal ('cold meat,
potatoes, just salad'). Another time he had a 'slight tragedy
in cooking potatoes, which boil dry'. He spent two hours one
morning on 'tremendous' household matters: 'fire clearing,
breakfast setting, getting & washing up, bed-making, washing
sorting, & sending away etc.'.

Two months in, Beth and Benjamin asked Mrs Traynor
to come every day, but she said she couldn't. So instead they
employed 'a terrible hag', Lena Magnus, to 'do' for them:
'She certainly is not prepossessing & has a loud & somewhat

raucous voice – but she is so eager to come & so willing to do everything wanted'. Lena 'the beautiful and silent' (as Britten facetiously described her) stayed on, with fish and chips her 'tour de force'.

When he set up a proper home of his own in The Old Mill, it was axiomatic that he would have a full-time housekeeper. So he did. Some years later the doughty Miss Hudson arrived at Crag House, on the Aldeburgh seafront, and stayed with Britten for a quarter of a century. Her assistant, Heather Bryson, joined as a young girl in 1961, and worked there continuously until her retirement in 2012.

Pears once said that Britten could just about boil an egg. It didn't stop him 'disclosing his most cherished culinary secrets' in a 1971 recipe book *The Food of Love*. He and Pears volunteered 'Miss Hudson's Soup', 'Soles Red House', and 'Dark Treacle Jelly'. But unlike most such celebrity contributors, Britten never imagined he would actually cook the dishes he'd chosen. He just ate them, very happily.

15
Britten's pets

One of Britten's fondest companions as a teenager was Caesar. With an Elgarian feel for word-play, Britten said he preferred to call him 'Seizer'. Although he had joined the family on 20 October 1929, Britten didn't meet this springer spaniel puppy until 2 November, when his parents drove to Holt to visit Benjie at school for a few hours. At Christmas, he found the dog had 'grown enormously' and was 'very full of life'. During the school holidays, Caesar cropped up almost daily in Britten's diary: he gave him an added incentive (not that he really needed it) to go for walks. Sometimes he went four times a day. The dog would plunge into ponds to chase a duck, or into the sea to chase gulls. This no doubt endeared him to the hydrophiliac Britten.

In February 1936 Caesar moved with Mrs Britten to Frinton in Essex. A year later, after her death, Britten inherited him. But the family clearly felt it was not fair on the dog to live in London, so he was temporarily dispatched to the school at Prestatyn in North Wales where Britten's elder brother Bobby was headmaster.

When Britten moved into The Old Mill at Snape, Caesar came too. He was presumably looked after by the housekeeper when Britten was away. His schoolboy friend Piers Dunkerley refers to Caesar being there in a letter of April 1938. The Old Mill also had a highly sexed tomcat in residence, called Vally, owned by his housekeeper, Mrs Hearn. 'He's too male for her liking', said Britten, after discussion with her had become rather stilted. 'We have continually to leave blanks in our conversations – "if he does — every night, he's so exhausted" – "if you'd had him – er – done – it would have been all right". I think she'd have liked the place littered with kittens & then I'd have had to do the drowning.' When

Britten went to north America, he presumably left Caesar in the care of his sister Beth and her family.

It was fifteen years before another dog made such an impact on the Britten household. In early 1954 a smooth-haired tan miniature dachshund arrived at Crag House. She had been bred by the choreographer John Cranko, who had worked with Britten on *Gloriana* the previous year. Britten told his librettist William Plomer that 'Peter has a new passion, the smallest Dachshund ever, called Clytie, & our lives are completely changed now'. But from photographs it is clear that Britten was equally devoted to her. In one of his dreams he imagined himself going through trials of fire and water (rather like Tamino in *The Magic Flute*), with Clytie hugging him round the neck throughout. 'He was quite a new man in the morning', Pears joked.

The dog's pedigree records her full name as Regency Clytie of Alderney: two of her grandparents were champions. Her mother rejoiced in the name of Moneymusk Petita, but Cranko called her Clytie. Like mother, like daughter – and Pears enjoyed the musical resonance of her sharing the name of his singing teacher in America in 1941, Clytie Mundy.

Britten referred to the dog's role in his composing life when writing to his boy companion Roger Duncan in summer 1955:

> You remember the piece I wrote in the garden (for the Punch Revue), with Clytie on my knee (just as she is now) [. . .] – well, they are very pleased with it, & think I'm clever! I told them it was only because I had something very handy to clean my india rubber on . . . it makes such a difference!

He and Pears of course had to leave Clytie behind when they set off on their world tour that winter. Their encounter with the island of Bali enchanted Britten – except for the appearance of the local dogs, which he described to Duncan as 'dirty thin & mangy; they obviously despise them. They say they are the ghosts of dead uncles & aunts! Shades of poor Clytie!

– I wonder who *she* is the ghost of; but someone nice I think, don't you?'

The following summer, Clytie had 'adorable' puppies. 'Even their puddles are adorable', Britten told Pears, '& Miss Hudson [their housekeeper, who owned a cat called Bang] worships them'. One of them was taken by the daughter of the owner of an Aldeburgh hotel – and was also named Clytie. But Britten and Pears kept one male puppy for themselves, a black one they called Jove. Britten said he was 'excessively naughty & attractive'. Their third miniature dachshund, born in 1965, was a cream bitch with the operatic name of Gilda, the heroine of *Rigoletto*. When Miss Hudson retired in 1972, Gilda went with her. But she lived in a house at the side of Britten's garden, so Gilda was never far away.

Another denizen of The Red House was Johnnie, who lived in the kitchen: he was a grey parrot with a red tail. As a boy, the composer Robert Saxton visited Britten in 1964, and was warned not to put his hands too close to its cage. 'What would your mother say', Britten pointed out, 'if she came to pick you up and your fingers had been bitten off?!'

16

Britten's ailments

After his serious illness at only three months old, Britten's health was always regarded by his mother as fragile. At school he was frequently unwell, and confined to bed. Yet Britten was all his life a keen sportsman: exercise was part of his daily routine – often several walks a day – and he swam whenever he could. Auden considered that his regular bouts of illness were psychosomatic or attention-seeking.

When he was diagnosed with the heart disease that eventually killed him, he said he'd always had a 'wonky heart'. Yet his childhood friend Basil Reeve, who became a medical practitioner, always contended that his heart problems were directly linked to his serious illness in the United States in early 1940, and argued that the original cause of this may have been syphilis, which was not correctly treated in the USA at the time.

The list of his recorded ailments is long and wide-ranging: it is hard to credit how much he achieved in his life despite them. But he liked to build illness into his timetable, as his music assistant discovered when planning his schedule in 1966. 'I'm always ill after a big piece', he warned her.

1914	February	Nearly dies from pneumonia
	early childhood	German measles: 'very ill with a high temperature and became delirious', according to Beth
1926	August	Diarrhoea and nausea
1929	January–March	Feverish cold: in sanatorium or at home for most of school term
	October	Gastric trouble
1930	February	Sore throat
	July	In sanatorium, where he writes *A Hymn to the Virgin*

1931	September–October	Nosebleeds
	December	Dental extraction
1932	October	'Filthy cold'
1936	April	Flu
	October	'Foul cold' and severe nosebleed ('a real *pourer*')
1937	January	Cold and high temperature, while his sister and mother are seriously ill
	March	Sprained ankle while playing squash
	June	Nosebleed
	December	Fainting fits, exhaustion: ordered to rest, but heart declared healthy
1939	March	Flu
1940	February–March	Severe nosebleed followed by strepto-coccal infection: his temperature reaches 107°F. Confined to bed for several weeks
	April	Urticaria: rash on face. Dental treatment
	June	Front tooth removed after abscess. 'Lousy cold & throat'. Boil on chin
	August	Further streptococcal infection
	September	Tonsillitis
	October	Tonsillectomy
1942	September	Flu
	November	High temperature: specialist says he has no resistance
1943	March–April	In hospital with measles; depression
	May	Bronchitis
	November	Flu and exhaustion: has to cancel thirtieth birthday party
1944	January	Flu
1945	August	Adverse reaction to typhoid injection
1946	January	Insomnia
1948	December	Suspected stomach ulcer; depression and nervous exhaustion: ordered to take three months' rest. Cancels all

		engagements and postpones work on *Spring Symphony* until March
1950	October	Throat infection and temperature
1951	January	Flu
	March	Laryngitis: doctor orders him to stop talking
	July–September	Cystitis
1952	October–November	Several bouts of illness
	December	'Filthy cold'
1953	August	Sprained ankle
	July–December	After two years of pain in right arm, bursitis is diagnosed: has short-wave treatment and manipulation. Has to rest it for several months, write with his left hand, and cancel concerts for six months
1954	March	Minor operation to relieve bursitis
	December	Toothache for three weeks
1955	January	Unspecified illness
	November	Upset stomach: cured by brandy and glucose
1956	January	Gallstones
	October	Anaemia
1957	January	Exhaustion: doctor orders rest at home for a month
	August	Upset stomach
1958	June	Pleurisy
1959	January–February	Flu and exhaustion: two months' rest
	December	Gastric flu and painful right arm
1960		Doctor detects aortic valve disease
1962	March	Operation for haemorrhoids
	April	Painful right shoulder (capsulitis)
	October	Stomach problems
1965	January	Takes sabbatical on medical advice
	August	Stomach problems caused by diverticulitis

1966	February	Operation for diverticulitis: convalesces in Morocco
1967	January	'virtually paralysed' by 'a chill in a nerve of my back'
	February	'Feeling as near death as only 'flu can make me'
1968	March	In hospital for four weeks with endo-carditis
	December	Feeling 'tired and ill'
1970	November	Hernia operation
1971	November	In hospital for extraction of several teeth
1972	August	Check-up reveals cardiac deterioration, requiring surgery, but Britten insists he must first complete *Death in Venice*. He can no longer climb the stairs without stopping
1973	January	Flu
	March	Sees heart specialist in Harley Street who recommends immediate hospital treatment
	April	In hospital for two weeks for 'energetic' drug treatment and cardiac catheter-isation
	May	Six-hour operation to replace aortic valve with homograft valve, complicated by slight stroke, leaving weakness on his right side which depresses Britten for many months. He remains an invalid for his final three and a half years, able to resume composing but unable to play the piano except with his left hand, or write without difficulty

Britten's death on 4 December 1976 was certified as having been caused by 'congestive cardiac failure' and 'aortic incompetence'.

17

Britten not at home

Britten's first journey beyond British shores came in March
1934, when he took the boat train from London Victoria with
his old schoolfriend John Pounder, to attend the International
Society of Contemporary Music festival in Florence. But his
foreign jaunt was interrupted by the death of his father in
Lowestoft. He returned to the continent later in the year with
his mother, and feasted on opera. During his life he visited
forty-two foreign countries, for work and for holidays – and
often a combination of the two.

1934	Paris, Florence and Siena; Basel, Salzburg, Vienna, Munich and Paris
1936	Barcelona
1937	Paris; Salzburg; Paris
1939	Brussels; Quebec City, Montreal, Toronto; Grand Rapids; New York, Woodstock; Toronto
1940	Chicago; Maine
1941	Escondido (California)
1942	Boston; Halifax (Canada)
1945	Paris; Germany; France
1946	Netherlands and Belgium; Switzerland; Tanglewood (Massachusetts); Netherlands
1947	Switzerland, Belgium, Netherlands, Sweden and Denmark; Italy; Netherlands, Switzerland; Ireland
1948	Switzerland, Italy and Netherlands; Netherlands
1949	Venice and Portofino; Switzerland, Italy, Austria, Belgium and Netherlands; USA and Canada
1950	Netherlands; Sicily
1951	Vienna; Wiesbaden; boat journey up the Rhine
1952	Austria and Wolfsgarten (West Germany); Paris; Copenhagen; France, Monaco and Salzburg

1953   Ireland; Denmark; Wolfsgarten
1954   Wolfsgarten; Venice; Switzerland, Belgium, Nether-
        lands and Sweden
1955   Belgium, Switzerland; Cannes; Schwetzingen (West
        Germany), Munich and Florence; Netherlands;
        Amsterdam, Dusseldorf, Stuttgart, Geneva, Zurich,
        Vienna, Salzburg, Yugoslavia, Istanbul, Ankara,
        Karachi, Bombay, New Delhi, Agra and Calcutta
1956   Calcutta, Singapore, Sumatra, Java, Bali, Bangkok,
        Hong Kong, Macau, Japan, Singapore, Ceylon,
        Madras, Bombay; Wolfsgarten; Paris; Netherlands;
        Munich, Switzerland, West Berlin; West Germany
1957   Paris; Austria and Italy; Milan and France; Ansbach;
        Canada; West Berlin; Wolfsgarten, Darmstadt
1958   Amsterdam; West Germany; France; Switzerland
1959   Bavaria; Sweden, Copenhagen; Venice; Dubrovnik
1960   Greece; West Germany and Switzerland
1961   Canada; Dubrovnik; West Germany and Poland
1962   Greece; Canada; Hamburg; Stockholm; France, Swit-
        zerland, Dubrovnik; W. Germany; Venice; W. Berlin
1963   Greece and Switzerland; USSR; Frankfurt and
        Strasbourg; France; Geneva; Italy
1964   Venice; USSR; West Germany, Budapest and Prague;
        Netherlands; Aspen (Colorado); USSR and Vienna
1965   India and Ceylon; Dordogne; USSR; Helsinki
1966   Marrakesh; Dordogne; Austria; USSR
1967   Antigua, Nevis; Montreal, New York, Mexico, Peru,
        Chile, Argentina, Uruguay, Brazil; Netherlands
1968   Venice; Copenhagen
1969   Bavaria; New York and Boston
1970   Australia and New Zealand; Iceland
1971   France; USSR; Venice
1972   Wolfsgarten; Orkney and Shetland
1973   Bavaria; Wolfsgarten
1974   Wolfsgarten
1975   Venice
1976   Bergen

18

Britten, the Court and two Queens

William Walton once happened to see a large photograph of Britten displayed in the window of a music shop in Lucerne at the time of the first performance there of *Peter Grimes*. According to his wife, Walton calmly walked in, reached into the window, removed the photograph and placed it face-down on a chair. He dusted off his hands in satisfaction, and left. Walton was then a composer in his mid-forties, with the success of *Façade*, *Belshazzar's Feast* and his First Symphony behind him. Such was the irrational jealousy that Britten's high profile provoked.

Britten did rather ask for it. Auden had warned him about his 'nest of love' back in 1941. 'You probably always will be surrounded by people who adore you, nurse you and praise everything you do' – and that is precisely what had happened. Britten's coterie of friends and admirers almost worshipped him. When he walked into a room, all eyes turned to him. Those who fell out of favour were cut adrift. In mitigation, there was the wonderful music that streamed from his pen. But his enemies spoke of the court of a medieval monarch, and indeed the Court was a concept familiar to Britten.

Another composer colleague, Michael Tippett, also not part of the Aldeburgh set, said that Britten had once confided in him: 'I would have been a Court composer, but for my pacifism and homosexuality'. Britten envied the opportunities that a court role had afforded Haydn two centuries earlier. He did write a number of 'royal' works, including an opera to mark the coronation of Queen Elizabeth II, and several arrangements of the National Anthem. The British royal family is not much linked with classical music in the public mind, but Britten became a friend of royalty, and had much closer contacts with the Queen than many have ever appreciated.

It wasn't always like that. Despite his conventional middle-class upbringing, Britten's lively contempt for so many things as a young man was readily extended to royalty, though his feelings were always ambivalent. At twenty-one he was unimpressed by the radio broadcast of George V's Silver Jubilee service. But he had been listening. He was already involved in the Jubilee through *The King's Stamp*, a film about the commemorative postal issue, for which he was writing the music. He consoled himself with the thought that it was 'only half-serious luckily'.

Britten's diary records the watch he kept during the King's last hours in January 1936. At 9.38 p.m. there was a 'very dramatic announcement' from the BBC: 'King Dying'. He monitored the news bulletins every quarter of an hour from then on (adding facetiously 'really this King *won't* die'), until he switched off the radio at midnight and carried on working at the orchestration of his *Te Deum*. Next morning the radio told him there was a new King. He noted in his diary:

> obviously considering the feelings of the BBC announcers
> & engineers, [George V] died at 11.55 last night. Great
> excitement – black round papers – tremendous eulo-
> gies – flapping black ties in buses & tubes. I can't feel any
> emotion – never having had any contact with the man – &
> disagreeing with Royalty on account of propaganda in
> Imperial & National directions.

'He may be a good man', he added, '& he certainly was very busy all his life – still, he was well paid! Anyhow now – long live Edward VIIIth.' This was followed a week later by facetious references to George V's funeral: 'father of nation, what what'.

He had high hopes of the new King, but he was disappointed by his broadcast to the Empire in March. He felt that he was 'more of a personality than his father' and he had reckoned that 'he would at least say something interesting'. But in the aftermath of Mussolini's adventures in Africa there was no reference to foreign affairs or the League of Nations –

crucial omissions for someone of Britten's emerging political sensibility.

His sympathies did lie with Edward VIII and Mrs Simpson during the abdication crisis. 'Obviously', he said, 'they wanted to get rid of a King with too much personality & any little excuse sufficed'. When Edward broadcast to the nation after his abdication, Britten found it

> a most moving affair. Very well spoken, very simple & direct – containing some good home truths only slightly disguised & ending with a terrifying 'God save the King' that made one shiver in one's shoes. If he had only been allowed to broadcast a week ago (as he wished to, but as it now transpires, the Ministers didn't think it 'advisable') there would have been no abdication.

He found the coronation of George VI frustrating because of the crush in the streets, 'crowds gaping at the literally hideous decorations' and the repetition of 'the same bla, bla, bla – of empire, loyalties, one big family (that is 'fine feeling' if expressed by the upper classes – 'damned cheek' if by the lower!)'. After listening to a Coronation Revue and the King's coronation address ('the poor man masters his stutter well'), he mockingly recorded that he spent 'a coronation evening, writing coronation letters & retiring to a coronation, if lonely, bed'.

Premieres of contemporary music were not King George's métier. But he did manage one by Britten. He sat through (looking 'very bored') the full ten minutes of Britten's *Wedding Anthem*, which the composer conducted in cassock and surplice at the society wedding of his friend Marion Stein to the King's nephew, George, Earl of Harewood, in 1949. By now his strong friendship with Harewood, and his growing reputation as a national composer, had led him to modify his attitude to royalty. He soon found himself giving private recitals at Harewood House near Leeds, in the presence of George Harewood's mother, the then Princess Royal, sister of the King. He was staying there over Christmas in 1950 when the Stone of Scone was stolen from underneath the Coronation

chair in Westminster Abbey. The Princess remarked at breakfast that it had perhaps been stolen by communists who had
taken it away in a small boat. Britten thought she was jok-
ing, and roared with laughter. 'What a *wonderful* idea, Ma'am!
Wouldn't it be funny if they had?' '*Funny?* . . .' exclaimed
the Princess. There was 'a ghastly silence', as Britten later
told Imogen Holst. Then the Princess added: 'I am *most*
displeased!'

Britten survived this faux pas, aided perhaps by the consign-
ments of fresh North Sea herrings he had taken to sending
the Princess, in sufficient quantity to supply her, her lady-in-
waiting and her household. These were much appreciated in
the days of postwar austerity, and the Princess complimented
him on the premiere of *Billy Budd*, to which she had listened
on the radio.

One of Britten's later recitals at Harewood House featured
his new friend, the cellist Mstislav Rostropovich. The Russian, who had never met a princess before, decided he should
curtsy before her, and began to practise ever more elegant
flourishes. Once again Britten took this as a joke. Once again
he was mistaken. On the way to Leeds Britten realised Rostropovich was serious, and belatedly tried to dissuade him.
The cellist reluctantly agreed to restrain himself, but on condition that Britten wrote him three more works for the cello.
The 'contract' was signed on a restaurant menu, and the three
Cello Suites were the eventual result. When they arrived at
Harewood House, Rostropovich was nonplussed to find his
hostess was an old lady who crocheted throughout their performance of Schumann, not the beautiful young princess of
his fevered imagination.

It was Britten's friendship with George Harewood that
so incensed the anglophobic American composer Virgil
Thomson. He attributed Britten's success to his links with
royalty – a rather off-the-nail accusation, since his biggest
royal commission (admittedly achieved through Harewood's
intervention) was the Coronation opera *Gloriana*, and that –
in establishment terms – was a flop.

The Queen herself made every effort to get to grips with *Gloriana*. Before the Coronation, she and Prince Philip attended a private run-through of the opera's highlights, performed by Britten at the piano with the two principal singers, Joan Cross (as Elizabeth I) and Peter Pears (as her lover Essex). It was held at Harewood's London home. According to Cross, it was a sticky evening: 'I don't think *they* enjoyed the evening any more than we did'.

The notorious premiere at Covent Garden got off to a bad start, with the National Anthem conducted by Walton. Half the orchestra started playing too soon (presumably that half included Walton), while the rest knew they should wait until the royal party had all found their seats. The opera itself went more smoothly, and the Queen was seen to applaud enthusiastically for eight minutes at the end. Britten reported that she was 'delighted and flattered' (her words, presumably), even if the critics and most of the bigwigs in the stalls weren't. He called them 'stuck pigs' – the exact phrase used by his equal in prickliness, Elgar, after similar people sat on their hands at the premiere of his Second Symphony.

For someone whose musical sympathies, according to royal myth-pedlars, extended no further than Gilbert and Sullivan (as if that were a crime anyway), the Queen maintained surprisingly regular contact with Britten. He was invited to lunch at Buckingham Palace and later went to stay at Sandringham. In 1958 the Duke of Edinburgh (who called him 'Ben') pressed him to write a setting of Mattins for St George's Chapel, Windsor Castle. At first Britten pleaded pressure of work, as he was in the thick of *A Midsummer Night's Dream*. Then he warned the Duke that 'to try and make bricks out of the Morning Prayer straw would be a step into the past – the whole tendency is towards the People's Mass'. (What Britten's low-church mother would have made of that, after the weekly Mattins routine at St John's, Lowestoft, one can only guess.)

Prince Philip persisted. He called Britten and the Dean of Windsor to a meeting. He said he was happy to commission a congregational mass as well, but only when Britten had

written the Mattins service, adding that, if Britten heard from
any clergyman or musician that it was a bad idea, he should
pay no attention!

After two years Britten set Psalm 100 (the *Jubilate*), and
embarked on a *Te Deum*. But he never completed it, and instead
suggested that his 1934 setting in the same key (C major)
would go with the *Jubilate*, which the score says was written
'at the request of HRH The Duke of Edinburgh'. Only after
Britten's death did it become clear that he'd also written a
Venite (Psalm 95) at the same time – so he almost managed the
full Mattins set. Prince Philip responded the following year
by going to Aldeburgh to open the Festival Club, and the two
men exchanged the occasional telegram thereafter.

By then the Queen herself had become involved with the
Aldeburgh Festival. When the Harewoods divorced in 1967,
and Britten ended his friendship with the Earl, it might have
put paid to the royal connection. But by now another cousin
of the Queen, Prince Ludwig of Hesse, had become close
friends with Britten and Pears, and Queen Elizabeth the
Queen Mother had recently attended the Festival to see *The
Burning Fiery Furnace*. So when Britten wrote to Buckingham
Palace to ask the Queen to open the Festival's brand-new
concert hall at The Maltings, he received a handwritten reply
from the Queen herself. She clearly wanted to come, and
promised to be as persuasive as she could when her private
secretary was drawing up the royal engagement diary.

On 2 June 1967 the Queen and the Duke went to lunch
with Britten at The Red House, to which he had added a front
porch as a more imposing entrance. She then cut the meta-
phorical Maltings ribbon, and heard Britten conduct his new
overture *The Building of the House*, as well as works by Delius,
Holst and Handel. The afternoon began with Britten's unusual
arrangement of the National Anthem: the first verse is sung
pianissimo in the low key of E flat, while the second is a fifth
higher and fortissimo, with bell-like overlapping cries of 'God
Save the Queen' at the end. Simple changes, but remarkably
cunning ones, which make the anthem feel almost unbuttoned.

When the Maltings burned down in the middle of the 1969 Festival, Britten and Pears embarked on frenzied fundraising to enable the rebuilding of the hall by June 1970. The Queen telephoned Britten personally, and he invited her to return for the first concert in the rebuilt hall. He might have worried that it would be a case of 'once burnt, twice shy'. Not at all: the Queen again replied by hand (this time to 'dear Ben'), and suggested a date that would fit. She and Prince Philip arrived as promised, this time for some Purcell, Mendelssohn and three scenes from *Gloriana*.

Two months later Britten and Pears volunteered their services for a private recital at Sandringham for the Queen Mother on her seventieth birthday. They had already been to stay there at her invitation, and she had attended the first performance they'd given of his Pushkin song cycle *The Poet's Echo*. She had also listened in the silence of her Scottish redoubt, the Castle of Mey, to the discs of *Curlew River* and *Les Illuminations* which he had sent her. The Queen Mother also heard the last recital Britten and Pears gave in Britain. At St James's Palace in February 1973, in aid of the Royal Academy of Music, they performed Britten's youthful cycle *On This Island* for the first time in almost twenty years. Two months later, with his score of *Death in Venice* complete, he underwent the first round of hospital treatment for his heart.

The Queen Mother kept a watchful eye. Her lady-in-waiting, the highly musical Ruth Fermoy, who sometimes played piano duets with Britten, was a valuable go-between. Queen Elizabeth sent him a message in hospital, before the operation, with the hope that 'the will to get well' would be stronger than the doctor's predictions. Later in the year, after the operation, Britten and Pears sent her congratulations on an honorary musical degree she had received. Her telegram in reply was designed to bring a smile to Britten in his frailty:

MAY AN IGNORAMUS OF A MUS DOC HONORIS CAUSA
SEND HER GRATEFUL THANKS TO TWO BELOVED
MUSICIANS FOR THEIR CHARMING MESSAGE OF WELCOME

SHE ALSO WOULD ADD A HOPE THAT THEY WILL SPEND
A HAPPY AND JOYOUS CHRISTMAS ELIZABETH R QUEEN
MOTHER

Britten next asked her to become Patron of the Aldeburgh
Festival. She responded with alacrity in her own hand: 'I don't
really feel that I am half musical enough' to be Patron of 'your
glorious Festival', she said, 'but I accept with joy'. She com-
miserated with him over his recuperation: 'The hours pass so
slowly when one is not well, and you must be longing to get
back to what in "horse parlance" is called strong work'.

In June 1975 the Queen Mother paid one of her occasional
visits to the Aldeburgh Festival, with a champagne reception
at The Red House first. She listened to Berlioz, Mozart and
the first performance of Britten's *Suite on English Folk Tunes*,
his first orchestral music since his heart operation. An encouraging thank-you letter to 'Dear Ben' followed, in her elegant
handwriting:

> The concert was pure bliss, and I was deeply moved by
> your glorious new piece [. . .] It is so marvellous that you
> are feeling stronger, and I hope that you will continue to
> feel better & better, & that more wonderful music will
> come pouring out, to delight & enchant us all.
>
> With my warmest thanks to you and to Peter for so
> much kindness,
>
> I am, ever yours,
>
> Elizabeth R.
>
> PS Ruth & I came home all aglow!

She little knew that plans had already been laid to bring on
'more wonderful music'. Her daughter, the Queen, had been
in direct touch with Britten. This correspondence, in the last
eighteen months of Britten's life, is the most significant of all
the royal contacts over the years.

In a handwritten letter from Buckingham Palace on 12 January 1975, the Queen pointed out that her mother was going
to be seventy-five in August. She thought it would be lovely

to have some music dedicated to her mother for her birthday, and asked Britten if he would take this on for her. She indicated it wasn't a formal royal commission but a 'you and me' request, from daughter to composer. The idea, it transpires, had originally come from Princess Margaret of Hesse (Prince Ludwig's widow), who felt Britten was depressed by his illness and needed a commission to restore his confidence and creative energy.

Britten accepted immediately, with the proviso that he couldn't manage anything large-scale. So he proposed a Robert Burns song cycle for voice and harp. In her reply from Wood Farm at Sandringham on 22 January, the Queen said she was delighted he couldn't write a symphony! The Burns poems were a wonderful idea, she said, but she urged him not to write anything long, because everyone would be only too pleased if the birthday bouquet was short and musically satisfying.

With this encouragement, Britten set to work, and on 7 March sent the Queen a recorded-delivery letter with his proposed selection of poems for the work that would become *A Birthday Hansel*. He also started on the music, but became alarmed that he had not had royal approval for the poems, so he sent an urgent prompt to the Queen's private secretary, although she had had them only a fortnight. The result was an apologetic reply from the Queen by return of post – another handwritten 'Dear Ben' letter from Buckingham Palace.

Clearly she had pondered Britten's selection of poems: she said her mother knew two of them well, and she herself picked out four others she particularly liked. Fortunately she did not react against any of the poems – just as well, since Britten had in fact already completed the score.

It has always been assumed that the published score replicates the poems Britten originally set. But closer examination of his archive now reveals that he originally wrote two further songs – of which the manuscripts survive. The first of these was 'O Why the Deuce', which the Queen had picked out: Britten planned to open the cycle with it. 'Ae Fond Kiss', one

of the poems the Queen Mother knew well, was designed as
the last song but one. In writing song cycles, Britten often left
some 'orphan songs' behind, after winnowing his work down
to a coherent whole, but nowhere else are they found already
woven into the structure of the sequence.

Not for long, however. He dropped 'Ae Fond Kiss' altogether (it was a personal thrill to unearth only recently this
virgin fragment of late Britten), and adapted the opening song
with more suitable words. He chose instead a poem Burns had
written for 'John Maxwell Esq., of Terraughty, on his Birthday'. But he felt Burns's first line, 'Health to the Maxwells'
veteran Chief', needed some adjustment, so he wrote to the
Queen with two alternative suggestions – either 'Health to
the Black Watch Veteran Chief', in recognition of the Queen
Mother's role as Colonel-in-Chief of the Scottish regiment,
or 'Health to our well-loved Hielan Chief'. In her reply the
Queen plumped for the latter, wryly adding that she wasn't
sure that 'Health to the Black Watch Veteran Chief' would
go down too well. Britten also tweaked the start of the second
verse to make it more appropriate: instead of 'Farewell, auld
birkie', he wrote 'All hail, auld birkie' – not the most common
nomenclature for the Queen Mother, but meaning nothing
worse than 'old fellow'.

This detailed collaboration over one of Britten's most
charming late works extended to its title. Britten's formulation
was *A Birthday Hansel*: the Queen gave her approval, although
she had never heard the word 'hansel' (meaning a first gift to
wish someone luck). She liked the choice of the final song,
'Leezie Lindsay', a gay (in the traditional sense) reel, and she
told Britten she was sure the whole thing would be lovely.

The Queen and the Duke of Edinburgh then left on a
two-week foreign tour, of Jamaica, Hong Kong and Japan. In
May 1975, two weeks after their return, she wrote to Britten
again, but on a quite different personal matter. She needed
a new Master of the Queen's Musick (she used the ancient
spelling, even though this had been officially dropped more
than forty years earlier), and asked Britten to take the position

on. Few people would imagine that the feeler would come direct from the sovereign in her own hand, but she made it clear that, because of his illness, she was making an informal 'between you and me' approach to see whether he would like to be asked officially. She said that the job wasn't onerous – he could do as much or as little as necessary – but for the coming Silver Jubilee he might have to do a special little something. She asked him to think about it, but hoped he would accept.

Britten and Pears worked together on his reply. He had never had any of the 'regular' honours such as CBE, and the assumption has been that he declined a knighthood. But he had accepted two honours in the sovereign's personal gift. In 1953, before he was forty, he was made Companion of Honour, presumably in recognition of *Gloriana*, and he joined the Order of Merit (one of only twenty-four members) in 1965, three years younger than Elgar and twelve years younger than Vaughan Williams had been when they became OMs. Now he was being offered further royal recognition. Fifty years earlier, Elgar had become Master of the King's Musick after canvassing rather brazenly for the job: Britten had never done that, but the draft of his response to the Queen's offer makes clear it was something that had crossed his mind.

Madam,
    I was very touched and honoured by Your Majesty's letter, since I have thought very deeply about it. The position of Master of the Queen's Music is an important one [here Britten has added in pencil: 'not just a title'] and I feel should be held by the liveliest, most public spirited composer one can think of: one who can write appropriate music, attend and preside over public social occasions, and generally lead the musical profession. Alas Your Majesty knows that I am not in that position. Of course I could try and write an occasional suitable piece (if my wretched heart will oblige me) but I can rarely get to London, and social occasions are quite beyond me. I should hate to accept it, and then seem to show I was not

interested. [This sentence is replaced by a note, the first three words of which were written by Britten, the rest by Pears: 'I would only accept such a responsibility if I thought I could fulfil the implied conditions'.] So would Your Majesty forgive me & accept my refusal? – only I *would* like to write something for the Silver Jubilee [as he did, in *Welcome Ode*].

The Birthday Hansel is finished and I was most happy about a first run-through with Peter Pears & [the harpist] Osian Ellis the other day. I do hope the recipient will like it.

A few months later the Australian composer Malcolm Williamson (rather than a veteran such as Walton or Tippett) was appointed Master of the Queen's Music, apparently on Britten's recommendation.

On 4 August, the Queen Mother turned seventy-five, and among her presents was Britten's manuscript of *A Birthday Hansel*. 'I don't think that I have ever had a more wonderful surprise in my life', she wrote from the Castle of Mey, 'than the moment when I set eyes on your Birthday Hansel'.

I am absolutely thrilled and delighted by this glorious birthday gift, and I do want to thank you with all my heart for your kindness in composing this very special & exciting music. The poems are so touching & beautiful, and Ruth has just been playing the harp music on our old upright here!

She responded in detail to his choice of poems, singling out 'A rose bud by my early walk' for Burns's 'touching love of little birds like linnets'. She went on:

I have never heard 'My Hoggie' poor Hoggie, what a charming little poem. And I love 'Flow gently, sweet Afton', what lovely things you have chosen for your lovely music.

I honestly do not think that anything in my life has given me greater pleasure than your birthday gift.

It is very precious to me, and will I am sure give joy to
your countless grateful admirers.

If *A Birthday Hansel* was designed as a tonic to lift Britten's
spirits, it worked. That same August he wrote his dramatic
cantata *Phaedra* for Janet Baker, and followed on with the
most profound of his late utterances, the Third String Quartet. In part at least, we have the Queen to thank for both.

In January 1976 Britten and Pears drove to Uphall in Norfolk for a private performance of the songs at the house of
Lady Fermoy. Pears and Ellis had tested them out at a public
concert in Bavaria five days before: now their audience was a
select one, comprising the Queen Mother, her two daughters,
the composer and his nurse, Rita Thomson. They recorded
them the following month.

Britten's own birthday, his sixty-third, came on 22 November, less than two weeks before he died. He was very weak, and
confined to bed. The previous night he had needed oxygen.
But in the morning he asked a few friends round for champagne. They gathered downstairs, and went up one by one
to speak to him – in effect, to say their goodbyes. At this late
stage there was one piece of unfinished business. The Decca
recording of *A Birthday Hansel* had been issued in July, but
copies had still not been sent to either the Queen Mother or
the Queen. So he asked his music assistant Rosamund Strode
to rectify this.

The next morning she sent the discs by recorded delivery.
'Yesterday', she wrote, 'Benjamin Britten most particularly
requested that you should be sent a copy of the recording of
A Birthday Hansel, made by Peter Pears and Osian Ellis in The
Maltings earlier this year. Assuring him that the matter would
be attended to at once, I now have the honour of sending Your
Majesty the record, as he wishes.'

The Queen Mother was fully aware that time was now
of the essence, and she replied by return of post in words
that are deeply touching in their sensitivity, as an unspoken
adieu:

Dear Ben

I was so thrilled and delighted to receive the record of
A Birthday Hansel, and I send you my warmest thanks for
such a kind thought on your part. I shall never forget that
happy day when you & Peter & Osian Ellis came over to
Norfolk, & we sat in Ruth's little house listening to the
lovely music. It was a wonderful experience, and when I
play this record, I shall think of that day, and of the great
happiness that you gave me – with thanks which are from
my heart.

Ever yours

Elizabeth R.

It was effectively her turn to adapt the Burns quotation:
'Farewell, auld birkie'.

PART THREE
The artistry of Britten

I like performing for several reasons. I enjoy the contact with the audience, and I find it valuable for my activities as a composer to see how listeners react to the music. I also enjoy rehearsals – especially if I am working with sympathetic and intelligent musicians – delving deeper and deeper into the great music of all ages, and learning a lot from it. There are some composers whose music I do not like, but performing it makes me analyse my reasons for the dislike, and so prevents it from becoming just habit or prejudice.

Benjamin Britten, 1944

19

Conductor

One of the reasons Britten turned down the music director-ship of Covent Garden in 1952 was that he felt he wasn't a conductor. Imogen Holst tried to insist that he was, but he would have none of it. By then he had conducted twenty per-formances apiece of *Albert Herring* and *The Beggar's Opera*, nine of *Les Illuminations*, eight *Saint Nicolases*, seven *Serenades* and *Billy Budds* (including the premiere), five *Rapes of Lucre-tia*, four *Peter Grimeses* and *Spring Symphonies*, and a clutch of *Sinfonias da Requiem*. So he was not exactly a novice.

But at that point he hadn't conducted much other music. In the late 1940s he had taken on three early performances of his friend Lennox Berkeley's *Stabat Mater*. At the first Aldeburgh Festival in 1948, he eased himself in gently with some Purcell, Handel and Frank Bridge. The following year came four Bach cantatas, some Holst and Pergolesi, and more Purcell. Then he moved on to Schütz, Monteverdi and Mozart – three or four symphonies (including the G minor, no. 40), his beloved *Sinfonia Concertante* in E flat, and the concertos for clarinet and for flute and harp. This was perhaps why Imogen Holst suggested that he could conduct a Mozart opera season at Covent Garden for three years in a row, which would 'make a difference to music'. But Britten countered that he would do that only in Aldeburgh's Jubilee Hall. (In the end he never conducted more than one Mozart opera, *Idomeneo* – initially in 1969 in Blythburgh Church, instead of The Maltings, which had burned down seventy-two hours before.)

Britten had long since learnt the ropes. Composers often end up conducting their own music, because they think no one else either will or can. To an extent, Britten was no excep-tion. He conducted his *Sinfonietta* as a student, and *A Boy was Born* and *Simple Symphony* when he was barely twenty. His first fully professional conducting engagement was at the 1936 Norwich Festival, when he handled the premiere of his almost avant-garde work *Our Hunting Fathers*. At the end of one rehearsal he said he was 'pretty suicidal' after 'the most catastrophic evening of my life':

> The orchestra is at the end of its tether – no discipline at all – no one there to enforce it. I get thoroughly het up & desparate [. . .] I get a lot of the speeds wrong & very muddled – but I'm glad to say that in spite of the fooling in the orchestra & titters at the work – the 'Rats' especially brought shrieks of laughter – the rehearsal got better & better.

For several months Britten had endured a fairly grim apprenticeship with an amateur orchestra in the Suffolk town of Bungay. He called it the 'BBBB (Benj. Britten Bungay Band, alias the Hag's Band)'. The playing was 'execrable', and the only advice he wanted to give was 'go away and learn to play your instruments'. His own learning curve continued in America, as the salaried conductor of the semi-professional Suffolk Friends of Music Orchestra, where one player remembered him saying: 'Gentlemen, what I hear sounds vaguely familiar, but I find nothing like it in my score!'

After rejecting the Covent Garden offer, Britten expanded his conducting commitments and never let up until his heart gave way. He conducted at least 170 different works by 40 different composers, plus 49 works of his own, 37 of which are preserved in his definitive recordings. (Those totals do not include all the incidental music he conducted in the studio and the theatre.)

Despite his love of Verdi, Tchaikovsky and Berg, he never conducted any stage works apart from *Idomeneo* and Purcell's *Dido and Aeneas* (28 times) and *The Fairy Queen* (7). He was presumably too busy with his own. He notched up 50 performances of *The Turn of the Screw* between the 1954 premiere in Venice and the Maltings revival in 1972. Tours with the English Opera Group meant he frequently conducted *Albert*

Herring (26 performances), *The Beggar's Opera* (24) and *Lucretia* (13). He conducted his troublesome ballet *The Prince of the Pagodas* at the Royal Opera House and at La Scala. He never conducted *Peter Grimes* in the theatre, which makes the dramatic force of his gramophone recording, and then the television production late in life, all the more remarkable. He conducted *The Little Sweep* only once on stage (and again in the recording), and *Noye's Fludde* only in the studio. *A Midsummer Night's Dream* clocked up four Britten performances, and *Owen Wingrave* two. He supervised the Church Parables, but had expressly ruled out the need for a conductor. He never tackled *Gloriana* in full, and by the time of *Death in Venice* he was too ill to conduct.

Among his concert works, Britten conducted 25 *War Requiem*s (usually as conductor only of the chamber orchestra, though in his recording the whole ensemble is under his thumb), and 17 performances of *Les Illuminations* between 1941 and 1970. Next in line were *Spring Symphony*, *Cello Symphony* and *Sinfonia da Requiem* with a dozen each. He clearly liked to try out all his orchestral and choral works at least once: *The Young Person's Guide* managed five performances by him, the *Four Sea Interludes* seven, and the Frank Bridge Variations only three (but then all three works were being conducted everywhere by other people). Through Richter's advocacy of the Piano Concerto, Britten was inveigled into raising his conducting total to six (matching the six performances he'd once given as the soloist). Even the Violin Concerto, which Britten always underrated, scored two. The only mature pieces of his own that he failed to conduct before his final illness took hold were *Young Apollo* (which he had blotted out of his memory), *Mont Juic*, *Ballad of Heroes*, some of the smaller choral pieces and *The Golden Vanity* (though he provided the piano accompaniment in the recording). Is it any wonder he suffered from bursitis in his right shoulder?

Among the substantial pieces he undertook from the pen of others were Bach's *St John Passion* (six times) and *Christmas Oratorio*, Elgar's *The Dream of Gerontius*, Haydn's *The Creation*,

The Seasons and *Harmoniemesse*, plus a clutch of his symphonies and the two cello concertos, Holst's *Egdon Heath* and *Hammersmith*, some of Mahler's orchestral songs and bits of his symphonies (only one, the Fourth, in full), Mozart's *Coronation Mass*, his *Requiem* and a number of his symphonies, serenades and piano concertos, Prokofiev's *Classical Symphony*, Purcell's *Ode for St Cecilia's Day*, Schumann's Cello Concerto and *Scenes from Goethe's Faust*, and the symphony that Shostakovich dedicated to him, the Fourteenth. (He never conducted any others: by his own admission, they never spoke to him as 'closely and personally' as the chamber music.) He also directed Tchaikovsky's *Rococo Variations* and *Francesca da Rimini* and Vivaldi's *Four Seasons*. Only two concert pieces did he conduct ten times or more: Purcell's *Chacony* in G minor, and Monteverdi's *Il Combattimento di Tancredi e Clorinda*. It is an eclectic list.

Musicians and singers who performed under Britten's baton still refer fondly to his encouragement, his sure pacing, and his sense of musical architecture. Joan Cross, the original Ellen Orford in *Peter Grimes*, said that *Albert Herring* became inspired when Britten was conducting, because of his sense of humour and his energy.

By 1960 Britten himself had relaxed into the role.

> I like conducting my works. Whether I'm good or not remains to be seen [. . .] but I've certainly had a lot of experience. But I don't agree that composers aren't good conductors [. . .] I mean Berlioz for instance was a remarkable one. No, I think composers can be very good, and if they are it's inclined to help their music [. . .] A performer is better if he's a composer, and a composer is better if he's a performer.

20

Instrumentalist

The alacrity with which Britten tackled the solo parts of viola concertos, and adapted the Beethoven cello sonatas for viola, when he was a mere sixteen, to play with his mother or his friend Basil Reeve, suggests a high degree of technical skill. He was happy to work through the viola parts of Beethoven's Ninth Symphony, or Schumann's Piano Quintet, and would play along with gramophone recordings of Brahms's Fourth Symphony or the Mozart 'Jupiter'. He leapt at the solo parts in Mozart's *Sinfonia Concertante*, or Walton's Viola Concerto, and played Brahms's Clarinet Sonata in a viola arrangement, at the time he wrote his *Reflection* and *Elegy* for viola. After listening to Brahms's third string quartet, he opined that it was 'the purest music in the purest of possible forms. What a marvellous craze for the viola Brahms had!'

As Britten headed off for North America in 1939, his mentor Frank Bridge must have had a premonition that his absence would become more than temporary. In an emotional gesture at the quayside in Southampton, he gave Britten his own viola to take to the New World. It turned out to be their final farewell.

The viola emerged from time to time in later years. He spent an evening in 1952 playing viola sonatas with Erwin Stein at the piano: by this time he had turned against Brahms, but he got out the viola arrangement of the Clarinet Sonata because 'there wasn't anything else to play except some *very* bad pieces by Schumann'! He also joined amateur players in the Aldeburgh Music Club, and Imogen Holst tellingly described him scraping away on open strings like a small boy when he wasn't getting his way. The Club gave concerts of Bach, Handel or Purcell, with Britten playing viola and Pears the piano. He only rarely played professionally, but he did take the viola part in a recording of Purcell's *Fantasia on One Note*, and performed it literally across the world – in Aix-en-Provence, Amsterdam, Bordeaux, Brussels, Cannes, Chicago, Cologne, Copenhagen, Djakarta, Düsseldorf, Florence, Geneva, Haywards Heath, Henley, Hitchin, Hong Kong, Hull, Maastricht, Macau, Munich, Naples, New York, Paris, Salzburg, Stockholm, Toronto and Vienna, and Aldeburgh too.

While in Tokyo in 1956 he was photographed playing the Japanese *shō*. But he first tackled a wind instrument a few years earlier, when Imogen Holst introduced him to the recorder. He played duets, with Pears on the tenor and even bass recorder, and they both took part in amateur ensembles with the Aldeburgh Music Club. This meant being cast adrift with a choir of recorders on the Meare at Thorpeness, with only Imo to guide them with her baton, while the Aldeburgh Festival audience listened at a safe distance on the bank.

His hands-on experience led him to write two minor works, *Scherzo* and the *Alpine Suite*, for himself to play with friends, plus the substantial role for massed recorders in his children's opera *Noye's Fludde*, and the sopranino (piccolo) recorders in the onstage band of *A Midsummer Night's Dream*. Britten practised and practised the recorder, even in bed. But his main problem was that he kept getting the giggles: 'his eyes swell, his ears grow scarlet, and his whole face is suffused with tears', said one friend.

Britten extended his prowess on the piano (and harpsichord too, when playing continuo in Bach's *St John Passion*, for instance) to the more obscure keyboard instrument, the bell-like celesta. He played it in a 1942 Wigmore Hall concert of modern French chamber music by Louis Durey and Germaine Tailleferre. Britten had first scored the celesta in *Paul Bunyan* the previous year, and went on to use it to great effect in *Peter Grimes*. But as a teenager he'd been wary of its 'sugary' effect in Holst's suite, *The Planets* – and the wartime concert seemed to reinforce this view. He called it a 'pukey little instrument – I nearly pushed it over trying to make a noise on it!' Uncharacteristically, he lost count of the bars and earned himself a glare from the conductor, Reginald Goodall.

Singer

The precise, deep bass of Britten's speaking voice hinted at a fine singing voice among his musical capabilities. But it was more hint than reality. There are only two known recordings of him singing: one is a film clip of him rehearsing a choir in his choral overture *The Building of the House* – and that at least shows that (unlike many conductors) he could sing rather than croak the notes. The second is an amateur recording of *Noye's Fludde* made by Britten and his friends round the piano, which was sent out to local schools as a rehearsal aid. Britten is mainly preoccupied with playing the instrumental parts, and his vocal interjections are mercifully occasional.

He did of course sing at school, and as a music student in London he was a bass in the English Madrigal Choir, run by Arnold Foster. Thursday evenings became a ritual for three years: after fortifying themselves with tea at Selfridges, he and his sister Barbara, the choir secretary, went on to rehearse madrigals at 6 p.m. They branched out for a concert with the conductor Iris Lemare, in which they sang some Manx folk-songs by Foster, and settings of Osbert Sitwell by Elisabeth Lutyens. But 'the choir was poor', he noted.

Thereafter Britten was otherwise engaged, although during their tour of the Far East in the 1950s, he and Pears were photographed taking part in a rehearsal of the Tokyo Madrigal Singers. Britten has his head well buried in the score!

22

Pianist

At the US premiere of Britten's Piano Concerto in Chicago in 1940, the soloist muffed his first entry. He stood up and stopped the orchestra. 'Something's wrong with the piano', he said. The piano tuner was called on stage. It turned out that earlier on the tuner had not settled the front fillet of wood correctly on the piano, so it had been impossible to depress the keys properly. Once the piano was fixed, the conductor raised his arms to restart the concerto, but the soloist stood up again. He turned to the audience and said with a smile: 'I hope you don't think I was to blame!'

This would have been nerve-racking for the most battle-hardened soloist: in Britten's case (for he it was) it must have been a nightmare. He suffered acutely from nerves before a performance, and he had given only five concerto perform-ances before – all of them of his own piece. He had also giv-en two broadcasts of a shorter piece for piano and strings, *Young Apollo*. The Chicago experience turned out to be his last bravura concerto appearance: from then on he occasionally played Mozart piano concertos (and no others) in the much more intimate setting of Aldeburgh, when he was conduct-ing as well. He did tackle some double piano concertos (by Mozart and Poulenc, plus his own *Scottish Ballad*), but there he had Clifford Curzon or Poulenc himself to hold his hand, as it were. Even these concerto appearances stopped in 1956. From then on he confined his piano recital outings to light-hearted duos and duets, such as Schubert's *Marche Militaire* or Brahms's *Liebeslieder-Walzer*.

Britten's nerves often resulted in attacks of nausea before he went on stage. Sometimes he tried to calm them with large slugs of brandy – which for most musicians would spell dis-aster. For Britten it seemed to enhance the orchestral colours he coaxed from the piano, and the 'shimmer of sound, like a shudder of electricity' that other people noticed. Nearly four decades on, musicians and singers still speak with awe of his pianistic skill, and how he never needed to practise.

Normally it's the accompanist who has to bolster the singer or instrumentalist before a recital. With Britten it was the other way round. Peter Pears had to inveigle his partner on to the stage when the audience was waiting. No one today is quite sure when they gave their first public recital. But Pears once said that it had been in Cambridge in 1937, to raise funds for the republican cause in the Spanish Civil War. He claimed they had performed a group of Schubert *Lieder*, some of Britten's new Auden songs *On This Island*, and some songs by Gustavo Durán, a Spanish musician who became a general in the republican army at the age of twenty-nine.

Although Britten occasionally accompanied other singers of the English Opera Group, he and Pears gave well over 350 recitals together, and performed Britten's first song cycle written for Pears, the Michelangelo Sonnets, 106 times – mostly during and immediately after the war. Next in the rankings was *Winter Words* (49 performances, including their last recital at Snape), followed by *The Holy Sonnets of John Donne* (30). But what featured in just about every single Britten–Pears recital were his folksongs – often as encores, and therefore unlisted. On dozens of occasions they did pro-gramme 'The Salley Gardens' (109 listings, so it therefore takes the palm), let alone 'Sweet Polly Oliver' (73), 'The Bonny Earl o' Moray' (72), and Shield's 'The Plough Boy' (66). 'Oliver Cromwell' scores just nineteen, but it is ideal as a final encore, so there were probably many more perform-ances that never appeared on concert programmes. The same goes for their signature song 'The Foggy, Foggy Dew', which has only ten official listings.

As far as songs by other composers are concerned, the Britten–Pears formula was often a group of Elizabethan songs in the first half by John Dowland and others (until the arrival of Bream's lute in the 1950s, whereupon Britten abandoned the inauthentic piano accompaniments), and a Schubert group in the second. Their favourite Dowland song was *In darkness let me dwell*, which they sang 57 times, followed by *Awake, sweet love* (29) and *Sorrow, stay* (23). Another favourite was *Have you seen but a white lily?* by an unknown composer (50). They sang complete cycles of Schubert's *Die Winterreise* 28 times, but only during the final decade of their partnership, whereas *Die schöne Müllerin* (19) spanned most of their working life. But the Schubert song they performed most of all was *Im Frühling* (78), closely followed by *Der Musensohn* (77). *Nacht und Träume* came a distant third with 41.

There was often a Purcell group too, latterly in arrangements by Britten. In fact, he accompanied more than 800 performances of Purcell songs across a thirty-five-year span. *There's not a swain* was the outright winner, with 118 outings. *Man is for the woman made* was a regular (sung tongue in cheek, of course) with 75, while *I'll sail upon the dogstar* managed 70.

Britten accompanied solo songs by no fewer than ninety-nine different composers, though only once did Brahms feature (in 1939), and Stravinsky and Vaughan Williams never – with the exception of four performances and a recording of the latter's cycle for voice and piano quintet, *On Wenlock Edge*. Haydn (*Six Canzonets*), Wolf and Schumann were often on the menu (Pears sang *Dichterliebe* with Britten thirty-eight times in twenty-eight years), Debussy occasionally (the Villon ballads). There were operatic excerpts of Verdi, Berlioz, Gluck and Mozart. They gave the premiere of Tippett's cycle *The Heart's Assurance* and sang it on sixteen occasions thereafter. They even gave Webern songs a try, but neither of them enjoyed it. As Pears said:

> We've performed them in public at least four times, if
> not more – I know that in each performance I have sung
> a different set of notes; I have not sung the right notes,
> although I have spent hours and hours practising them.
> And you see, nobody notices, virtually. The avant-garde

boys come up to one with tears in their eyes, saying:
'We've never heard this Webern sung like this'. Indeed
they probably haven't! But I mean that's not the point –
they think it's absolutely marvellous. And if they don't
know the difference between the right and the wrong, well
now who does?

Apart from his work in the film studio and theatre, where
he frequently played the piano in his own incidental music,
Britten joined chamber-music groups to perform Beethoven
piano trios, the piano quartets of Mozart (with the Amadeus
quartet) and the piano quintets of Dvořák, Franck, Schumann, Shostakovich and Schubert (the 'Trout', though he is
only known to have played that once).

He accompanied solo instrumentalists such as the violin-
ists Antonio Brosa and Yehudi Menuhin, the cellist Mstislav
Rostropovich, and the clarinettist Gervase de Peyer. One of
my most treasured recordings is of Britten and Rostropovich playing Schubert's Arpeggione Sonata, where they are so
entwined in their music-making that each seems to be playing
the other's instrument as well as his own.

The final British recital with his proud songster Pears ended
with *Winter Words*. When it was broadcast on the radio later,
Britten was so overcome that he switched off the folksongs
with which they had rounded off the evening. That recital
was in September 1972, and soon the race was on to complete
Death in Venice before the doctors insisted on a heart operation. But still he carried on performing, despite the risks.

He went on a recital tour in Bavaria for ten days in January 1973, where he and Pears performed their last Schubert
Winterreise, some Haydn and Mozart, Britten's first Canticle
and his Scottish cycle *Who are these Children?*, as well as some
folksongs. With members of the Amadeus, he played the
Schumann Piano Quartet. In Munich he and Pears were due
to perform his Hölderlin settings, but Pears was felled by flu,
so Britten had the added strain of helping an unfamiliar young
German tenor, Heiner Hopfner, sing them from the copy. He

also played piano duets by Schubert and Mozart with a local professor.

Pears had recovered in time for a private fund-raising event at St James's Palace in February, in aid of the Royal Academy of Music. It featured, in touching symmetry, *On This Island*, the set of songs by Britten they had worked on together soon after they first met in 1937: now, thirty-five years later, it rounded off their performing partnership. Their only subsequent performance was of piano duets by Schubert at the sixtieth birthday party of Princess Margaret of Hesse, a fortnight before Britten's heart surgery.

After his stroke, he tried for a while to rebuild the strength of his right hand by playing Mozart duets with a friend, Patricia Nicholson. But when he realised he was making no progress, he gave up. The music-making was over.

No one observed Britten the pianist so closely over so long a period as Pears:

> You could watch Ben holding his hands over the piano preparatory to playing a slow movement, a soft, soft chord – and you could see his fingers alert, alive, really sometimes even quivering with intensity. It was amazing what colours he could get. He thought a colour and he could do it.

This is confirmed by Pears's niece, Sue Phipps, who was sometimes even closer as Britten's page-turner. She says that watching his hands 'a-quiver' was terrifying:

> You thought 'how is he ever going to put a key down?' and then finally the finger met the key and this glorious sound came out. It was just extraordinary.

PART FOUR
The influences on Britten

23

Britten's private passions

No composer enjoys having his or her music picked apart, and the sources of its inspiration identified, let alone analysed. Britten was no exception. But he was not writing in a hermit's cave, nor in a hermetically sealed bubble. In his early years he voraciously devoured music of all sorts – in the concert hall, on the wireless, on disc, at the piano, and on the printed page; even as a schoolboy he would read scores in bed as though they were Sherlock Holmes stories. Some of this music he swallowed whole, some he spat out in disgust, some was 'good in spots', as he used to say. But it all fed his own musical personality as it developed in his teens and twenties.

He did occasionally acknowledge the influences on him. In one extraordinary letter, written to the composer Alan Bush in August 1936, he was surprisingly candid. He had just completed *Our Hunting Fathers*, of which he was justifiably proud: he said he'd be quite happy if all his previous work were destroyed. He felt he was going through a process of 'mental spring-cleaning' at a 'mental cross-roads', caused by four things:

> my discovery of Mahler, an increased understanding of
> & affection for (if possible) the works of Beethoven, yet
> another ISCM Festival [a contemporary music festival
> in Barcelona that spring], and hearing of too much con-
> temporary music at BBC contemporary concerts & odd
> societies.

He felt modern music had become too 'introspective, too self-consciously original': all composers laboured to find some 'watertight style' of their own, instead of drawing what they wanted from any other period or style and giving it their own voice. As a result, he said,

modern music has become the meat for only the cultural
few. Why is dance music now divorced from serious
music? Why should serious composers only use the dance
form for satire? It is partly for this reason that I spend so
much time writing for films and theatres.

Then, in a remarkable passage, he spelt out which ways he was
pointing at his crossroads.

My greatest influences are: Beethoven (from the beginning), Mahler, Stravinsky & Berg (increasing rapidly).
    The three greatest works of this era I feel are: Das Lied
von der Erde [Mahler], Psalm Symphony [Stravinsky], &
Wozzeck [Berg] (not knowing Lulu enough to say whether
it surpasses the earlier opera or not – tho' I have a feeling
it does). That those works might stand up to three works
of any era I feel sure.

Because Britten was such a squirrel (he hardly ever threw
anything away), we are able to piece together his reactions to
music – his enthusiasms and his pet hates – almost day by day.
His diaries and letters have plenty to say about the cupboards-
ful of music he owned, and the records he so avidly collected.

Britten was never marooned on the BBC's desert island,
and Radio 3's *Private Passions* had not been invented. But for
his sixtieth birthday in 1973 the BBC did ask him to choose
some gramophone records of which he had 'particular memories'. His list (with his comments in italics) does not include
his own music, nor any Purcell or Shostakovich.

1 Beethoven, *Coriolan* Overture

*Beethoven was my earliest love; until I was in my teens, he dwarfed
all other composers.*

Britten was given the miniature score by his brother when he
had just turned thirteen. He went to several performances,
including one conducted by Bridge when he was eighteen,
which he described as 'electric'. He also went to a 'great'
performance by Toscanini in 1937, when he said it stood out

for 'its colossal welding inspiration, technique, & philosophy. One of the number one works of the world.'

It is interesting that Britten at the age of sixty picked out the *Coriolan* Overture in this way, because ten years earlier he had been very rude about it. He said he had been listening to it 'only yesterday', and went on:

What a marvellous beginning, and how well the development in sequence is carried out! But what galled me was the crudity of the sound; the orchestral sounds seem often so haphazard. I certainly don't dislike all Beethoven, but sometimes I feel I have lost the point of what he's up to.

He added that, between the ages of thirteen and sixteen, he knew every note of Beethoven and Brahms, and that 'receiving the full score of *Fidelio* for my 14th birthday' was 'a red letter day in my life'. But, rather ungraciously, he said he had never forgiven either composer for leading him astray in his own musical thinking.

Britten protested a bit too much. The *Fidelio* score was given to him at sixteen, not fourteen, and he was still besotted with Beethoven well into his twenties. He later told the musicologist Hans Keller that as a boy he had had the uncanny feeling that he had written some of Beethoven's music. At the age of eighteen, Beethoven's Ninth was 'the most marvellous musical thrill of my life yet'; when he turned twenty, he was enthusing about the *Missa Solemnis* as 'the acme of beauty'. He felt it was 'impossible to conceive music greater than this'. By the time he saw *Fidelio* in Paris in early 1937, he was increasingly responsive to Mahler and Berg, and had enjoyed some Shostakovich. But he found Beethoven's opera 'a very deep religious & exhilarating experience. Well as I know the incredible music, I did not realise what a tremendous dramatic thrill it was.' Soon afterwards he wrote, of the late B flat major string quartet (op. 130), 'it is works like this that make one decide to go on living after all', and waxed lyrical about the Third and Sixth symphonies. So Beethoven was much more than a teenage fad.

2 Songs my mother used to sing, such as:
Roger Quilter, *Now sleeps the crimson petal*
Cyril Scott, *Lullaby*
Schubert, any of the better-known songs
Who is Sylvia?; *Hark! Hark! the lark*; *Heidenroslein*

3 A movement from the Ravel String Quartet

This was the first music I heard non-domestically, so to speak –
played by the Norwich String Quartet.

His viola teacher, Audrey Alston, played in the Norwich Quartet and got him tickets. He probably heard this shortly before he saw Bridge conduct his orchestral work *The Sea* in October 1924. Years later, when his own First String Quartet was premiered in Los Angeles (1941), the Ravel quartet was also on the programme.

4 Brahms, Double Concerto (Thibaud and Casals)

We had this recording at Gresham's, and I used to devise methods
of getting hold of it.

He noted in his diary that listening to this at school in January 1930 was 'the only cheering thing'. He said he adored the first two movements, 'but not 3rd as yet'. He later acquired his own copy of this recording (made in 1929), which is still at The Red House. At this point he was still passionate about Brahms, but he fell out of love with him during the early 1930s, and barely ever performed any, apart from the *Liebeslieder-Walzer* as a bit of fun. But it is intriguing that Brahms made it through to this 1973 list.

5 Mozart, 'Dove sono' from *Figaro*

This completely shattered me, and destroyed most of my early gods.

Britten's diaries document this 'road-to-Damascus' moment. Although the overture to *The Marriage of Figaro* was one of his first miniature scores, it was on Wednesday 11 November

1936 that he was 'knocked flat' by seeing the opera at Covent Garden. 'It is without exception the loveliest thing I have ever seen on any stage', he wrote. 'This simple beauty (expressing every emotion) is withering to any ambitions one might have – & yet it is good to have lived in a world that could produce such perfection.' He decided to be extravagant and go home by taxi: 'You can't scramble on a 13 bus after Figaro!' Two days later he said the opera was 'haunting me beyond words. Wed night was a landmark in my history.' He bought a score of the whole opera, and then a complete recording 'which I play often later in the day, and adore more than I can say'.

He went to many performances thereafter, and wrote a press review after seeing it at Covent Garden in 1952. He said he left 'overwhelmed anew by the enchantment of Mozart's score'.

6 Madrigals, particularly Wilbye, *Sweet honey-sucking bees* (Wilbye Consort, directed by Peter Pears), or *Draw on sweet night* (ditto)

While I was at the RCM I used to sing in the Arnold Foster Choir, of which my sister [Barbara] was the Secretary. This gave me my first experience of sixteenth century music.

Britten's copy of *Sweet honey-sucking bees* seems to date from his first term at the Royal College. He sang bass in the choir, though he was never known for his singing ability. In 1953, he used the opening of a Wilbye madrigal, *Happy, O happy he*, in one of Essex's lute songs in *Gloriana*.

7 Stravinsky, *Symphony of Psalms* (conducted by Stravinsky)

For a long time this was my favourite record.

Indeed it was: he kept these 78s all his life. He bought them on 20 July 1932, just after he had completed his *Sinfonietta*, and listened to them frequently. 'Epoch-making', 'really colossal', he wrote. He once listened to the piece side by side

with *Parsifal* and compared them as religious music. He found
Wagner attracted by the sensuous side – 'the incense, ritual,
beauty of sound & emotion', whereas Stravinsky was drawn
by 'the moral, the psychological side, yet tremendously influenced by the ritual side as well'.

He had first heard the work a few months before, when his
teacher Frank Bridge took him to hear it: he later recalled
that 'when everyone around was appalled and saying how
sad about Stravinsky, Bridge was insisting that it was a masterpiece'. He himself wrote at the time that it was 'marvellous', but added: 'Bits of it laboured I thought, but the end
was truly inspired'. In September 1934 he put it on a par
with Beethoven's *Missa Solemnis* as he listened to the records
of both 'incredible masterpieces'. He bought a full score in
April 1936.

8 Berg, *Lyric Suite*, first movement

*I heard the first performance (?) of this in 1936 at the ISCM
Festival in Florence.*

Not quite right . . . He did hear the 'magnificent' *Lyric Suite*
in Florence, but it was in 1934, and it was not the premiere
(which had been in 1927). Britten had already been captivated by the piece on the radio a year before, which seems
to have been the first time he had heard any of Alban Berg's
music. He found it 'astounding', and wrote in his diary that
'the imagination and intense emotion of this work certainly
amaze me if not altogether pleases me' – an interesting distinction. That very day (13 February 1933) he had started
a string quartet of his own, *Alla Marcia*. It is tempting to
imagine that his miniature score of the *Lyric Suite* dates from
this time.

He heard the version for full string orchestra in 1935, and
blamed the conductor Adrian Boult for 'a Kensington drawing room apology for the wild, sensuous and beautiful music'.
Poor Boult was always a whipping-boy, when perhaps Britten
needed to allow for the difference in character between the

quartet and orchestral versions – he recognised this at another performance six months later, conducted by Webern. He then bought the 78 rpm recording of the quartet version (by the Galimir String Quartet), and played the 'wonderful' discs over and over again, and never got rid of them.

9 Mahler, Fifth Symphony (Waltz movement)

Heard on the radio from Hilversum in the early thirties; this started a passion for Mahler.

Britten's memory in 1973 conflicts somewhat with his diary entries from the early 1930s. The Mahler pieces that preoccupied him at the time were *Kindertotenlieder* and the Fourth Symphony, rather than the Fifth. But he did record hearing Bruno Walter conduct it in a 1934 concert from the Concertgebouw in Amsterdam, presumably on Dutch radio. After Mozart's 'superb' Symphony no. 40 in G minor ('surely the loveliest bit of music ever conceived'), he found Mahler's Fifth 'enormously long but I was interested & thrilled for the full 1 hr & 10 mins'.

By June 1936 his passion for the work was growing. He wrote of going to bed at 11.30 pm 'to revel in Mahler's 5th', and studied the score a few days later. He bought a record of the *Adagietto* movement (Willem Mengelberg's 1927 recording) which he called 'a miracle', and played it to his fellow composer Grace Williams, who 'surrenders completely to it'. The next day he listened to it late at night and went to bed 'with a nice (if erotic) taste in my mouth'. He said he supposed there were more beautiful bits of music than Mahler's Fifth – 'but I don't know them'. Frank Bridge gave him a miniature score for Christmas 1936.

The record of the *Adagietto* is still in Britten's house. But it is interesting that for this programme he chose the scherzo movement: perhaps he was aware of how heavily Visconti's film of *Death in Venice* had relied on the *Adagietto*.

10 Frank Bridge, String Quartet no. 3

Written while I was a pupil of his.

Bridge completed this astringent, almost atonal, quartet in 1927, just at the time he started giving Britten lessons. The boy bought a score of it in September 1929, and said a few days later that he was finding it 'very entertaining'.

The eventual BBC programme was broadcast on Radio 3 on Sunday 25 November 1973, under the title *Britten's Choice*.

24

Britten's music library

Britten naturally amassed piles of sheet music for piano, and dozens of vocal and orchestral scores. He was so proud of his boyhood collection of miniature scores that for seven years he numbered them in order, from 1 (Beethoven's 'Eroica') to 137 (Stravinsky's *The Rite of Spring*). His sheet music was not catalogued like this, but even so his diary often makes clear when it was acquired. Most of the piano music, and much of the chamber music, has pencil markings by Britten, indicating that he had worked at it.

This list of all the scores we know he acquired between the ages of eight and twenty-five, when he left for his three-year sojourn in North America, is supplemented with extracts from the notes he sometimes made after hearing the works in performance. Some of these are the superficial reactions of a schoolboy, but others are useful insights into his creative mind at a volatile but receptive stage in his gestation as a composer. Combined, they enable us to attempt a provisional tabulation of his early musical experiences and influences. (Where I have made deductions about either the score numbering or the dates, I have used square brackets.)

- **Coleridge-Taylor**   *Petite suite de concert*   Dec 1921
                           for piano
- **Chopin**   *Polonaises*   Jul 1922
  This is inscribed by the eight-year-old composer: 'E B Britten from his Darling Mummy and Daddy for passing the Elementary Exam (with Hounours) 21 Kirkley Cliff Road, Lowestoft'
- **Beethoven**   **Favourite Waltzes**   c.1923
  and Schubert
- **Beethoven**   15 **Waltzes**   c.1923

- **Beethoven**　　**Piano Sonatas (ed. Liszt)**　　Nov 1923
  This edition (inscribed 'E. B. Britten, Nov 1923, from
  his mother and father') places the thirty-two sonatas
  in ascending order of difficulty, rather than in the order
  in which they were composed. The boy Britten marked
  the real number of the sonata at the top of each, and
  proudly added 'Hammerklavier' to the last.
- **Beethoven**　　**Symphonies nos 1–9,**　　1923?
  　　　　　　　　　　arranged for piano duet
  The instrumentation in Italian has been written in at the
  start of each symphony. For the Ninth, instruments have
  been noted in pencil throughout the work (in both piano
  parts), suggesting Britten did this after acquiring the
  miniature score in 1928.
- **Rachmaninov**　**Selected piano music**　　Sep 1924
- 1 **Beethoven**　　**Symphony no. 3, 'Eroica'**　　1925
- 2 **Beethoven**　　**Symphony no. 6, 'Pastoral'**　　1925
- 3 missing
- 4 **Stravinsky**　　**Suite, *The Firebird***　　1925
- 5 **Wagner**　　　**Overture, *Tannhäuser***　　1925
- 6 **Beethoven**　　**Symphony no. 5**　　1925
- **Chopin**　　　**Waltzes**　　Aug 1925
- **Elgar**　　　　***The Dream of Gerontius***　　Oct 1925
  This vocal score, bought by Britten at the age of eleven,
  was used by Peter Pears for his performances. He sang
  Gerontius twice in the 1940s, and twice in the 1960s
  before going on to sing the role in the 1971 Aldeburgh
  Festival, and in the Decca recording, both conducted by
  Britten.
- 7 **Schubert**　　　**Symphony no. 8, 'Unfinished'**　1925–6
- 8 **Mozart**　　　**Overture, *The Marriage of***　　1926
  　　　　　　　　Figaro
- 9 **Mozart**　　　**Overture, *The Magic Flute***　　1926
- 10 **Tchaikovsky**　**Violin Concerto**　　1926
  Britten inscribed this: 'E. B. Britten from Miss Austin
  (Laulie)', his godmother.
- **Brahms**　　　**Piano Sonata in F minor**　　Apr 1926

| 11 | Wagner | Prelude, *Die Meistersinger* | 1926 |
| 12 | Wagner | Prelude, *Lohengrin* | Aug 1926 |

Britten noted that this was 'bought with money of prize sold to Daddy'.

| – | Beethoven | Piano Sonatas | Sep 1926 |

The omnibus edition of the sonatas given him by his piano teacher, Miss E. M. K. Astle, on 23 September 1926 (the start of a new term at South Lodge). She in turn had received it as a present thirty years before. Britten has annotated the score with analytical comments such as 'Sonata Form', 'Rondo Form', '1st Subject', 'bridge passage', 'recapitulation'.

13	Beethoven	Two Romances for Violin & Orchestra	1926
14	Haydn	Symphony no. 94, 'Surprise'	1926
15	Beethoven	Fugues for string quintet, op. 137	1926
16	Wagner	*Siegfried Idyll*	1926
17	Bach	*Magnificat*	1926
18	Wagner	*Tannhäuser*	Nov 1926

His first full operatic score is inscribed: 'Edward Benjamin Britten with best wishes for his 13th birthday from Mum & Daddy Nov 22 – 26'.

| 19 | Beethoven | Overture, *Coriolan* | 1926 |
| 20 | Wagner | Overture, *The Flying Dutchman* | 1926 |

Scores 19 and 20 are inscribed: 'E. B. Britten from RHMB' [his brother Bobby].

| 21 | Wagner | 'Venusberg Music', *Tannhäuser* | 1926 |

Britten has corrected misprints in the score.

| – | Schumann | *Faschingsschwank aus Wien* | Dec 1926 |
| 22 | Beethoven | Symphony no. 2 | Jan 1927 |

A present from Mabel Austin ('Laulie'), his godmother.

23	Beethoven	Symphony no. 4	Jan 1927
24	Weber	Overture, *Der Freischütz*	Jan 1927
25	Weber	Overture, *Oberon*	Jan 1927
26	Haydn	Symphony no. 45, 'Farewell'	Jan 1927
[27]	Haydn	String Quartet in C, op. 76 no. 3, 'Emperor'	Jan 1927

–	Haydn	Cello Concerto in D	[1927–28?]

In 1931 Britten used this piano score to rearrange the
solo part for viola.

28	Wagner	'Prelude and Liebestod'	1927
		from *Tristan und Isolde*	
29	Mozart	Symphony no. 41, 'Jupiter'	1927
30	Mendelssohn	Overture, *The Hebrides*	1927
31	missing		
32	missing		
33	Mendelssohn	Symphony no. 3, 'Scottish'	1927
34	Wagner	Introduction to Act III,	1927
		Lohengrin	
35	Beethoven	String Quartet in F,	Apr 1927
		op. 59 no. 1	
36	Beethoven	String Quartet in C minor,	Apr 1927
		op. 18 no. 4	
37	Beethoven	Violin Concerto	Apr 1927
–	Ireland	*Decorations*, for piano: 'The	Jul 1927
		Island Spell', 'Moon-glade',	
		'The Scarlet Ceremonies'	
38	Mendelssohn	Overture, *A Midsummer*	Aug 1927
		Night's Dream	
39	Beethoven	String Quartets: E flat,	Sep 1927
		op. 74; F minor, op. 95;	
		E flat, op. 127; B flat, op. 130;	
		C minor, op. 131; A minor,	
		op. 132; B flat, op. 133,	
		Grosse Fuge; F, op. 135	

A present from his mother on 16 September 1927, two
months before his fourteenth birthday. He was just
beginning his last year at South Lodge, and had been
made Head Boy.

40	Brahms	*Alto Rhapsody*	Oct 1927
41	missing		
42	Rimsky-Korsakov	*Capriccio espagnol*	Oct 1927
43	Strauss	*Till Eulenspiegel*	Oct 1927
44	Wagner	'Good Friday Music', *Parsifal*	Oct 1927

45	Wagner	'Wotan's Farewell' from *Die Walküre*	1927
46	Beethoven	Overture, *Leonora* no. 3	1927
47	Beethoven	Piano Concerto no. 4	Nov 1927
48	Schubert	String Quartet in D minor, 'Death and the Maiden'	1927
49	Beethoven	Symphony no. 1	Dec 1927
50	Haydn	Symphony no. 104	Dec 1927
51	Beethoven	String Quartet in E minor, op. 59 no. 2	Dec 1927
52	Beethoven	String Quartet in C, op. 59 no. 3	Dec 1927

Britten noted that scores 49–52 were bought with money from the Badminton Prize at South Lodge School. He heard the E minor quartet at a recital in Norwich, which he described as 'absolutely ripping'.

| 53 | Brahms | *Ein' deutsches Requiem* | Dec 1927 |

A Christmas present from his mother and father.

	Bach	15 three-part *Inventions*	[before 1928]
	Bach	48 Preludes and Fugues: Book 2	[before 1928]
54	Schubert	Overture, *Rosamunde*	Jan 1928
55	Beethoven	String Quartet in G, op. 18 no. 2	Jan 1928

Britten was at a concert performance of this quartet on 5 January.

| 56 | Wagner | A Faust Overture | Jan 1928 |
| 57 | Wagner | 'Wood Scenes', *Siegfried* | Jan 1928 |

Both these Wagner scores were a gift from 'Mrs Turner'.

| – | Mozart | Piano Trio in E flat, K498 | Mar 1928 |

His mother ordered the parts for this Trio, which he practised with her and Charles Coleman (son of the church organist) over the spring and summer.

| 58 | Beethoven | String Quartet in F, op. 18 no. 1 | Apr 1928 |

Bought with money given him by his mother at Easter. He was writing his own F major quartet at this time.

59	Ravel	*Introduction and Allegro*	Apr 1928
–	Beethoven	*Choral Fantasia*	Apr 1928
–	Beethoven	*Missa Solemnis*	Apr 1928

Britten heard both Beethoven works performed by the Royal Choral Society at the Royal Albert Hall in London, and had bought the vocal scores in Lowestoft a few days before..

| 60 | Bridge | *The Londonderry Air*, for string quartet | Apr 1928 |

Inscribed: 'Yours sincerely, Frank Bridge'.

| – | Mozart | **Piano Sonatas** | May 1928 |

A present from his piano teacher Miss Astle. He used it to perform the D major sonata (K311) in 1931, yet the number of his pencilled fingering marks is minimal. There are no rings round notes, or other markings to assist his piano practice.

–	Grieg	*Peer Gynt Suite* no. 1, arr. for piano	[before 1928]
–	Quilter	**Three Studies for piano**	[before 1928]
–	Schubert	**Four Impromptus, D899**	[before 1928]
–	Schumann	*Kinderszenen*	[before 1928]
–	Scriabin	**33 Piano Pieces**	[before 1928]
–	Handel	**Judas Maccabaeus, vocal score**	[before 1928]
–	Ravel	'Noctuelles' from *Miroirs* I	Jun 1928

Given by his mother, shortly after he had begun work on his *Quatres chansons françaises*.

| 61 | Tchaikovsky | **Symphony no. 6, 'Pathétique'** | Jul 1928 |

Given by 'Miss Austin (Laulie)' on his final day at South Lodge.

| – | Franck | **Violin Sonata** | [Aug 1928] |

On 19 August 1928, with his brother Bobby (who played the violin), Britten attended a recital in Lowestoft by the violinist Albert Sammons and the pianist Mark Hambourg. It excited much the most detailed response to music thus far in his daily diary. He said he had

always liked Sammons, but 'Hambourg thumped and
banged, until it was literally painful. He altered the
Fran[c]k sonata, putting in chords, taking no notice
whatsoever of dynamic marks.' The Britten brothers
sometimes played the Franck sonata at home.

62   Beethoven   Overture, *The Creatures of*   Sep 1928
                   Prometheus
Bought on 7 September, the day he heard the overture
played at the Proms, conducted by Sir Henry Wood.

[63] Beethoven   Symphony no. 9   [Sep 1928]
The flyleaf has a press cutting glued to it, with a
photograph of a statue of Beethoven by Francesco
Jerace in the concert hall of Naples Conservatoire.

64   Beethoven   Overture, *Egmont*   Sep 1928
65   Mozart   Ten String Quartets: K387,   Nov 1928
                   K421, K428, K458, K464,
                   K465, K499, K575, K589, K590
66   Mozart   Piano Concerto in C minor,   Nov 1928
                   K491
Both Mozart scores were a present on his fifteenth
birthday from his 'mother and father R. V. & E. R.
Britten, Nov. 22nd 1928'. It was his first birthday away
from home, and at Gresham's he retired to bed with a
sick bug.

67   Beethoven   Symphony no. 8   Nov 1928
A birthday present from 'the Maids' at Kirkley Cliff
Road, Alice, Ruby and Dost.

68   Beethoven   Symphony no. 7   Nov 1928
A birthday present from his godmother Laulie.

68   Ravel   String Quartet   Dec 1928
Britten noted this as 'a wonderful work, I love it', and
listened to a record of it two days later. Britten's numbering went awry, leading to two scores numbered 68.

69   Beethoven   String Quartet in D, op. 18   Dec 1928
                   no. 3
70   Beethoven   String Quartet in B flat,   Dec 1928
                   op. 18 no. 6

71 Brahms   **String Quartet in C minor,**   Dec 1928
                  op. 51 no. 1

The three string quartets (69–71) were a Christmas
present from his godmother. When inscribing them, he
changed the way he wrote his name from 'E. B. Britten'
to 'E. Benjamin Britten', and this form persisted for the
next two years.

72 Honegger   *Pacific 231*   Dec 1928
73 Beethoven   **String Quartet in A, op. 18**   Dec 1928
                  no. 5

Both 72 and 73 were acquired at Christmas.

–   Beethoven   **Cello Sonatas,**   Jan 1929
                  arranged for viola
–   Mendelssohn   *Rondo Capriccioso* in E and   1928–9
                  Fantasia on an Irish Song

Britten played the *Rondo Capriccioso* at a school concert.

74 missing
75 Brahms   **Symphony no. 4**   Apr 1929

Britten recorded this purchase in his diary, with a one-
word comment: 'Ecstasy!'

–   Schumann   *Andante and Variations*,   Apr 1929
                  arranged for two pianos
76 Brahms   **String Quartet in B flat,**   Apr 1929
                  op. 67
–   Beethoven   **Piano Concerto no. 2 in**   [Apr 1929]
                  B flat, arranged for piano
                  (four hands)
77 Borodin   **String Quartet no. 2 in D**   Apr 1929
–   Haydn   **String Quartet no. 17 in F,**   Apr 1929
                  op. 3 no. 5

Britten bought the parts, for rehearsal with friends
between May and July.

–   Beethoven   **Piano Quartet in E flat,**   May 1928
                  arr. from Piano Quintet, op. 16
[78] Mozart   *Ein musikalischer Spass*   22 May 1929
–   Liszt   **Two Concert Studies:**   Aug 1929
                  Waldesrauschen and *Gnomenreigen*

79   **Bridge**   **String Quartet no. 3**   Sep 1929
     A few days after buying the score, he said he was finding
     it 'very entertaining'.

–   **Bach**   **Cantata no. 147:** *Herz und*   [1929]
                       Mund und Tat und Leben

80   **Weber**   ***Invitation to the Dance***   Sep 1929

81   **Haydn**   **String Quartet in G minor,**   Sep 1929
                       op. 74 no. 3, 'Cavalier'

82   **Beethoven**   **Overture,** *The Ruins of*   Sep 1929
                       Athens

82   **Brahms**   **Symphony no. 3**   Nov 1929
     A birthday present from his sister Barbara. Once again
     there is a mistake in the numbering.

83   **Beethoven**   *Fidelio* **(and Overtures,**   Nov 1929
                       Leonora **nos. 1–3)**
     This handsomely bound score was a sixteenth birthday
     present. It is inscribed by his father: 'To Benjamin /
     From "Mum" & "Pop" / November 22 – 29', with, on
     the reverse, an inaccurate quotation from the American
     sports journalist Grantland Rice (an interesting
     acknowledgement of Britten's keenness on sport):
     'When the last great scorer comes / to write against
     your name: He / writes – not whether you won or / lost
     – but how you played the game!' (Some three decades
     later this verse was quoted by Alan Bennett in a *Beyond
     the Fringe* sketch mocking the Church of England.)

84   missing

85   **Wagner**   **'Siegfried's Funeral Music'**   Nov 1929
                       from *Götterdämmerung*
     Another birthday present, from 'Bette'.

86   **Tchaikovsky**   **Symphony no. 4**   Nov 1929
     A birthday present from his godmother, Laulie Austin.

[87] **Schubert**   **Octet**   Dec 1929

88   **Brahms**   **String Quartet in A minor,**   Dec 1929
                       op. 51 no. 2

–   **Brahms**   **Two Songs for voice,**   [before 1930]
                       viola and piano, op. 91

-   **Brahms**   **Horn Trio in E flat, op. 40**   Dec 1929
    He bought this two days after Christmas, and practised
    it with his friends Basil Reeve (violin) and Charles Cole-
    man (piano). To judge by the bow markings, he played
    the horn part on his viola. This involved a feat of trans-
    position at sight, from the horn in E flat to the alto-clef
    viola. They must have played some of it at the musical
    evening Mrs Britten held at home on New Year's Day.
    He preferred 'our Philistine viola version' to Brahms's
    original, which he said was 'horn – horn – nothing else'!

89 **Brahms**   **Symphonies nos. 1 and 2**   Jan 1930
    The day after the Brahms evening, he purchased these
    scores for 7s 6d (reduced from ten shillings), from the
    £1 Christmas present from his aunt Julianne, who was
    his other godmother. The next day he started work on
    his *Quartettino* for string quartet.

90 **Brahms**   *Variations on a Theme of*   Jan 1930
                       Haydn

91 **Delius**   *On Hearing the First Cuckoo*   Mar 1930
                       in Spring; Summer Night
                       on the River

92 **Smetana**   **Overture, *The Bartered Bride***   Apr 1930

-   **Schoenberg**   *Six Little Piano Pieces*, op. 19   Apr 1930
    He noted in his diary for 14 April (the day he bought this
    music): 'I am getting very fond of Schönberg, especially
    with study'. He played these six pieces a fortnight later at
    another of Mrs Britten's musical evenings.

93 **Mendelssohn String Quartet no. 3 in D,**   Apr 1930
                       op. 44 no. 1
    Bought two days before he went to hear the Norwich
    String Quartet play it.

-   **Bridge**   *Melodie* for cello and piano   May 1930
    Britten bought this in Lowestoft, with the intention of
    arranging the cello part for himself to play on the viola.

-   **Brahms**   **Clarinet Sonata in F minor,**   Jun 1930
                       arranged for viola
    His viola teacher at school procured this arrangement

for Britten. A few weeks later she played it through, with
Britten accompanying her on the piano. 'Bliss!', he said.

94	Strauss	*Don Quixote*	Jun 1930
95	Rimsky-Korsakov	Suite, *The Golden Cockerel*	Jun 1930
96	Strauss	Five Songs with Orchestra: *Cäcilie, Morgen, Liebeshymnus, Das Rosenband, Meinem Kinde*	Jun 1930
–	Schoenberg	*Pierrot Lunaire*	Jun 1930

In his last term at Gresham's, Britten was awarded the
Wyndham Birch Prize for music. He spent the prize
(£2 10s) on four scores (nos. 93–5, plus *Pierrot Lunaire*
which he omitted to inscribe or number), as well as the
Oxford Book of English Verse, and two volumes of plays
by the contemporary poet and playwright John Drink-
water. These were presented to him at Speech Day on
28 June, when the headmaster, Mr Eccles, paid tribute
to his musical prowess. Only a few days earlier, Britten
had won an open scholarship to the Royal College of
Music.

| 97 | Bridge | *Three Idylls* for string quartet | Aug 1930 |
| – | Bridge | *A Prayer*, for choir and orchestra | Aug 1930 |

He was pleased to get his score of *A Prayer* for one
shilling and fourpence instead of two shillings. Later in
the year he played the piano in a concert performance
of it in Lowestoft. He regarded both Bridge scores as
'wonderful' works. He took a theme from the second
Idyll as the basis of his Variations for string orchestra in
1937.

| – | Walton | *Sinfonia Concertante*, arranged for two pianos | Sep 1930 |
| 98 | Beethoven | Overture, *Namensfeier* | Sep 1930 |

Both the Walton and Beethoven scores were the fruit
of another school prize at Gresham's – this time for
Maths. The new RCM student heard the Walton piece

at a Queen's Hall Prom the next day, and described it as
'quite good, but immature'.

- **Palestrina**   *Missa assumpta est Maria*   Oct 1930
- **Palestrina**   *Missa Brevis*   Oct 1930

   Britten bought the Palestrina masses while struggling
   with the counterpoint demands made by his new
   composition teacher John Ireland, who he said was 'very
   severe & the Palestrina things I have written weren't
   much to his liking'.

- **Ireland**   *Merry Andrew*   Oct 1930
- **Ireland**   *Spring will not wait*   Oct 1930

   He described both pieces by Ireland as 'marvellous'.

[99] **Ravel**   *Boléro*   Oct 1930

   Britten had just been to an LSO concert at the Albert
   Hall, conducted by Willem Mengelberg, which
   featured Brahms's Third symphony and Ravel's *Boléro*.
   'The Brahms was thrilling, and so was the *Boléro*, in
   which I was nearly hysterical!' he said. He wrote out its
   melody and rhythm for his mother, adding that he was
   'so mad that I can scarcely keep still'.

- **Tchaikovsky Piano Concerto no. 1**   Oct 1930

   Bought on the day he was due to hear Artur Rubinstein
   play the concerto.

100 **Bach**   *Brandenburg Concerto* no. 2   Nov 1930
101 **Bach**   *Brandenburg Concerto* no. 3   Nov 1930
102 **Bach**   *Brandenburg Concerto* no. 4   Nov 1930
103 **Bach**   *Brandenburg Concerto* no. 5   Nov 1930
104 **Bach**   *Brandenburg Concerto* no. 6   Nov 1930

   Five days after buying these Bach scores, he was taken by
   Frank Bridge to hear all six *Brandenburgs* conducted by
   Sir Henry Wood. He particularly enjoyed nos. 3, 5 and 6.

105 **Brahms**   *Song of the Fates*   Nov 1930

   A birthday present, inscribed 'E. Benjamin Britten Nov.
   22nd 1930 From Nanny & the Maids No 105'.

106 **Brahms**   *Song of Destiny*   Nov 1930

   A birthday present from Miss E. E. Hayes, his father's
   secretary, affectionately known to the family as 'Lazy'.

107 **Brahms**   **Piano Concerto no. 1**   Nov 1930
This arrived by post from his godmother Laulie two
days after his birthday. The three Brahms scores were
presumably not a coincidence, but specific requests by
Britten, particularly as he bought two more with his
birthday money. His parents gave him a picture of
Brahms for Christmas a month later. He was clearly in
his Brahms 'phase'.

108 **Schubert**   **Symphony no. 9 in C major**   Nov 1930
Britten elected to buy this with money from his aunt
Julianne, even though a month before he had been
annoyed by its 'ceaseless repetitions. Beautiful in parts',
he added, 'but 1000 times too long'.

109 **Beethoven**   **Serenade, op. 25**   Nov 1930
110 **Brahms**   **String Quintet no. 2 in G**   Nov 1930
  – **Brahms**   **Piano Concerto no. 2**   Nov 1930
He had been to hear Rubinstein perform the concerto
a month before: 'his playing', he said, 'and the heavenly
music makes me feel absolutely hopeless'. He was
pleased to buy this and scores 108–10 for a total of
eight shillings and sixpence.

111 **Delius**   *Brigg Fair*   Dec 1930
112 **Weber**   **Overture, *Euryanthe***   Dec 1930
Both 111 and 112 were Christmas presents.

  – **Schumann**   *Papillons*   Jan 1931
113 **Handel**   **Concerto Grosso in**   Jan 1931
                       E minor, op. 6 no. 3
He listened to this on the wireless on 14 January.

114 **Mendelssohn** **Violin Concerto in E minor** Jan 1931
115 **Schumann**   **Overture, *Manfred***   Jan 1931
116 **Mozart**   **Symphony no. 39 in E flat**   Jan 1931
[117] **Mahler**   *Lieder eines fahrenden*   Jan 1931
                       Gesellen
His first Mahler score, bought in London on 24 January.
He went to a performance in May, when he described the
songs as 'lovely little pieces, exquisitely scored – a lesson
to all the Elgars and Strausses in the world'.

208   THE INFLUENCES ON BRITTEN

–	Beethoven	Piano Sonata in D, op. 10 no. 3	Jan 1931
118	Berlioz	*Symphonie fantastique*	Feb 1931
119	Debussy	*Prélude a l'après-midi d'un faune*	1931

A birthday present from his brother Bobby, perhaps
given (or chosen) several weeks late.

| – | Brahms | Piano Variations on an original theme, op. 21 no. 1 | Feb 1931 |
| – | Prokofiev | Prelude for piano, op. 12 | Feb 1931 |

Britten worked at both these piano scores, and played
the Prokofiev to friends at home on 25 April, along
with part of Beethoven's D major piano sonata he had
bought in January.

| [120] | Dvořák | Cello Concerto in B minor | Mar 1931 |
| – | Beethoven | Rounds and Canons | Apr 1931 |

Sung at a musical evening hosted by Mrs Britten on
18 April and again a week later: he and his friends had
'a very hilarious time, if we don't give perfect perfs of
these lovely little creations'. The compositional device
of canon appealed to Britten all through his life.

| 121 | Saint-Saëns | Piano Concerto no. 4 | May 1931 |

Britten went the following day to a Queen's Hall
performance by Alfred Cortot.

| – | Beethoven | Piano Sonata in E flat, op. 27 no. 1 | May 1931 |
| – | Ravel | *Sonatine* | May 1931 |

Britten's piano teacher Arthur Benjamin had given him
these pieces by Beethoven and Ravel to study.

| – | Kirbye | *O Jesu, Look* | May 1931 |

This five-voice anthem, which Britten was rehearsing
as part of the small choir he had joined, may have been
partly to blame for what Bridge called the 'too vocal'
counterpoint in Britten's D major string quartet, in
progress at this time.

| 122 | Bach | Suite no. 2 | May–Nov 1931 |
| – | Schumann | Piano Sonata no. 1 in F sharp minor, op. 11 | Jun 1931 |

- **Howells** *Madrigal* Jul 1931
  and three other songs
- **Walton** **Viola Concerto** Sep 1931
  Britten bought the reduction for viola and piano the
  day before he heard a radio broadcast of Lionel Tertis
  playing it at the Proms. 'Wonderful', he said: 'it stood
  out as a work of genius'. He played through bits of it
  with Basil Reeve at home. Four years later, he decided 'a
  lot of it wears so thin'.
- **Franck** *Symphonic Variations* Oct 1931
  Britten was learning the solo piano part with Arthur
  Benjamin, after hearing Myra Hess play it at the Proms
  the previous month, when he found it a 'delightful work
  (his masterpiece)'. He played it at a musical evening in
  Lowestoft the following January.
- 123 **Haydn** **Symphony no. 103** Nov 1931
  His faithful godmother, Mabel Austin, gave him this for
  his eighteenth birthday.
- **Bridge** **String Sextet** Nov 1931
  A birthday present from the composer, who inscribed it:
  'B. B. from F. B.'
- **Delius** *Hassan*: 'Serenade', Nov 1931
  arranged for cello and piano
- **Walton** *Belshazzar's Feast* Nov 1931
  Britten bought the vocal score of Walton's oratorio for
  the London premiere the same evening (25 November),
  conducted by Adrian Boult. He found it 'very moving
  and brilliant', especially the first half, but 'over- long and
  too continuously loud'.
- **Bridge** *The Christmas Rose* Dec 1931
  Frank Bridge gave Britten a vocal score of his one and
  only opera, which was being performed at the RCM a
  few days later. His pupil was loyal about this 'darling
  little work', and saw it three times, though he did add
  that it 'may not be an excellent opera from the stage
  point of view, but when there is little action the music is
  always sublime – and that is O.K. for me!'

- **Bridge**   **Piano Trio**   Dec 1931

  A Christmas present from Bridge: 'I am very bucked as it is a most interesting and beautiful work'. He rehearsed it in the New Year with his RCM contemporary, the violinist Remo Lauricella.

124 **Stravinsky**   *Petrushka*   Dec 1931

  A Christmas present from 'Mum & Pop'. Early in the New Year he bought the first two 78 rpm discs (all he could afford) of this 'marvellous music', and bought the rest six weeks later. He played them repeatedly.

125 **Wagner**   **'Ride of the Valkyries',**   Dec 1931
                    from *Die Walküre*

  'From Nanny, Alice, Ruby, Phillis' [the Maids].

126 **Mozart**   ***Sinfonia Concertante* for**   Dec 1931
                    violin and viola, K364

  His godmother Laulie gave him the score of what became a favourite Mozart work. He was soon rehearsing it for a musical evening at Kirkley Cliff Road in January.

- **Bridge**   *Graziella, Hidden Fires*   Jan 1932
- **Brahms**   **Piano Sonata no. 1 in C**   Jan 1932
- **Rachmaninov** 13 **Preludes for piano, op. 32** Jan 1932
- **Bach**   *Italian Concerto*   Jan 1932

127 **Ireland**   *Mai-Dun*   Feb 1932

  He heard this later the same day, and found it 'magnificent'.

128 **Beethoven**   **Overture, *King Stephen***   Feb 1932

  He attended a performance straight after buying the score, but found the overture 'miserably played' under his least favourite conductor, Adrian Boult.

129 **Debussy**   **String Quartet in G minor**   Feb 1932

  Bought just before attending a performance by the Brosa Quartet. He heard another on the radio a week later.

- **Bridge**   *Phantasy*, **Piano Quartet**   [Mar 1932]

  Britten heard this on the radio in March 1932, shortly after completing his own *Phantasy* for string quintet.

130 **Dukas**   *The Sorcerer's Apprentice*   Apr 1932

  Acquired the day after buying Toscanini's recording.

–	Bach	*Jesu meine Freude*	May 1932
131	Walton	**Overture**, *Portsmouth Point*	May 1932
132	Bridge	*Novelletten* for string quartet	May 1932

To buy scores 131–2 he dipped into the Cobbett Prize
money of thirteen guineas awarded by the RCM for his
Phantasy string quintet.

[133] Wagner   *Tristan und Isolde*   May 1932

This miniature score of the complete opera was
inscribed by Britten: 'Bought 26th May 1932, 2nd hand
from Reeves, London'. Only two weeks before, he had
heard a 'disgraceful' performance of the Prelude
conducted by Thomas Beecham at Covent Garden.
In October he called the opera 'this wonder of the
world', and six months later he saw it for the first
time. 'Dwarfs every other art creation save perhaps
[Beethoven's] 9th', he said.

| 134 | Falla | *El amor brujo* | Jun 1932 |
| 135 | Stravinsky | *Berceuses du chat* | Jun 1932 |

Scores 134–5 are further booty from the Cobbett
Prize. The Falla piece was the last work he conducted
in public, in 1972.

| – | Schumann | *Phantasie* in C for piano, op. 17 | Jun 1932 |

[136] Kodály   *Psalmus Hungaricus*   Jun 1932

Later in life, Britten met Kodály several times (he was
an honoured guest at the 1965 Aldeburgh Festival)
and seemed to remember fondly the first British
performance of this work in 1927. When he bought
the score (on the day he started work on 'a bit of a
chamber symphony' – which would become his
Sinfonietta), Britten called it a 'marvellous work', and
found that he was 'too full of Psalmus to write music!'

| – | Stravinsky | *Symphony of Psalms* | Jul 1932 |

Britten bought Stravinsky's own recording of the
'great Psalm Symphony' on 20 July and, fired up by
the records, bought the vocal score ten days later with
the remainder of the money from his Cobbett Prize.

137 Stravinsky   *The Rite of Spring*   Sep 1932
The day after buying the records, he spent twenty-
four shillings on the score of 'the world's wonder' –
money from the Sullivan Prize of £10 which the RCM
had given him for his *Sinfonietta*. This was the last of
his numbered miniature scores.

– Bach   Concerto (for keyboard)   Sep 1932
**   in D minor, BWV 1052**
In October he started studying the piece with Arthur
Benjamin, and in November attended a performance by
his former teacher, Harold Samuel.

– Bridge   *There is a willow grows*   Dec 1932
**   *aslant a brook***

– Tchaikovsky *Francesca da Rimini*   Dec 1932
Both scores were Christmas presents from Frank
Bridge. The Tchaikovsky work was a favourite of his:
a month later Britten went to a performance he
conducted, and said he made it 'sound terrifying'.

– Haydn   Symphony no. 101   Jan 1933
Britten heard Bridge conduct this symphony at the
same concert as the Tchaikovsky.

– Chopin   Complete piano music   1933

– Debussy   *L'isle joyeuse*   Jul 1933
Studied by Britten for his ARCM exam.

– Stravinsky Three pieces from *Petrushka*,   Jan 1934
**   arranged for piano solo**
Having loved the score for several years, Britten now
worked up these pieces as piano solos.

– Bridge   *April, Rosemary, Valse*   Jan 1934
**   *Capriccieuse***

– Berg   *Wozzeck*   Apr 1934
Britten bought the vocal score in Florence, having
heard three movements of the 'magnificent' *Lyric Suite*
at the ISCM Festival there. He had first heard the
'sincere and moving' *Wozzeck Fragments* at a Henry
Wood concert a year before, and then listened to a
crackly radio broadcast of the first UK performance of

the whole opera, conducted (in concert) by Boult. Some
of the music was, he said, 'extraordinarily striking'.

– **Bartók**   **Rhapsody no. 1 for violin**   Apr 1934
                   and piano
He also bought this 'amusing' score in Florence after
hearing Joseph Szigeti play it.

– **Mendelssohn Scherzo, Intermezzo,**   Aug 1934
                   Notturno, from *A Midsummer*
                   Night's Dream

– **Humperdinck** *Hänsel und Gretel*   Aug 1934
Britten had heard a studio performance of the opera on
the radio in June, and the role of children in it appealed
to him. 'What heavenly music this is – perfectly done. I
simply revel in it. Some of it, I could wish performed
otherwise – I wish they could get simpler voices for the
children – but on the whole a good show.' At Christmas
1936 he saw this 'glorious work' at Sadler's Wells with
Piers Dunkerley and Grace Williams, and said he adored
every bar.

– **Stravinsky**   *Duo concertante*   Sep 1934
At the time he was writing his own piano suite *Holiday
Diary*. Britten found the Stravinsky piano part 'a blight-
er to play', though he liked the work, and did perform it
with the violinist Antonio Brosa in 1936.

– **Strauss**   *Ein Heldenleben*   Oct 1934
Acquired on his European tour with his mother. He
heard Strauss's tone-poem in Basel conducted by
Weingartner: it had 'some really thrilling moments.
The love section was stiff & cold (for Strauss) – but
what a work! In spite of its egotism, I admire it now
wholeheartedly.'

– **Mahler**   **Symphony no. 4**   Nov 1934
After moving on to Vienna, he bought his first score of
a Mahler symphony the day before hearing Mengelberg
and the Vienna Philharmonic perform it. He had first
heard it in a Prom broadcast four years before, when he
found it 'much too long but beautiful in parts'. In April

1933 he had listened to the composer Webern conducting it – how intriguing that must have been! – and
commented: 'This work seems a mix up of everything
that one has ever heard, but it is definitely Mahler. Like
a lovely spring day.' On this occasion he spotted with
displeasure that Mengelberg had made some changes to
the scoring: Mahler 'of all people', he said, 'knew to the
nth degree what he wanted' – rather like Britten himself.
But even so he enjoyed it 'enormously' and found that
only the third movement outstayed its welcome. The
next day, in his Vienna hotel room, he started work on
his Suite for violin.

– **Stravinsky**   *Les Noces*   Nov 1934
His next Vienna purchase was the second-hand score of
'a great work' he had heard on the radio, when he was
thrilled by 'the exciting rhythms and colours; splendid
architecture and the beautiful end'.

– **Verdi**   *Requiem*   Nov 1934
Verdi's greatest non-dramatic work was Britten's next
Viennese quarry, but at the last minute the concert was
postponed. Two months before he had heard a broadcast
from Rome, and found it 'theatrical but very effective'.
Almost three decades later, he was ready to acknowledge
the debt of his own *War Requiem* to Verdi.

– **Wagner**   *Siegfried*   Nov 1934
His musical feast in Vienna continued with performances of *Die Meistersinger* and *Siegfried* – the first time
he had seen any of Wagner's *Ring* cycle on stage. Before
that, his experience had been mostly confined to 'bleeding chunks' in concert. He bought the score, read it,
and saw it on stage – all on the same day, 15 November.
'The scenic effects were wonderful', he wrote, 'and the
dragon fight, far from being ludicrous, was very exciting;
and the last act was touchingly beautiful'. Then, foreshadowing his own distinctive writing for the horn, he
added, 'the horns (esp. the horn call) were just incredible. And the Music . . . . !!!'

- **Bruckner**   **Symphony no. 4**   Nov 1934
  Bruckner does not normally feature on the map of
  Britten. In Vienna he heard Hans Knappertsbusch conduct it at the Musikverein, and said he had never heard
  such string or horn playing, but he felt this was wasted
  on 'a dismal work, with very very few redeeming patch-
  es'. Nonetheless, he kept his second-hand score.
- **Johann Strauss** *Die Fledermaus*   Nov 1934
  This full score was a twenty-first birthday present from
  his mother, just after he had wrenched himself away
  from Vienna to travel to Munich. They had been to see
  the opera earlier in the month, which he called 'inimitable' and 'delightful'. It was, he said, 'inspired from
  beginning to end'.
- **Schubert**   **Piano Sonatas**   Nov 1934
- **Schumann**   **Duos and Pieces for viola** Nov 1934
                   and piano
- **Strauss family Waltzes**   Nov 1934
- **Beethoven**   **Songs (including** *An die* Dec 1934
                   ferne Geliebte)
  A twenty-first birthday present from Marjorie Fass,
  friend of the Bridges, which was awaiting his return
  from his European travels.
- **Debussy**   *Pelléas et Mélisande*   Dec 1934
  Another piece of the musical education provided for his
  twenty-first birthday, and inscribed 'For Benjamin Britten
  wishing him all good luck. November 1934, affectionately
  Frank Bridge'. Bridge followed up with the discs of the
  complete opera at Christmas, which Britten described as
  'marvellous stuff – but so sensitive and intangible'.
- **Ravel**   *Pavane pour une infante défunte* 1935
- **Mahler**   *Seven Last Songs*   1935
- **Mendelssohn Octet**   1935
- **Gibbons**   **Pavans and Galliards**   1935
- **Mahler**   *Des Knaben Wunderhorn*   1935
  He was 'thrilled' by the recording he bought of the
  Wunderhorn songs in March.

- **Beethoven   Piano Trios (complete)**   Apr 1935
  An Easter gift from his old piano teacher, Miss Astle.
  He noted in his diary: 'Miss Ethel presents me with all
  the Beethoven trios – very welcome indeed'. The markings on the piano part indicate that Britten practised
  them conscientiously.
- **Johann Strauss Waltz selections,**   May 1935
  for violin and piano
  He noted in June that he was supposed to be working on
  his film score for *Coal Face* – 'but finding piano free the
  temptation of Strauss Waltzs is too much'.
- **Stravinsky   *The Soldier's Tale***   Jun 1935
- **Milhaud   *Le bœuf sur le toit*,**   Jul 1935
  arranged for piano duet
  His comments about Milhaud's music in his diaries are
  almost all negative. 'Singularly unedifying', he said.
- **Françaix   String Trio**   1935
- **Stravinsky   Violin Concerto**   Aug 1935
  He had been rehearsing this work with Antonio Brosa,
  and bought the score for a Prom performance he
  attended: 'so musical and such style', he said.
- **Bridge   *Sir Roger de Coverley***   Sep 1935
- **Busoni   *Rondo Arlecchinesco***   Sep 1935
  Purchased in connection with a Prom performance he
  attended, when he found the work 'very exciting'.
- **Mendelssohn Symphony no. 4, 'Italian'**   1935
  He may have bought this after hearing it conducted by
  Bridge at the Proms: 'Very charming and really beauti-
  fully wrought'.
- **Glinka   Overture, *Ruslan and Lyudmila*** Sep 1935
- **Stravinsky   *Fireworks***   Sep 1935
  'Brilliant', Britten wrote after hearing a broadcast three
  months later. 'More original than people think.'
- **Moeran   *Nocturne*, for baritone,**   [1935]
  chorus and orchestra
  Both Moeran and Britten signed this score. Britten was
  at the work's first performance in April: he said it was

'rather lovely – tho' v. influenced by Delius, yet somehow stronger'.

- **Berlioz**   *Grande Messe des morts*   [Mar] 1936
Britten was excited by the work: 'what power and imagination!', he wrote.
- **Stravinsky**   *Capriccio* **for piano and**   [Mar 1936]
                    orchestra
Britten probably acquired this two-piano arrangement
in connection with the performance he attended at the
end of March, when Stravinsky himself conducted this
'engaging' work, together with the *Pulcinella* and *Firebird*
suites. 'A great man is Stravinsky – sans doute', he added.
- **Stravinsky**   *Symphony of Psalms*   Apr 1936
After the discs and the vocal score, there came finally
the full score of an 'epoch-making work'.
- **Berlioz**   *Harold in Italy*   1936
- **Webern**   **String Trio, op. 20**   1936
- **Mahler**   *Das Lied von der Erde*   1936
While working on *Our Hunting Fathers*, Britten read
the scores of Mahler's great song cycle and his First and
Fifth symphonies. At a concert later in the year he said
Das Lied von der Erde moved him more than any other
music – certainly of the twentieth century.
- **Bruckner**   **Symphony no. 7**   [Oct] 1936
At a concert by the Vienna Symphony Orchestra, he
concluded: 'Bruckner's 7th does not convert me. The
organist in his loft dreamily improvising – very lovely
sounds the occasionally lovely ideas (the beginning is
lovely) – but the construction, the aimless wandering,
the appalling lack of invention.'
- **Mozart**   *The Marriage of Figaro*   Nov 1936
Britten bought the miniature score after seeing the
opera at Covent Garden, and being 'knocked flat'. It was
'a landmark in my history'.
- **Berg**   **Violin Concerto**   Nov 1936
Britten had heard the premiere in Barcelona, several
months after Berg's death. 'Just shattering', he said,

'very simple and touching'. Six months later, in a fit of
extravagance, he bought the full score: 'My God, what
a sublime work', he wrote. After a further concert performance, he said it had 'an extremely moving effect on
me like no other stuff. It is so vital & so intellectually
emotional' – unlike the 'frightful' Second symphony of
Brahms which preceded it: 'dull, ugly, gauche'. He said
it was difficult to go back home and work on his *Temporal Variations* for oboe, 'but it had to be done'.

– **Mahler**   **Symphony no. 5**   Dec 1936
    Inscribed by Frank Bridge: 'Benjy / Love from me /
    F. B. / Xmas 1936'.
– **Mahler**   **Symphony no. 6**   1937
– **Rimsky-**   ***Sheherazade***   1937
      Korsakov
– **Elgar**   ***Introduction and Allegro***   Jun 1937
    Britten's involvement with this work is fascinating.
    In November 1931 he said it had 'nice spots' but was
    'terrible'. A year later, it made 'some nice sounds' but
    the form seemed 'so unsatisfactory'. In May 1937, after
    seeing Toscanini conduct it, he said, 'not for me'. But a
    few days later he bought the score, just at the time he
    was starting his own string orchestra piece, *Variations on
    a Theme of Frank Bridge*. Perhaps he wanted to learn how
    another 'old magician' made his effects. He certainly
    came round to them when in 1969 he conducted and
    recorded the work, and wrote of the novelty of Elgar's
    'subtle sonorities', contrasting and combining the quar-
    tet and the orchestra.
– **Debussy**   ***Ibéria***   Jun 1937
    With score in hand, he saw Toscanini give 'a worthy
    show of a great adorable piece of music'. Sibelius's *En
    Saga* was 'as bad as that was good (in every way)'.
– **Bartók**   ***Music for Strings, Percussion***   Jan 1938
                      and Celesta
    He attended a BBC performance of this 'very interest-
    ing' work on 7 January.

- **Webern**   *Das Augenlicht*   Jun 1938
- **Mendelssohn** *Erste Walpurgisnacht*   1938
- **Haydn**   **String Quartets**   Nov 1938

These six enchanting volumes, containing all eighty-three string quartets by the man who invented the form, are like prayer books, with green marbled boards, red marbled endpapers, and white leather title-blocks and gold tooling on the spine. They were a twenty-fifth birthday present from his would-be lover, Lennox Berkeley, and are touchingly inscribed: 'From L. B. / to his little friend / Benjamin Britten / November 22nd, 1938.'

- **Mahler**   **Symphony no. 9**   Dec 1938

This Christmas gift from Peter Pears is inscribed: 'An meinen liebsten Ben. Weihnacht. 1938 / Peter.'

25
Britten's record collection

Britten was tart at times about the lack of effort which he thought gramophone records entailed: 'Anyone, anywhere, at any time, can listen to the B minor Mass. No qualification is required of any sort – faith, virtue, education, experience, age.' He railed against cocktail-party background music available at the flick of a switch. Perhaps this was a throwback to his child-hood, when his father refused to have a radiogram in the house, for fear that it would replace the live music-making by his wife and sons.

Britten did, however, leave behind a huge collection of long-playing records. At its core is his own historic legacy – recordings of his own music as either conductor or pianist. Then there are the many recordings he made of other com-posers' music. There are also several hundred discs which other people made of his music – or of their own – which they presumably thought he might like to hear. The cellophane wrappers on some of them are still intact.

Before the LP had been invented, Britten was ravenous for records at school, at college, and as a young composer find-ing his musical bearings. So, with the exception of a few discs owned by Pears, the surviving collection of some 200 record-ings on 78 rpm discs (listed here in summary) is likely to be his own choice – a fascinating indication of music that caught his fancy. Some of them we know he played again and again.

ADAMS
The Holy City   Clara Butt

BACH
Chromatic Fantasia   Wanda Landowska   1940
    and Fugue
Organ music   Albert Schweitzer   1936

BEETHOVEN
'Battle Symphony'   Berlin Orch./Weissmann
A Christmas present in 1936: 'There are some very exciting & picturesque things in it – & the end is gloriously naive.'

Missa Solemnis   Berlin Philharmonic/ Kittel   1931
It's interesting that Britten never threw out this first ever recording of the complete Mass. He bought the discs in 1933, only to find the soloists 'excruciating', and the chorus 'pretty bad'. However, he persevered and, by adjusting the tone control on his gramophone, 'managed to make the soloists sound normal', he said. 'But what music! The end of the Gloria drives me potty.' He repeatedly listened to these discs, and said 'it is impossible to conceive music greater than this'. It was 'above criticism'. He bought a new recording in 1935, when he called the Sanctus and Benedictus 'perhaps the most lovely and greatest music of the world'.

Overture, *Prometheus*   LPO/Weingartner
Piano Concerto no. 5,   Backhaus, Ronald   1928?
'Emperor'
Piano Sonata in E,   Denis Matthews
op. 109
Piano Sonata in A flat,   Edwin Fischer
op. 110
Piano Sonata in B flat,   Louis Kentner
'Hammerklavier'
Piano Trio in B flat,   Cortot, Thibaud, Casals   1936?
op. 97
String Quartets   Léner String Quartet   1939?
String Quartets   Capet String Quartet
Symphony no. 3   Vienna Philharmonic/Furtwängler
Symphony no. 4   LPO/Weingartner
Symphony no. 5   Paris orchestra/Schuricht
Symphony no. 7   Philadelphia/Stokowski   1936?
Symphony no. 8   RPO/Weingartner
Symphony no. 9 (exc.)   Berlin State Orch./Fried   1941
Symphony no. 9   Vienna Philharmonic/Karajan

| Violin Sonata in A, 'Kreutzer' | Thibaud, Cortot | 1940? |
| Violin Sonata in G, op. 96 | Rostal, Osborn | |

BERG

| *Lyric Suite* | Galimir String Quartet | 1936 |
| **Three Fragments** from *Wozzeck* | Ribla, Philadelphia/Ormandy | 1949 |

BERLIOZ

| **'Hungarian March'** | Berlin Philharmonic/ Furtwängler | 1932 |

BISHOP

| *Lo, here the gentle lark* | Amelita Galli-Curci | 1929 |

BRAHMS

| **Songs** | Lotte Lehmann | 1936 |
| **Double Concerto** | Thibaud, Casals/Cortot | 1929 |

BRIDGE

Idyll no. 1	Virtuoso String Quartet	
Novellette no. 3	Virtuoso String Quartet	1929
Cherry Ripe, Sally in our Alley	London Chamber/Bernard	1931

These were favourites of Britten's – but then so was everything by his mentor. He had recordings of the same pieces in their original version, for string quartet.

BRUCKNER

| **Symphony no. 4:** **Scherzo** | Vienna Philharmonic/ Krauss | |

BUXTEHUDE

| **Prelude and Fugue in D minor** | Ralph Downes | 1937 |

CLAY

| *I'll sing thee songs of Araby* | Ben Davies | 1932 |

DEBUSSY
La Mer Boston SO/Koussevitzky 1939

DONIZETTI
Don Pasquale (exc.) Tito Schipa

DUKAS
The Sorcerer's Apprentice New York PO/Toscanini
 He bought the 'v. fine' discs in Lowestoft on 22 April 1932, and the miniature score the next day.

FAURÉ
Cygne sur l'eau, Lise Daniels/Benvenuti 1939
 Reflets dans l'eau

GARTNER
Trusting Eyes Enrico Caruso 1914

HUMPERDINCK
Hansel and Gretel (exc.) Berlin State Opera/Weigert

LISZT
A Faust Symphony Paris Philharmonic/ 1936
 Meyrowitz

MAHLER
Das Lied von der Erde Thorborg, Kullman/Walter 1937
'Rheinlegendchen', Schlusnus/Weigert 1931
 'Tambourg'sell'
 These two songs from *Des Knaben Wunderhorn* were often performed by Pears and Britten in the 1940s.
Symphony no. 5: Concertgebouw/Mengelberg 1927
 Adagietto
Symphony no. 9 Vienna Philharmonic/Walter 1938

MENDELSSOHN
Hear my Prayer Ernest Lough, Temple Choir 1927
 In April 1931, when Britten was seventeen, his father had still not relented on allowing a gramophone in the house, so it was at a friend's house that he was struck by the famous treble's 'beautifully sung' recording of the Mendelssohn anthem, which includes 'O for the Wings of a Dove'. More than a million copies of this disc were

sold – one of them to Britten a few days later.

MILHAUD
Suite d'après Corrette   Trio d'Anches de Paris

MONTEVERDI
Il Combattimento di   Angelici, Peyron/Meili
  Tancredi e Clorinda
Orfeo   Calusio   1940

MOZART
The Marriage of Figaro: Helletsgruber/Berlin State Orch.
  Act I excerpts
'Dove sono' (*Figaro*)   Joan Cross/Sadler's Wells   1940
The Magic Flute: arias   Heddle Nash
Songs   Lotte Lehmann   1936

MURRAY
I'll Walk Beside You   Gigli/Covent Garden   1947

O'HARA
Your eyes have told me   Enrico Caruso   1938
  what I did not know

POULENC
Le Bestiaire,   Pierre Bernac, Poulenc   1946
  Montparnasse

PUCCINI
La bohème, Madam   Joan Cross
  Butterfly: excerpts

RAVEL
Boléro   Boston SO/Koussevitzky   1930
Introduction and Allegro Virtuoso String Quartet etc.
  Britten had a score of this 'delicious' work at the age of
fourteen, in 1928. He bought the recording on 22 August
1931, with Bridge's third *Novellette*. He described them as
'absolutely thrilling!' A few days later, he got 'stuck' writing his ballet *Plymouth Town*, because he was 'saturated in
Ravel'.

SATIE
Gymnopédie no. 1   Boston SO/Koussevitzky   1930

SCHUBERT
Crusade   Therese and Artur Schnabel
Der Hirt auf dem   Ritchie, Moore, Kell
  Feisen
Im Abendrot,   Lotte Lehmann, Balogh   1936
  Ungeduld

SCHUMANN
Der Nussbaum,   Karl Erb
  Mondnacht
Die Kartenlegerin,   Lotte Lehmann, Balogh   1936
  Waldgespräch

STRAUSS J.
Die Fledermaus (exc.)   Elisabeth Schumann

STRAUSS R.
Ein Heldenleben   NYPO/Mengelberg
Till Eulenspiegel   Berlin Philharmonic/Furtwängler
Purchased on 4 February 1933, when he was nineteen. He had gone to buy them the previous July, but came away instead with Stravinsky's *Symphony of Psalms*. He had had the miniature score since 1927.
Traum durch die   Lotte Lehmann
Dämmerung, Ständchen
Der Rosenkavalier (exc.)   Lehmann   1928
These are probably the Strauss recordings he bought in March 1935. He noted two years later: 'I have such a passion for sopranos that I may some time become "normal"'.

STRAVINSKY
Apollon musagète   Boyd Neel String Orchestra
Symphony of Psalms
Petrushka   LSO/Coates   1932?
Britten was thrilled to get the miniature score from his parents at Christmas 1931, and bought this recording in the New Year. He could afford only discs one and two at first, so he had to wait a week for the other two. 'Marvellous music', he said.

SULLIVAN
The Lost Chord   Clara Butt

TIPPETT
Symphony no. 1   [test pressing]

VAUGHAN WILLIAMS
'The Roadside Fire'   Gervase Elwes
On Wenlock Edge   Elwes

VERDI
Ernani: **Act I excerpts** Rosa Ponselle
Rigoletto **(excerpts)**   Tito Schipa

WAGNER
Siegfried: **Act III duet** Laubenthal, Leider
Tristan und Isolde: BPO/Furtwängler   1931
    Prelude
Britten bought this 'superb' recording on 3 January 1934
– he had had the score of the Prelude since 1927, and the
full score since 1932. He loved the opera all through his
apprentice years, and described Act II as a 'wonder of the
world'. In May 1933, after seeing it with his sister Beth, he
was effusive about 'the glorious shape of the whole, the perfect orchestration: sublime idea of it, & the gigantic realisation of the idea'. He was 'somewhat dazed' and couldn't do
much work for several days afterwards: he lent his score to
a friend 'to get rid of the wretched thing'.
Die Walküre: Hartmann, Berlin State   1929
    Act I scene iv   Opera

WALTON
Overture,   New English SO/A. Bernard
Portsmouth Point
These discs were lucky to survive. As soon as he bought
them on 11 August 1932, he decided he was disappointed by the piece: 'ineffective & apparently bad & careless
workmanship', though he had had the miniature score
since May.

WEINBERGER
Schwanda the Bagpiper Berlin State Orch./Blech
  (excerpts)

WOLF
Songs   Lotte Lehmann, Balogh   1936

We know that he once owned some other 78 rpm recordings, but they no longer form part of the collection: Berg's
Wozzeck, for example, Debussy's *Pelléas et Mélisande*, Delius's
Brigg Fair, Honegger's *Pacific 231*, Mahler's *Kindertotenlieder*, and Stravinsky's *Firebird* and *The Rite of Spring*.

Britten died before the age of the compact disc, but his collection of LPs is formidable, and too extensive to list here.
Among the chief items of interest are: Beethoven's piano
sonatas played by Artur Schnabel; the Debussy piano preludes
played by Walter Gieseking; a boxed set of Elgar conducting his own works; various pieces by Gustav Holst, normally
given as presents by Imogen Holst; Janáček's *The Cunning
Little Vixen*, *Katya Kabanova* and his string quartets; Mahler's
symphonies nos. 1, 3, 5, 7, 8 and 10 (most of them conducted in the 1950s by Hermann Scherchen; these are the only
recordings by Scherchen that Britten owned – with Mahler
an interesting emotional context for the inevitable private
reminders of Britten's affair more than a decade earlier with
Scherchen's teenage son, Wulff); Messiaen's *Turangalîla* Symphony; Schoenberg's piano and violin concertos; recordings
of *Die Winterreise* and other Schubert *Lieder* sung by Dietrich
Fischer-Dieskau with Gerald Moore; Shostakovich's symphonies nos. 4, 6, 10, 14, and some of his string quartets (some
discs given by the composer and inscribed in Russian); numerous Tchaikovsky recordings, including a well-thumbed boxed
set of *Eugene Onegin* conducted by Rostropovich; Vaughan
Williams's *Tallis Fantasia*, conducted by Karajan; Britten's own
Young Person's Guide with the spoken commentary in Arabic;
and a copy of *A Hard Day's Night* by the Beatles.

Round Britten Quiz IV

ANSWERS ON PAGE 411

1 At Sunday lunch at The Red House, what usually came after roast beef?
2 Which two Britten operas refer to sherry?
3 At the age of twenty-two, what did Britten regard as one of the most thrilling stories ever, adding that it was good to be able to get such a thrill at his age?
4 Why did Josef Krips withdraw as conductor of the premiere of *Billy Budd*?
5 Just before he turned fifteen, who did Britten say had risen one place in his list of composers, to 'either second or third'?
6 What costume did Britten wear at the 1950 fancy dress ball to raise funds for the English Opera Group?

PART FIVE
The music of Britten

The full works

Britten was an incredibly fast worker. He wrote most of his pieces in his head first, and only later came the laborious task of writing them down. He was rather proud of his progress with his two-and-a-half-hour opera *A Midsummer Night's Dream*. He said it took him 'seven months for everything, including the score. This is not up to the speed of Mozart or Verdi, but these days, when the line of musical language is broken, it is much rarer. It is the fastest of any big opera I have written.'

His total output amounts to some seventy-five hours of music (and counting, because more and more of his manuscripts are being unearthed and published). Its range and variety is impressive: each piece is distinct and different. There are very few potboilers here: you hardly ever feel he is on auto-pilot.

Opera dominated the last thirty years of his composing life. But from the first twenty there was a good deal of chamber music, and music for film and radio. Threaded through it all is a feast of songs which, with his intuitive understanding of the music of language, is a Britten hallmark. He was inspired throughout by individual artistry, whether the cello of Rostropovich, the soprano of Sophie Wyss, the violin of Toni Brosa, the harp of Osian Ellis, the percussion of James Blades – or the tenor of Peter Pears. And he was captivated by the energy and potential of children.

I have been presumptuous – and foolhardy – enough to grade Britten's music, purely on the basis of the pieces I most value and enjoy. The top ranking, as with the best hotels, is *****. Some pieces don't merit a star, but are still worth highlighting. His folksong arrangements are not graded in this way.

I have also pointed up with a key-sign (𝄞) particular short pieces or movements which those looking for a key to unlock the mysteries of Britten's music are recommended to explore. In truth, there are many more key moments than those marked, because Britten was never ashamed of making his music accessible.

I have listed recordings that are particularly worth having, but the selection is far from exhaustive. New Britten recordings are constantly being added to the catalogue. Older recordings disappear without warning, while others just as suddenly reappear. So I have chosen only those discs available at the time of writing. Both Decca and EMI offer bargains for those preferring the 'big bang' approach to building a CD library. Decca's CDs work out at five or six pounds each, EMI's at two or three.

R 'Britten conducts Britten'
Decca 475 6020/6029/6040/6051: 35 CDs in four volumes, featuring thirty-seven works (including all the operas) that Britten either conducted or accompanied, plus one or two extras conducted by other people.

R 'Benjamin Britten: The Collector's Edition'
EMI 217 5262: 37 CDs, featuring more than a hundred different works, large and small, performed by artists other than Britten.

Symphonies and concertos

Britten only ever completed one 'proper' symphony – a massive work in D minor (with eight French horns!) which has never yet been heard. He was thirteen at the time, his favourite age. Later he was perhaps put off by all the symphonies written by British composers for whom he had little time – Elgar, Vaughan Williams and Bax, let alone Parry and Stanford. His mentor Frank Bridge never felt the symphonic urge, and in Britten's eyes Bridge could do no wrong. However Britten did use some form of the title on five occasions, whether for chamber, choral or concertante pieces. So those are included here, as are other orchestral works featuring solo instruments – alongside the 'proper' concertos he composed.

Double Concerto ** 1932

In this astonishing score Britten's true orchestral personality flowers for the first time. Four years earlier his *Quatre chansons françaises* had put the green shoots of fluency and sensibility on vivid display; in his 1931 ballet *Plymouth Town* the Britten buds had formed. But in this concerto for violin and viola we meet the mature Britten as a youth of eighteen.

He had learnt the viola part of Mozart's *Sinfonia Concertante* for the same two soloists, which was a lifelong favourite of his. He had had the miniature score the previous Christmas, and two months later heard it in a concert which he described as 'the most marvellous musical thrill of my life yet'. So Mozart was probably this concerto's godfather. Britten supplemented Mozart's orchestra with flutes, clarinets, bassoons, trumpets and timpani, and allowed himself his favourite percussion extravagance of this period, a suspended cymbal.

He never wrote out the full score, because he was diverted by what he regarded as a more ambitious work, his *Sinfonietta*. So the concerto's first performance in 1997 was derived from the (very detailed) compositional sketch in his archives. Its brisk opening leads into a rhapsodic slow movement, while the final tarantella (a favourite form of his at this time) is the longest movement of the three. The way he ends the work – in pensive, rather than hectic, mood – is both surprising and effective.

R   Kremer, Bashmet, Hallé/Nagano, recorded 1998
Warner Classics 25646 94521 (with *Young Apollo*, *Sinfonietta*, *Two Portraits*)

Sinfonietta, op. 1 *   1932

Britten numbered this work as his opus 1 presumably because he was proud of it: he regarded it as the first piece of his maturity, the fruit of his recent interest in Schoenberg. He wrote its three linked movements in three weeks during his second summer at the Royal College of Music. Large or small, it's not really a symphony at all, despite the use of sonata form in the first movement. The instrumental line-up (a string quintet and a wind quintet) formed the template for all Britten's chamber operas, with the addition of harp, percussion and piano, until the Church Parables in the 1960s.

Apart from his *Phantasy* string quintet, the *Sinfonietta* was the only piece of his rehearsed at the RCM during his three years there, and even that was pain and grief for him. His contemporary, the oboist Evelyn Rothwell, told me how short-tempered he was in rehearsal, not least because the same players rarely turned up for two rehearsals running, and on each occasion they were usually two or three instruments short. This rankled: many years later Britten bumped into the bassoonist from that student ensemble, and the temperature dropped ten degrees.

It is indeed a remarkably assured piece for an eighteen-year-old, but austere too. Only the hectic tarantella of the third movement tickles the palate, and smells like vintage Britten.

R   Nash Ensemble/Friend, recorded 1995
Hyperion CDA 66845 (with *Phaedra, Lachrymae* etc.)

R   Hallé/Nagano, recorded 1998
Warner Classics 25646 94521 (with *Young Apollo, Double Concerto, Two Portraits*). Nagano records the version for small orchestra, in which Britten added a second horn part: the presence of full strings, rather than a string quintet, leads to a softening of the work's astringency, but also of its potency.

Simple Symphony, op. 4 *   1933–4

Few composers at the age of twenty would resort to recycling their juvenilia, but Britten was unabashed. His childhood was always so important to him that he seemed to carry it round in a back-pack for most of his life. He certainly stored (and filed) all his early manuscripts, and would occasionally dig them out for fun – as he did for this four-movement symphony. For his raw material, he took eight tunes he had written for piano or voice between the ages of nine and twelve, transposed and arranged them for string orchestra, and signed them 'E. B. Britten' as he'd always done until he was almost fifteen.

Most young composers would have run a mile from their early jottings, but Britten was proud of them: 'not too uninteresting', he said – rather like Elgar turning his childhood ideas into the *Wand of Youth* suites, and giving them phoney opus numbers '1a and 1b'.

It was a good business decision too. *Simple Symphony* has proved the most lucrative of all his early scores for his then publishers, Oxford University Press, because the piece is charming – if musically undemanding – and easily playable by school orchestras. Even today the work provides Britten's estate with about £45,000 a year in royalties.

R   Northern Sinfonia/Hickox, recorded 1987
Resonance CDRSN 3043 (with *Variations on a Theme of
Frank Bridge* and *Prelude and Fugue*)

R   Maggini String Quartet (quartet version), recorded 1998
Naxos 8.554360 (with String Quartet no. 3, *Alla Marcia* etc.)

Piano Concerto, op. 13 **   1938, revised 1945

Late in life, Britten said that he'd been told so often that his
piano and violin concertos were no good that he'd ended
up believing it himself. Now, however, there are nine or ten
recordings available of the Piano Concerto alone. It was written for the Proms, and Britten himself gave the premiere with
Sir Henry Wood conducting the BBC Symphony Orchestra.
The BBC marked the occasion by broadcasting it live on radio
and the nascent television service, though without pictures!

It's a flamboyant piece, with echoes of the piano concertos
by Prokofiev and Ravel. It was a wow with the Proms audience, but Frank Bridge and his friends sat with glum faces.
They felt it was all show and no music, though they didn't
dare say so at the time. They were greatly relieved when the
concert moved on to Dvořák's Eighth symphony – music at
last, and beautifully made, as one of them said. Britten could
not understand all the fuss. He said the concerto was simple
music that one liked or disliked, and there was no need to
hunt for 'meanings and all that rot!'

It is without doubt a crowd-pleaser: the composer Constant
Lambert said it had one 'sterling merit – it is never boring'.
It opens with a Toccata (as Vaughan Williams's concerto had
done seven years earlier, though Britten would not have relished the reminder). It's brash, but rather fun, with a cascade
of notes for the pianist, although the orchestra's quiet entry
at the end of the cadenza adds some Ravelian magic. After
the intermezzo-style Waltz, Britten originally wrote a Recitative and Aria, an ill-fitting mixture of rhapsody and parody. In
1945, perhaps reacting to his friends' criticism, he replaced it

with an ironically named Impromptu, which revolves round a *Romeo and Juliet*-style theme pinched from his *King Arthur* incidental music. Complete with blaring brass and bass drum, the finale marches to a bombastic conclusion guaranteed to bring the house down. But what is wrong, as one critic of the time said, with a young composer 'sowing a few wild notes'?

R Richter, ECO/Britten, recorded 1970
Decca 473 7152 (with Violin Concerto)

R MacGregor, ECO/Bedford (with both third movements), recorded 1990
Naxos 8.557197 (with *Johnson over Jordan* suite)

Young Apollo, op. 16 ** 1939

This fanfare for piano solo, string quartet and string orchestra is unique in Britten's output. Shortly after arriving in North America, he wrote it for himself to perform, which he did twice (on Canadian and New York radio stations), but never again. Throughout its eight minutes it glitters in A major – though with a prominent flattened seventh – and while the piano seems almost high on a torrent of rising scales, the strings thrill in rich Messiaenic harmonies.

Britten said it was inspired by his discovery of 'such sunshine as I've never seen before'. He appended lines about young Apollo from Keats's unfinished poem *Hyperion*, and went on to describe how Apollo, as the new god of beauty, 'stands before us – the new, dazzling Sun-god, quivering with radiant vitality'. The music is a perfect match. What he did not disclose was that his own young Apollo was Wulff Scherchen, the handsome flame he had left behind in England, only to find him hard to extinguish, even after he'd begun his affair with Peter Pears. In its closing bars he asserts the primacy of beauty through an emphatic succession in the strings of twelve A major chords – his insistent tonic – and A major, as he kept demonstrating (with his 'lovely boy' in the *Nocturne*, and with Tadzio in *Death in Venice*) was his essential key for male beauty. Perhaps the withdrawal of the piece was the only way he could close this chapter in his life. Perhaps Pears insisted on it.

R   Osborne, BBC Scottish SO/Volkov, recorded 2008 Hyperion CDA 67625 (with Piano Concerto and *Diversions*)

Violin Concerto, op. 15 **** 1939; revised 1950, 1954, 1965

Britten opens his concerto with conscious homage to that of his hero Beethoven, whose solo drum-beats in the first bar so startled his audience. Britten's drum rhythms then permeate the work – a foil to the intensely lyrical cantilena of the solo violin. For a long time this piece languished on the sidelines: it was seen as gawky and difficult on the ear – heaven knows why. Today the number of available recordings is in double figures.

It is predominantly a Spanish piece, written as it was for Antonio Brosa, whom Britten greatly admired and often partnered in recitals. He persuaded Brosa to follow him from Britain to New York, where he gave the first performance under Barbirolli's baton. Brosa was a refugee from Franco's Spain, and the menace in the work has more to do with the Spanish Civil War (which had so exercised Britten) than the world war that broke out just as he was completing the score. Brosa said the first movement's drum rhythms were Spanish, and it is significant that the final movement is built round a passacaglia, one of the first of many times the mature Britten used this form of ground bass and variations: the passacaglia originated in Spanish dance music.

The concerto is unusual in having a single fast movement sandwiched between two slow ones, instead of the other way round. The violin writing is at first beautiful, and then (in the central scherzo) energetic and exciting with its gypsy inflections, from which the cadenza emerges to take us into the finale. This startles the first-time listener with the belated appearance of the trombones: they announce the solemn tread of the passacaglia, and instead of the normal finale heroics we embark on an extended lament, with the falling lines of the woodwind in counterpoise to the soloist's attempts to rise higher. A plangent climax is reached in D major, but it cannot last, and the orchestra subsides into an uncertain open fifth, while the violin hovers inconclusively between major and minor – a haunting end to a remarkable work.

R Zimmermann, Swedish Radio SO/Honeck, recorded 2008 Sony 88697 439992 (with Szymanowski Violin Concertos)

R Marwood, BBC Scottish SO/Volkov, recorded 2011 Hyperion CDA 67801 (with Double Concerto and *Lachrymae*)

Sinfonia da Requiem, op. 20****   1940

No other Britten masterpiece began life so truly misbegotten. Only a political innocent or a musical ostrich could have accepted, a few weeks into the Second World War, a commission from the Japanese government to celebrate the 2,600th anniversary of the Mikado dynasty. But Britten was in the United States, and perhaps out of touch. He set to work on what he regarded as his '1st Symphony', and began to imagine a visit to Tokyo for the premiere, apparently oblivious of the risk of hostilities breaking out with Japan. He consoled himself with the idea of making his symphony 'just as anti-war as possible'.

The deafening thunderclaps on the timpani at the start (first-time listeners should beware of damage to their speakers or headphones, let alone eardrums, but it is a key Britten moment ♪) reflect the darkening clouds of war which shroud much of the symphony. This is a piece of uncompromising, biting intensity, with little chance of requiem until the comfort of the last movement. It was not music to bring a smile to the Emperor's lips, particularly as its three movements (written in memory of Britten's parents) were given Latin titles from the Catholic Requiem Mass, which spoke of death, wrath and tears. Shortly before Pearl Harbor, the Japanese authorities refused to accept the work, which was probably just as well for Britten's reputation, damaged as it already was by his pacifism. He thought the publicity from the Japanese bridling at a work for being Christian would be 'a wow'. In public, the Japanese were diplomatic: it had arrived, they said, too late for adequate rehearsal. And they never asked for their money back.

Britten had a similar experience many years later when he was asked to write a national anthem for the newly independent Commonwealth state of Malaysia. His score was rejected by its chief minister. But once again the agreed fee (£50 in this case) was paid. Britten asked for the score back. 'After all', he said, 'it might come in handy for some other Eastern nation'. (It was finally performed in 2007 under the title *Sketch for Malaya*.) In the case of the *Sinfonia da Requiem*, the piece came in handy for Barbirolli and the New York Philharmonic, and we have Emperor Hirohito to thank for what is perhaps Britten's greatest orchestral utterance.

R   New Philharmonia Orchestra/Britten, recorded 1964
Decca 425 1002 (with *Cello Symphony*, *Cantata Misericordium*)

R   LSO/Previn, recorded 1973
EMI 562 6152 (with *Four Sea Interludes* and Holst *Egdon Heath* and *The Perfect Fool*)

Diversions, op. 21 **   1940; revised 1950, 1953–4

For a composer who was rather stingy with solo works for his own instrument, the years 1938–41 were positively bountiful. After the Piano Concerto and *Young Apollo*, but before his trio of two-piano works, came this second piano concerto, written for the left hand only. Commissioned by the disabled pianist Paul Wittgenstein, Britten devised it in one of his favourite formats, theme and variations – the fifth of at least twelve works he crafted this way.

Unlike the famous Ravel Concerto for the left hand, Britten chose to create a single line rather than the illusion of two hands. All the same, the illusion persists – which is surely right, as it can then be judged as a musical rather than a technical feat, though the amount of virtuoso display is surprising. These eleven variations deploy some typical Britten ideas – a caustic March, a hypnotic Nocturne – but, after all the brilliant ingenuity, the emotional heart of the piece is the long Adagio which eases us into the whirlwind of the concluding Tarantella.

R   Fleisher, Boston SO/Ozawa, recorded 1992
Sony Classical SK 47188 (with Ravel and Prokofiev concertos for left hand)

Scottish Ballad, op. 26   1941

Thundered out on two grand pianos, the chords of the Scottish tune 'Dundee' (often used for the hymn 'Lord in thy name thy servants plead') are just the first episode in this weird piece for piano duo and orchestra. For a moment, we have entered the world of Vaughan Williams's *The Pilgrim's Progress*, which a decade later was to begin with another loud tune from the Scottish Psalter (in that case, 'York'). But then the might of both Britten's pianos pulls the tune apart, as he begins a long funeral march, into which he threads other Scottish melodies and a pentatonic lament. 'Long' is perhaps not the word: 'eternal' might be better. A short piece it may be, but it does go on. Eventually it slips into a Scottish reel, which cuts a dash – and that is it. The whole piece is quite fun, moment by moment, and Britten enjoyed it enough to tackle the ivories himself twice (with Clifford Curzon) during the war, and to conduct it at Aldeburgh near the end of his life. But why this supreme narrative composer counted it a 'Ballad' I cannot fathom.

R   Donohoe, Fowke, CBSO/Rattle, recorded 1982
EMI 573 9832: *Rattle conducts Britten* (2 CDs, with *Ballad of Heroes*, *Canadian Carnival*, *Diversions* etc.)

Movements for a Clarinet Concerto *   1942;
                                                arr. 1989, 2008
In memoriam Dennis Brain   1958
Rondo Concertante   1930

Three fresh Britten pieces which will have escaped many afi-
cionados are now available on a single recording. In America, Britten heard and admired the jazz clarinettist Benny
Goodman playing the Mozart concerto, but was struck by
his nervousness – with which Britten, as a fellow sufferer,
would have sympathised. Perhaps that lay behind the taut
opening of the clarinet concerto he started writing for him
in 1942. It settles into a languid second idea, before nervous
interjections from the soloist above muted strings suggest
the 'Night' sea interlude he was to write for *Peter Grimes*
two years later.

Britten's sketches for this movement were seized by jittery
customs officers when he set sail for home, and were only
extricated some months later. By then his mind was occu-
pied by *Grimes*, and the moment had passed. But in 1989 his
one-time assistant, the composer Colin Matthews, converted
the sketches into a full score. Now he has built on to that
an enchanting slow movement, effectively an orchestration of
Britten's piano duo piece from 1941, *Mazurka Elegiaca*, and a
finale taken from an untitled sketch of this period (perhaps for
his projected Sonata for Orchestra), with falling sixths in the
clarinet solo and nervous string figures underneath. At one
point there is another presage of *Grimes* – this time of the
scoring of the 'live and let live' refrain. All this is not Britten's
clarinet concerto – that remains a might-have-been – but it is
an attractive addition to the clarinet repertoire, nearly all of it
made from Britten's music of the time.

The young horn virtuoso Dennis Brain had so inspired Britten that his sudden death in a car crash was a bereavement. In
tribute, Britten devised a piece for four horns and orchestra,
but his two brief sketches are incomplete. With echoes of the
Dirge in the *Serenade* for tenor, horn and strings, a tolling

bell prompts urgent, anguished outbursts from the horns. It promises eloquence, but remains a tantalising torso.

The sixteen-year-old music student at one time thought of his unfinished *Rondo Concertante* as a piano concerto. Its opening is electrifying, with the orchestral bows hunting as a pack as they bounce furiously on the string. The piano almost somersaults in, but then these abrasive gymnastics settle incongruously into a quasi-Rachmaninov idyll. The nine-minute slow movement consists almost entirely of steady octaves moving in thirds – on the piano alone for the first three minutes, and then on the strings while the piano offers the occasional chord instead. It's strange stuff, which the teenager (perhaps prompted by his teacher John Ireland) abandoned in mid-flow – but intriguing as a piece of musical archaeology.

R Collins, Thompson, Watkins, Francomb, Griffiths, Hind, Northern Sinfonia/Zehetmair, recorded 2008
NMC NMCD140: 'Unknown Britten' (with *Les Illuminations*, Variations for piano etc.)

Spring Symphony, op. 44 ***** 1948-9

Every time I hear this symphony, it comes up tingling fresh. It is brimful of inventive ideas, many of them unique to this work, and makes the world seem a better place. It is really a large song cycle which Britten roughly modelled on his beloved *Das Lied von der Erde* (Mahler's would-be ninth symphony), but with the larger forces of three solo singers, boys' choir, mixed chorus and orchestra. Its only claim to symphonic status is its four parts (introduction, slow movement, scherzo and finale). But it's bound together by fourteen English poems which shape the season or mood of spring.

The opening gave Britten a lot of trouble in conjuring up the drear cold of winter from which the joys of spring were to emerge. The glacial lines of the chorus with sharply dissonant harmonies, the chattering teeth of the woodwind, and the magical use of the vibraphone to give a sinister, clammy

244   THE MUSIC OF BRITTEN

resonance to the orchestral chords – these combine to suggest
an alien, spooky world of arctic gloom, from which Spenser's
'The merry cuckoo' bursts out with relief: a tenor solo with
a trio of trumpets. Nashe's 'Spring, the sweet spring' features
snatches of birdsong from the soprano, contralto and tenor
soloists, which they take in their own time – an example of
aleatoric music years before Stockhausen or Lutosławski tried
it, and before the term had been coined. (Britten needed his
curlew-sign here, as a way of gathering the songbirds together
again – but he hadn't invented it yet.) After a teasing, whistling duet between soprano and boys' choir (with prominent
tambourine and tuba!), the first section ends with Milton's
'The Morning Star', which bewitches and thrills by turns – a
wonderful piece of choral writing with only brass and percussion, powered by an almost repressed rhythm and ending the
work's first part on a chord of F major which is lanced by a
forward-looking B flat from the altos. This is a movement
which unlocks a door into Britten.

The musician Erwin Stein pointed out that, although the
Spring Symphony was scored for full orchestra, at any one time
Britten employed only the instruments he really needed. The
soft tinkling of woodwind and harps in Herrick's 'Welcome,
maids of honour' gives way to Vaughan's 'Waters above', in
which the tenor has only the violins for company, playing
mostly on the bridge as they hover round the unusual keynote of A sharp. Then comes the only modern poem, and the
last setting he ever made of Auden's words. 'Out on the lawn'
begins with the lazy haze of an early summer evening, into
which the developing pain of Poland in 1939 makes an unwel-
come intrusion – an edgy end to the 'slow movement'.

The 'scherzo' begins with a furious tug of war between lower and upper strings, as the tenor sings 'When will my May
come?', before tenor and soprano chase each other in canon
round Peele's 'Fair and fair' until they are finally caught in
unison. Then the men, women and boys of the chorus compete in separate verses of Blake's 'Sound the Flute', leaving the
orchestra to sprint to the finish in triumph.

The finale is an extended extract (the speech of the May-lord) from Beaumont and Fletcher's *The Knight of the Burning Pestle*. You might think it was time for Britten to pull things together and tie up some loose ends. Not a bit of it: this exhil-arating romp of a morris dance lacks nothing in fresh inven-tion, reckless momentum and sheer physical dash. It begins with a summons by cowhorn, to the same repeated appoggiat-ura as Claggart would use to call 'your name!' in *Billy Budd* two years later. Then it launches into the absurdly rubicund verse – but a composer who had managed to navigate Auden's word games in the *Paul Bunyan* libretto didn't blink at setting 'Fly Venus and phlebotomy'. In fact you can almost hear him giggle as he turns it into a long-jump challenge for the boys' choir, with two octave-leaps. Eventually words fail, with the company swaying increasingly drunkenly to a wordless waltz, until the boys (supported by the horns) ride heroically to the rescue by pounding out the thirteenth-century tune 'Sumer is i-cumen in'. It all fits perfectly. Indeed it's the crowning moment – in C major (Britten's key for roast beef and sher-ry trifle) – and always takes the breath away. This is sheer bravura, easy to mock, but unique and unafraid.

R   Armstrong, Baker, Tear, St Clement Dane's Choir, LSO and Chorus/Previn, recorded 1978
EMI 764 7362 (with *Four Sea Interludes* from *Peter Grimes*)

Cello Symphony, op. 68 ****   1962–3; revised 1964

Shortly after completing his *War Requiem*, Britten received a letter from his new Russian friend, the cellist Mstislav Ros-tropovich, asking him for a concerto. Britten responded with enthusiasm, and embarked initially on a 'Sinfonia Concer-tante', which then mutated into a Symphony for Cello and Orchestra, in recognition of the soloist's role as the orchestra's partner rather than competitor. It was Britten's first orchestral work to be based on sonata principles since his *Sinfonia da Requiem* almost twenty-five years before.

For years I found it hard to get under the skin of this remarkable piece, but perseverance brings its reward. With the opening flourishes on the cello set against a dark bass texture in the orchestra – from the tuba, contrabassoon and double basses – the complexity of Britten's musical palette is revealed. As with the bass sonorities in *Billy Budd* or the treble sound world of *The Turn of the Screw* or *A Midsummer Night's Dream*, Britten explores contrast between different shades of the same colour, rather than between different colours.

The violence of the first movement is succeeded by a short, scurrying scherzo, before the eloquent Adagio, dominated by the timpani. But most striking of all is the concluding Passacaglia, which the trumpet opens in a cheerful D major. For once this is not a lament, but a high-spirited finale in tune with the ebullient character of its original soloist.

R   Rostropovich, ECO/Britten, recorded 1964
Decca 425 1002 (with *Sinfonia da Requiem* and *Cantata Misericordium*)

R   Watkins, BBC Philharmonic/Gardner, recorded 2010
Chandos CHAN 10658 (with *Gloriana Suite* etc.)

Lachrymae (orchestral version), op. 48a ***   1976

In the last year of his life Britten again took up the poignant viola piece he'd written twenty-five years before: a set of ten variations (or 'reflections', as he had called them) on a song by the Elizabethan composer, John Dowland. The 1950 version had been for viola and piano (see chapter 32, 'Solo instrumental music'): this time he rewrote the accompaniment for string orchestra – but without the first violins. As a viola player himself, he wanted to avoid them swamping the solo part, used as they are to soaring away on the top line.

The switch from piano to strings makes it sound a different piece. The six piano chords in the second variation, for instance, become six ethereally sustained comments in the orchestra. The third variation is a Venetian nocturne, and the original viola harmonics in the ninth are extended into the orchestra to create an other-worldly slow movement before the gripping drive to the finish in the final variation. This, with the slow tread in the bass, subsides inevitably into Dowland's full melody and harmonies for *If my complaints could passions move*. This is an apt summation of a piece which, in the strings version, has a wistful tenderness that the more abrasive character of the viola-and-piano original cannot reach.

R Power, BBC Scottish SO/Volkov, recorded 2011
Hyperion CDA 67801 (with Violin and Double Concertos)

R Chase, Nash Ensemble/Friend, recorded 1995
Hyperion CDA 66845 (with *Phaedra* etc.)

Other orchestral works

Britten's use of the full orchestra was fastidious and distinctive. He was determined to avoid what he regarded as the hectic, exciting 'gestures' in some Beethoven, the thickness of Brahms's orchestral textures, or the amateurishness of Vaughan Williams's orchestration. 'I don't want to use the orchestra as it's normally constituted', he said in 1964. That particular kind of sound 'became the bread and butter of the 19th century. It isn't *my* bread and butter.'

Lennox Berkeley often used to marvel at how precisely and economically Britten voiced orchestral instruments. He would open a Britten score and point out how naked it looked. 'How could so few notes possibly register?' he would say. But because those that were there were so precisely placed, in terms of both the natural tessitura of the instrument and the architecture of the score, 'they always sound utterly right'. That chimes in with what Britten himself said: 'All that is important is that the composer should make his music sound inevitable and right'.

Two Portraits [originally **Sketches nos. 1 and 2**]** 1930
His schoolfriend David Layton probably never knew at the time that Britten had captured him in a nine-minute movement for strings. But this first *Sketch* is more than its title. It's a keenly felt, intricately moulded portrait, highly chromatic and full of energy, as befitted his tennis and cricket nets partner. Towards its end, the tempo slows and romantic Mahlerian textures emerge, replete with falling ninths, although Britten was writing a month before his first hearing of Mahler. Then the vigorous opening idea returns, but set this time above a faint C major chord. The second *Sketch* was

of Britten himself, represented by his own instrument, the viola, which spins a sad, solitary melody above the rest. If only the real Britten had been that simple!

R   Hallé/Nagano, recorded 1998
Warner Classics 25646 94521 (with *Young Apollo*, *Sinfonietta*, *Double Concerto*)

Russian Funeral or *War and Death* *   1936

This short funeral march for brass, drums and cymbal is based on a Soviet revolutionary theme which Shostakovich also used in his Eleventh symphony. Its grim progress belongs more to Mahler than Shostakovich, however, particularly at the climax of its seven minutes. One of the high-water marks of Britten's communist sympathies as a twenty-two-year-old (and superior to his 1936–7 *Pacifist March*), it was first conducted by the overtly communist composer, Alan Bush – and perhaps prompted the fascinating exchange of letters later that year, in which Britten confessed his penchant for Mahler. It was first performed as *War and Death, An Impression for Brass Orchestra*. Faber Music changed the title when it was finally published in 1981.

R   London Collegiate Brass/Stobart, recorded 1986
CRD 3444 (with brass works by Walton, Tippett and Ireland)

Soirées Musicales, op. 9   1936
Rossini Suite **   1935
Matinées Musicales, op. 24 *   1941

From early on, Britten always knew how to turn an honest penny, and his orchestration of Rossini melodies as *Soirées Musicales* was a shrewd move. It was first played on radio, and repeated regularly, and Henry Wood conducted it at the 1937 Proms – so it became something of a popular classic. The idea came from the Brazilian film producer Alberto Cavalcanti, who first signed Britten up at the GPO Film Unit. For *The Tocher*, a film about the Post Office Savings Bank, Cavalcanti suggested Britten use some Rossini tunes. The result was the *Rossini Suite*, which set two melodies from the opera *William Tell*, and three from Rossini's collection of songs and duets, 'Soirées Musicales', with which both Liszt and Respighi had also dabbled. At Britten's disposal were three wind players (flute, oboe and clarinet), two percussionists and a pianist (himself presumably).

Five months later, he rescored three of these tunes for full orchestra, added two more, and then assigned the new work its own opus number. With full brass and strings, let alone a percussion section that really lets rip, it feels coarser than the simple *Rossini Suite* which gave it birth. The fastidiousness hadn't yet set in.

The *Suite*'s raw originality makes it attractive and different. It could almost be one of Stravinsky's ventures into musical history, but for the addition of a boys' choir in two movements. The way Britten underscores the boys' wordless melody with occasional notes on the glockenspiel, his deft use of tambourine and xylophone, his shrewd understatement of the melody – all this seems more characteristic than the showier orchestral work. With a recent recording, the *Suite* has at last been released from its long incarceration in the poor-quality soundtrack of the original film.

Almost five years later he supplemented the orchestral work with five more Rossini numbers, to make a short ballet *Divertimento* for the American Ballet Company. The resulting *Matinées Musicales* are less inflated (and less well known) and he gives himself a freer hand in the transcriptions, notably in the high jinks of the concluding *moto perpetuo*.

R   *Soirées Musicales* and *Matinées Musicales*: National Philharmonic/Bonynge, recorded 1981
Decca 425 6592 (with *Young Person's Guide* and *Four Sea Interludes* conducted by Britten)

R   *Rossini Suite* (*The Tocher*): Birmingham Contemporary Music Group/Brabbins, recorded 2006

NMC NMCD 112: 'Britten on Film' (with *Night Mail* and *Coal Face* etc.)

Variations on a Theme of Frank Bridge, op. 10**** 1937

The massive plucked chord that opens these variations is an assertive declaration. 'I've arrived!', Britten seems to be saying – not just as a British composer, but on the European stage.

The conductor Boyd Neel had a problem when his crack string orchestra was invited to the 1937 Salzburg Festival on condition that it brought with it a new British work for strings. (Such was Salzburg in 1937!) Time was short: the concert was booked for August, and it was already May. But Neel knew whom to ask. He'd been highly impressed the previous year by the speed at which the young Britten scored the film *Love from a Stranger*. This time the composer turned up on his doorstep within a week with a completed sketch of a twenty-minute work! The full score took a further month, but there were still six weeks in hand. Even now there are one or two musicians alive who played in that premiere, and remember the tousle-haired composer tweaking the score as he heard it in rehearsal. It made a great impact at the time (much more so in Salzburg than later in London), perhaps because Britten seemed to be affirming his bond with the international heritage of Bartók, Mahler and Stravinsky, as well as his debt to the English composer who had embraced European modernism, Frank Bridge.

The *Variations* begin with the theme, played 'with tenderness' and taken from Bridge's second *Idyll* for string quartet. Britten at one stage wanted his ten variations to illustrate different aspects of Bridge's character, but his one-time teacher dissuaded him, so the movements stand on their own musical feet. Britten finds rich variety in his palette of string tone and texture: the fierce, short March ('his energy') switches to a nostalgic Romance ('his charm' – perhaps a nod to the concerts of light music that Bridge used to conduct), followed by an absurd Aria Italiana ('his humour'), where most of the orchestra furiously thrum their instruments as if they were guitars, a brisk neo-classical Bourrée, an affectionate paro-dy of the Viennese waltz (Bridge and Britten both enjoyed Johann Strauss), and then an impassioned Funeral March, the longest variation, where the lower strings take one of the ideas in the theme (a falling fifth) and turn it into the drum-beats of the cortège. This is followed by 'Chant', where the fragments of melody on the violas (the instrument of both Bridge and Britten) are set in relief against high, sustained harmonics on the violins.

When the eleven-part fugue begins with an angular, jag-ged subject, we may think (with the benefit of *Young Person's Guide* hindsight) that we know where Britten is going. But he takes a quite different turn. The fugue moves offstage, as it were, to allow a solo quartet to take over with a long, flowing melody – the most heartfelt expression in the piece, where the ghost of Elgar seems to hover, perhaps out of respect for his mastery of string textures in the *Introduction and Allegro*. But it was Bridge who took centre stage in Britten's mind, even if in no one else's. Indeed it was only decades later that anyone spotted the further homage Britten paid him in the finale. There were quotations from five other Bridge works: *The Sea* and *Enter Spring* (both of which Britten had heard in Norwich as a young boy), *Summer*, his piano trio, and *There is a willow grows aslant a brook* (which Britten had once arranged for viola and piano). This homage remained a secret between them. Bridge acknowledged it in his note of thanks (a touch Elgarian in its self-pity): 'It is one of the few lovely things that has ever happened to me'.

R   LPO/Jurowski, recorded 2008
LPO 0037 (with *Double Concerto* and *Les Illuminations*)

R   Northern Sinfonia/Hickox, recorded 1987
Resonance CDRSN 3043 (with *Simple Symphony* and *Prelude and Fugue*)

Mont Juic, op. 12*   1937

The composer Lennox Berkeley struck up a friendship with
Britten at the contemporary music festival in Barcelona in
spring 1936. It led on their return to this joint composition
– a suite of Catalan dances, named after the hill where they
first encountered them and scribbled the notes down on the
backs of envelopes. Berkeley later told his son Michael how
impressed he was by Britten's 'Mozartian dexterity in getting
instantly every nuance and decoration down on paper in such
a way that, back in England, it came bouncing back off the
page full of life and expression'. Broadly speaking, the first
two numbers are by Berkeley, the latter two by Britten. As
the slow movement, Britten wrote an impressive Lament in
C minor, to mark the Spanish Civil War which broke out
soon after their visit – but also, perhaps, to commemorate
their mutual friend Peter Burra, who died in an air crash just
after this work was begun. The tearaway finale is a typically
virtuosic piece of Britten orchestration.

R   ECO/Bedford, recorded 1989
Naxos 8.557198 (with *Canadian Carnival* and Violin Concerto)

Canadian Carnival (Kermesse Canadienne), op. 19** 1939
An American Overture   1941
Occasional Overture, op. 38   1946

No sooner had Britten arrived in Canada in May 1939 than he
began to respond to the wide open spaces of the North American landscape. They were a metaphor for the new artistic
and emotional horizons he was seeking. *Canadian Carnival* is
a one-movement suite, based on French Canadian folksongs,
which he wrote after the Violin Concerto and in tandem with
Sinfonia da Requiem. It opens with a dawn haze on suspended
cymbals, over which a set of characteristic rising B flat triads
emerge on offstage solo trumpet, soon to be joined by sustained high violins. The second section features scalic scurrying by the strings, with some teasing bitonality, while the

succeeding slow waltz (marked *Andante amoroso*) is almost a lazy lullaby, revelling in its expansiveness. A disquieting passage in the strings leads to the final section, based on '*Alouette, gentille alouette*', the well known folksong in which the rather jaunty tune clothes the (to English ears) gruesome words about plucking a dead skylark. Britten's adaptation emphasises the grotesquerie on brass and xylophone, before the opening arpeggios return on trombones as well as trumpets.

Despite its transatlantic genesis, the piece was first heard only on wartime British radio – a sort of postcard home – and not in concert until Britten conducted it in Cheltenham in 1945, just six days after the tumultuous premiere of *Peter Grimes*.

Even before reaching the USA, Britten was excitedly saying he was into his 'American period, and nothing can stop me'. Two years later he had so absorbed the culture ('enterprising and vital', he said) that he wrote an American overture bursting with Bernstein-like buoyancy. For some reason it was never performed, and meant so little to him that years later he had no memory of it, and had to be shown the manuscript and admit to his own handwriting. It's a vibrant, enjoyable piece, as is his later (and rather more English) *Occasional Overture* in C major, laden with trills to launch the BBC's Third Programme. Soon after, he withdrew the piece. This time he remembered it, but evidently not with pleasure.

R Warren, CBSO/Rattle, recorded 1982
EMI 573 9832: 'Rattle conducts Britten' (2 CDs, with *Sinfonia da Requiem*, *Young Apollo* etc.)

Prelude and Fugue, op. 29**   1942

This string orchestra piece has always lain in the shadow of the Frank Bridge Variations. Yet it is a remarkable work, written once again for Boyd Neel's band, this time celebrating its tenth anniversary. It was wartime, so the orchestra was dispersed, but Britten wrote expressly for the eighteen players who could make it to the celebratory concert – indeed, in the

fugue each of them has a separate part. Its predominant tonality is E major, yet the flattened seventh of D natural provides
tension in the bass, and fights G sharp in the violins – making an augmented eleventh, the unsettling tritone. It was the
first work on which Britten embarked after arriving home
from his three years in America, and it seems far larger than
its eight-minute duration or reduced instrumentation suggests. It's a much darker-hued piece than the glad, confident
morning of the *Variations*. Once again the fugue resolves into
slow arpeggiated triads, with a Mahlerian ambiguity between
minor and major.

R   Festival Strings Lucerne/Fiedler, recorded 2007
Oehms OC723 (with *Variations on a Theme of Frank Bridge*
and *Simple Symphony*)

Four Sea Interludes from *Peter Grimes*, op. 33a*****   1945
Passacaglia from *Peter Grimes*, op. 33b*****   1945

It says a lot for Britten's business sense that he was adept
(and why not?) at extracting snippets from his operas and
publishing them separately: seven vocal or choral moments
from *Peter Grimes* were proliferated in this way. The much
more substantial suite he crafted from its orchestral interludes needs no singers, yet captures the essence of the opera
– indeed it has become even more popular and famous than
the opera itself.

It is a miracle of orchestration and rhythm that through
Britten's music we can hear the drag of the retreating waves
on the shingle of the Aldeburgh beach, or see the glints of
light on a completely flat North Sea at night. If you're a
newcomer to Britten, there is nowhere better to begin than
here ☞ , but the *Sea Interludes* are not cheap cuts. You will
find they haunt you for the rest of your life.

Much less well known is the extraordinary Passacaglia which
forms the fourth interlude in the opera, to cover the journey
of the rancorous male townsfolk to Peter Grimes's hut. This is

'another marvel', as Britten builds layer upon layer of unease, through a long cantilena on the cellos, the sinister jauntiness of the woodwind, the barking brass, the anguished violins – and all the time the ground bass beats away ominously on the timpani. The climax subsides into the chilling sound of the celesta tinkling away beneath a high melody on the cellos – a foretaste of the developing tragedy on the clifftop. Another key to Britten ♪→, without question.

R Ulster Orchestra/Handley, recorded 1986
Chandos CHAN 10426X: 'Works of the Sea' (with works by Bax, Bridge and Stanford)

The Young Person's Guide to the Orchestra, op. 34 **** 1945

Britten's signature piece was written for an educational film, *Instruments of the Orchestra*, hard though it is today to imagine public money being assigned to such a project. The music was first heard in concert in Liverpool, conducted by Malcolm Sargent, six weeks before the film premiere in London at the Empire Theatre, Leicester Square. The whole concept fitted Britten like a glove. Eight years later he took great delight in explaining it to his twelve-year-old friend David Hemmings. Take a tune by (his beloved) Purcell, toss it round the orchestra to introduce the different sections (wind, brass, strings, percussion), and then let each instrument play a short variation on the tune (with chamber accompaniment from one or two others). Cue chirpy flutes, plaintive oboes, and then duetting clarinets with playful arpeggios, and marching bassoons. The strings race in, section by section (not forgetting the nimble double basses), then horns, harp, galloping trumpets, stately trombones and tuba, followed by ten or eleven different percussion instruments, culminating in a gong and three strokes of the whip. Whereupon the circus comes round again, in the same order but this time with a most elaborate tearaway fugue (thanks to his former teacher, John Ireland, who kept his nose to the counterpoint grindstone). Just when things couldn't get any better, Purcell's grand theme (from his music for *Abdelazer*) sounds out fortissimo on the trombones, crowning the fugue (still beavering away) in a quite different time-signature – but it all locks together perfectly. 'That's the champagne moment!', David Hemmings once told me. 'F---ing great!' Indeed it is 𝅘𝅥𝅮➔.

R   Everage, Melbourne SO/Lanchbery, recorded 1998
Naxos 8.554170 (with works by Poulenc and Prokofiev)
But if you prefer not to have Dame Edna as compere, or indeed any compere at all, try:

R   Bergen Philharmonic/Järvi, recorded 1988
BIS/Conifer BISCD 420 (with *Cello Symphony* and Pärt's *Cantus in memoriam Benjamin Britten*)

Symphonic Suite 'Gloriana', op. 53a*   1953
Variation on an Elizabethan Theme   1953

Compiling a concert suite from an opera is harder than it sounds. Composers must dispense not only with voices, but with most of the intricate psychological drama that is fundamental to opera. Instead they have to pull out the plums. The *Four Sea Interludes* from *Peter Grimes* were almost an off-the-peg fit: all Britten had to do was reorder them and tweak the ending. With *Gloriana*, he worked with his evocations of the Tudor period, and was not so successful. The suite opens with the jousting tournament, and moves on to the chordal hymn to the Queen, 'Green leaves are we', in which he typically makes a five-in-a-bar melody seem the most natural thing in the sixteenth-century world. The slow movement of the suite features one of the opera's greatest moments, the dreamy lute song 'Happy were he', where the tenor voice of the Earl of Essex can be replaced by an oboe: this returns in the finale, from the last scene of the opera. But the suite collapses in the third movement, itself a suite of five dances. Both shape and pace are lost as it meanders on for about ten minutes. It might have been more effective

to rework the burlesque duet for soprano and tuba from the
third scene of Act II.

The *Variation* is another offshoot of *Gloriana*. To mark the
Coronation at the 1953 Aldeburgh Festival, Britten asked five
leading composers to write a short variation for strings on a
popular dance from Gloriana's time, 'Sellenger's Round' – and
contributed a sixth himself, in which he also quotes a theme
from the opera.

R   Murray, BBC Philharmonic/Gardner, recorded 2010
Chandos CHAN 10658 (with Cello Symphony etc.)

Suite on English Folk Tunes: 'A time there was . . . ', op. 90 **
1966, 1974

If there was any concern that Britten's physical debility after
his heart operation would impair either his facility or his
response as a composer, this suite confounded it. The ribald
vigour of 'Cakes and Ale' sets the pace – the first of five movements, in which he reworks ten traditional songs and dances.
The abrasive centrepiece for wind and drums, 'Hankin Boo-
by', was the first-born: it had been written for the opening of
the Queen Elizabeth Hall in 1967. Now Britten provided it
with some siblings: racing strings in 'Hunt the Squirrel' and
an unusually pastoral number, 'The Bitter Withy'. Only the
finale, 'Lord Melbourne', betrays Britten's infirmity. In earlier
years he might have ended the work with a triumphant flourish; instead it fades away in melancholy, as the wise and wistful sound of the cor anglais takes a longer view of life, in the
spirit of the Hardy poem 'Before life and after' which provides
the suite with its subtitle and harks back to Britten's favourite
song cycle *Winter Words*.

R   Bournemouth SO/Hickox, recorded 1993
Chandos CHAN 9221 (with *Young Person's Guide*, *Four Sea
Interludes* etc.)

Choral music

Of all the music Britten wrote, it is probably his choral work that has connected with the greatest number of people – in the sense that anyone who sings will probably have taken part in at least one of the works listed in this section. School choirs, church choirs, village choirs, choral societies – he was always alive to the importance of children and amateurs in music-making. That doesn't mean it's always easy: his choral variations *A Boy was Born* comprise one of the toughest pieces in the choral repertoire. He never stopped writing for choirs – from the very first work he had published, *Three Two-part Songs*, to the last piece he wrote, *Welcome Ode*.

Friday Afternoons, op. 7*	1933–5
Three Two-part Songs: 'The Ride-by-nights',	1932
'The Rainbow', 'The Ship of Rio'	
Fancie *	1961; revised 1965
A Wealden Trio: The Song of the Women	1929–30; rev. 1967
The Oxen	1967
The Sycamore Tree *	1930; revised 1934 and 1967

The short, predominantly unison, songs for children's voices and piano, *Friday Afternoons*, were written over an eighteen-month period just after Britten had graduated from the Royal College of Music. For such a speedy and prolific composer, this was a surprisingly long gestation. The first four songs were tossed off in a fortnight, and they fizz with striking ideas to make them fun for children to perform. Then came the best of the lot, 'Old Abram Brown', a funeral march in four-part canon. But he struggled to complete the set, and the later songs have a bland inconsequence which dilutes the impact of the others – though Britten was shrewd enough to minimise this by interspersing them among the earlier songs.

His three two-part settings of Walter de la Mare are entertaining exercises in canon, a musical form that fascinated Britten, with his mathematical mind, all his life. *Fancie* is a gem of a unison song, with a lively piano part. It lasts just under a minute, and sets words from *The Merchant of Venice* ('Tell me, where is fancy bred?') which Poulenc and Kodály also set at the same time. The first two subsequent carols have a rare specification in Britten: they are for women's voices alone. The third is his own setting of 'I saw three ships': not quite the famous repetitive carol, but five imaginatively crafted verses of distinction.

R   New London Children's Choir/Corp (all except *The Sycamore Tree*), recorded 1994
Naxos 8.553183 (with *A Ceremony of Carols*)
R   *The Sycamore Tree*: The Sixteen/Christophers, recorded 1992
Coro COR 16034 (with *A Boy Was Born*, *Missa Brevis* etc.)

Two Part-songs: 'I lov'd a lass' and 'Lift Boy' *   1932–3
Philip's Breeches **   1936
May   1934
Am stram gram   1954

The part-songs were originally published under the alluring title *Two Antithetical Part-Songs*. They are for four-part mixed chorus and piano. 'Lift Boy', a practical-joke poem by Robert Graves, brings out Britten's ever-ready fifth-form humour, particularly with the plunging sevenths as the lift apparently crashes down the shaft, and the sung laughter that follows. His sympathy with the larky lad in confronting a pompous adult passenger is immediate – one of the earliest of Britten's children.

In *Philip's Breeches* we meet another. Charles Lamb's Victorian poem to mark the moment a small boy graduates to long trousers was a perfect fit for Britten. It seemed to provoke

him into another energetic, light-footed setting – a witty yet
tender treatment of 'my little mannikin'. The strange thing is
that Britten actually wrote the music first, and only six months
later, on New Year's Eve, found the right words to put to it.
With Britten, that is no accident – it was he, after all, who
believed that Schubert wrote his famous 'Trout' melody (in
the song and piano quintet) only after he had already devised
the accompaniment. *Philip's Breeches* is a delightful piece from
his early maturity which has not yet been performed, as far as
I can tell, let alone recorded.

Two years earlier came *May*, which he called 'a part-song
for boys' (though in fact it's in unison throughout), while *Am
stram gram* is a tiny theatrical curiosity in French, which can
be sung in unison with piano, or as a four-part canon.

Ballad of Heroes, op. 14 **   1939
Advance Democracy   1938

Britten himself may have become embarrassed by the rather
unsubtle propagandist tone of some of his work in the 1930s,
when he was in the brief but full flush of youthful radicalism
and rebellion. The three-movement *Ballad*, with large orchestra (triple woodwind and five trumpets for a start), was written for Alan Bush's Festival of Music for the People in April
1939, where Constant Lambert conducted the LSO. It was
for a left-wing audience, but was not a pacifist piece: quite
the opposite. In the poems it set, by Randall Swingler and W.
H. Auden, it honoured British members of the International
Brigade who had volunteered in the Spanish Civil War, which
had just ended. It was overtaken by events – and by the rest of
Britten's life – and had few, if any, outings thereafter.

But it is more than an occasional piece, because of the point-
ers in the music. In shape and tone, it foreshadows the *Sinfonia da Requiem*, which he began writing only six months later.
It also experiments with effects and ideas (like the offstage
fanfares) he was to perfect in the *War Requiem* two decades
on. The second movement, 'Dance of Death', prefigures the

extended battle scene towards the close of the later work. It
is actually a passacaglia, but a frantically furious one – indeed
it is some of the angriest music he ever wrote. 'It's farewell to
the drawing-room's civilised cry' is the apt first line, written
by Auden as he left for Spain himself in 1937. It deserves a
key mark ♮⟶ for the clues it gives to Britten's gift for sheer
violence in music, though you have to hold on tight when the
bass drum is given its head. If Auden's words are to have any
chance, they have to be spat out. Quite how the twelve Co-
operative and Labour Choirs managed it in 1939, when there
were only six days between the work's completion and the premiere, hardly bears thinking about.

In the rather over-ominous Funeral March which opens the
work, they had an easier time. It is all in a unison C minor,
much of it on one note, until a short harmonic flowering in the
closing bars. But the final Choral (like the lullaby that concludes
Sinfonia da Requiem) offers a gentler, though not kinder, landscape. A solo tenor sings a recitative to more Auden, accompanied by grim brass and percussion until they are replaced by
the *a cappella* choir singing Swingler's 'Europe lies in the dark'
in an artful fusion of the texts. 'Pardon them their mistakes',
the choir sings with passion. There is more than a hint here of
Vaughan Williams's *Dona Nobis Pacem*, written a few years earlier, and *Ballad of Heroes* deserves to be rescued from its current
obscurity. I'm not sure I feel the same about the earlier Swingler piece, *Advance Democracy*. Its three unaccompanied minutes have a number of vivid choral moments. But the words are
not for fainthearts – unless, perhaps, they're sung in Russian.

R   *Ballad of Heroes*: Hill, LSO and Chorus/Hickox,
recorded 1991
Chandos CHAN 8983/4 (2 CDs, with *War Requiem* and
Sinfonia da Requiem)

R   *Advance Democracy*: The Sixteen/Christophers, recorded
1992
Coro COR 16038: 'Fen and Meadow' (with *Five Flower
Songs*, *Sacred and Profane* etc.)

*AMDG****   1939

In June 1939 Benjamin Britten and Peter Pears became lovers in the USA, and shortly afterwards Britten began these settings of religious poems by Gerard Manley Hopkins as a gift for Pears to perform with the four-voice Round Table Singers he proposed to found in London. The plan at that stage, once the summer was over, was for Pears to resume his career back in Britain, while the other Britten would stay on in North America for a while. In the event, the war intervened and both stayed on for almost three years. So *AMDG* rather went off the boil, and was never performed in Britten's lifetime. Drafts of its seven part-songs were completed just before war broke out: they were given an opus number (17), but not prepared for publication, so Britten's intended order of the songs is unclear. Since 1984, when the work was released for performance, the seven songs have been given in various sequences. But the Round Table Singers were intended to be a quartet rather than a choir, so it would be good to hear this piece sung that way.

This is vivid choral writing, a worthy successor to *A Boy was Born*. In 'The Soldier' Britten creates a military band from the four voices, while in 'Heaven-Haven' (surely a convincing final movement) the distilled simplicity of the harmony ends with a rapt mention of Britten's beloved sea. The last song to be composed was 'O Deus ego amo te' (My God, I love thee), two days before the Nazi invasion of Poland, and it captures the feverish, almost ecstatic, religious ardour of Hopkins's verse. In 'God's Grandeur', the continual repetition of individual words allows Britten to savour the poem's assonances and rhythms. But the movement deserving the key mark ♦━▸ is 'Rosa Mystica' where, with the almost muttered words over a single-note pedal which lasts almost throughout the song's four minutes, the music enters a trance. If there is such a thing as glossolalia in music, this is it.

Why Britten put the incomplete work aside is unclear. At the end of his life it paid the price by surrendering its opus number to the previously unnumbered operetta *Paul Bunyan* (which was completed almost two years later, and should therefore have been op. 24 – but before being given a number it too was withdrawn). *Bunyan* won Britten's belated favour, while *AMDG* (the abbreviation of the Jesuits' Latin motto, meaning 'To the greater glory of God') was never rescued from his out-tray. Luckily he never tore manuscripts up.

R   London Sinfonietta Chorus/Edwards, recorded 1988 Virgin Classics 7 90728-2 (with *A Boy was Born* and *Hymn to St Cecilia*)

Hymn to St Cecilia, op. 27 *****   1942

It was a happy accident (presumably, although his mother was always ambitious on his behalf) that Britten was born on the feast day of the patron saint of music, and he readily paid his debt later in life by conducting works written for St Cecilia by Handel and Purcell. But before that, in his early twenties, he was looking for suitable words about St Cecilia to set to music himself. The quest ended with a delightful, expansive poem that W. H. Auden wrote for him in New York in 1940–1, which Britten immediately turned into an exquisite miniature for unaccompanied chorus (or, as first envisaged, for vocal quintet).

This is surely the most perfect of all the Auden–Britten collaborations. It was almost strangled at birth, when overzealous customs officials confiscated the score as Britten set sail for England in March 1942. (They no doubt thought the musical hieroglyphics were some sort of code – as indeed they were.) But its vivid memorability ensured that he could write it all out again during the transatlantic voyage home (where equally vigilant officials once again impounded the manuscript!) He responded with extraordinary vitality to Auden's imaginative poems, each concluding with an appeal to St Cecilia to 'startle composing mortals with immortal fire'. She certainly obliged with Britten. The opening magically captures Cecilia as she 'poured forth her song in perfect calm', and Aphrodite as she 'rose up excited'. The words derive extra power from the echoes produced by the two-speed writing which rocks gently between the keys of E major and C major (a typical Britten progression). The breathless canonic scamper through the middle scherzo exemplifies his unmatched skill in really fast music, while the long final threnody in A minor is interrupted tellingly by the 'dear white children casual as birds', who prompt Britten to lapse into his beauty-key, A major, crowned with a soprano solo. This is a piece you never want to end. As it does inevitably subside into a final E major chord spread across three octaves (and, it seems, across the universe), its key mark 𝄞 is unarguable.

R   London Sinfonietta Voices (quintet version), recorded 1988
Virgin Classics 7 90728-2 (with *AMDG* and *A Boy was Born*)

R   Tenebrae/Short (choral version), recorded 2005
Signum SIGCD 085: 'Allegri *Miserere*' (with choral works by Holst, Harris, Rachmaninov, Tavener)

*The Ballad of Little Musgrave and Lady Barnard*****   1943

How did Britten get this wartime score to its intended performers inside a German prisoner-of-war camp? (By posting microfilm, actually, page by page.) And how did those British prisoners then manage to stage a Britten world premiere, let alone put on a symphony concert with a twenty-nine-piece orchestra? More important, how did Britten manage to colour so vividly the almost cinematic narrative of this old ballad, with only a three-part male voice choir and a piano to help him? The prisoners of war found it rather a rum piece – not the simple rollicking part-song they might have imagined – but warmed to it after several performances. It would be hard not to 𝄞. This touching little drama – eight minutes of adulterous love, betrayal, revenge and remorse – is a feast of

invention which encapsulates the emotional power and range
that Britten found in the slenderest of resources.

R   The Sixteen/Christophers, recorded 1992
Coro COR 16038: 'Fen and Meadow' (with Choral Dances
from *Gloriana*, *Sacred and Profane*, *A Wedding Anthem* etc.)

A Shepherd's Carol   1944
Chorale after an Old French Carol**   1944

Both pieces for unaccompanied choir set words Auden originally intended for a huge Christmas oratorio, with the strange
working title 'For the Time Being'. He was keen to launch a
new Auden–Britten collaboration, and a (far too) large libretto was drafted and discussed during the war. But no music was
written and the project foundered, much to Auden's dismay.
Britten did, however, use these two texts for a BBC feature,
The Poet's Christmas. The verses of the first, sung as solos, are
almost folksongs in contemporary language, with a traditional
choral refrain to the words, 'O lift your little pinkie . . .' He
told Pears it would make him smile. The second is a sustained arc of choral virtuosity, which restores the hymn tune
'Picardy' ('Let all mortal flesh keep silence') to its origins as a
French carol. In the second verse, the parts move at different
speeds, producing a kaleidoscope of glistening sound. It is a
special piece 🔑 for choirs that can manage it.

R   *Chorale after an Old French Carol*: Polyphony/Layton,
recorded 2000
Hyperion CDA 67140 (with *Five Flower Songs*, *AMDG* etc.)

Saint Nicolas, op. 42 ***   1947–8

He called it a cantata, and indeed *Saint Nicolas* (Britten's
account of the original Santa Claus, the fourth-century
bishop of Myra) often brings Bach to mind, with its chorales,
the impassioned aria that Britten writes for Nicolas's advice to
his flock from prison, and the audience/congregation partici-

pation in well-known hymns which – just as in the Bach Passions – are seamlessly interwoven to articulate the underlying meaning of the narrative. But he also has much more fun than Bach would have done, with the ingenuous fast waltz describing the saint's development from infancy to manhood in 'The Birth of Nicolas'. This catchy tune flips simply between the keys of A and E, and comes off best when sung by young children, as the composer intended. It is interrupted by cries from the boy Nicolas – 'the youngest boy in the choir', Britten said, although when he came to record it, he wisely couldn't resist using David Hemmings's fruity thirteen-year-old treble voice. The movement may strike some as too candied for comfort, but that awkwardness is another key 8→ to Britten.

Today the work is given usually by professionals, but it was actually written for the boys of Lancing College (Pears's old school, with Nicolas as its patron saint). His writing for tenors and basses in the storm scene of the saint's journey to Palestine – a fascinating foretaste of the sailors' choruses in *Billy Budd* – was exactly tailored for sixth-formers who had just come off the football pitches. It doesn't work half as well in the mouths of choral scholars from Oxbridge colleges. Britten, perhaps optimistically, reckoned his string parts could be handled by amateurs (with a string quintet's professional stiffening), and the only other instruments involved are piano, organ and multiple percussion (one player should be professional). With these arrangements *Saint Nicolas* is a precursor of *Noye's Fludde*, the children's opera he wrote a decade later, and the opening of the final movement, 'The Death of Nicolas', brings *Fludde* to mind. The more ecclesiastical writing (when Nicolas becomes a bishop, for example) is rather prosaic, but the final scene, with the tenor's farewell above the plainsong of the Nunc Dimittis, is masterly, leading (inevitably, it feels) to the hymn 'God moves in a mysterious way', in which Britten characteristically avoids the dominant-tonic perfect cadences one expects, and often holds insistently the tonic key.

R   Rolfe Johnson, Briggs, Corydon Singers, ECO/Best, recorded 1988
Helios CDH 55378 (with *Hymn to St Cecilia*)

Five Flower Songs, op. 47 **	1950
Choral Dances from *Gloriana* **	1952–3

The *Flower Songs* were a silver-wedding present for two musical benefactors, both of them great gardeners. Britten's choice of poems, by Robert Herrick, John Clare and George Crabbe, is an admiring floral tribute for an *a cappella* choir – as delightful to sing as to hear. He is never daunted – not even when Crabbe's stinging nettle gets a look in. After the floating idyll of Clare's 'The Evening Primrose', the anonymous 'Ballad of Green Broom' comes bounding in ♪♪ , with the choir imitating the chords on the ballad-singer's lute. The story describes how an old woodcutter forces his lazy son Johnny out of bed to cut a bundle of green broom, only to lose him to a 'lady in full bloom'. When she propositions him, Johnny gives up his new day-job and weds her (his father's reaction is not recorded). As the ballad races to its ebullient conclusion, church bells ring out in Britten's ever-inventive choral writing. What lovelier gift could there be for a silver-wedding couple?

Even though *Gloriana* received a dusty response from the cognoscenti after the Coronation and disappeared from view for almost ten years, Britten adopted his normal (and prudent) practice of publishing a few titbits from it separately. As well as Essex's lute song, and the *Symphonic Suite*, Britten extracted the dances from the masque in Act II, which Queen Bess observes during her royal progress through Norwich, and issued them as six unaccompanied choruses.

Although the pageant's place in the opera was criticised, these Choral Dances are full of Tudor flavour and, at the same time, pure Britten. The first honours the god Time ('a sunburnt and heroic-looking young man', rather than a grim reaper), and Britten's tease is to have the boisterous choral lines working in parallel time-zones, as it were, until they all meet in 'Behold the sower of the seed!' In sharp contrast, the second dance demurely represents Time's wife, Concord: naturally, Britten cannot resist writing the entire piece in concords – no counterpoint, no discords. Then follow dances of tongue-twisting abandon: the rollicking, angular lines of women's voices in 'Sweet flag and cuckoo-flower' seem to be an overspill from the *Five Flower Songs*, yet these are William Plomer's words, freshly minted. They all resolve in the gentle, chorale-like farewell as the Queen goes on her way.

R   Polyphony/Layton, recorded 2000
Hyperion CDA 67140 (with *Sacred and Profane* and *AMDG*)

Cantata Academica, Carmen Basiliense, op. 62 *   1959

In this anniversary piece for Basel University, Britten cocks a snook at musical pedantry, with one of his many variants on the serial composition method of some of his more earnest contemporaries. The twenty-minute cantata opens with toppling brass fanfares and a grand chorale, and he then divides up the eleven further movements between four solo singers, the different sections of the orchestra (including piano) and a four-part chorus. Britten plays with these combinations variously with assurance, but not much enthusiasm. All is sung in vulgate Latin, and the German and English translations provided in the score are expressly forbidden to be used in performance. The eighth movement is marked *Tema seriale* – a tuneful theme which beguiles the ear into disowning its serial origins. It certainly beguiled several young British composers, who took it as the basis of a set of variations they wrote for Britten's fiftieth birthday a few years later. The tenth contains an attractive *canto popolare*, the term Elgar used for a tune emanating from the Italian countryside in *In the South* (a piece that Elgar, like Britten, composed in his head: 'all that was left', he said, 'was the dreary bit of writing it down'). In Britten's case the tune came from tavern tables in the town – just as when Joe went fishing in *Peter Grimes*, or just as the student chorus comes roistering in near the end of this cantata. As a birthday shindig, it's a work that both had and has its moment(s).

The Bitter Withy*   1962

This short work for tenor, boys' choir and piano is even shorter than intended, because Britten never finished it. He thought of it as his fourth Canticle, but abandoned it after realising it was too much of a challenge for the London Boy Singers, for whom it was planned. Its origins are in folksong as a kind of carol, mixing the religious and the secular. But it is really an original Britten work, in the style of The Golden Vanity, and well worth hearing, despite the missing three final verses. Britten returned to this tune for his orchestral Suite on English Folk Tunes in 1974.

R Langridge, Wenhaston Boys' Choir, Norris/Barnett, recorded 1995
Naxos 8.557222: 'Folk Song Arrangements 2' (with songs for voice and harp, etc.)

War Requiem, op. 66*****   1961–2

The early plaudits for the War Requiem turned after a while to complaints that the work was too accessible, the message too obvious, and the music derivative or formulaic. How dare they? This must be the outstanding piece of twentieth-century choral music, in terms of its ability to communicate with, move and shatter the public, way beyond the normal confines of the concert hall. Its premiere in the new Coventry Cathedral, rising out of the wartime ashes of the old, was a news event. The subsequent recording (issued shortly after the Cuba missiles crisis) sold, amazingly, 200,000 copies in a year, and won three Grammy Awards. Its utterance is direct, in that it speaks forcefully to everyone first time round, yet at the same time complex, in the way it allows repeated fresh discoveries.

Britten's stroke of genius was to take the words of the Latin requiem mass, and intersperse the often bitter war poetry of Wilfred Owen. That alone was inspired enough, but he went further: the precise points at which he made the interpolations allowed one text to comment powerfully on the other. So the last trump on judgment day is partnered with the sad bugles in Owen's trenches; the kneeling in contrition (in 'Oro supplex') is countered with the rising 'long black arm' of Owen's 'great gun towering t'ward Heaven'; the dust of earth in the 'Lacrimosa' is intercut with the poet's 'Was it for this the clay grew tall?', and God's promises to Abraham 'and his seed' with the slaughter of 'half the seed of Europe'.

Many commentators have interpreted the structure of the text to mean that the poetry indicts organised religion. But I think Britten is much more concerned to counterpoint private and personal suffering with public and general. He has three separate spaces in this requiem – not two. The first belongs to the individuals, with their intimate experience of war, expressed by Owen's poetry through the tenor and bass soloists and the chamber orchestra (that shattering line about slaying 'half the seed of Europe' is immediately personalised with the words 'one by one'). In the second are the public onlookers – the chorus, the soprano solo, and the full orchestra – seeking (and often failing) to find refuge in the traditional words of the liturgy. The boys' choir and organ occupy the third, somewhere between this world and the next, and therefore offstage, with a reminder of ultimate aspiration, or perhaps of 'a time there was . . .'

The idea that the chorus and orchestra are confident in their wrong-headed piety is repeatedly disputed by the music. From the instability of the opening tritone – that unsettling interval between C and F sharp – accompanied by the tolling of warning bells, to the rudderless prayers of the female chorus in 'Recordare', when they simply sound lost, and the sobbing of the 'Lacrimosa', these onlookers are troubled and uncertain. The way that their opening tritone eventually resolves into a major chord for the arrival of the boys singing

'Te decet hymnus' is significant, as is the way the boys' cheerful plainsong is picked up by the tenor, as he describes the boys saying farewell on their way to war.

There are so many extraordinary passages in this music that it is otiose to list them all. Of course there are many hints of Verdi's great Requiem here, such as the opening mutters of 'Requiem aeternam', the thumps of the 'Dies irae' or the fluttering soprano in 'Tremens factus sum ego': Britten was unabashed by this, and always said how important it was to study how other composers had worked their magic. But the tumult in the crowd before the ecstatic outburst of the 'Sanctus' is a striking Britten invention, as is the poignant reference to his own setting of *Abraham and Isaac* when he comes to Owen's brutal but telling distortion of that Old Testament story. The short 'Agnus Dei' ♪— , to which the tenor adds Owen's heart-rending poem 'At a Calvary near the Ancre', is Britten's supreme achievement here, culminating in one of the most beautiful – and difficult – lines in the lyric tenor repertoire, to the words 'Dona nobis pacem'.

Then follows the last, gruelling, movement. To experience this in concert (whether as singer or listener) is literally terrifying, with everyone inexorably drawn into the bloody battle, and the choir moaning 'Libera me', just as the infantry must have wailed prayers for deliverance as they went over the top. Out of the turmoil, the cordite and smoke, the tenor stumbles down the 'profound dull tunnel' of Owen's signature poem 'Strange Meeting' (rather as, in *Peter Grimes*, the fisherman's mad scene emerges from the tumult of the manhunt). He meets the enemy he killed the day before, and the two combatants find release and reconciliation in death, and a major tonality. The choir adds its benediction with 'In Paradisum', but, as soon as eternal rest is mentioned, the boys – with their uncluttered perception of truth – bring back the tritone, to remind us that such rest can only be unstable and uncertain. It is an inconclusive end to a deeply disturbing piece. It was also the end of a chapter for Britten. Never again did he take such a public stage, never again paint such an enormous canvas. The

War Requiem seems to have exhausted him, and he moved into thinner air, with more transparent textures.

It is far better to encounter this work for the first time in a live performance, rather than on an iPod or CD player. Recordings (and there are many good ones) cannot do justice to the spatial separation of the forces, or the different impacts of the full ensemble and of the chamber orchestra. This is visceral music, demanding a physical response. Encounters with it should be reserved for exceptional occasions.

R   Vishnevskaya, Pears, Fischer-Dieskau, Melos Ensemble, LSO and Chorus, Bach Choir, Highgate School Choir/ Britten, recorded 1963
Decca 475 7511 (2 CDs): included are some out-takes of Britten rehearsing and talking to the performers. He was furious this had been done behind his back, but it is an invaluable part of musical history.

R   Dasch, Taylor, Gerhaher, Festival Ensemble Stuttgart/ Rilling, recorded 2008
Hänssler HAEN 98507 (2 SACDs)

Psalm 150, op. 67*   1962

This is a curiosity – a work that is hard to imagine anyone else writing, least of all just after the *War Requiem*. Faced with the centenary of his old school, South Lodge, by now reincarnated more grandly as Old Buckenham Hall, Britten came up with a setting of the psalm that glorifies all sorts of musical instruments. But it is a piece entirely for children (of relatively ordinary musical ability), and can be played with any instruments that come to hand, and sung by a two- or four-part children's choir. The only things that Britten says are essential are 'a treble instrument, some sort of drum, and a keyboard instrument'. But, he adds, 'the more instruments there are, the merrier'. He clearly is hoping for a recorder or two, a violin, a flute, oboe or clarinet, plus a trumpet, a bass instrument and a cymbal player.

The five-minute piece consists of a simple march in C major, a lively trio section in 7/8 time, a short four-part round, and a reprise of the march. On the way there are some really scrunchy chords, and a great shout on the word 'cymbals'. There is one commercial recording which is crisp and perfect – and completely wrong. It needs to sound a bit raw, like Britten's own recording, in which the side drum and cymbals are rather too enthusiastic. But this is the way the piece works. Just as in his children's opera *Noye's Fludde*, its charm relies on the notes being a little out of tune, and not quite together at times – Britten's take on 'aleatoric' music!

R Boys of Downside School/Britten, recorded 1966
Decca E4363942 (with *A Ceremony of Carols*, *A Boy was Born*)

Cantata Misericordium, op. 69 **   1963

For the centenary of the Red Cross, a musical version of the parable of the Good Samaritan was the perfect choice. But the idea of setting it in Latin was odd. Presumably Britten felt it was a universal language for an international organisation (though surely English laid better claim to that); then again, Stravinsky had set *Oedipus Rex* and *Symphony of Psalms* in Latin, and extolled its virtues as the language of ritual. But here, where the compassionate message of the story is all, Latin seems a barrier, and a strange choice by a composer normally so addicted to the vernacular.

Musically, it is a rewarding and touching piece. He achieves great intimacy in the story by the use of string quartet, offset against the full string orchestra, and with the addition of piano, harp and timpani he is fully equipped for his tale of violence, disdain and consolation. In the aftermath of his heady success with the *War Requiem*, he wrote once again for Pears and Fischer-Dieskau, who he knew could convey the vocal humanity he wanted. There are echoes too of the larger work – notably in the Samaritan's farewell lullaby 'Dormi nunc, amice', which is in the vein of the *Requiem*'s final duet 'Let us sleep now . . .'

R   Pears, Fischer-Dieskau, LSO and Chorus/Britten,
recorded 1963
Decca 425 1002 (with *Cello Symphony*, *Sinfonia da Requiem*)

Voices for Today, op. 75 *   1965

Few composers would turn up their nose at a commission for
a completely international work, to be performed in three
countries at once, in support of a noble cause. Britten was
asked by the Secretary-General of the United Nations to write
such a piece for the UN's twentieth anniversary, and produced
what has turned out to be one of the least performed of all his
works. The main problem is the words. Britten chose fifteen
peace-loving authors, from the Roman poet Virgil to the Chinese philosopher Lao Tzu, from Shelley to Yevtushenko, with
the result that he could set little more than a slogan from each.
They are sung by an unaccompanied, fully mixed choir (men,
women and children), who have to cope with lines like 'Force
is our enemy!' They smack of Tippett at his most worthy and
ungainly. Despite this, there are some wonderful sounds in
the piece. As in his *War Requiem*, Britten uses the offstage
children's voices as an angelic parabola to encircle the world,
though by today's standards it seems somewhat deficient to
define a threefold 'global' premiere simply by simultaneous
performances in New York, Paris and London.

Overture, *The Building of the House*, op. 79 ***   1967

This sparkling five-minute piece was written for the opening
of the Snape Maltings concert hall in 1967. Britten's eyes lit
on the first words of Psalm 127: 'Except the Lord build the
house: their labour is but lost that build it' – although divine
involvement must have been hard to acknowledge when
the hall burned down two years later. Britten sets the words
homophonically to the seventeenth-century chorale melody,
'*Vater unser im Himmelreich*', but with typical Britten élan sur-
rounds them with bustling activity of his own in the orchestra

– musical craftsmanship which paid proper tribute to that of
the builders and carpenters. A short film clip survives of Britten rehearsing for the first performances – an illuminating
insight into his method, although it did not prevent the choir
singing the first phrase a semitone sharp on the day. He later
specified that the choral part could be taken instead by organ
or trombones.

R   CBSO and Chorus /Rattle, recorded 1990
EMI 573 9832: 'Rattle conducts Britten' (2 CDs, with
Sinfonia da Requiem, *Young Apollo* etc.)

Children's Crusade, op. 82   1969

Britten was never so grim as in this piece, which sets a Bertolt
Brecht story about a group of orphans wandering through the
debris of Poland at the start of the Second World War. There
is no happy ending – even their dog starves to death – and
Britten responds with a huge percussion orchestra of some
twenty-seven different instruments, played by children, with
two pianos and a chamber organ to help the children's choir
keep its pitch. There's no doubt it gives children a great kick
to be allowed full welly on the bass drum or gong, and it is
a fearsome noise at times. But it batters, rather than cajoles
or moves, the audience with its bleak pacifist message, and I
wonder whether it has won many hearts.

R   Christ Church Cathedral (Oxford), Driskill-Smith/
Darlington, recorded 2002–3
Lammas LAMM 146D (with *The Golden Vanity*, *Missa Brevis*
etc.)

Sacred and Profane, op. 91 **   1974–5

Eight medieval lyrics were set by Britten on the basis of one
voice to a part, although they can also be sung by a larger choir.
They are highly demanding, and require plentiful reserves of
vocal stamina and dexterity. The Old English words might as

well be a foreign language, but Britten relishes them, whether in the ecstasy of 'St Godric's Hymn', the interrupted sentences of 'Carol', or the gallows humour of 'A Death', with which he closes the work. The painful enumeration of the afflictions of old age might have been near the bone for the ailing composer, but he is clearly enjoying himself.

R Polyphony/Layton (choral version), recorded 2000
Hyperion CDA 67140 (with *Five Flower Songs*, *AMDG* etc.)

Welcome Ode, op. 95 *   1976

In the last piece he was to complete, Britten returned to the children and young people he held so dear. This cheerful, short cantata (five movements in eight minutes) is far removed from the intensity of his Third String Quartet a few months before. It was designed for school choirs and orchestras to play to the Queen during her Silver Jubilee visit to Ipswich in 1977. With march, jig and canon, this is familiar Britten terrain. But it is moving to find that, when his physical strength was failing for the final time, the bounce in the music was as exuberant as ever. There is more than a hint of the maypole of 'merrie Englande' here, but it is Britten at his most generous. The closing phrase, 'all day long', recalls the wit and panache of the end of *Spring Symphony*: 'and so, my friends, I cease'.

R City of London School for Girls Orchestra and Choir, and other choirs/Hickox, recorded 1990
Chandos CHAN 8855 (with *Spring Symphony* and *Psalm 150*)

Praise We Great Men   1976

In 1959 Edith Sitwell wrote a magnificent poem at Britten's request for the tercentenary of Purcell's birth. Perhaps inspired by the biblical passage, 'Let us now praise famous men', it is (like Auden's 'Hymn to Saint Cecilia') a paean to the glories of musical instruments and 'the gods of sound'. Sitwell always hoped Britten would set it to music, but it was not until twelve years after her death that he did, in the form of a cantata for four solo singers, chorus and orchestra – a gift to Rostropovich for his inaugural concert as conductor of the Washington Symphony Orchestra the following year. It was to be the first piece he had written for such large forces since *War Requiem*. Sadly it was too late, and he completed only six minutes of music before he became too ill to work.

This torso has been recorded, and now published, and we can hear Britten still enjoying the gamelan techniques of Balinese music. The slow section (which perforce forms the conclusion) has a majestic, cavernous quality not unlike that in Vaughan Williams's *Sinfonia Antartica* (though it may be heresy to say so), in which expansive sixths mark Britten's final utterance for solo tenor.

R   Hargan, King, Tear, White, CBSO and Chorus/Rattle, recorded 1985
EMI 573 9832: 'Rattle conducts Britten' (2 CDs, with *Ballad of Heroes*, *Canadian Carnival*, *Diversions* etc.)

30

Church music

Although Britten counted himself a supporter of Christianity, even if not a churchgoer for much of his adult life, he wrote relatively little music for the church. He knew that some of his forerunners as English composers had written little else, and he had so much more to say and do. But much of what he did write is so strikingly original and fresh that it has become essential to the mix of any church choir's repertoire.

Although *War Requiem* was written for Coventry Cathedral, I have counted it as choral music rather than church music. On the other hand his three short stage works, the Church Parables, belong here, because they were always intended to be performed inside the hallowed doors.

*A Hymn to the Virgin*****   1930; revised 1934

This jewel of an anthem – a macaronic carol to medieval words – was tossed off in a few hours in the sick bay during Britten's last school term at Gresham's. It is tiny and apparently simple, but perfect. His imaginative use of a semi-chorus almost as an echo reveals an alert ear, even at the age of sixteen. The third verse is written in two speeds – an effective device he was often to use thereafter. It may well have had more performances than almost any other Britten piece, but because most of these have been at church and carol services, they largely escape the official tally. New Britten listeners can start here ☛, but it still works for old hands too.

R   Westminster Cathedral Choir/Hill, recorded 1988
Hyperion CDA 66220 (with *A Ceremony of Carols*, *Missa Brevis* etc.)

Christ's Nativity or *Thy King's Birthday**   1931
'Sweet was the Song'   1931; revised 1966

The first seedling to sprout in this Christmas suite was the carol 'Sweet was the Song', a cool lullaby for women's voices, written when Britten was just seventeen and a new student at the Royal College of Music. Four more carols followed, and only gradually did Britten group them together mentally, first as a 'choral symphony', and then as a suite originally entitled *Thy King's Birthday*. He was sufficiently proud of it that he showed it not only to his composition teacher John Ireland, but to Frank Bridge and Arthur Benjamin as well.

Written for unaccompanied double choir, with soprano and mezzo soloists, it was an important staging-post *en route* for *A Boy was Born* two years later, although its dense choral textures often obscure the words, which just race by, too plentiful and indistinct. The suite was not performed or published entire in his lifetime. But the two carols that Britten did allow into the Aldeburgh daylight in 1955 and 1966 turn out to be the best: 'New Prince, New Pomp' and 'Sweet was the Song'.

R   Gritton, Wyn-Rogers, Holst Singers/Layton, recorded 1992 Hyperion CDA 66825 (with *A Boy was Born* and other Christmas music)

A Boy was Born, op. 3 ****   1932–3; revised 1950s
Corpus Christi Carol   1961; original version 1932–3

It took six months to complete this *tour de force* for unaccompanied choir. The piece takes the form of theme and variations, using a range of medieval texts mostly from a volume called *Ancient English Christmas Carols*. Britten uses the unusual combination of an eight-part mixed-voice choir and a boys' choir – which tips the sound balance into the treble register. At times the writing seems simple, but only because it beguiles the ear. The texture is frequently complex – and a tough sing for all but the most accomplished choirs. Britten acknowledged this in the 1950s when he provided an optional organ part to help choirs maintain their pitch – an interesting choice of instrument, because it was not conceived as a church piece. It was first sung on the radio on the day Elgar died, and the first concert performance was in a London theatre some months later.

The uncompromising challenges of the piece are demonstrated in the ferocity of the Herod variation, and in the raw chill of the one venture into modern English, the Christina Rossetti carol 'In the bleak mid-winter'. People familiar with the fireside glow of the settings by Gustav Holst and Harold Darke will find no comfort in Britten's brittle version. With his treble sonorities, earth and water are frozen solid, and the frosty wind really moans. He then artfully joins it to an anonymous fifteenth-century carol about the suffering Saviour (which he later published separately for voice and piano as the *Corpus Christi Carol*). *A Boy was Born* culminates in a richly woven nine-minute finale, 'Noël', where the closing refrain of 'Sing hosanna' is set to the same chord progression as are the Alleluyas in the opening theme. It resolves into a simple major chord, striking for its lack of tonic.

The Observer's renowned critic, A. H. Fox Strangways, recognised an important new musical voice in this work:

> It has one mark of mastery – endless invention and facility. He takes what he wants, and does not trouble about what other people have thought well to take. He rivets attention from the first note onwards: without knowing in the least what is coming, one feels instinctively that this is music it behoves one to listen to, and each successive moment strengthens that feeling. He inspires confidence; there is no wondering what is coming next; whatever that may be, and whether we 'like' it or not, we shall agree with it.

R   London Sinfonietta Chorus, Choristers of St Paul's Cathedral/Edwards, recorded 1988
Virgin Classics 7 90728-2 (with *AMDG* and *Hymn to St Cecilia*)

Jubilate Deo in E flat	1934
Te Deum in C	1934; revised 1936
Jubilate Deo in C	1961
Venite	1961
Festival Te Deum in E, op. 32 *	1944

Britten's low-church origins are evident in these settings for
Mattins. He responded well to their somewhat bracing cheer-
fulness, as he did to cold showers before breakfast. He could
hardly have guessed that his 1934 *Te Deum* (striking in its very
soft opening and close) would result a quarter of a century
later in a royal summons to write a companion piece, the *Jubilate*, for the choir at Windsor Castle. He added a *Venite* for
good measure. These, as well as the earlier *Jubilate* and later
Te Deum, are still sung regularly by cathedral choirs, the latter piece being a rather more substantial work (he gave it an
opus number, after all) with a characteristic dance rhythm in
the middle section, and a soaring treble solo at the peaceful
close. He wrote this in the middle of scoring *Peter Grimes* –
for which, of course, he set part of another Mattins canticle,
the *Benedicite*, in the first scene of Act II.

R   *Te Deums* and *Jubilate* in C: The Sixteen/Christophers,
recorded 2002
Coro COR 16006: 'Blest Cecilia' (with *Rejoice in the Lamb*,
Britten's four *Hymns* etc.)

R   *Te Deums* and *Jubilate* in C: Choir of St John's College
Cambridge, Farrington/Robinson, recorded 2000
Naxos 8.554791: 'English Choral Music' (with *Missa Brevis*,
Hymn to St Cecilia etc.)

| *The Company of Heaven* * | 1937 |
| *The World of the Spirit* * | 1938 |

Although Britten had for some time abandoned regular
churchgoing, his two big scores for the religious affairs department of the BBC betray his long familiarity with the church's

seasons. *The Company of Heaven* was designed for Michaelmas, and *The World of the Spirit* for Pentecost, with the texts of each assembled by Ellis Roberts at the BBC. At a time when Britten had been experimenting with chamber ensembles for film and theatre, the BBC commissions allowed him to keep his hand in with a much larger orchestra.

Britten's music for *The Company of Heaven* is intensely dramatic – whether in the primeval chaos he conjures up (like Haydn in *The Creation*) at the start, the angular lines in the first (mostly unison) chorus 'The Morning Stars', or the violence of 'War in Heaven', where strings, percussion and organ battle it out, while the men of the chorus declaim the famous words from the book of Revelation in fortissimo *sprechgesang*. Although Britten said he couldn't see the significance of the programme when he listened to it, he rejoiced in the words he'd had to set, and found the 'War in Heaven' movement 'thrilling'. 'My stuff all comes off like hell', he went on. His setting of Emily Brontë's 'A thousand, thousand gleaming fires' was the first piece Britten wrote specifically for the tenor voice of Peter Pears, whom he'd first met only a few months before. It's a slight number, which belongs more to a musical than a cantata (as if Britten at that stage thought that was where Pears's light tenor belonged), and is written almost entirely in a note-per-syllable fashion, with few of the melismas Britten wrote for Pears later on. But the piece that most engages him here comes after the narrator's account, in words of Ellis Roberts himself, of a nineteenth-century road accident which killed a young boy – and the belief of one onlooker that, at the moment of impact, an angel had intervened. This touching story drew from Britten an extraordinary miniature, a 'Funeral March for a Boy' for strings and timpani. It is imbued with the spirit of Mahler – perhaps the result of his repeated listening to his records of *Kindertotenlieder* – 'music that I think I love more than any other', as he had written a few months before. The march's dark B minor switches to the major at the end, a moment of Mahlerian transfiguration.

When he wasn't referring to it as his 'big BBC Holy show', Britten called *The World of the Spirit* an 'oratorio in the grand style'. It is a forty-five-minute sequence of readings and music about the Holy Spirit, with words both sacred and secular. Britten was given the BBC Orchestra and Chorus to play with, plus four solo singers and organ. As the texts are an anthology, so is the music – with styles that range unblushingly from a Bach chorale and arioso to cod-Walton of *Belshazzar's Feast* vintage.

The whole piece was broadcast twice in the thirties, but was largely forgotten till the 1990s. He frames it with plainsong (the hymn 'Veni, Creator Spiritus'), just as he was to do later on with *A Ceremony of Carols* and his three Church Parables. But then he had sung a plainchant psalm every day in the chapel at Gresham's. In between are some nuggets to discover: 'The sun, the moon, the stars' is his first mature setting of Tennyson, and there is a sharp-edged, Prokofiev-style approach to Hopkins's 'The world is charged with the grandeur of God'.

R   *The Company of Heaven*: Pope, Dressen, London Philharmonic Choir, ECO/Brunelle, recorded 1989 Virgin Classics VC 7 91107-2 (with *Paul Bunyan* excerpts)

R   *The World of the Spirit*: Chilcott, Stephen, Hill, Varcoe, Britten Singers, BBC Philharmonic/Hickox, recorded 1996 Chandos CHAN 9487 (with *King Arthur* suite)

A Ceremony of Carols, op. 28 *****   1942; revised 1943

The noisy and sweaty cabin on his transatlantic voyage in a Swedish freighter, dodging icebergs and U-boats, was hardly the ideal place to compose this set of medieval carols for treble voices and harp. Yet this is one of Britten's supreme creations. Each of the nine carols has its distinctive challenge for his boy singers, rather like an old-fashioned obstacle race on sports day – whether it's the octave leap at the end of 'Wolcum Yole!', the smooth homophonic triplets of 'There is no Rose', the breathless canonic lines of 'As Dew in Aprille' (he who hesitates is lost), the chromaticism of 'That Yongë Child', the major-minor shifts of 'Balulalow', the intricate yet smudgy three-part canon of 'This Little Babe' ♪♩ emerging into a rollicking unison, the aching, arching onomatopoeia of 'In Freezing Winter Night', or the taut rhythms of 'Deo Gracias'.

Every boys' choir worth its salt has tackled these carols – though they are far from easy – and they must be one of Britten's most recorded works. But the composer's own recording in 1953 is peerless, not least for the insight it gives into the treble sound that Britten liked. He chose the Copenhagen Boys' Choir, who he said were 'like angels': 'They sang my *Ceremony of Carols* as I never thought it could be sung'. He wrote to Pears about a rehearsal with them, 'which I must say was heaven – meaning, of course, the way they sing'. Their treble sound has the sweet clarity of spring water on a sunny day, bubbling with a little vibrato – as far removed from the breathy English treble voices so common at that time as the Vienna Boys' Choir he so admired. The English vowels may be a little strange, but the Copenhagen boys have a taut discipline (without ever sounding strait-laced) that reveals the full glory of Britten's part-writing. With the experience of these recording sessions so fresh in his mind, it is no wonder he singled out David Hemmings two months later as his favoured boy soprano for *The Turn of the Screw*. Hemmings had the same unchurchy, virtuoso confidence.

R   Copenhagen Boys' Choir, Simon/Britten, recorded 1953 Decca 436 394-2 (with *A Boy was Born*, *Friday Afternoons*, etc.)

R   Westminster Cathedral Choir, Williams/Hill, recorded 1988 Hyperion CDA 66220 (with *Missa Brevis* etc.)

Rejoice in the Lamb, op. 30***   1943

While in America, Britten was introduced by W. H. Auden to the bizarre eighteenth-century poem '*Jubilate Agno*' by Christopher Smart. It had just been discovered in a private library, and was first published in 1939. Smart was famous for approaching people in the street and asking them to pray with him, which in those days (just as now) was reason enough to lock him up. (Dr Johnson did say that he would as willingly 'pray with Kit Smart as any man living'.) He was confined to a madhouse for seven years, and ended his short life in a debtors' prison. His poem grabbed Britten's imagination, and he better than anyone was able, in this choral work, to reveal Smart as more visionary than lunatic, and his poem as a wonderfully imaginative *Benedicite*. It may not be orthodox or biblical to see the creative wonder of God in tigers, bears, bassoons, clarinets, and letters of the alphabet – but, Britten smilingly asks, why not?

'I will consider my cat Jeoffrey', Smart writes, 'for he is the servant of the living God', and Britten responds with wondrous feline curlicues on the organ. When the next verse describes the mouse as 'a creature of great personal valour', we know Smart has foreseen *Tom and Jerry*. Yet Britten never goes for the cartoon, but rejoices in the richness of Smart's own creative landscape. When various biblical figures come forward with wild animals, he puts the choir on its mettle as it dodges and weaves with seven, then six, then nine quavers in a bar.

At the emotional core of this work is Smart's acknowledgement of his own 'madness': 'For I am under the same accusation with my Saviour / For they said, he is besides himself'. The mocking cries of 'Silly fellow!' accompanied by full organ lead to the anguish of his being in 'twelve hardships'. But soon the joy of creation returns, and Smart and Britten delight in the rhyming vowels which illustrate different musical instruments, before the work closes with its own 'Hallelujah Chorus' – subdued, but with suppressed energy in the stressed athletic quavers of its dotted rhythms.

Most composers would have looked away, embarrassed by the outpourings of an eccentric, but Britten, who was never scared by naivety, embraces and transfigures them. Thanks to his music, 'malignity ceases, and the devils themselves are at peace', and it is hard not to be moved.

R   Finzi Singers, Lumsden/Spicer, recorded 1996
Chandos CHAN 9511: 'Britten Choral Edition vol. 2' (with
Hymn to St Cecilia, Choral Dances from *Gloriana* etc.)

A Wedding Anthem (Amo Ergo Sum), op. 46 *   1949

This ten-minute anthem for choir and organ (or 'little cantata' as its author, Ronald Duncan, called it) was written for
the wedding of Britten's friends, the Earl of Harewood and
Marion Stein. It proved too much for one of the guests, King
George VI, who Duncan noticed was bored. Royal protocol
had already almost torpedoed it, because Duncan's original
words were deemed too Catholic for the King. It took interventions from Downing Street and an Anglican bishop to persuade Duncan to refer to the Virgin Mary's intercession for
the couple, rather than to her blessing.

Britten's setting is affectionate and personal, with bell-like
peals of 'Ave Maria' ringing out (despite the censors). He
himself conducted it at the wedding, with solo parts for Pears
and the soprano Joan Cross. Their unconventional duet –
an engagingly halting, breathless canon – perfectly captures
Duncan's idea of bride and groom, hesitant yet eager: 'These
two are not two / Love has made them one'. For reasons that
remain obscure, a copy of the manuscript was laid beneath the
foundations of the Royal Festival Hall in 1951.

R   The Sixteen/Christophers, recorded 2005
Coro COR 16038: 'Fen and Meadow' (with *Sacred and
Profane*, *Five Flower Songs* etc.)

Hymn to St Peter, op. 56a   1955
Antiphon, op. 56b ***   1956
A Hymn of St Columba   1962
Deus in adjutorium meum *   1944–5

Britten takes plainsong further in his *Hymn to St Peter*, which
is based on the chant 'Tu es Petrus'. It was written for the

church in Norwich where C. J. R. Coleman (by this time
in his mid-seventies) was organist. He had been organist at
St John's, Lowestoft, for many years, and his son and Britten used to make music together as boys. So with this short
anthem Britten is paying his childhood dues, although he
doubtless also had his own 'rock', his own Peter, in his mind.

The companion piece, the rarely heard *Antiphon*, is a glistening miniature which hides its light under the bushel of a
bland title. It sets a hymn of praise by George Herbert, with
an antiphonal and antithetical duet between angels and men
that was ideally tailored for Britten's ear. Each three-line verse
begins with energetic, syncopated dance rhythms for choir
and organ, followed by short, soaring treble solos offset by
deep bass comments from the men – a variant of the 'great
gulf fix'd' approach to the last song in *Winter Words*. The final
chorus ends with the angels applying Britten's insistent tonic
of F major against the dissonant chords of the men. Six times
they insist, until finally the men conform. Hearing *Antiphon*
sung at Britten's memorial service in Westminster Abbey was
a visionary moment.

The *Hymn of St Columba* is also a rarity, a setting for choir
and organ of words by the Irish saint. Its main idea is a rising
arpeggio on an E minor chord, which appears first in a choral
unison, with disturbed rumblings underneath on the organ
pedals, before flowering into four-part harmony.

The anthem Britten wrote for unaccompanied choir at the
end of the war, a setting of Psalm 70, comes from his incidental music for the play *This Way to the Tomb*. Given that it was
written for this specific dramatic context, I am not sure it's
right to extract it as a piece of church music. It is largely built
on imitative phrases, with the curling semitones in one section offering an interesting foretaste of the 'Libera me' choral
lines in the *War Requiem*.

R   Choir of St John's College Cambridge, Farrington/
Robinson, recorded 2000
Naxos 8.554791 (with *Rejoice in the Lamb* etc.)

R *Deus in adjutorium meum*: Britten Singers/Hickox,
recorded 1991
Chandos CHAN 8997 (with *Cantata Misericordium* and
works by Holst and Finzi)

Noye's Fludde, op. 59****   1957–8

The high-water mark of Britten's music for children is the
story of Noah's Ark, performed almost entirely by children
– and not prodigies either: there are parts here for absolute
beginners. It's easy to dismiss this as kiddies' stuff, but a big
mistake. In my experience it chokes an adult audience every
time – much more than any other dramatic work of his.

The sound is unique, based as it is on an army of recorders
and strings, played by children, with supplementary roles for
bugles, handbells, and an array of other percussion, including
slung mugs, sandpaper and wind machine. Ten adults provide
a professional anchor. Similarly the singers are children, apart
from Noah and his wife: they all sing in medieval English,
taken from the Chester Miracle Play.

Magic moments abound in this story of the building of the
ark, the animals going in two by two, the storm and flood,
Noah's discovery of dry land, and the appearance of the rainbow as God's promise never to repeat the Flood. The procession of scores (occasionally hundreds) of masked children
into the ark as leopards, camels, mice and so on, to bugle
fanfares, is a wonderful theatrical coup. They never sing
in time – but the marvel of Britten's score is that it doesn't
matter. The handbells ringing out with the rainbow provide
another heartstopping moment. Underpinning everything is
the audience (or congregation, as Britten calls them), who as
one part of his musical 'holy trinity' (with composer and performers) join in three well-known hymns to which Britten
adds his own harmonies and counterpoint. He could never
have foreseen in 1958 that these hymns would start falling
out of common currency, and it will be a problem for the
work (as for *Saint Nicolas*) if they do not immediately strike

a chord of memory in everyone present. But fortunately that is still some way off.

R   Brannigan, Rex, Anthony, EOG, children of East Suffolk/ Del Mar, recorded 1960
London 436 397-2 (with *The Golden Vanity*)

Missa Brevis in D, op. 63 ****   1959

Britten was pressed by various people to write a mass for liturgical use, but apart from two teenage attempts, he only ever produced one. The *War Requiem* doesn't count as church music: it may harness the text of the Catholic requiem mass, but it was never designed for worship. The *Missa Brevis* is a short setting for boys' voices and organ, which is now a core part of the repertoire of most cathedrals – partly because it so challenges the boys, but also I suspect because it gives the adult choristers a night off. It is one of Britten's finest scores, with an unmistakable sonority.

He was struck by the bright, focused sound that George Malcolm coaxed from his trebles at Westminster Cathedral, and the work, for three treble lines, depends on it. The vocal writing is crisp, precise and effortful: Britten is not interested in the echoes of dreaming spires, but in the shrieks of boys running in the playground. The organ most of the time reinforces rather than complements this pungency in the voices. In the opening Kyrie (marked 'passionate'), the boys command, rather than plead for, divine support. The Gloria finds them turning plainsong into jazz, with vigorous 7/8 syncopations. In the Sanctus, the singers become change-ringers – perhaps, in Britten's mind, wielding the handbells from *Noye's Fludde* the previous year. Yet, at the same time, each bar is a twelve-note row, set against a constant pedal of a D major chord, but a pedal in the voices' own register – an extraordinary effect. The Benedictus, for three solo voices, is a bitonal canon, ending in an insistent D major once again.

The 'slow and solemn' Agnus Dei at the end is only two

minutes long, but an intense experience ♦━┓. Many composers have set these words as a gentle, comforting prayer to conclude the mass, but Britten follows Beethoven's example in another great Mass in D, the *Missa Solemnis* he so adored as a young man. It becomes instead a terrified plea for mercy and peace, all too aware that the sinful turmoil of the world makes it unlikely to be granted. The plea is always urgent – whether as a pulsating fortissimo or breathless pianissimo. Throughout the organ is rooted in the dark terrain of D minor, with an unceasing ground bass of a rising five-note arpeggio. Above that are discordant interjections on a reed – mini-fanfares that perhaps echo the bugle calls of conflict in the Beethoven model. Even when Beethoven's B minor Agnus Dei finally sinks into the comfort of D major harmonies, the military echoes keep breaking back in. In Britten, there is no yielding to the major key, and the final staccato whisper is truly forlorn.

R   Christ Church Cathedral choristers, Driskill-Smith/
Darlington, recorded 2002–3
Lammas LAMM 146D (with *The Golden Vanity*, *Children's Crusade*, *A Ceremony of Carols*)

Curlew River, op. 71 *****   1964

It began with sniggers in Japan in 1956, when Britten first encountered the stiff rituals of the Noh play. But the giggles faded as he absorbed a starkly different cultural ethos and found that it fed a fresh creative stream. In *Curlew River*, he took the Noh masks and ceremonial, and imported them into a medieval monastic context in East Anglia. He mixed oriental music (the gamelan techniques of Bali are again prominent) with Christian plainchant, and used a tiny chamber orchestra quite different from that of his post-war chamber operas. Instead of adding a string quintet to a wind quintet and stirring in some percussion, he concocted a much weirder ensemble of flute, horn, viola, double bass, harp, chamber organ, bells, gong and untuned drums. As Vaughan Williams said of Elgar's First Symphony, 'it looks all wrong, but it sounds all right. Here indeed is a mystery and a miracle.'

Miracle and mystery are the exact words William Plomer uses in his libretto to describe this affecting tale of a madwoman searching for her lost son. She tries to cross the fenland river – significantly the dividing line between west and east – but her hysterical grief is derided by the ferryman and the other passengers. As they all eventually cross the river, the ferryman describes the death of a boy he had taken across a year before, and they all come to realise that the madwoman is the boy's mother. On the eastern bank, they gather at his grave: they hear, and then see, the boy's spirit, which releases his mother from her derangement. The whole story is enacted by monks (which is why the madwoman is sung by a tenor), who open and close proceedings with plainsong. Lacing it all is Britten's acute awareness of human frailty.

Once heard, this work is never forgotten. At first the long sustained clusters on the organ, with drums tapping away during the scene-setting narration, may be disconcerting, but they soon lead us into a new Britten sound-world, dominated by the rising fourth of the curlew's cry. There are ideas which echo other Britten works: when the men gang up on the madwoman and insist she sing for their entertainment, it recalls the baying of the mob in *Peter Grimes*, while the hieratic canonic lament as the ferryman guides the madwoman to the tomb reminds us of *Lucretia* or *The Ballad of Little Musgrave*. But the score is brimming with new musical ideas, whether the stuttering keen of flute and horn to match the madwoman's crying, or the rising and falling glissandos on all instruments which suggest the ferryman plying his craft across the river. The use of bells in the scene at the tomb is inspired, and heightens the senses for the gradual emergence of the boy's voice from the men's clangorous chanting – one of the greatest of many redemptive moments in Britten.

In *Noye's Fludde* eight years earlier, Britten allowed for a children's orchestra not being perfectly synchronised – indeed the piece loses something if it is. In *Curlew River* and the other two Church Parables, the small instrumental group has no conductor, and Britten makes a virtue of unsynchronised, entangled sound, very much on the model of the Balinese gamelan which had entranced him on his travels eight years before. So the same melodic ideas are played simultaneously by different instruments at different speeds, and chords change gradually on the chamber organ, note by note: it is a different way of playing – and of listening. He devised a special sign to denote the moments at which these deliberately wayward lines should be pulled back into order: the curlew-mark ⌒ .

R   Pears, Shirley-Quirk, Drake, Blackburn, EOG/Britten, recorded 1965
London 421 858 2

The Burning Fiery Furnace, op. 77 ****   1965–6

For his second Church Parable, Britten turned to the Old Testament book of Daniel, and its story of the three Israelites condemned by Nebuchadnezzar, King of Babylon, to be burned alive for not worshipping his pagan god, and of their miraculous survival in the furnace. Britten adopts the same format as in *Curlew River*, though this time the mystery play (on the model of the Japanese Noh play) has no fenland overtones. The story is enacted by a group of monks, and both framed by and based on plainsong. The eight musicians are also costumed, and themselves play a part in the hour-long drama.

It follows a simple path: once the monks have put on their masks and costumes, the three Israelite princes (Ananias, Misael and Azarias) are presented to Nebuchadnezzar, who appoints them as governors of three of his provinces in Babylon, and gives them Babylonian names, Shadrach, Meshach and Abednego. There was clearly no place for multiculturalism in the Babylon of the sixth century BC. But the Israelites spurn the king's food and drink, and refuse to worship the pagan golden image he has set up, so an angry Nebuchadnezzar and his wicked astrologers adopt a policy of ethnic cleansing. The youths are thrown into a furnace (with the thermostat turned up to seven times its normal level). The king sees a fourth figure walking with them in the fire, in divine form, and is converted to Judaism when the three Israelites emerge unscathed. Britten's monks then disrobe and leave.

Some of the sonorities here are unique in his output. His sole percussion player has his work cut out playing five small untuned drums, an anvil, two tuned woodblocks, a lyra glockenspiel (that is, a vertical one in the shape of a lyre), a Babylonian drum and a whip, so Britten asks the double bass player to help out by playing a drum too, and the organist to strike the cymbals! All the instruments are on display when the whole troupe moves in procession round the church, worshipping Nebuchadnezzar's golden image. But the thunder is stolen by the unusual sound of the alto trombone. Coupled with slithering instrumental glissandos and the wild top notes of the singers, its strained high wailing captures perfectly the frenzy of the pagan worship in Babylon. Just when you start to reckon the devil has all the best tunes (the most colourful ones, anyway), the trio in the furnace start their homophonic chanting of the words of the *Benedicite*. Capped by the seraphic cries of a boy angel, it stops you in your tracks. It certainly stopped Nebuchadnezzar. Israel's got talent, quite clearly.

The Church Parables will not appeal to those who sit waiting for a good tune. This is opera with a difference, a rarefied sound and manner that was quite new to Britten. *The Burning Fiery Furnace* has flashes of humour (as when the boy acolytes poke fun at their Babylonian elders – who themselves are revealed as pathetic yes-men). But the musical rewards will be greatest for those who patiently let the oriental manner and flavour of the piece wash over them.

R   Pears, Drake, Shirley-Quirk, Tear, Dean, Leeming,
EOG/Britten, recorded 1967
London 414 663-2

The Prodigal Son, op. 81   1967–8

The prodigality of Britten's invention meant that, although
philosophical themes would recur, he rarely repeated himself
in the musical expression of his ideas: he always had fresh
things to say. *The Prodigal Son* is the unfortunate exception.
As the chanting monks entered Orford Church in the 1968
Aldeburgh Festival, then robed and masked themselves in
character during a long instrumental introduction, there must
have been a feeling of 'here we go again'.

Britten hit on the idea of setting this story (the only Gospel
parable of the three Church Parables) after seeing a painting
at the Hermitage in Leningrad. In his and William Plomer's
treatment, the Prodigal Son is lured away from a dull but virtuous life on the farm with his father and elder brother by a
Tempter, who urges him to investigate the pleasures of wine,
women and gambling. He ends up destitute and despondent,
and returns home to beg forgiveness. His father kills the fat-
ted calf in welcome, to the chagrin of the more dependable
elder brother.

There are new, distinctive, sounds here, it is true: the high
trumpet in D is a persuasive choice to summon the tempta-
tions in the mind of the younger son, and the mirror-dialogue
between him and the Tempter (who is his shadow) is a rare
Britten example of a duet for two tenors. But the use of treble voices to lead him on to 'nights of ecstasy' is risible, or
worse. Indeed, the temptation scene is toe-curlingly tame,
particularly when acted out in a church. No wonder the much
less puritanical Vaughan Williams insisted, in his Vanity Fair
scene in *The Pilgrim's Progress*, that it must be staged in a theatre, not a church, and that strippers be hired.

There is a pious quality to this work (rather as there is in
Owen Wingrave) which acts as bleach to both drama and music.

Compared with *Curlew River*, the audience is left uninvolved
with any of the characters, and at the end the Elder Son's
unbiblical capitulation in being reconciled with his brother
seems simply feeble.

Round Britten Quiz V

ANSWERS ON PAGE 411

1 How many times did Britten represent Apollo in music,
  and how?
2 When he was fifty, Britten named three living composers he
  most admired: Stravinsky, Shostakovich and Tippett. Who
  was the fourth?
3 Who was the best wolf whistler at The Red House?
4 Which orchestral instrument did Britten say (in an interview) he wasn't aware he had any predilection for?
5 Which Britten work features the ukelele?
6 What did Britten record that he had done three times on
  Easter Day 1928?

31

Chamber music

Like most aspiring composers, Britten wrote large quantities
of chamber music when he was young, for the simple reason
that performances were easier and cheaper to arrange than
of orchestral music. He adapted these skills to the small-
scale ensembles he used in much of his film music, and then,
after the war, to the chamber operas that became such a Britten hallmark. This had the paradoxical effect of staunching
the flow of chamber music proper for thirty years after the
Second String Quartet, until the Third emerged at the end
of his life.

String Quartet in F	1928
Rhapsody for string quartet	1929
Quartettino	1930
Movement for wind sextet	1930
String Quartet in D	1931; revised 1974
Phantasy for string quintet	1932

The delightful F major quartet (first heard in 1995) shows
no sign of a distinctive Britten voice, but its fluent and dis-
ciplined technique suggests the mature craftsman, unlike
the relevant entry in his diary in April 1928: 'Begin string
quartet in F. End of term. Mark reading. Am top of VIth
by only 44 marks. Come home for Hols. Hooray.' He was
only fourteen. The opening Allegro has the sweetness and
vigour of Dvořák, with its first subject built round an F
major chord – an early sign of Britten's lifelong addiction
to triads. The Delius-like slow movement casts a mysterious
spell, although it doesn't really fit with the other three: in
fact he had pinched it from some string quartet pieces he'd
written a few months earlier.

By the time of the single-movement *Rhapsody* the following year, he was gorging himself on intense chromaticism like
that of Schoenberg's *Verklärte Nacht*. Yet there are Warlockian
English harmonies too. The piece is notable for its fluency
and variety of texture, and it never lacks a sense of forward
movement.

Compared with the ten days he spent on the F major
quartet, his three-movement *Quartettino* of 1930 caused him
trouble. He worked on it for almost four months, before
sending it off to the Royal College of Music as part of the
portfolio that helped win him a scholarship. It foreshadows
the most important work he wrote as an RCM scholar, his
Sinfonietta. So does the movement for wind sextet he wrote
in his last term at Gresham's, presumably also for his RCM
portfolio: it has a Schoenbergian flavour perhaps designed to
impress the examiners. It is an interesting curiosity from a
sixteen-year-old boy who had recently discovered Schoenberg
(in particular *Pierrot Lunaire* and the *Six Little Piano Pieces*).
It is intriguing that this so influenced his instrumental writing for a short while, but not his choral: *A Wealden Trio* and
A Hymn to the Virgin were written at the same time, but are
characteristic Britten.

After his open-heart surgery in 1973, Britten went rum-
maging in his cardboard boxes to dig out his juvenilia, and get
himself back to composing. His eyes lit on the D major string
quartet that he had written at the age of seventeen. He smart-
ened it up a bit, made a big cut in the last movement, and
had it performed and published. It is much more original than
the quartet in F, though still an apprentice piece. At the time,
Frank Bridge criticised its counterpoint for being 'too vocal'
(Britten was then singing in a madrigal group). But his official
composition teacher at the Royal College, John Ireland, disa-
greed – and indeed there are harmonies in this quartet that
owe him much. It coincided with a fruitful phase of Britten's
often volatile relationship with Ireland. After completing the
first movement, he had a 'good & instructive' lesson. When
he showed him the slow movement a week later, he endured

Ireland's 'most damning (tho' v. good) criticism', tore it up and started again the following morning. Ireland was much happier with the second attempt, and the quartet also won the approval of his piano professor, Arthur Benjamin.

The one-movement *Phantasy* in F minor has the distinction of being the sole Britten composition given an RCM performance during his three years there. It won him the College's Cobbett Prize for chamber music written in the form of a one-movement fantasy, and he spent the proceeds (thirteen guineas) on scores by Walton, Falla, Stravinsky and Bridge. The quintet's harmonies have a traditionally English tinge, but the faster music shows more individuality. It became the first Britten piece to be broadcast, in February 1933, and three days later Elgar's friend and biographer, Basil Maine, said in a public lecture that this 'boy of nineteen' would be one of 'the lights of the future'. So is it too fanciful to imagine that, in the last year of his life, Elgar became aware of Benjamin Britten?

R   String Quartets in F and D: Sorrel Quartet, recorded 1998 Chandos CHAN 9664 (with String Quartet no. 2)

R   *Quartettino*: Maggini String Quartet, recorded 1998 Naxos 8.554360 (with *Alla Marcia*, String Quartet no. 3 and *Simple Symphony*)

Phantasy for oboe quartet, op. 2 **   1932

The quartet for oboe and string trio was the first Britten score heard overseas: Leon Goossens played it at the 1934 ISCM Festival in Florence. It had been well received at its premiere the previous year, when one critic called it 'uncannily stylish, inventive and securely poised for a composer reported to be still in his teens' (the performance had been on 21 November, the day before he turned twenty!). The dominating figure of the opening march was an idea that Britten simply couldn't get out of his head. He used it further in *Alla Marcia*, his next completed piece, and again in *Les Illuminations* several years later.

R   Francis, Delme Quartet, recorded 1995
Helios CDH 55154: 'Music for Oboe, Music for Piano'

Alla Marcia   1933
*Three Divertimenti***   1936

These works for string quartet are various incarnations of
the same material under the broad heading *Alla quartetto
serioso*, emanating from Britten's love of physical exercise, his
excitement about the film of *Emil and the Detectives*, and his
empathy with the Shakespearean subtitle 'Go play, boy, play'.
The history of their composition is confusing, and not really
worth the effort of investigation. Britten dedicated parts of
the works at various times to different schoolboys, and clearly
had 'P. T.' (physical training), dancing at a party, and 'ragging'
in his mind. In their final form the *Three Divertimenti* feel part
of Britten's mature output, although he never published them
in his lifetime, perhaps because they attracted 'sniggers and
cold silence' at their Wigmore Hall premiere. 'Why, I don't
know. Perhaps they are worse than I had hoped.' In his diary
he then adds the intriguing comment: 'They are not great
music – but I did feel that they are interesting & quite brilliant'. After reading an unfavourable press notice, he went on,
'I feel like a spanked schoolboy'.

His own assessment was spot on: the opening fanfare on
strings commands attention, as it leads through repeated glissandos to a distinctive March, some of which plays on harmonics. The succeeding Waltz, of graceful charm, has a spare
texture, with the occasional English cadence, and the final
Burlesque (the original ragging movement) demonstrates
once more Britten's facility for fast music. This is the musical
sportsman at work, and the players have their work cut out
as the music almost topples over itself in a race to the finish.

R   Sorrel Quartet, recorded 1995
Chandos CHAN 9469 (with String Quartets nos. 1 and 3)

String Quartet no. 1 in D, op. 25 ****   1941

The arresting opening sets the scene for what was perhaps
Britten's most inventive instrumental work to date. The violins and viola struggle high up on the fingerboard with a
sustained cluster of notes, D, E and F sharp, while the cello
plucks D and F sharp in the bass. The other-worldly, time-
less way he floats what is essentially a D major chord (at first
without any presence of an A) is a foretaste of what Britten called the 'million-dollar' opening of his second Canticle, *Abraham and Isaac*. It is still such an original sound for
a string quartet, and in hearing it you know you are in for a
treat. This opening is interrupted by an energetic, rhythmic
Allegro, back at a pitch where the instruments have their
feet on the ground. But the interchange between these two
opposite ideas provides Britten with surprising raw material for a reworking of traditional sonata form. After a short
scherzo which fizzes with invention and physical exertion
comes the slow movement, marked *Andante calmo*. This is
the almost static, moonlit surface of the sea he was to depict
in *Peter Grimes* a few years later – a ten-minute nocturnal
meditation, which is the heart of the quartet. A short, tum-
bling last movement ends exuberantly in D major, with a
wit and snap that Haydn would have enjoyed. Luckily it is
well worth the gold medal it was awarded before Britten had
finished writing it!

R   Maggini String Quartet, recorded 1998
Naxos 8.553883 (with Quartet no. 2 and *Three Divertimenti*)

String Quartet no. 2 in C, op. 36 ****   1945

The string quartets demonstrate, as does his cello music, how
original and creative Britten was when writing abstract music,
and how wrong it was to criticise him for relying on words to
produce his best music. He in turn complained that his audience better understood his *Holy Sonnets of John Donne* (written
a month earlier than his second quartet, but premiered the

following night), because they could latch on to the words, whereas the quartet was the more significant work, in marking the 'greatest advance' he had yet made.

Once again the opening commands attention with a long melodic line in unison above a bass drone, revolving round the unusual interval of a tenth. Many composers would have been content with a third, but Britten – always the wiry athlete – opts to vault the extra octave. This makes the static end of the first movement all the more magical, in hazy but sure C major chords. But the chords are missing the dominant – they have no G in them, and rely entirely on thirds (or tenths). It's how he opened the First Quartet, and would open *Abraham and Isaac*.

The scampering Scherzo on muted strings in the second movement leads into the enormous finale, which is an anniversary tribute to Purcell, first performed exactly 250 years on from the day he died. He takes the Purcellian device of a chaconne (or passacaglia), a jagged Shostakovich-like unison theme, and ingeniously constructs a sequence of twenty-one variations on it, with solo cadenzas, across a span of almost twenty minutes. The limpid, lyrical start of the third set of these variations has a strange preview of the passacaglia theme in his third quartet thirty years later. Just when the original 'chacony' seems to have been forgotten, he brings it back in the cello, and this extraordinary work reaches a triumphant conclusion with Britten's insistent tonic – a profusion of C major chords (twenty-three of them!) reasserting the quartet's home key against all comers.

R   Belcea Quartet, recorded 2004
EMI 5181 822 (2 CDs, with String Quartets nos. 1 and 3, *Three Divertimenti*)

Canticle III: Still Falls the Rain – The Raids, 1940, Night and Dawn, op. 55 *** 1954

For his third Canticle, Britten set the anguished poem by Edith Sitwell, which, in bloodstained imagery, compares the Blitz with the Crucifixion. Written for tenor, horn and piano, the music is a perfect match for the uncompromising power of the words. Woven through it by repetition is a talismanic chord of a fourth in the piano's treble register – it sounds almost like an air-raid warning – with the melismatic line sung above it: 'Still falls the rain'. Britten's response to Sitwell's words seems born of experience, and yet of course he had not himself undergone the bombing raids of 1940. His continuing religious sensibility is evident in the way he embraces Sitwell's conclusion: the voice of Christ saying, 'Still do I love, still shed my innocent light, my Blood, for thee'. Britten signals this redemptive moment with an unexpected hymn-like texture that catches the breath. In musical shape, the Canticle is both sequel and heir to his opera *The Turn of the Screw*. It holds another key ⌐→ to his inspiration: indeed Britten himself knew its importance. The poem, he said, had 'dragged something from me that was latent there, and shown me what lies before me'.

R   Pears, Tuckwell, Britten, recorded 1961
Decca E425 7162: 'The Canticles'

Alpine Suite * 1955
Scherzo 1954

It may be only a trifle, but the *Alpine Suite* for three recorders demonstrates how, in Michael Tippett's phrase, music simply 'sprang out' of Britten's fingers and mind. The six short movements were written on a Swiss skiing holiday, to occupy his friend Mary Potter after an ankle injury had confined her to their chalet. In the evenings, she, Pears and Britten could play through the *Suite*, and enjoy the whirring mechanism of Britten's 'Swiss Clock', the growing confidence on the 'Nursery Slopes', or the wistful lament of 'Farewell to

Zermatt'. His *Scherzo* for recorder quartet, written a few months earlier, has Britten's characteristic *sportif* energy.

R   The Flautadors, recorded 2003
Dutton CDLX 7142: 'Rubbra and Britten, The Complete Recorder Works'

Fanfare for St Edmundsbury *   1959

Britten the mathematician loved conundrums. This short fanfare for three trumpets was written for a pageant held in the precincts of the cathedral at Bury St Edmunds in Suffolk. One after the other, each trumpet plays its own melody – three different time-signatures and three different keys (F, C and D). Then they play all the melodies at once, and hey presto, they fit snugly together!

R   Hjelm, Nilsson, Tilly, recorded 1993
BIS BISCD 031 (with *Nocturnal*, *Songs from the Chinese* etc.)

Gemini Variations, op. 73   1965

Britten was so taken by the twin thirteen-year-old boys he met in Budapest – both keen musicians – that he wrote them a 'quartet for two players'. Gábor and Zoltán Jeney played the violin and flute respectively, and both played the piano, so these twelve variations on a theme of their veteran national composer Zoltán Kodály used all eight musical combinations possible (violin solo, flute solo, two piano solos, flute and violin, flute and piano, violin and piano, and piano duet). This no doubt appealed to Britten's mathematical mind, as did the two variations where one part mirrors the other. They came to Aldeburgh to perform the piece, and then recorded it. But it is more circus trick than music: when performed by four players rather than two, it barely holds the attention.

R   Schulz, Kussmaul, Koenen, Hellwig, recorded 1999
Campanella C130038: '*Musik mit Oboe*'

String Quartet no. 3, op. 94 ***   1975

Choosing between Britten's three mature string quartets is almost impossible: it depends which one you are listening to at the time. In my view, the third just steals the palm, not least because its middle movement (of five) contains the most utterly beautiful – and fascinating – sounds that Britten ever wrote. It's not often that one of a composer's final utterances holds the key for a newcomer to unlock his music, but 'Solo', as it is called, does just that ♪. It features a long, haunting cantilena from the first violin, interrupted only by the sweetest birdsong, while his three colleagues produce other-worldly sounds from a mixture of harmonics, pizzicatos, glissandos, arpeggios and trills. With such a rich sound palette, it is hard to believe it is simply a string quartet – you could swear there are wind instruments here, and others not yet invented.

At the very end of his life, Britten was refining and simplifying his technique. The work has a sense of summation and resignation, perhaps reflecting his own belated acceptance that he would never be well again. It may not be fanciful to spot a moment in the second movement when the viola (Britten's own instrument) looks back to the opening idea of one of his early string quartets, *Alla Marcia* (1933), or to hear in the rocking theme of the final Passacaglia an echo of the thirteenth variation of the chaconne in his Second Quartet. But there is resistance as well as resignation. Either side of 'Solo' are two short, fast movements: both burst in with a ferocity that belies the composer's frailty.

The quartet's subtitle is 'La Serenissima' – and the outermost movements in particular refer directly to the world of *Death in Venice*. It begins with 'Duets', in which the overlapping seconds suggest the water rippling against the banks of a Venetian canal. In the final Recitative and Passacaglia, there are direct quotations from the opera, before the theme is endlessly repeated, with simple decoration in the other parts. It may be in E major (Aschenbach's key), but the mood is one of poignant farewell. The music just ebbs away, in tandem with Britten's own life, and is matched almost perfectly by Pears's description of his dying partner: 'He is slowly fading, taking his time, uncomfortable but not in great pain, calm and loving all the time, drowsier each day but surprising us too with sudden questions'. The quartet ends with one of those questions, but the brief surge of chordal power subsides unanswered, as the cello holds a D natural after the E major has faded. It is a far cry from the exuberant affirmations that conclude the two earlier quartets.

R   Elias Quartet, recorded 2009
Sonimage SON10903 (with Quartet no. 2 and *Three Divertimenti*)

R   Coull Quartet, recorded 2006
Somm SOMM 065 (with *Three Divertimenti* and Nicholas Maw's String Quartet no. 3)

32

Solo instrumental music

Britten was drawn to particular solo instruments through particular people. He wrote for the violin only when he was dazzled by the artistry of Antonio Brosa in the late 1930s, and for the cello when he encountered Mstislav Rostropovich in the early 1960s. In the case of the oboe it was Sylvia Spencer and then Joy Boughton; the harp, Osian Ellis; the horn, Dennis Brain; the guitar, Julian Bream. He never wrote a solo work for clarinet (though he began one for Benny Goodman), flute or bassoon, trumpet or trombone. The piano was a special case. It was, after all, his instrument.

Five Walztes	1923–5; revised 1969
Three Character Pieces	1930
Twelve Variations	1931
Holiday Diary, op. 5 **	1934
Sonatina Romantica	1940
Night Piece (Notturno) *	1963
Variations for piano	1965

By the time he died, Britten had published only three works for solo piano: a youthful suite on holiday themes, a test piece for a piano competition, and a set of five waltzes dating from his early childhood. From someone with such a reputation as a pianist, it seemed a niggardly list – but pianists could take comfort from the dozens of piano accompaniments he had left.

Perhaps, when he decided to give up performing solo, he felt solo compositions were best avoided; perhaps, like Bruckner the great organist who wrote next to nothing for the organ, he was such a good improviser that it was a chore to write the notes down; or perhaps he was just too absorbed in opera, songs, choirs and chamber music. Pears once said that Britten had 'very mixed feelings' about the piano, and Britten himself said he preferred the piano as a background instrument rather than a melodic one. 'I find that it's limited in colour', he went on (quite rich, coming from one of the greatest conjurors of colour from the instrument). 'I don't really *like* the sound of a modern piano.'

His *Five Walztes* may chafe a little, enjoyable as they are, because of the twee way an eleven-year-old's misspelling was retained when Britten revived them at the age of fifty-five. But in recent years more and more solo piano music has been surfacing – much of it from these childhood and apprentice years, but some from his early maturity – and there is more to come. He began *Three Character Pieces* just as he started at the Royal College of Music as a student of sixteen: of these three portraits of his friends, the third ('Michael') grabs attention for its Ravelian exuberance. His *Twelve Variations* the following year show Britten entering his atonal period and experimenting with a range of styles to produce resonances of Satie, Hindemith and Shostakovich.

Holiday Diary is pre-eminent for its inventive illustrations. The opening 'Early Morning Bathe' 🔊 depicts the nervous swimmer stumbling across sharp pebbles into the bracing water of the North Sea (something that Britten at one stage did five times a day): once immersed, he settles into a rhythm as he breasts the waves, represented by fluid arpeggios and an effortful theme in the piano's left hand. With the return of dry staccato chords, we know he is tottering on the pebbles again, until the final triumphant flourish shows the warm glow of satisfaction as he wraps himself in his towel. The placid, lyrical patterns of 'Sailing' set the second movement clearly on the Norfolk Broads rather than the North Sea, although a breeze creates a brief disturbance in the middle section. The exhilarating 'Funfair' is a brisk toccata in rondo form, and would have made the perfect end to the suite, except that Britten went on to add a second slow movement, 'Night'. There's no clubbing here for the twenty-year-old composer: night is a much more staid affair. Indeed almost four minutes go by before anything happens – certainly not a finale to bring the house down.

He did write a four-movement piano sonata (or, rather a *Sonatina Romantica*) in 1940 as a personal study for a friend in New York, but it was not performed in public until after Britten's death, and even then only the first two movements ('Moderato' and 'Nocturne') have been published. The other two movements are 'Burlesca (*allegro con fuoco*)' and 'Toccata (*presto possibile*)'. The only post-war piano solo he completed was *Night Piece*, for the first Leeds Piano Competition. It was designed to test competitors' musicianship rather than their technical bravura. At times it evokes Bartók, Debussy and even Messiaen, but its nocturnal terrain is Britten's own – surprising only because his solo piano sound world is still so unfamiliar. He did start a set of variations in 1965 for the second Leeds competition, but seems to have lost interest. Rolf Hind's recent recording on NMC's 'Unknown Britten' disc reveals the six he completed as terse and compressed.

R   Stephen Hough, recorded 1990
EMI 567429 2: 'The music for one and two pianos'

R   *Holiday Diary*, *Five Walztes*, *Night Piece*: Michael Dussek, recorded 1995
Helios CDH 55154: 'Music for Oboe, Music for Piano'

Suite for violin and piano, op. 6**   1934–5
Reveille **for violin and piano***   1937
Elegy **for solo viola**   1930

Britten was seventeen when he first heard Antonio Brosa (a friend of Bridge) play the violin. He was captivated, and, although the Suite was not written for Brosa, its first complete performances were entrusted to him, notably at the ISCM festival in Barcelona in April 1936, where it had been selected by a panel that included the composer Anton Webern and the conductor Ernest Ansermet. Webern was perhaps impressed by Britten's flirtation with Schoenbergian sonorities at this time, particularly in the crisp March that opens the Suite. This unfamiliar work is well worth searching out, especially for his original take on the Waltz in the finale, and the languid Lullaby that precedes it. Britten retained enough affection for the work to prepare a revised version in the last months of his life. As well as his later Violin Concerto, Britten wrote a five-minute concert study for Brosa, entitled *Reveille*. Its somnolent feel until the last fifteen seconds accurately suggests the violinist was not a morning person.

The melancholy viola piece was written in the two days after the end of his final term at school, and has been taken as a comment on the misery of his schooldays. But he was happier at Gresham's School than he let on, and rather nostalgic as he left, so perhaps it is actually an exercise in school-sickness. It was presumably designed for Britten to play to himself – unusually, he never even gave it a title (*Elegy* was the publisher's choice in 1985). It rather outstays its welcome.

R   Violin Suite: Mireille and Lydia Jardon, recorded 2003 AR Ré-Sé AR 20036: 'English Impressions' (with sonatas by Bridge and Rawsthorne)

Two Insect Pieces *	1935
Temporal Variations ***	1936
Six Metamorphoses after Ovid, op. 49 **	1951

The short, witty *Insect Pieces* were the first of three significant contributions Britten made to the oboist's repertoire. In 'The Grasshopper' the oboe leaps around perkily, while 'The Wasp' has more than a hint of *The Flight of the Bumble Bee*. The pieces were written for his friend Sylvia Spencer when Britten was only twenty-one, but not publicly performed until her memorial service more than forty years later. Britten said he was 'very pleased with the little pieces'. Another three insects were planned, but never emerged. But the *Temporal Variations* (originally *Temporal Suite*) are of much greater consequence, and a work of striking originality. It is built round a simple, pleading motif of a rising second followed by a rising sixth, and all eight variations (for oboe and piano) are of strong character. A March is followed by toccata-style 'Exercises'. A 'Commination' (how's that for a musical title?) leads to a quiet Chorale, an unorthodox Waltz, and then a cocky Polka. In the final 'Resolution', the motif is confined to repeated appoggiaturas, which assert the tonality of D. *The Daily Telegraph* said 'Mr Britten is again a sly and nimble Harlequin of music', but *The Times* thought it 'a triviality'. Why this work was withdrawn after its first performance is unfathomable: since it was rescued in 1980, it has justly become a staple of the repertoire.

The *Metamorphoses* display the full versatility of the solo oboe. Britten takes six mythical characters from Ovid's poems, each of whom underwent some transformation. He expresses this musically in his adaptation of the distinct musical idea with which each movement opens. In 'Narcissus', the mirror-sounds in the music match the youth's fascination with his own reflection, as he turns into a flower. We hear Phaeton's hectic ride to disaster, or Bacchus's boozy hiccups, or Arethusa's glistening fountain – if on paper it reads as a bit obvious, it sounds wonderful. They are testing pieces, but their rhapsodic form allows the soloist plenty of individuality.

R Francis, Dussek, recorded 1995
Helios CDH 55154: 'Music for Oboe, Music for Piano'
(with *Phantasy* oboe quartet etc.)

R *Metamorphoses*: Gordon Hunt, recorded 1996
BIS BISCD 769: 'Soliloquy' (with works by Gordon Jacob, Nicola LeFanu etc.)

Introduction and Rondo alla Burlesca, **op. 23 no. 1** **   1940
Mazurka Elegiaca, **op. 23, no. 2** **   1941
Lullaby   1936
*Lullaby for a Retired Colonel**   1936

The first two works (for two pianos) were written separately,
but both are war pieces. The *Introduction and Rondo* is full of
foreboding, with a burlesque element that is far from frivo-
lous – much more in the Shostakovich mould of grim irony.
Its ambivalence between D minor and E flat is unresolved
even in the final chord. The *Mazurka Elegiaca* of the following year is a tribute to the Polish politician-pianist, Ignacy Jan
Paderewski, replete with references to Chopin's Mazurkas.
But in the context of the time it's also a lament for Poland's
predicament: its tenderness is tinged with violence, and in the
middle the piece seems to hang by a thread.

The two lullabies were written in gentler times for an audi-
tion Britten had at the BBC as a prospective piano-duo performer. The first teeters in true Gallic style on the verge of
parody, while the second is merciless in its proposition that
the cure for military insomnia is to hear bits of 'The British
Grenadiers', 'Men of Harlech', the *Marseillaise* and the Last
Post – all at once: a two-minute treat.

R Hough, O'Hora, recorded 1990
EMI 567429 2 (with *Holiday Diary* etc.)

R *Introduction and Rondo alla Burlesca*, *Mazurka Elegiaca*:
Curzon, Britten, recorded 1944
Pearl PRL 9177 (with Michelangelo Sonnets, *Serenade* etc.)

Prelude and Fugue on a Theme of Vittoria   1946

This five-minute organ piece was written in a hurry three days
before St Matthew's Church, Northampton, was due to mark
its patronal festival. Walter Hussey, the vicar, had been badg-
ering Britten to write a St Matthew's Day anthem to words
by Auden: the poet obliged, but not the composer. Instead he

dashed off this nondescript piece – his only solo work for the organ. The organ accompaniment he provided for his *Missa Brevis* showed much greater originality.

R Iain Farrington, recorded 2000
Naxos 8.554791 (with *Rejoice in the Lamb*, *Missa Brevis*, *Hymn to St Cecilia* etc.)

Lachrymae, op. 48 **   1950

The Elizabethan composer, John Dowland, was the driving force behind the set of variations Britten wrote for the viola player William Primrose to perform at the 1950 Aldeburgh Festival. After the viola and piano open in unison, part of the original Dowland theme is heard on the piano underneath the viola line. It comes from the song *If my complaints could passions move*, but does not appear in full until after the tenth and final variation, when it is played poignantly by both instruments, complete with sixteenth-century harmony. Another Dowland song, *Flow my tears*, appears in the sixth variation, and gives the Britten work its title. The variations generally last less than a minute each, and range widely in mood and vim. A deceptively simple piece, Britten reworked it for viola and strings at the end of his life (see chapter 27, 'Symphonies and concertos').

R Koll, Inui, recorded 2004
Naxos 8.557606: 'The Art of the Viola' (with works by Beethoven, Schumann and Hindemith)

Timpani Piece for Jimmy   1955

This 'silly little piece' (as Britten called it) was written 'in the maddest hurry' in Istanbul in December 1955 for his favourite percussionist, James Blades – although Blades used to say that he and Britten had first discussed the sketch for it during a train journey to Venice. It's a three-minute frolic for timpani and piano: it begins and ends in D minor, but the

middle section in B major requires swift pedalwork to change
the pitch of the drums.

Sonata in C for cello and piano, op. 65 **   1961
Suite for Cello op. 72 ***   1964
Second Suite for Cello op. 80 **   1967
Third Suite for Cello op. 87 ****   1971
Tema Sacher   1975

Britten wrote more works for the Russian cellist Mstislav Rostropovich than for any other individual, save Peter
Pears. The *Cello Symphony* and the five instrumental works
all stemmed from a London concert at which Rostropovich
had performed Shostakovich's First Cello Concerto. Britten
was in the audience, and was so excited by the performance
that the very next day he promised a work for Rostropovich,
on condition that he gave the premiere at the next Aldeburgh
Festival. The sonata was the result.

The questioning at the start reflects perhaps the tenta-
tive start of a friendship, before it leads on to a dialogue that
is vigorous and languid by turns. After the impish Scherzo
comes an Elegy, in which the piano is sometimes the dominant partner, then a fast, heavy March, before a concluding
Moto perpetuo where jagged unison quavers hurtle towards a
final chord of C major.

At their first meeting the two men forged an instant bond,
even though Britten spoke no Russian, and Rostropovich
no English. They communicated in very bad German, and
through liberal supplies of both music and alcohol. Ciné film
of them larking around (as two middle-aged men) on railway lines, trying to keep their balance, demonstrates their
shared sense of the absurd. But the musical partnership was of
immense significance. Their recording of Schubert's Arpeggione Sonata, for instance, demonstrates an almost unique
rapport: cellist and pianist seem to be thinking, playing, even
breathing, as one. This closeness bore extraordinary fruit in
Britten's work: in a (by then) rare departure from music for

the voice, he embarked on three suites for solo cello – which are arguably the most important unaccompanied works for the instrument since J. S. Bach composed his six suites 250 years earlier. This is why they are among the most frequently recorded Britten works: some twelve recordings of each suite are currently available, as well as fourteen of the sonata.

Bach's supreme achievement in writing for an instrument which cannot sustain more than two notes at a time was to create a space in which the listener's mind fills in the gaps, and adds the harmonies to the cello line. Britten does the same, and takes it further. So he manages to write a fugue in each suite, although only one instrument is playing: he uses rests as spaces in which to place other lines of music. The player will often be doing three things at the same time: in the fifth movement of the First Suite, for instance, the cellist's right hand is bowing rapid semiquavers on one string, while maintaining a drone on another, and plucking notes with his left hand on a third. It may sound tricksy (it is certainly difficult technically!), but it results in music of imagination and complexity.

Other movements in this suite are a slow Lament, a non-stop pizzicato Serenade, and an enchantingly witty March, in which the cello switches between major arpeggios on harmonics (a fairyland fanfare) and rhythmic drum-beats tapped out with the wooden part of the bow held upside-down. Woven throughout the work is the repeated idea (a different kind of *cantus firmus*) of a slow melody continuously achieved through double-stopping the strings. The cellist sets off on the final furlong with galloping semiquavers – but bit by bit the *cantus firmus* returns, along with Bachian arpeggios. It is an emotional homecoming as the cello, with one final burst of energy, crosses the G major threshold in triumph.

The Second Suite has a different flavour of flamboyance. It opens by declaiming a phrase that surely derives from the opening of Shostakovich's Fifth symphony. Then come fugue, scherzo, slow movement, and a long chaconne, in which he repeatedly tips his cap to Bach. It requires virtuosity that both startles and satisfies.

The Third Suite is the most intimate of the three, and less concerned with bravura writing. Its nine continuous movements seem to reach down into the depths of the soul. There is not much wit here – rather more anguish. Once again there is a Fugue and a fast *Moto perpetuo*, and a Barcarolle that belongs to the spirit of Bach – indeed this movement, with the gentle song which precedes it, presents another key ⊶ to unlock Britten's secrets. The climax comes with yet another Britten Passacaglia, in which the ground bass goes constantly round, with ever more elaborate decoration above, until the movement subsides into the utter simplicity of three Russian folksongs and finally the sobbing melody of the Kontakion (the Orthodox Church's hymn for the departed). We may not have realised that the work has been based on these tunes all through, but subconsciously we experience the emotion, once again, of returning home, as the melodies are played complete, and straight – the themes coming after, not before, the variations. Britten had done something similar with his viola *Lachrymae*, and his guitar *Nocturnal*, both of which are based on songs by John Dowland – with the Dowland theme emerging in full glory only at the end. He surely also remembered his excitement in hearing the Bach chorale at the end of the Violin Concerto by Alban Berg – he had been at the work's first performance in 1936. It is brave for any composer to let another one have the last word – but here the impact is overwhelming.

It was three and a half years before the Soviet authorities allowed Rostropovich to travel to Aldeburgh to perform the Third Suite for the first time. By then Britten was seriously ill. The associations of this most personal music, ending with the prayer 'Grant repose, together with the saints', was too much for Rostropovich. He wept, and after Britten's death seldom performed it again.

Rostropovich did squeeze one final cello piece out of Britten, *Tema Sacher*. This one-minute theme to honour the conductor Paul Sacher is built around the musical notes of his surname: E flat (S), A, C, B natural (H), E and D (Ré). Rostropovich's idea was that eleven other composers would add variations on it, but it is hard to imagine Pierre Boulez agreeing to work with anything by Britten, and indeed he didn't. He wrote a separate piece, as did the others.

R   Cello Sonata and Suites for Cello nos. 1 and 2:
Rostropovich, Britten, recorded 1961 and 1970
Decca 421 8592

R   Suites for Cello nos. 1–3: Watkins, recorded 2003
Nimbus NI 5704

R   Cello Sonata: Wispelwey, Lazic, recorded 2002
Channel CCS 20098 (with sonatas by Shostakovich and Prokofiev)

Nocturnal after John Dowland, op. 70***   1963

Slivers of Dowland's song *Come, heavy Sleep, the image of true Death* glint in the musings – as if improvised there and then – that open this magnificent twenty-minute virtuoso piece for the guitar, which Britten subtitled as 'reflections' on the Dowland song. Once again he is caught up in the world of sleep – this time as an anaesthetic for grief – but still finds scope for fast, edgy music, to capture the agitation of sorrow, the restlessness of insomnia, and the tossing and turning of semi-consciousness, before the pace slows, and sleep finally does 'close up these my weary weeping eyes'. Then, in the key eighth section of the work ♪—♪ , comes one of Britten's masterly passacaglias, based on a single descending scale in the key of the passacaglia in Brahms's Fourth symphony which had so excited him as a boy, E minor, but here with flattened supertonic. This lament is the expressive core of the work: it is new-minted Britten, yet the form and cadences of the Elizabethan original begin to take shape, until the guitar slips, inevitably and almost imperceptibly, into E major for the pure Dowland melody and harmony at the end. It is a precious part of the guitar repertoire, which is why there are about a dozen recordings currently available.

R   Stephen Marchionda, recorded 2003
Chandos CHAN 10305 (with *Songs from the Chinese* and
works by Dowland and Maw)

Suite for Harp, op. 83 *   1969

The harp had a special appeal for Britten: he began writing
for it as a prep-school boy, when he recognised the extra colour it could give large orchestral scores such as his Symphony
in D minor, or his *Quatre chansons françaises*. At the end of his
life, when he could no longer accompany Pears on the piano,
he chose the harp as the instrument most compatible with
Pears's voice. This was largely due to the important role the
harp had played in the small ensemble for his three Church
Parables in the mid 1960s. The charming Harp Suite followed
close behind. Far from being all glitter and shimmer, the harp
has a sinister feel in the central Nocturne, another Britten
night piece akin to the mood of *A Midsummer Night's Dream*.
The Suite ends with variations on a theme: but as so often
Britten teases his audience by revealing the theme only at the
end. It is 'St Denio', the Welsh tune for the hymn 'Immortal,
invisible, God only wise' – a compliment to the Welsh harpist
for whom the suite was written, Osian Ellis.

R   Ellis, recorded 1976
Meridian CDE 84119 (with *Tit for Tat*, *Six Metamorphoses
after Ovid* etc.)

33
Songs

With a total of some 170 solo songs to his name, let alone the folksongs he reworked, Britten must be the greatest English writer of art songs since Purcell – of whose songs he also made many arrangements. Indeed it was one of his ambitions as a young man 'to try and restore to the musical setting of the English language a brilliance, freedom and vitality that have been curiously rare since the death of Purcell'. Few would deny him that achievement.

Beware!	1922–6; revised 1967–8
O that I had ne'er been married	1922–6; revised 1967–8
Epitaph: The Clerk	1922–6; revised 1967–8

Beware! was first written when Britten was nine years old, but there are numerous subsequent manuscripts, indicating that he liked it enough to keep fiddling with it. Even at his tender age, Britten managed to convert the rather ungainly metrical shape of Longfellow's poem into a successful musical pattern. Perhaps he was engaged by the danger of a maiden 'fair to see', who can 'both false and friendly be', and his major-minor shift at the end is an apposite touch. It is the best known of these three early songs, which Britten readied for publication near the end of his life. Its first public performance was by Pears in a lecture in Norwich in 1980 – when he accompanied himself.

R Monnaie Children's Choir/Menier, recorded 2004
Fuga Libera FUG 507 (with *Friday Afternoons*, *Three Two-part Songs* and *The Golden Vanity*)

Quatre chansons françaises **   1928

These remarkable songs for high voice and orchestra set poems that the prep-school composer found in his *Oxford Book of French Verse*. His choice of texts may have been influenced by their brevity: he chose the shortest poems by Victor Hugo and Paul Verlaine that he could lay his hands on. He was only fourteen – and a rather immature fourteen at that – when he set them in his final term at South Lodge and the ensuing summer holidays of 1928, and their musical language is largely derivative. Yet the songs are disconcerting portents of the mature composer's feeling for the mood, meaning and drama of words. For instance, the bitter-sweet pathos of Hugo's five-year-old child singing and playing nonchalantly in the garden, while its mother coughs herself to death inside, draws a dramatic response worthy of the later composer of *Curlew River*.

How could such a young boy, who had no access at home to gramophone records or the wireless, and had attended only a handful of orchestral concerts, have written for the orchestra with such assurance? The notes we hear now have not been edited or doctored by wiser heads: they are exactly those he heard in his own. The work sprang forth fully clothed and without warning, like the goddess Athena leaping fully armed from inside the head of Zeus. Britten never heard it played, but he signalled his belief in it by agreeing to the reproduction of one page of the score almost half a century later.

At fourteen, Britten loved Wagner, as he did for many years afterwards, and he owned a dozen miniature scores of 'bleeding chunks' from his operas, among them the 'Prelude and Liebestod' from *Tristan und Isolde*, which suffuses the fourth of these French songs. There are Richard Strauss moments too, although it was another two years before he soaked himself in Strauss's songs with orchestra. But the French words also coax modern French textures, such as Debussy (whose *Prélude à l'après-midi d'un faune* delighted Britten) and Ravel, whose *Introduction and Allegro* (particularly the use of the harp) and String Quartet had already made an impression on him.

R   Lott, RSNO/Thomson, recorded 1988
Chandos CHAN 10192X (with *Les Illuminations, Serenade*)

*The Birds***	1929–34
The Witches' Song – Jonson	1929
The Owl – Tennyson	1929
Diaphenia – Constable	1929
Chamber Music V – Joyce	1930
*The Moth** – de la Mare	1931
Sport – Davies	1931

The Birds reveals Britten's tenderness for his mother, to whom
this setting of Hilaire Belloc's poem was dedicated. He was
rightly proud enough to include it in his portfolio for his
Royal College of Music scholarship. It is infinitely touching,
without being sentimental, and must have jerked many tears
when it was heard at his mother's funeral.

The other songs in this engaging group from his apprentice years have been published only recently. The most startling of them is *The Moth*, in which Britten experiments with
atonality, as he was doing in instrumental pieces at the time.
The pianist's hands are in different keys, often in conflicting
rhythms, as they flit lightly and softly round the upper keyboard in wickedly fast arpeggios, evoking the moth's wings as
it is drawn to its doom in the flame. Interwoven with them is
the smooth vocal line – a thread of separate tonality.

R   *The Birds*: Leonard, Martineau, recorded 1997
Somm SOMM 213: 'A Century of English Song, vol. 1'
(with *On This Island* and songs by Walton, Tippett and
Berkeley)

R   *The Owl, Diaphenia, The Witches' Song, Chamber Music V*:
Swait, Bowman, Plant, recorded 2007
Signum SIGCD128: 'Songs of Innocence'

| *Tit for Tat** | 1928–31; revised 1968 |
| *Farfield 1928–30* | 1955 |

When Britten started reviewing his juvenilia for publication in his middle age, he was not interested in disclosing his youthful dalliance with atonality. Instead he chose six separate settings of poems by Walter de la Mare, with their literary insight into the child's mind. Some of them are indeed contemporary with his atonal experiments, yet these settings feel mostly at home in the world of Peter Warlock, one of the leading song composers of Britten's teens. The most vivid word-painting comes in one of the earliest songs, 'Silver'.

The little song he wrote for the 400th anniversary of his old school, Gresham's, bears the name of his boarding house and his years there. It's a whimsical reminiscence of boarding-school life, complete with strokes of the cane.

R   *Tit for Tat*: Shirley-Quirk, Ledger, recorded 1987 Meridian CDE 84119 (with Suite for Harp, *Two Insect Pieces* and *Six Metamorphoses after Ovid*)

To lie flat on the back	1937
*Night covers up the rigid land**	1937
*Fish in the unruffled lakes**	1938; revised 1942–3
The sun shines down	1937
What's in your mind?	1941
Underneath the abject willow	1936 and 1941?
Mother Comfort – Slater	1936

Some of these Auden settings may have been intended for a second volume of his collection *On This Island*. The first two songs set words that Auden had written about Britten himself. The second reveals his attraction to the composer. But his feelings were unrequited: 'so I must lie alone,' he says. Britten's music is unselfconscious, but tender – notable for its final falling ninth. *Fish in the unruffled lakes* is the only song of this group that Britten and Pears performed in public: it is an outstanding song – not least for the glinting, aqueous nature of the piano introduction. *Underneath the abject willow*, which Auden dedicated to Britten, was first set, together with the Montagu Slater poem, for soprano duet – perhaps as a way of concealing its direct appeal to Britten to give rein to his emotions and come out. 'Very light & Victorian in mood!', he noted in his diary. He later adapted the song for solo voice.

R   Langridge, Bedford, recorded 1997
Naxos 8.557204: 'Auden Songs by Britten and Berkeley'

Tell me the Truth about Love **	1938
Funeral Blues	1937
Johnny **	1937
Calypso *	1939

Hedli Anderson, for whom these light-footed cabaret songs were written, must have been quite an artist. Britten loved sopranos, and she certainly brought out the best in him. Thanks to an eyewitness account, we can picture the 'long-legged beauty' sitting on the piano, with the tense, earnest figure of Britten at the keyboard, as they performed these sensual Auden numbers, with their undoubted gay subtext, for their friends. She and Britten recorded *Johnny* (the best of the four) and *Funeral Blues*, along with two intriguing songs for which the music has now disappeared (*Give up love* and *I'm a jam tart*). The discs – Britten's first – were never issued, but what a discovery it would be if the masters turned up one day! *Funeral Blues* (the setting of 'Stop all the clocks') dates from the time of his mother's sudden death in February 1937; the poem has since become famous because of its use in the film *Four Weddings and a Funeral*.

R   Bourne, Holmes, recorded 2008
RCA 88697 293 432: 'The Truth About Love' (with songs by Martinů and Weill)

'Evening'**	1944–5
'Morning'**	1944–5
'Night'**	1944–5

These three songs written for the stage production of Ronald Duncan's *This Way to the Tomb* deserve to be better known. Their lyrics are pumped full of Duncan's purple imagery: 'Morning is only / a scarlet stallion / jumping the ocean', 'Eyes of mice, the stars, from the privacy of light peep into the darkness', 'Night is no more than a cat which creeps to the saucer of light'. 'Evening' teeters hauntingly between C minor and C major, while 'Night' is a mini-passacaglia in B minor. In between comes a crisp G major setting of 'Morning'.

R   Bostridge, Johnson, recorded 1995
Hyperion CDA 66823 (with *The Holy Sonnets of John Donne* etc.)

The Red Cockatoo – Po Chu-I, trans. Waley	1938
When you're feeling like expressing your affection *	
– Auden	1935
A Poison Tree – Blake	1935
Wild with passion – Beddoes	1942
If thou wilt ease thine heart – Beddoes	1942
Um Mitternacht – Goethe	1960
Not even summer yet – Burra	1937
Birthday Song for Erwin – Duncan	1945
Cradle Song (Sleep, my darling, sleep) * – MacNeice	1942

This miscellaneous collection has now been published as *The Red Cockatoo and Other Songs*. The title song is the shortest of the lot, but its forty seconds are vividly coloured. The next, a witty little number about the delights of using the telephone, was written for the GPO Film Unit, and captures the era of 'Button A' public call boxes, the flavour of the 1930s, and the deft touch of the twenty-one-year-old composer, all in just fifty seconds.

The austere Blake setting is Britten's first of a poet who became a favourite. He seems to have toyed with further settings of the nineteenth-century poet, Thomas Beddoes, but never went further than these two engaging songs, written on his transatlantic journey back to England in the war. Similarly, he marked up various Goethe possibilities, but *Um Mitternacht* is the only one he managed (not to be confused with the Rückert poem of the same title, which Mahler set).

Not even summer yet is a touching lament for Peter Burra, a friend of Britten's who was killed in an air crash. It was first sung by Burra's sister, Nell, at a memorial concert, but she had to pull out of a subsequent Wigmore Hall performance, because she found it too emotional. *Birthday Song for Erwin* was written for the music publisher Erwin Stein, who became a close friend, as did his daughter Marion – she only discovered this manuscript in 1986. It is particularly notable for its evocation of a gong – something that Britten had been practising since childhood, when he amazed his friend Basil Reeve by reproducing on the piano the harmonics of the family dinner gong. The Louis MacNeice song (also titled 'Cradle Song for Eleanor') strikes home the deepest here, but then sleep always brought out the best in Britten.

R   Bostridge, Johnson, recorded 1995
Hyperion CDA 66823 (with *The Holy Sonnets of John Donne*)

Our Hunting Fathers, op. 8 ****   1936

Britten's first – perhaps only – avant-garde work is utterly astonishing in its virtuosity. It came only five years after Walton's great oratorio *Belshazzar's Feast*, which was alarmingly modern to many ears in 1931, yet in terms of contemporary English music *Our Hunting Fathers* must have sounded as if it came from another planet, with its fierce, uncompromising subject-matter and musical language. 'It is Puck-like music', said one review, 'fantastically nimble and coruscating'.

The text – five poems about man's relationship with the animal kingdom – was devised and partly written by W. H. Auden. There is nothing cosy here: a plague of rats and the

rituals of falconry tempt Britten into feats of vocal and instrumental display. *The Daily Telegraph* wondered if it was an
'orchestral prank, in which the instruments lead a distracted
human voice into one embarrassing position after another'.
The terrifying 'Dance of Death' (not far removed from that
of Bartók's *Miraculous Mandarin*) must have had the country
sports enthusiasts of Norfolk choking on their pink gins. Britten even felt the rare displeasure of his ever-doting mother.
The Observer called it 'dire nonsense'. Perhaps none of them
grasped his subtext – a commentary on the unfolding brutality
of Nazism.

The Norwich concert also premiered a risqué work by
Vaughan Williams – the bawdy *Five Tudor Portraits*. VW and
Britten were never the best of pals, but the older man famously stood up for Britten at the first orchestral rehearsal, when
players were giggling and squeaking like rats in mockery of
Britten's music, and told them to behave. The tomfoolery was
the equivalent of the sniggers that can often greet contemporary music or minimalist scores today. Britten knew this was
his first really adult work: 'It's my real opus 1', he said. Everything that had gone before, with the possible exception of
A Boy was Born, was apprentice work, although that included
several fine scores which have lasted.

By a strange coincidence, *Our Hunting Fathers* and *Five
Tudor Portraits* met in the middle (as well as at the concert). As
a centrepiece both Britten and VW chose to write a funeral
lament for a dead pet – a monkey and a sparrow respectively.
Both are heartfelt rather than facetious.

From the first note – one of those hollow Britten wind
chords that feel like electric shocks – his orchestral mastery
is established. He turns his orchestra into a team of virtuoso
soloists: the spacing and colouring of every chord is meticu-
lously calculated. Take, for example, the chilling brass chords
at the words, 'if her monkey die'. The fast, scurrying second
movement, 'Rats Away!', deserves a key mark ♪— for wit,
agility and daring. The bleakness of Auden's epilogue is conveyed in chamber-like textures that owe much to his recent

discovery of Alban Berg, with the insistent brittle scale on that instrument of childhood, the xylophone, an early instance of lost innocence.

Thanks to Peter Pears, most of Britten's songs written in the upper register are associated with the tenor voice. But *Our Hunting Fathers*, like many of his early songs, was intended for Sophie Wyss, and some of the most effective modern recordings are by sopranos.

R   Harper, LPO/Haitink, recorded 1979
LPO 0002 (with Elgar *Enigma Variations* and *Introduction and Allegro*)

On This Island, op. 11 **   1937

So generous was the applause after the first performance of these songs at a BBC Concert of Contemporary Music in November 1937 that Britten concluded they were 'far too obvious and amenable for Contemporary Music'. His settings of five Auden poems (a year after *Our Hunting Fathers*) were his first published group of songs for voice and piano – in this case the soprano, Sophie Wyss, and his own piano accompaniment. They broadly relate to the theme of Home – and indeed the work is a step back from the avant-garde style of the previous Auden work. The opening declamatory fanfare of 'Let the florid music praise' has a boldness which Britten would match in his Michelangelo Sonnets three years later. The scurries of notes in 'Now the leaves are falling fast' suggest the sudden gusts of wind in autumn, while the cabaret style of the final song 'As it is, plenty' feels a touch discordant with the rest of the set: it may, as Pears once said, have a pertness that points to its shallow nature, but it also has a whiff of Britten manufacturing his own applause. The core of the work is the 'Nocturne', in which the trochaic rhythms of 'night's caressing grip' in C sharp minor allow 'sleep's healing power' to work. After slipping down to C minor with the 'traction engine, bull or horse', Britten holds the listener captive with the singer's surprising shift to top G sharp, as he pulls the song back to its home key.

R   Bonney, Martineau, recorded 2004
Onyx ONYX 4003: 'My Name is Barbara' (with songs by Barber, Bernstein, Copland, Quilter)

Les Illuminations, op. 18**** 1939

Britten's settings of the French visionary teenage poet, Arthur Rimbaud, were also written for soprano, but it was Pears who made them famous – so much so that many have thought some of the sexual allusions (deriving from the seventeen-year-old Rimbaud's torrid affair with his older colleague, Paul Verlaine) related to the affair between Pears and Britten, which began during the work's composition. The most overt of these references is in 'Being Beauteous', the longest of the cycle's ten sections, which was indeed dedicated to Pears, but only as an afterthought. It was the first to be written, in March 1939, when Britten was besotted not with Pears, but with his own teenage (would-be) poet, Wulff Scherchen. 'Written two good (!) songs this week', Britten told Scherchen. 'French words. Arthur Rimbaud – marvellous poems. I'll show you them later. Much love to you my darling – I think of you all day.' When 'Being Beauteous' was performed the next month, Britten told Scherchen he'd been thinking of him 'so much during it'.

Britten's writing in these songs (accompanied by string orchestra) is utterly delicious. At the start he summons the singer with a bitonal fanfare on the strings – alternating between the remote keys of E major and B flat major. The music for 'Villes' has boundless vitality, whereas the static, graceful arpeggios of 'Antique' (with a concealed dedication to Scherchen) clothe the '*gracieux fils de Pan*' in a sensual innocence. In 'Royauté', the strings cunningly conjure up people shouting in the streets; in 'Parade' he reworks ideas from his *Alla Marcia* for string quartet six years before; but the predominating orchestral glitter subsides into music of

Mahlerian depth and poignancy for the closing 'Départ'. He told his first soloist, Sophie Wyss, to sing this quietly and very slowly, to 'bring tears to the eyes of even the programme-sellers at the back of the hall!' – and he was right.

R   Lott, RSNO/Thomson, recorded 1988
Chandos CHAN 10192X (with *Serenade* and *Quatre chansons françaises*)

R   Matthews, LPO/Jurowski, recorded 2008
LPO 0037 (with *Double Concerto* and Frank Bridge Variations)

R   Bostridge, Berlin Philharmonic/Rattle, recorded 2005
EMI 558 0492 (tenor version, with *Serenade* and *Nocturne*)

Seven Sonnets of Michelangelo, op. 22 ****   1940

After *On This Island*, Britten composed no songs in English until the *Serenade* in the middle of the war. In between he returned to French in *Les Illuminations* and embarked on Italian for the first and only time in the Michelangelo Sonnets. This allowed him a clean break from what he saw as the inadequacies of word-setting by other English composers, but was also a convenient disguise for what were otherwise overt love-songs for his new musical and sexual partner, Peter Pears. Michelangelo wrote about his young lover Tommaso dei Cavalieri so passionately that, when his grand-nephew published the poems some years later, he felt obliged to change the gender of the pronouns. Britten, however, worked from a text of the original, uncensored Italian words, beside which was printed an honest Victorian translation by John Addington Symonds.

When Pears started singing the Sonnets, he produced for his audience his own modern translation, which was designed once again to obscure the homosexual tone of the erotic poetry, and therefore the nature of Pears and Britten's relationship. The collaborator in this translation was their host during their three-year sojourn in America, Elizabeth Mayer

– who thus gave Pears convenient female 'cover' for what
might have been a risqué exercise.

Even so, Pears and Britten did not (dare to?) perform these
songs publicly for almost two years after they were written. A
few private performances and a private recording (now issued
on the NMC label) sufficed. Only back in England, in September 1942, did the songs come nervously out into the open,
although Britten thought it would be 'cruel to parade them in
the cruel light' of the Wigmore Hall. He need not have worried. The work was an immediate success, they were booked
the same evening for an HMV recording, and repeated the
performance at a lunchtime concert at the National Gallery
in October.

It was a while before most people grasped the thrust of the
cycle, arising from the sonnets that Britten had chosen. Critics
and audience alike had the benefit of Pears's doctored translation in the concert programmes, but not of the actual Italian
texts, so only those who knew their Michelangelo poetry cot-
toned on. Indeed the *Sunday Times* critic, Ernest Newman,
complained about this: the words, he said, had sped by at
so rapid a pace that he could only record a general impression of the piece. The *Times* critic said blandly that there was
'nothing to perplex the listener', and they were 'fine songs for
singing'. No one knew that day that Britten's manuscript was
headed 'To Peter' – direct evidence that Michelangelo was
speaking for Britten about the new love of his life. Only the
most sharp-eared would have spotted Britten laying his cards
on the table at the end of the first song, where he deliberately repeats Michelangelo's earlier phrase, '*Signor, mie car*'.
In his translation, Pears could have rendered this as 'my dear
lord': instead he opted for the neutered phrase, 'dear love'.
For two artists already in the firing-line for their pacifism, the
Pears translation was an artful and calculated device in those
straiter-laced days. It minimised the risk of the work's content
causing collateral damage to its undoubted musical merit.

This talisman from the peak of their affair was to become
the Britten work they performed together more than any

other – more than a hundred performances all told, twice as many as any other song cycle. This is no surprise, because of the allure of these intense songs, arresting in their ardour, whether in the passionate declamation of the first (Sonnet 16), or the playful florescence of the second (Sonnet 31), where the Italian words speak suggestively of the naked poet in bondage to his 'armed cavalier'. In Sonnet 32, Britten creates the agitation of a lover desperate to repair a relationship after a row, while Sonnet 24 ('*Spirto ben nato*') concludes the cycle with its noble keynote phrase of a rising major third, followed by a falling fifth. The third (Sonnet 30) is without doubt one of the most sublime songs Britten ever wrote, in which a long, slow *bel canto* line is spun by the singer above repeated triadic chords played by the pianist's left hand – a direct foreshadowing of 'Before Life and After', which thirteen years later was to end the set of songs with the strongest rival claim to be Britten's most personal, and most successful, *Winter Words*. Pears regarded the third Sonnet as a type of song that 'had never been done by an Englishman before; it was this Sonnet and the last one of the set which, in the early performances of these songs, opened the eyes of his audience to what vocal writing could be.'

R   Anthony Rolfe Johnson, Graham Johnson, recorded 1986
Helios CDH 55067 (with *Canticle I* and *Winter Words*)

Serenade for tenor, horn and strings, op. 31 *****   1943
Now sleeps the crimson petal***   1943
Nocturne, op. 60 ****   1958

'It is not important stuff, but quite pleasant, I think', wrote Britten disingenuously about his *Serenade*, an undisputed masterpiece. This work, above all others, is the gateway to understanding Britten's mind and music. It makes an immediate impact, but also benefits from deeper acquaintance. The whole piece must have a key mark 𝄐 , but if time is short, the final three vocal movements ('Dirge', 'Hymn' and 'Sonnet') are particularly recommended.

All through his life, Britten was drawn to the edgy world of dreams, darkness and night. He initially conceived of the *Serenade*'s six poems as Nocturnes (one of his favourite titles – he used it in seven other works as well, including the orchestral song cycle of 1958). He establishes the mood with the prologue for solo horn (which one early critic said was out of tune – failing to realise that Britten had specifically asked for the discomfiting sound of the natural, valveless horn).

With the help of a small string orchestra and the horn, the tenor gets to the languid heart of Cotton's 'Pastoral' ('The day's grown old'), and moves on to Tennyson's evocation of bugle calls echoing across a crepuscular landscape in 'Nocturne'. In Blake's 'Elegy', feverish repeated chords in the upper strings sustain the long horn melody, with ominous pizzicatos in the lower strings. This is the cycle's longest movement, yet shortest song: eight brief lines about a beautiful crimson rose destroyed by the worm at its heart. It leads remorselessly to the anonymous fifteenth-century 'Dirge', in which the tenor's nine verses of a constant, mournful melody are enveloped in increasingly elaborate string textures: a fugue emerges, with complicated key relationships, and the horn breaks in at the climax. This is hallmarked Britten: through his artistry, the clever complexity of the writing sounds utterly simple. Ben Jonson's 'Hymn' is a fast, almost skittish, paean to the moon, with the horn in hunting mood. As in his later night-cycle *Nocturne*, Britten turns to Keats for the climax of the work – in this case his sonnet 'O soft embalmer of the still midnight'. Here tenor and strings on their own evoke the imprecise contours of semi-consciousness, the brink of sleep. This is music of taste, smell, touch and sight, as well as sound, which in its perfect marriage with Keats's words stirs the very depths of the spirit. After this, how can anyone seriously say that Britten was a clever composer of musical devices who could not write from the heart? As he seals 'the hushed casket of my Soul' in a magical D major, the only response is silence – except for the hushed reprise of the natural horn solo offstage.

A decade after Britten's death, the manuscript of a seventh song for the *Serenade* turned up – a setting of Tennyson's 'Now sleeps the crimson petal'. His friend Marion Thorpe found it among her family papers. Britten wrote it in March 1943, at the same time as the others, but discarded it (as he often did) when ordering the songs into a cycle. It is a peach of a song, and its gently rocking opening on the strings captures perfectly the breathing rhythm of someone asleep – ideal for this erotic poem, in which the poet appeals to his lover, 'waken thou with me'.

Fifteen years later, Britten resurrected this breathing idea, and used it to open his next orchestral song cycle, *Nocturne*. Not only that: the Tennyson setting and the new cycle share the same key (D flat), and the Tennyson poem ends with the horn on a C – thereby setting up the *Nocturne*'s ambivalent oscillation between C and D flat, which is the key to its restless nature.

The *Nocturne*'s basic premise is that the singer is accompanied by string orchestra, with extra solo instruments colouring the texture – one for each nocturnal poem. For the Shakespeare sonnet which concludes the cycle, all the solo instruments play together with the strings, to weave a richer orchestral tapestry. As so often with Britten, it is a simple idea, but one that holds the listener spellbound.

First in is the bassoon, to conjure up Tennyson's sleeping subterranean monster, 'The Kraken', in the rich, doleful key of B flat minor (rare in Britten). The beast expires on a top A natural for the tenor – a note that, in this context, is both surprising and inevitable. This movement deserves a key mark ♭⟶ , along with the two that follow. In the first the harp suggests both the glitter of moonlight as Coleridge's 'lovely boy was plucking fruits' and the danger of his being out 'alone, by night, a little child', while the second portrays multifarious animal activity at the stroke of midnight in a poem by Thomas Middleton. Dog, cat, mouse, cricket, raven, owl and nightingale – all are ensnared by Britten's solo horn. The timpani convey the menace and violence afflicting Wordsworth's dreamer in 'The Prelude', which rudely dispels any risk of cutesiness as it rises to a terrifying climax. This leads straight into the funeral march of Wilfred Owen's 'The Kind Ghosts', led by the cor anglais. Then flute and clarinet chirrup through Keats's 'Sleep and Poetry', until the ear is lifted by the unexpected, magical re-entry of the strings in C major on the word 'sleep', and we are once again reminded of the kinship of *Nocturne* and *Serenade*. Just as Keats had concluded the earlier work, here Shakespeare's Sonnet 43 ('When most I wink, then do mine eyes best see') provides an intensity that owes much to Berg and Mahler, with the advent of the full ensemble. The entire sonnet is propelled by chiasmus and oxymorons in the way it continually plays with night and day, light and shade – the perfect literary parallel to the work's C–D flat oscillation.

R Prégardien, Lanzky-Otto, Tapiola Sinfonietta/Vänskä, recorded 1991
BIS BISCD 540 (with *Sinfonietta*)

R *Serenade* and *Nocturne*: Pears, Tuckwell, LSO/Britten, recorded 1963 and 1959
Decca 436 3952 (with *Les Illuminations*). The premiere recording in 1944 with Pears, Britten and Dennis Brain is also available (Decca 468 8012).

R *Serenade*: Rolfe Johnson, Thompson, RSNO/Thomson, recorded 1988
Chandos CHAN 10192X (with *Les Illuminations* and *Quatre chansons françaises*)

R *Nocturne* and *Serenade*: Langridge, Lloyd, ECO/Bedford, recorded 1994
Naxos 8.557199 (with *Phaedra*)

The Holy Sonnets of John Donne, op. 35 ** 1945

In mid-July 1945, still glowing from his triumph with *Peter Grimes*, Britten met Yehudi Menuhin for the first time, at a party thrown by his publishers, Boosey & Hawkes. Menuhin was about to leave for Germany, to play to refugees and Holocaust survivors, only two months after the bombing had stopped and the Third Reich had been destroyed. Britten was moved by this gesture of reassurance and reconciliation by the violinist (who at twenty-nine was perhaps the most famous young fiddler in the world), and pleaded with him to take him as his accompanist. Gerald Moore had been booked, but withdrew with apparent good grace in Britten's favour.

It is sometimes described as a tour of concentration camps, but in reality they played in villages and towns (the ruined city of Münster was one), giving seven recitals in four days, as well as two more to the still bewildered survivors of Belsen, where they played Bach, Debussy, Beethoven's 'Kreutzer' Sonata and the Mendelssohn Violin Concerto. They stayed the night there, and saw over the hospital.

Years afterwards, Britten said the experience was so shocking that it had coloured all his subsequent music. It certainly drove the cycle of nine sonnets by John Donne, into which he plunged only two days after his return. Whereas the Michelangelo Sonnets had been about love, the Donne cycle was about death. Fired by his first-hand brush with suffering, and by a high post-tour fever, it is perhaps the blackest, most obsessive music he ever wrote – a stark contrast with the Second String Quartet and *The Young Person's Guide*, which followed. From the fierce pounding of F sharp octaves in the piano, which open the work, this is heavy, demanding music – not the sort of thing to while away a lazy weekend afternoon. Much of it dwells on a tension between B minor and C minor – indeed those notes form a slow trill in the gentler third sonnet. The pace varies, but seldom the mood: there is little scope for wit, as Britten embraces Donne's almost apocalyptic language. There is brief respite with a soothing major key in the sixth sonnet. 'Death be not proud' ends the cycle in a funeral march (using Britten's favourite device, the relentless tread of a passacaglia). Only on the final word of 'death, thou shalt die' does the cycle settle on an affirmative chord of B major. He completed it in two weeks, and it was first performed on Britten's thirty-second birthday.

R   Langridge, Bedford, recorded 1995
Naxos 8.557201 (with *Winter Words*, Michelangelo Sonnets)

R   Padmore, Vignoles, recorded 2008
Harmonia Mundi HMU 907443 (with *Winter Words* etc.)

Canticle I: My Beloved is Mine, op. 40***   1947

The first of the five Canticles is a setting of 'A Divine Rapture' by the seventeenth-century poet Francis Quarles, which Pears and Britten performed in London in November 1947 and broadcast three weeks later. The poem entwines erotic and religious imagery, in the vein of the biblical Song of Songs, which it paraphrases in what becomes almost a refrain: 'So I my best beloved's am, / So he is mine!' Britten dispenses with Quarles's title (which would surely have worked well), and instead takes the exact biblical quotation, 'My Beloved is Mine, and I am His', never actually used by Quarles. In so doing, he seems to be advertising even more openly than in the Michelangelo Sonnets his relationship with his singer. The quotation's biblical flavour gives him some shelter, but not as much as Quarles's original title would have done. The discrepancy in the published score over the use of capital letters for the possessive adjectives 'mine' and 'his' perhaps mirrors a confusion in Britten's mind over whether they had human or divine meaning – a confusion already inherent in the sensual ambience of the poetry of both the Song of Songs and Francis Quarles.

The five Canticles all set poetry that is in some sense religious, and the musical shape derives from some of the extended vocal works of Purcell, such as the *Divine Hymns*

which Britten had been working on shortly before the first
Canticle. This freely expressive seven-minute cantata is com-
prised of four continuous sections or movements, ranging
from the delightful rippling of shallow water over pebbles
(with which it opens) to the ecstatic chords which mark the
union of two souls: 'Ev'n so we met and after long pursuit /
Ev'n so we joined. We both became entire.' This could perhaps be taken as a metaphor for spiritual union with God, but
to more worldly ears (both then and now) it tells of a human
bond: 'For I was flax, and he was flames of fire'. Pears himself
said five years later that this work was Britten's 'finest piece of
vocal music to date'.

R   Anthony Rolfe Johnson, Graham Johnson, recorded 1986
Helios CDH 55067 (with Michelangelo Sonnets etc.)

A Charm of Lullabies, op. 41 **   1947
A Cradle Song: Sleep, Beauty Bright – Blake   1938

At first glance this looks a rather milk-and-water confection,
but Britten managed to find a diversity of poems that challenges the very concept of lullaby. 'A Cradle Song' by Blake
(a different setting from the soprano–mezzo duet he'd written in 1938) is the first of five lullabies with piano intended
for his friend, the mezzo Nancy Evans. It has a cool rocking
motion to calm a restless baby on the edge of wakefulness.
But in Burns's 'The Highland Balou', the dancing rhythms
(anticipating his Burns settings in *A Birthday Hansel* nearly
thirty years later) keep the infant eyes wide open, as do the
bouncing piano figures in 'Sephestia's Lullaby', in which the
refrain's haunting chord transformations in the piano prefig-
ure the train whistles in *Winter Words*. The furious commands
of 'Quiet! Sleep!' in Britten's setting of Thomas Randolph's 'A
Charm' are threatening (and today would interest child protection officers): here Britten tries out the chords he would
use a few years later when Flora tells her doll to go to sleep
in *The Turn of the Screw*. In his simple descending scale for the

voice, he also reminds us of Ellen in Act I of *Peter Grimes*. The traditional soothing nature of the lullaby returns for 'The Nurse's Song' at the end, though shaded with melancholy in its dactylic rhythm. These songs are now also available in an orchestral version by Colin Matthews.

R   Murray, Martineau, recorded 2005
Avie AV2077 (with *Cabaret Songs* and songs by Mahler and Schumann)

R   Connolly, BBCSO/Gardner, recorded 2010
Chandos CHAN 10671 (with *Phaedra*, *Lachrymae* etc.)

Canticle II: Abraham and Isaac, op. 51 ****   1952

The plight of the boy Isaac, as he encourages his father to proceed with preparing a sacrifice, without realising that he himself is to be the burnt offering, rang many bells with Britten. In this Canticle, he plays the story straight, as conveyed in the medieval mystery play he used for the text. It was only when he returned to it in the *War Requiem* that he gave vent to his feelings about the treachery of Abraham, and his intended slaughter of an innocent boy (emblematic of the millions of young men slain in the First World War).

The Canticle was written for some fund-raising song recitals that Britten and Pears were planning with the contralto Kathleen Ferrier. The two singers played the father and son in the story, but Britten also needed to represent the voice of God calling Abraham. He hit on the idea of combining the two voices in unison or close harmony, accompanied by soft, rippling piano arpeggios in E flat – without any modulation. The consequent effect is of an unearthly shimmer round this insistent tonic, which compels the attention. Britten knew it was a stroke of genius: he told Michael Tippett it was 'worth a million dollars'.

The only recording made of the Ferrier–Pears performances was lost by the BBC, much to Britten's fury. But eight years passed before he tried performing (and recording) it with a boy alto, John Hahessy. It changed perceptions of the piece: the vulnerability of a boy's voice about to break was a perfect match for the plight of Isaac. Once heard like this, the Canticle loses some of its power when Isaac is sung by an adult, however brilliant the contralto (or, as often today, the counter-tenor) may be. But, whichever way Isaac is cast, this heart-stopping miniature is worth crossing several roads to hear. For its insights into Britten's concern for the young, and the spell he sustains with the simplest of resources, it effortlessly wins a key mark ☞.

R   Hahessy, Pears, Britten, recorded 1961
Decca 425 7162 (boy alto version, with the other Canticles)

R   Chance, Rolfe Johnson, Vignoles, recorded 1991
Helios CDH 55244 (counter-tenor version, with the other four Canticles and three Purcell realisations)

Second Lute Song from *Gloriana* **   1953

The enchanting song for the Earl of Essex, one-time favourite of Queen Elizabeth I, uses the historical Essex's own words: 'Happy were he . . .' Not only that, Britten begins it with a phrase from an Elizabethan madrigal by John Wilbye: 'Happy, O happy he'. This concert arrangement of the song from Act I scene ii of the opera is for tenor and guitar, but has also been arranged for piano and for harp. It is one of Pears's most rapt moments.

R   Pears, Ellis, recorded 1975
Australian Eloquence 442 9448 (with *A Birthday Hansel*, *Canticle V*, *Sacred and Profane* etc.)

Winter Words, op. 52 ****   1953

After the exertions of writing and performing *Gloriana*, Britten turned to the poetry of Thomas Hardy for these extraordinarily moving 'lyrics and ballads' for high voice and piano.

They form Britten's most intimate set of songs. Each poem he has chosen refers in some way to childhood, and most of them have a disconcerting and often gloomy perspective on history and time. The uneasy first song, 'At Day-close in November', uses trees to reflect on the permanence of nature through the eyes of children. As the other bookend of the set, the last song harks back to the age of nescience, a time when 'all went well, none knew regret, no sense was stung', and longs for its return. 'Before Life and After' is one of Britten's most profound, yet simple achievements: soaring, aching lines for the tenor and the right-hand octaves in the piano, while the left hand trudges away in the worldly murk of dense triads in the bass clef – a musical device first hinted at in the third of the Michelangelo Sonnets.

Britten counters the prevailingly depressing nature of Hardy's themes with the vivid sound-images he conjures out of voice and piano. Perhaps the most famous is the remarkable Doppler effect of the locomotive whistle in 'Midnight on the Great Western', coupled with the uneven rattling of the train crossing the points on the track, and the swaying of the carriages heard in the melismas of the vocal line. But beneath these evocative sounds is a more disturbing picture, anchored in C minor, of a boy journeying 'to a world unknown', undertaking 'this plunge alone' (at which point the comforting chuntering of the carriage vanishes) through a 'region of sin'. This idea of innocence on the edge of corruption is the single most consistent theme of Britten's work.

In 'Wagtail and Baby', Britten's witty word-painting seems almost footling at first. The bird is unperturbed by the appearance of three potentially alarming animals: it takes the arrival of the 'perfect gentleman' (heralded by music of suave refinement) to scare it away. But the bird's surprising perception of relative danger is watched by a human baby, which in its wisdom (marked by Britten's telltale triads) is set 'a-thinking'. The vocal and pianistic creaks of 'The Little Old Table' are the only clues to a long-gone love story, while 'Proud Songsters' is almost fierce in applying the poet's dust-and-ashes philosophy to birds. In 'At the Railway Station, Upway', the piano takes the role of the violin in Hardy's vivid account of a little boy on the station platform giving a handcuffed prisoner a glimpse of freedom through his fiddle-playing. This redemptive power of music is the central feature of 'The Choirmaster's Burial', a quintessential Britten song ♫, Purcellian in the way it features four musical episodes in its three and a half minutes. The simple story tells how, even in death, the love and devotion of the choirmaster outwits the blundering pomposity of the parson. With typical yet affecting sleight of hand, Britten weaves into the piano accompaniment the hymn tune the old choirmaster liked best, 'Mount Ephraim', partly concealed by being in a different rhythm and key from the tenor's line.

Each song in this set is outstanding, so its cumulative power overflows at the culmination, with the anguished, repeated cry: 'How long?' This is one of the most emotional, heart-rending moments in all Britten's music. It is no wonder that, when Britten himself heard Pears singing this on the radio twenty years later, he was utterly overcome. He was moved to send Pears (who was abroad) a letter of touching devotion – which stands out as the most voluble declaration of their long and abiding partnership. For Britten, *Winter Words* was so personal that he was originally reluctant to put it into the public domain at all.

In the Britten catalogue of published works, *Gloriana* should have been given the opus number 52, and his next piece, *Winter Words*, number 53, but Britten wanted to honour *Gloriana* with the number that matched Coronation year. So he swapped the numbers round. The confusing result is that the later piece, *Winter Words*, has the earlier opus number, 52.

R Anthony Rolfe Johnson, Graham Johnson, recorded 1986 Helios CDH 55067 (with *Canticle I* and Michelangelo Sonnets)

Three Rimbaud songs: 1939
    Phrase
    Aube **
    A une raison *
Two Hardy songs: 1953
    If it's ever spring again *
    The Children and Sir Nameless *
Three Soutar songs: 1969
    Dawtie's Devotion
    The Gully
    Tradition
Three Sitwell songs: 1957
    Where are the seeds of the Universal Fire?
    We are the darkness in the heat of the day
    So, out of the dark

These orphan songs are rejects from Britten song cycles. He would usually write more songs than he wanted for the cycle, perhaps for reasons of quality control, or perhaps because it was only when he had written them all that he could see how the cycle would best hang together as a whole – and that meant some songs had to be dropped.

Huw Wheldon, the legendary editor of the BBC arts programme *Monitor*, was fond of telling his television producers to slaughter their darlings. Any composer who could wantonly sacrifice songs of such quality as these Rimbaud settings was destined for greatness. They were drafted alongside the ten other songs that comprise *Les Illuminations*. *Aube* is a piece of real substance, and Britten responds generously to Rimbaud's sensual imagery. The final line, describing waking at noon after the poet's encounter with the goddess, is ecstatic, and ends longingly on a dominant seventh. The third song has a Straussian voluptuousness, but Britten's original passion for Strauss had waned, and that may have sealed its fate.

When compiling his Hardy cycle *Winter Words*, Britten excluded two songs. *The Children and Sir Nameless*, in almost undiluted bouncing triads, tells of a pompous knight determined to banish 'wretched children romping in my park' who 'yap and yell from early morn till dark'. But the children have the last laugh, centuries later, as they unwittingly deface his marble effigy. This song, while lacking the gentle melancholy of the cycle, does speak to its two themes, whereas *If it's ever spring again* barely touches on either. But its simple, spare texture deserves independent life.

The songs to texts in Scots dialect by William Soutar were written for Britten's final cycle, *Who are these Children?* Each lasts less than a minute. While *The Gully* has a rhythmic playfulness, Britten's heart is not really in the wit of *Tradition* – though he manages, in the last two bars of both songs, to win himself a little audience chuckle. All three are potential encores, but not more.

The Sitwell songs are not rejects, but additions to Britten's third Canticle, *Still Falls the Rain*. For the 1956 Aldeburgh Festival he made it the centrepiece of a concert sequence entitled *The Heart of the Matter*, for which he added three new songs, some horn fanfares and spoken poems by Edith Sitwell. The middle song, for tenor and piano, is unique in Britten's output in that the piano chords simply reinforce and harmonise the melodic line, which is written in a note-per-syllable form. The outer songs, with the addition of the horn, form prologue and epilogue to the sequence, and are not really suited to separate performance.

R   Rimbaud songs: Piau, Northern Sinfonia/Zehetmair, recorded 2008
NMC NMCD140: 'Unknown Britten' (with *Movements for a Clarinet Concerto* etc.)

R   Hardy, Soutar and Sitwell songs: Mackie, Tuckwell, Vignoles, Scottish Chamber Orchestra/Bedford, recorded 2001
EMI 5 74346 2: 'The Heart of the Matter' (2 CDs with *Serenade, Canticle III, Rossini Suite* etc.)

Songs from the Chinese, op. 58*   1957

The rather tight-lipped title may in part explain why these charming songs (in English!) are seldom heard. The fatalistic tone of the Chinese poetry, translated by Arthur Waley, is off-set by the sparkle of the guitar accompaniment – a gift to the new recital partnership between Pears and Julian Bream. Britten teased Bream with his choice of a poem deriding the faded glory of the lute: in the sudden animation of its final line, Britten has the guitar imitating the chiff of a Chinese flute, which the poet finds so much more exciting. The wry lassitude of the proverbs in 'The Big Chariot' makes an attractive opening, and the abandon of the dance song about a unicorn rounds off this ten-minute work with delayed energy.

R   Langridge, Marchionda, recorded 2003
Chandos CHAN 10305 (with *Nocturnal*, and works by Maw and Dowland)

Sechs Hölderlin-Fragmente, op. 61***   1958

Friedrich Hölderlin didn't cut much ice with the great German *Lieder* composers, but Britten found him, as a Lutheran with a Hellenic aesthetic, a kindred spirit. Nearly twenty years after his song cycles in French and Italian, Britten now turned with confidence to German. These six songs are short – they last only just over ten minutes – and not well known. Yet they are well worth the effort of discovery. They articulate Britten's skill in song-writing – in absorbing the essence of a poem, not just its line-by-line meaning; in identifying its centre of gravity, or where the pivot points are; in finding specific ideas in the text to illustrate in the voice or the piano; and finally in deciding how to open and close each poem he set. This simple technique bore rich fruit here in the fourth song, 'Youth', where the bouncing, playful piano part enters the child's world without condescension. In 'The Middle of Life', the first verse is heavily perfumed to match the profusion of the poem. The third song – a Socratic dialogue about

the beauty of youth – has recitative and a single-note 'continuo', until the tenor blossoms lyrically as Socrates' eyes
light on Alcibiades. This leads to a heart-stopping top A flat
on the word 'beauty' – an approving nod from the composer
for the Greek philosopher's endorsement of the worship of
beauty. 'Home' is simple and nostalgic, with the right hand
of the piano echoing the fluid tenor line in canon (a favourite Britten device), while the left hand supplies pure water-
music – of which Britten can concoct more varieties than a
hydrologist. Last comes 'The Lines of Life', an extraordinary song written in plain minims without rhythmic variation, while the pianist climbs repeated scales. This spare
texture thickens in the final phrase, at the thought of divine
harmony and peace.

R   Pears, Britten, recorded 1963
Decca 468 811-2: 'Britten, The Rarities' (2 CDs, with
Canticle II [contralto version], *The Poet's Echo* etc.)

R   Gritton, Burnside, recorded 2007
Signum SIGCD122: 'Britten Abroad' (with *The Poet's Echo*,
Michelangelo Sonnets etc.)

Songs and Proverbs of William Blake, op. 74***   1965

The German baritone Dietrich Fischer-Dieskau made such
an impact with his participation in the *War Requiem* that Pears
suggested Britten write a song cycle for him. Not only that,
Pears even selected the poems, from Blake's *Songs of Experience*
and *The Marriage of Heaven and Hell*. Britten was always rather
frightened of Fischer-Dieskau (indeed Pears, who had first
sung with him in 1956, described him as 'very musical, but
grand'). But Pears's idea resulted in Britten's most elaborate
cycle, fashioned in a single arc of extraordinarily imaginative
gloom. The seven songs are interspersed with Blake's profound proverbs about humanity and eternity – presented in
ritornello form in the uninterrupted cycle, and using clusters
of notes in a twelve-tone scheme.

Britten heads the score 'for baritone and piano', although the vocal line is written in the treble clef as if for a tenor, and the vocal range (low B flat to top G flat) matches that of some of the songs he wrote for Pears. But the dark hues of the baritone's middle register work superbly for Blake. In the most famous poem, 'Tyger, Tyger', Britten couples them with the bass register of the piano (nothing in the treble clef, apart from a brief central interlude) in a way that would horrify any composition teacher. Yet the clarity of the texture is unmuddied, because of the ingenuity of the staccato scales in the piano (think 'In the Hall of the Mountain King' from *Peer Gynt*, but faster). As these relentless scales run up and down, in the compass of a single octave, broken only by smudged G sharp minor chords, we cannot but visualise this handsome beast pacing up and down, perhaps in a cage. Fischer-Dieskau's legato line weaves in and around these scales, delivered with scorching intensity – mostly pianissimo. It is literally hair-raising, and one of Britten's finest songs ♪ .

R Fischer-Dieskau, Britten, recorded 1968
Decca 417 4282 (3 CDs, with *Billy Budd* and Donne Sonnets)

The Poet's Echo, op. 76 *   1965

The six settings of Pushkin have rarely escaped the clutches of their first performer, the Russian soprano Galina Vishnevskaya. They were tailor-made for her while Britten was staying with the Rostropoviches in Armenia – so much so that the shrill, often unforgiving tone that characterised her singing seems woven into Britten's score. The gamelan techniques of the previous year's *Curlew River* reappear in the piano part of the first song, while the ticking of time (in major sevenths) in the final song belongs to the world of *Winter Words*. At the first private run-through in Armenia, she and Britten finished this song just as a clock outside chimed midnight. It sent a shiver down their spines.

R   Bullock, Martineau, recorded 2006
Avie AV 2117 (with songs by Prokofiev, Quilter, Rorem,
Strauss and Wagner)

Who are these Children?, op. 84 ***   1971

The least known of Britten's song cycles for tenor and piano
is only now coming into its own. For years it had a forbidding
aspect, caught perhaps in the slipstream of his grim morality tale *Children's Crusade*, which immediately preceded it.
Those not privy to the felicities of the Scots dialect of some
of William Soutar's poems may have been rather slow to discover the wit and playfulness of Britten's settings. Some of the
twelve songs are tiny, but each one excites his creative imagination – whether a riddle, a lullaby, a larking-song, or a grace.
One of them even achieves a time-signature of 18/16, which
must be a Britten first.

Two of the longer, more serious, settings capture the
uncomprehending stare of children in wartime: 'the blood of
children corrupts the hearts of men'. Two others treat of the
felling of trees: one 'bleeding beneath the axeman's stroke' as
the branches 'flowered with children's eyes', the other an old
oak tree, the victim (we presume) of age and weather. This
produces a *Winter Words*-like song of utter simplicity and
compression, a sequence of triads which starts '*pp*, heavily'
and ends on the saddest E flat major chord anyone ever wrote.

R   Padmore, Vignoles, recorded 2004
Hyperion CDA 67459 (with *Sechs Hölderlin-Fragmente* and
Tippett's *Boyhood's End*)

R   Pears, Britten, recorded 1972
Australian Eloquence 4768492 (with Michelangelo Sonnets,
Tit for Tat, *Winter Words*). This was from Britten's last
recording session, in November 1972. There is also a BBC
radio recording of the first complete concert performance a
year earlier, but be warned that this has quite a few mistakes
– not least the way Pears smooths out the rocking rhythms

in the first song by adding an extra beat in the bar. The composer, at the piano, presumably had no choice but to go along with him.

Canticle IV: Journey of the Magi, op. 86 **   1971

The overlapping vocal ranges of baritone, tenor and counter-tenor give this unusual trio with piano a close-harmony feel. No one voice predominates, and the three singers sometimes toss adjacent words from one to another, as if they were playing ball, or throwing dice. Eliot's poem has an eastern flavour, with cantankerous camel owners and 'silken girls bringing sherbet', and Britten's music matches this, with the uneven repetitions in its refrain conveying a slightly queasy camel ride. But this is no biblical tale of gold, frankincense and myrrh. The wise men complain bitterly of the winter cold and the unfriendly and mercenary people they meet. There is a corresponding chill in the music, as the Magi wonder whether they went all that way for birth or death – and observe three trees on the horizon, a portent of Calvary. The glint of something less earthbound is suggested, as frequently in Britten, by plainsong – strange how strong its impact was on a man of such low-church origins. In this case it is 'Magi videntes stellam' (the only time the star is referred to in the work), which emerges in the piano at their (merely 'satisfactory') encounter at the stable – and again at the end, when the grumbling trio return to their kingdoms and find that, in fact, their lives have changed.

R Daniels, Bostridge, Maltman, Drake, recorded 2001
Virgin 545 5252: 'The Canticles'

Canticle V: The Death of Saint Narcissus, op. 89 **   1974

'I haven't got the remotest idea what it's about', Britten said (perhaps defensively) of his second bite at the Eliot cherry, but he responded so readily to its shafts of sensual imagery that it

spurred him to write his first new piece since his heart operation of 1973. He set it for tenor and harp, or more specifically
for Pears and his new accompanist, Osian Ellis. Once Britten's
physical disability prevented him playing the piano in public,
he could not envisage another pianist taking his place – not
even Murray Perahia, who was giving recitals of Schubert
Lieder with Pears. So instead, he wrote songs for Pears to sing
with Ellis's harp.

It is a weird piece, but Britten's vivid understanding of Narcissus's self-absorption is compelling, whether in the florid
melismas that coalesce into the majestic hymn-like sweep of
him becoming 'a dancer before God', or in the delicate intimacy of his imagining that 'he had been a young girl'.

R   Pears, Ellis, recorded 1976
Decca 425 7162: 'The Canticles'

R   Langridge, Ellis, recorded 1995
Naxos 8.557202 (with *Canticles I–IV*, *The Heart of the Matter*)

A Birthday Hansel, op. 92 **   1975

Britten first set Robert Burns in *O that I had ne'er been married*
when he was only nine or ten. He tangled further with Scots
dialect in his folksong setting, 'The Bonny Earl o' Moray', and
much later with his Soutar song cycle, *Who are these Children?*
Here he embarked on a sequence of seven poems by Burns as
a seventy-fifth birthday tribute to the poet's compatriot, the
Queen Mother.

Deference to the 'Hielan' chief' is commanded from the
start, with the thrummed minor chords on the harp – a thrilling, dramatic opening to 'Birthday Song'. *A Birthday Hansel*
is not demanding listening, but weaves its own enchantment
– for instance, with the vocal melismas on the word 'morning' at the end of each verse of 'My Early Walk'. There is
plenty of wit here too, with the skittish 'Wee Willie Gray'
and the tongue-twister in its last line. 'The Winter' spins a
romantic line to warm the heart, and the final reel, 'Leezie

Lindsay', was designed to bring a birthday smile to the lips of the dedicatee, who might have been about to step forward for the Gay Gordons.

R   Pears, Ellis, recorded 1976
Australian Eloquence 442 9448 (with Harp Suite, *Sacred and Profane*, Folksongs with harp etc.)

R   Wilde, Owen Norris, recorded 2010
Naxos 8572706 (with *Who are these children?* and Britten's other Scottish songs)

34

Stage works

The operas are Britten's greatest achievement. With only the slenderest native tradition to build on, Britten managed to put English opera on the world stage almost from the word go. Yet after *Peter Grimes* in 1945 he didn't simply repeat a successful formula. He was canny enough to realise that the post-war world would not find grand operas an attractive financial prospect, and he experimented with different types of chamber opera instead. Such was his composing skill that these didn't feel pale or limp compared with the big pieces – quite the opposite. He creates an illusion of a large ensemble, while at the same time drawing audiences into a more intimate experience of opera than they were accustomed to. The Church Parables (discussed in chapter 30, 'Church music') took this to a new level: there is not even a conductor, and the singers and instrumentalists are left to coordinate things themselves. The stage works listed in this chapter begin with a small ballet, and include the much larger one which is one of his most intriguing orchestral scores.

Plymouth Town **   1931

One of the biggest scores of his teenage years, this half-hour ballet tells of a young sailor led astray by a Bad Girl, a 'sweet maid' who was 'mistress of her trade' in the folksong 'A-Roving', on which the score is based. She takes the sailor on a pub crawl and then robs him – an early instance of the perennial Britten theme of (male) innocence corrupted, pointing forward to his comic opera, *Albert Herring*, where another lad is led astray. From the arresting taut opening on timpani (which often play solo melodies here) *Plymouth Town* is full of vivid orchestral effects and Britten hallmarks such as canonic

writing and intervals of a second. Its assured dramatic pacing
suggests it arose from a wealth of stage experience. Only the
occasional bitty section, where the tension sags, reveals that
it was a student piece, dating from the weeks leading up to
his eighteenth birthday, and his first for the theatre. Britten
never heard the piece: indeed its first performance was only in
2004, and the sole recording (BBCSO/Llewellyn) was issued
by *BBC Music Magazine* in 2006 and is not yet available commercially. This is a fascinating harbinger of the mature Britten, with moments of wit and poignancy, all delivered with an
angular energy. It deserves wider currency and is well worth
tracking down.

Paul Bunyan, op. 17****	1939–41; revised 1974–5
'Lullaby of Dream Shadows'**	1941
'Inkslinger's Love Song'*	1941
Overture, *Paul Bunyan* *	1941

When the Wandsworth School Choir sang three ballads at
the 1974 Aldeburgh Festival, it was the first time anyone had
heard music from *Paul Bunyan* for thirty-three years. Back in
1941, it ran for a week at Columbia University, New York –
the one and only stage collaboration between Auden and Britten. There was no broadcast, no recording, and when the run
finished the score was tucked away deep in a bottom drawer.
Britten told the Wandsworth Choir's director that the operetta
had been 'a great flop'. People, he said, were always asking him
to revive it, but he had always said no. 'Now', he said, 'it's time
to do bits of it'. He wanted the choir to tackle the country-
and-western-style ballads which had carried the story along
between the scenes. 'What it needs is good old Wandsworth
fun', he said, 'with the accompaniments played on any guitars,
banjos etc that you can muster!' (In the event, the boys were
accompanied on the piano.) Later in the same Festival, eight
of *Bunyan*'s songs and ensembles were performed. But, at that
stage, Britten was against a full-scale revival, without a major
reworking of the score. He was still convinced it was a failure.

After those performances he did agree to make a few minor changes for a radio broadcast of the complete opera. That won him over. He was actually moved to tears, and said he simply hadn't remembered what a strong piece it was. By then Auden was dead, and he was free of much of the emotional baggage that had weighed it down in his mind, so he permitted a staging at the 1976 Aldeburgh Festival. But his initial refusal showed that composers are not infallible judges of their own work, because *Paul Bunyan* turned out to be more than an interesting archaeological find, filling a lacuna in his early career. It was a sparkling, essential part of his creative output, and no one could understand why it had been suppressed for so long.

People don't associate Britten with musicals, but that's what *Paul Bunyan* is. In 1940 he called it an operetta – in the line of Gilbert and Sullivan, presumably, of which he was such a great (and recent) admirer. 'What heavenly shows these operas are!' he wrote in 1932 after seeing *The Mikado*; a month later he listened to a broadcast of *The Yeomen of the Guard*; and just after Christmas 1936 he went to see *The Pirates of Penzance*. Now, in New York, he had in W. H. Auden a poet who was more than a match for W. S. Gilbert – and Britten was in his 'American period', after all. So a musical it was.

Paul Bunyan is a hero of modern American mythology. As both giant and lumberjack, he belongs particularly to the logging states of Michigan, Wisconsin and Minnesota. His benign presence oversees the change to an industrial society. The Prologue of the opera/musical is a prophecy of Paul Bunyan's birth at the next blue moon. The first act tells of his recruitment of lumberjacks from Sweden, and two cooks, and Johnny Inkslinger, the verbose book-keeper. Paul then gets married, has a daughter called Tiny, separates from his wife, who later dies. He replaces the cooks with a cowboy called Hot Biscuit Slim, and Tiny goes to help him in the kitchen. In Act II Paul is challenged by his top lumberjack, Helson, and they fight. Helson loses. Tiny and Slim fall in love. Paul and Helson are reconciled, and then Paul plans to move on to other forests. For those left behind, life opens up, in Hollywood, Washington and New York.

If this sounds inconsequential, it is. But then, as a modern morality tale about the industrial challenges in America, it is alien to British ears, which have never heard such a thing. It also works a great deal better when performed by American artists, rather than by disguised Brits. Highlights include 'Once in a while the moon turns blue', a magical number which Britten said wistfully at the end of his life represented Pears and the 'dream come true'. The Lumberjacks' Chorus has tremendous verve – indisputably a number for a musical. Listen out for the Cooks' Duet (with saxophone, bass clarinet, tuba and strings – the two singers ending in a B flat chord almost three octaves wide); the natural flair in 'The Blues – Quartet of the Defeated'; the witty lyrics of the 'Food Chorus'; and Bunyan's third 'Goodnight' – with yet another nocturnal soundscape from Britten (written in 1975), this time featuring barking dogs on the clarinets, and the cries of the roosting whippoorwill. It's a touching, heart-warming score, full of zest and wit, which have not faded with the passing years.

In Britten's 1975 revision, two substantial numbers fell by the wayside. One is the 'Lullaby of Dream Shadows' which originally ended the first Act. This opens and closes with an entrancing ensemble, based on a simple five-note scale and underpinned by hieratic staccato chords that provide the rhythmic anchor. It looks forward twenty years to the closing scene of *A Midsummer Night's Dream*. Britten is not content to shape his 'Lullaby' in 5/4 time: he interjects a feast of quick, wicked Auden rhymes. Just as he had thrilled a few years earlier to the Mikado's 'very humane endeavour / To make, to some extent, / Each evil liver / A running river / Of harmless merriment', he clearly relished Auden's equivalent:

> On beaches or in night-clubs I
> Excel in femininity [presumably pronounced 'tie']
> And I at all athletics;

> I pay attention to my hair,
> For personal hygiene I've a flair,
> The Hercules of underwear,
>   The Venus of cosmetics.

He made the point by mimicking each cadence straightaway in the orchestra, in true Sullivan style.

People often say that Britten found Auden's librettos impossible to set, because of their ridiculous wordiness. But that surely underestimates Britten. He was a man who fifteen years later was still delighting in his nonsense language, in which he put the letters 'arp' before every vowel. He used to converse with some of his boy companions in this way: Roger Duncan remembers, for instance, 'Arpi warpant tarpo plarpay tarpennarpis' as Britten's version of 'I want to play tennis'. So to be the composer who managed to set 'appendicectomy', 'anthropomorphosis' and 'psychokinesia' – which he does with great élan in 'Inkslinger's Love Song' – would have given him just as much pleasure as the record he held at South Lodge school for Throwing the Cricket Ball. We can hear in the music the sheer fun he has with crazy rhymes ('Papal Encyclicals / Are full of pricklickles, / Plenipotentiaries / Endure for centuries').

Britten may have excised these songs to improve the dramatic shape of the piece, but they work well as self-contained numbers, and his associates fortunately brought them back into circulation in the 1980s. No orchestral score survives of the original overture, but Britten's piano sketch was orchestrated by Colin Matthews to make an enticing taster for the whole show, complete with an intricate fast section that hints at the fugue in *The Young Person's Guide to the Orchestra* four years later.

R Lawless, Dressen, Nelson, Chorus and Orchestra of Plymouth Music Series, Minnesota/Brunelle, recorded 1987 Virgin Classics VCD 7 90710-2 (2 CDs)

R Overture, 'Lullaby', 'Love Song': Forbes, Mills, Murgatroyd, Smith, Dressen, ECO/Brunelle, recorded 1989 Virgin Classics VC 7 91107-2 (with *The Company of Heaven*)

Peter Grimes, op. 33 *****   1944–5

For a conductor to call out, 'This stop for Peter Grimes, the sadistic fisherman!' – as reputedly happened on a red bus in Rosebery Avenue – indicates the hold Britten's first full-blown opera had on war-weary London in June 1945. Its grip has barely slackened since. Once again Britten mastered a musical form with the minimum of apprenticeship (and *Paul Bunyan* was anyway a quite different animal), thanks to the numerous operas he had enjoyed and studied, and to an almost faultless instinct for pace and timing. *Peter Grimes* is probably the greatest British opera ever written, and is certainly one of the world's enduring operatic landmarks of the twentieth century.

Its beginnings were not auspicious. It was in a second-hand bookshop in Los Angeles that Peter Pears found a volume of poetry by the eighteenth-century Suffolk clergyman, George Crabbe. His poem 'The Borough' told of a child-murdering brute called Peter Grimes – an undiluted monster that Britten had the insight to turn into an ambiguous character who could excite our pity, or even sympathy. In his and Pears's mind, Grimes's situation as a lonely outsider matched their own as they came back to England as a couple of conscientious objectors in 1942. Their transatlantic truancy while Britain fought alone had been noted, and their homosexuality emphasised their 'otherness', although they were never exactly lonely.

But a search for close parallels between Britten and the Grimes he created will be fruitless. Rough and anti-social, the fisherman is in many ways his antithesis. They may have shared a poetic sensibility, but nothing in the score suggests Grimes is homosexual: in his unloving way he loves the schoolmistress, Ellen Orford, but he is perhaps asexual. The opera begins with an inquest into the death of Grimes's boy apprentice: the verdict blames 'accidental circumstances', but the townsfolk clearly think he is a child abuser. Grimes insists he still needs help at sea and, to the dismay of the crowd, Ellen volunteers to fetch his new boy apprentice. She sets off in a gathering storm, while he dreams of his future with her in an ardent A major aria, 'What harbour shelters peace?'.

Now the storm unleashes its full fury, and the townsfolk gather in the pub to calm their nerves. When the pariah Grimes enters, the turmoil turns into an awkward silence. He softly ruminates about grief and fate in one of the greatest of all Britten arias, 'Now the Great Bear and Pleiades', which is virtually all on one note, E. 'Who can turn skies back', he asks, 'and begin again?' It is a peerless demonstration of the elemental power of music, greater than any storm's, to stir the depths of the soul. But the pub crowd is unimpressed – frightened, perhaps – and turns nasty. Just in time, someone starts up a community song to relieve the tension – it sounds like a folk-song, yet it is freshly minted by Britten with an uneven seven beats in a bar! At the climax of the song the door swings open, and Ellen and the new apprentice arrive, drenched. Before they have time to recover, Grimes grabs the boy and heads off to his clifftop home. 'Home?' the crowd cries derisively, 'do you call that home?' – and the first Act hurtles to the buffers, ending one of the most gripping scenes in all opera ♪.

The second Act begins some weeks later, with Ellen discovering that the new apprentice has bruises. Word spreads among the townsfolk, who conclude that 'Grimes is at his exercise', and a group of men sets off to his hut on the cliff to investigate. Before they get there, Grimes clumsily attempts to comfort the tearful boy, and then both leave the hut to go fishing. But the boy slips down the cliff to his death, just as the search party arrives at the hut, noses around inside, and is disappointed to find it 'neat and empty'.

At the start of the third Act, the partying townsfolk believe Grimes and the boy are out at sea. They are soon whipped up by the discovery that his boat is in and they have both disappeared. Suspicions of foul play spread, and a manhunt begins. The way Britten ratchets up the tension in this scene is masterful: it culminates in the chorus shouting Grimes's name with blood-curdling malice (and with a faint, dissonant foghorn underneath – pure genius). Meanwhile Ellen and her friend Balstrode go looking for him. They find him on the beach, exhausted and distraught at what has happened. In his 'mad scene', he disjointedly reprises the events of the first two Acts, until Balstrode advises him to scuttle his boat, and go down with it. The following morning the townsfolk return to their daily routines. There is news of a boat sinking out at sea, but their passion is spent, and they barely notice.

In *Peter Grimes*, the chorus are principal players in the drama. The other main character is the sea. The opera is shaped round a sequence of orchestral interludes between the scenes, which capture different aspects of the ocean, but also comment on the drama. So the enchanting slow interlude that prefaces the third Act illustrates the play of the moon on a calm, flat sea – but is also a heart-rending threnody for a dead child, in which the glints of moonlight double as choking sobs.

The *Daily Express* reported on the first night that a 'slim, curly-haired young man in evening dress stood for three hours at the back of the stalls, too nervous to sit down'. He had no need to worry. Far from trying to write about himself, Britten had hit upon a great story with a complex character at its heart. The layers of meaning in both story and score ensure that no one production can exhaust this opera's capacity to hold an audience in thrall. The music moves seamlessly on, perfect in its dramatic timing. It shocks, it terrifies and it moves us, as the masterpiece it is.

R   Pears, Watson, Pease, Royal Opera House Orchestra/
Britten, recorded 1958
Decca Legends 467 6822 (2 CDs)

R   Langridge, Watson, Opie, City of London Sinfonia/
Hickox, recorded 1995
Chandos CHAN 9447 (2 CDs)

The Rape of Lucretia, op. 37 **   1946, revised 1947

Lucretia must have been quite a shock to the system for most of those who had cheered *Peter Grimes* the year before. It still is. Having proved himself conclusively in grand opera, Britten broke with convention to write a work in tune with the straitened post-war era. He opted for eight soloists, compared with *Grimes*'s twelve, no choral singers, and a pared-down orchestra of thirteen (twelve if the conductor plays the piano part). Compared with the pell-mell action of *Grimes*, the drama in *Lucretia* is often static, and framed by a Chorus of the Greek tragedy variety as narrator and compere, which often challenges the audience's full emotional involvement.

The plot is set in the sixth century BC, in the days of the last king of Rome, Tarquinius Superbus. At a military camp some distance from the city, the king's son (also called Tarquinius) is drinking with two of his fellow generals, Collatinus and Junius. They discuss the easy virtue of Roman women, and the one exception: Collatinus's wife, Lucretia, who is renowned for being faithful and chaste. The unmarried Tarquinius taunts Junius with being a cuckold, and in reply Junius tempts him with the idea of making Lucretia succumb to his charms – whereupon the excited Tarquinius rides off to Rome in the dark. The scene switches to Lucretia's house, where she and her servants are a picture of pure domesticity. Tarquinius arrives and demands shelter. Lucretia is disconcerted, but obliges him. Later in the night, Tarquinius tries to seduce her, rapes her and leaves. In the morning Lucretia emerges, overwhelmed with shame. Collatinus arrives and tries to console her, but she stabs herself. (I forgot to mention that Tarquinius was an Etruscan, which in Roman eyes was a Bad Thing. It leads to a lot of shouting offstage in Act II, to no apparent purpose, except to give three of the characters something to do.)

There are scenes of ravishing delicacy in this opera – far more so than anything in *Grimes* – as Britten's skilful restraint in using the instruments of his chamber orchestra results in magical colouring. His dextrous use of leitmotivs gives some of the music a seamless flow. Highlights include the second scene, where the three women are spinning and folding linen: the limpid use of harp forms a stark contrast with the fury of

Tarquinius's ride to Rome immediately before. The first Act ends with a hypnotic good-night ensemble ♪─♩ , based on four descending chords laden with foreboding in the dark key of C minor. Then there is Tarquinius's approach to Lucretia's bedroom (described by the Male Chorus in pitched speech rather than song, accompanied only by percussion), his almost tender aria, 'Within this frail crucible of light', as he tries to wake Lucretia, the fierce struggle between them before the rape, and the heart-wringing duet between Lucretia and Collatinus the next morning.

It's important to hold on to the promise of these (and many other) good things to come, because the start of the opera is bumpy. First comes dense, didactic recitative, as the Male and Female Chorus try to get us up to speed with rather too much information, but disconcert us with Christian moralising (Britten insisted on this) which recurs intermittently later on. Our interest briefly revives as Britten colours a sultry evening with sounds of crickets and frogs, and the generals uncork the wine. But their laddish trio is far too full of words, many of them incongruously high-flown, and I always find myself longing for this raucous scene to end. Indeed the whole libretto (by Ronald Duncan) suffers from an over-'poetic' flavour (which Britten unwisely bragged about beforehand). No wonder Michael Tippett, when he heard Britten was planning a comic opera next, advised him: 'For Christ's sake, don't use this librettist!' Indeed, apart from a small anthem, Britten never hired Duncan again.

There are some who claim *Lucretia* as Britten's finest opera. For me, it remains problematic. There have been recent performances of the original score before the 1947 revisions which Britten made to sharpen the pacing. But the problems are unresolved.

R   Baker, Luxon, Pears, Harper, Shirley-Quirk, Drake, ECO/Britten, recorded 1970
Decca 425 666-2 (2 CDs, with *Phaedra*)

Albert Herring, op. 39 *****   1947

It is all too easy to dismiss *Albert Herring* as a period piece, an Ealing comedy of opera – easy, and a serious mistake. This is one of Britten's most inventive scores, a delight for performers and audience alike, and in its way a musical miracle.

Britten's eldest sister Barbara was always supportive of her brilliant brother, but not highly musical herself. He once gave her a recording of Puccini's light-footed comedy *Gianni Schicchi* – which surprised me, because he was never very fond of Puccini (he once said he was sickened by the 'cheapness and emptiness of the music' in *La bohème*). Britten also owned a full score of *Schicchi*, given to him by Pears and inscribed 'To my one and only' and signed 'P'. It's hard to believe Pears would have given him a Puccini full score on the off-chance: Britten must have asked for it. My theory (and it is just that) is that Britten studied this opera as a model for *Albert Herring*. Both are comic operas, both are ensemble operas – and Britten did once remark, revealingly: 'What makes Puccini a greater composer of operas than (in my humble opinion) a great composer, is that he knows how long it takes a person to cross the room'.

Herring, like *Grimes*, is set in a small Suffolk town, with the thin disguise of an invented name, Loxford – although the story derives from a French short story by Guy de Maupassant. In Eric Crozier's hands, the libretto has a strong (absurd) English flavour. The town's worthies, headed by the *grande dame* Lady Billows, cannot find a girl virtuous enough to be crowned Queen of the May at the annual carnival, so they decide to nominate the greengrocer's inoffensive assistant, Albert, as May King instead. Albert is a plodder, tied to his mother's apron, and has little idea about Life. Two cool 1940s dudes, Sid and Nancy, reckon it's time he found out, so at the carnival they spike his lemonade (presumably all Lady Billows would permit) with rum. Albert is crowned to a chorus of 'Albert the Good, Long may he reign' (and we forget now that the then King George VI had always been known by his first name, Albert). But no sooner has he choked on the toast to Her Ladyship than he decides to break out. He runs off with his prize money (more than £700 by today's values) and disappears. A search is organised the next morning, and when his coronation wreath is found crushed in the road the town presumes the worst and goes into mourning. Whereupon Albert comically wanders in at his own funeral, as it were, rather the worse for wear. The worthies turn on their fallen May King, but Albert is a happier and wiser young man.

Albert typifies the innocent on the threshold of experience – the aspect of adolescence that so fascinated Britten. He also knew from his own life the perils of maternal suffocation, from which he had escaped only ten years before. But it is unwise to try to force *Herring* into a straitjacket of Britten moralising. This is a comedy, and Britten is audibly having fun. (So too did some members of the cast one night, when Pears was playing the part of Albert. They replaced his lemonade with neat gin. Pears swigged it, and didn't blink.)

Britten doesn't waste time: the opening is masterly in its concision, and we know Lady Billows before we see her (when the 'Good mornings' remind us of *Peter Grimes*). The orchestra is the same size as in *Lucretia*, and offers even greater riches as it moves effortlessly from parody to pathos, from sentiment to near-slapstick. The horn at times sounds like trumpet or trombone, the violins whistle with their glissandos and harmonics. This score often touches us and even moves us, so we know the comedy has hidden depths. The 'First of May' ensemble at the end of the first scene is built round a simple triad (one of Britten's favourite devices), but its brilliance and ingenuity as it moves towards a triumphant C major are undeniable. The quarrel between Albert and his mother after they've been told of the May King plan is a *tour de force* (echoes of Puccini here), as is the handbrake turn from E major to G major in the closing bars of Act I.

Other highlights include the genuinely funny singing lesson, when the tiresome schoolmistress, Miss Wordsworth, struggles to hold the attention of the three children while rehearsing them in 'Glory to our new May King'. Their eyes keep wandering to the sausage rolls, treacle tarts and trifles laid out on the trestle tables (and this was austerity Britain, in the grip of food rationing). Then there is the music for Sid and Nancy, as they 'refresh' themselves in the 'pleasures of love' – with greater understanding of the boy-girl relationship than Britten often showed. The spiking of the drink has Wagner's famous '*Tristan* chord' as a comic reminder of the danger in love potions, and chromatically suggestive after the diatonic simplicities of 'Albert the Good' just before. It is played at first on the viola – with the choice of his own instrument Britten perhaps identifies himself with Albert. There's a hint of Tchaikovsky's *Nutcracker* when Albert describes himself as 'your sugar-plum of a prodigal son'. His insurgent grievance is aptly captured in the low frequencies of bass flute and bass clarinet, while smooching strings for Sid and Nancy's kiss mark the moment of Albert's awakening. The orchestral interludes were designed to cover scene-changes, but are fascinating in their own right, yet only rarely heard on their own. The pacing throughout is spot on – Britten certainly knew how long it took to cross a room, and a great deal more. The climax comes with the threnody for the departed Albert, 'In the midst of life is Death' ♪. It is profoundly moving – with another Wagnerian echo perhaps: the quintet before the final scene of *Die Meistersinger*. But here there are nine voices, each with his or her own perspective on Albert. The reality of grief serves only to deepen the bathos of Albert's sudden return. I could go on. But this is a good starting-point for any Britten opera novice.

R Barstow, Palmer, Gritton, Savidge, Kale, Lloyd, Finley, Taylor, Gillett, Jones, Northern Sinfonia/Bedford, recorded 1996
Naxos 8.660107-08 (2 CDs)

The Beggar's Opera, op. 43 **   1948

For his third chamber opera, Britten went back to the eighteenth-century ballad opera (or musical) *The Beggar's Opera*,
for which the original creators Gay and Pepusch had themselves turned to a number of popular airs of the time. Britten,
however, did much more than arrange the original score: he
re-composed it in his own language, while using and respect-
ing the existing tunes – in the same way he had treated folksongs for the previous eight years or so.

In the 1920s Frederick Austin's arrangement of the work
had been highly popular. It ran on the London stage for three
and a half years, and 1,463 performances. Britten's version
broke many conventions (not least in his quirky orchestration,
with prominent percussion), and freed an Old Master from
years of grime. When he took it on tour to Holland, he was
relieved to feel that his version would avoid constant compari-
son with Austin's – and reckoned that a European audience
would already be attuned to the much more radical treatment
Gay's work had had from Kurt Weill in *The Threepenny Opera*.

The difficulty today is that nearly all the sixty-nine tunes
have slipped from public memory, so the piece has lost that
popular resonance, while the bawdy, gun-toting and liquor-
swilling plot is tame by modern standards. The satire on the
politics of the time – and on the conventions of Italian opera –
has also lost its edge. Mind you, it wasn't easy to stage in 1948:
the role of Macheath, the butch braggart wenching his way
round London, was not exactly tailor-made for Peter Pears.

Macheath is a highwayman, whom Mr and Mrs Peachum
are horrified to discover has secretly married their daughter
Polly. They decide the only solution is to get him arrested
and executed, and leave Polly a widow. Polly tips him off,
but he is so enamoured of flirting with a group of his old
flames that he leaves his escape too late, not realising that
that they are all in on the plot. Peachum arrives to arrest him.
In prison, Macheath bemoans the treachery of women. His
jailer's daughter, Lucy Lockit, who is pregnant by him, taunts

him and accuses him of betrayal because of his marriage to Polly. He tries to deny this, whereupon Polly turns up, and both women are furious. In the last Act, Lucy has arranged Macheath's escape from prison, but he has returned to Polly. Peachum however contrives the re-arrest of Macheath, but an execution was deemed too grisly an end for those Georgian times, so a royal pardon is effected in the nick of time to save him from the gallows.

The orchestra consists of just twelve players – the same as in *Lucretia* and *Herring*, minus the piano. The effects he creates from such lean resources are once again almost incredible: by choosing his instruments carefully, he finds fresh sonorities for each song. So, for example, 'In the days of my youth' is scored for high-pitched piccolo and violin harmonics, with bassoon and double bass growling along at the bottom, whereas 'Come sweet lass' has a bizarre accompaniment of downward arpeggios on the clarinet, with sharp stabs on the horn, bassoon and strings, and soft cymbal strokes in between. When Macheath speaks to all his wenches one by one, they are individually characterised by a single instrument – almost as if Britten is writing his own *Enigma Variations*, with 'friends pictured within'.

Only rarely does he pull his forces together, as in the slow march to the Old Bailey, where the fortissimo horn suggests a whole brass choir. As the Beggar/compere explains just before the end, no opera is complete without a scene in a condemned cell: in this case it is the most extended scena for the tenor Macheath, as he awaits his execution – rather like 'Billy in the Darbies' in *Billy Budd* a few years later. The melancholy strains of 'Greensleeves', or a variant of it, are heard over the top – but when the royal pardon arrives the mood changes. Britten engineers a triumphant end, but in G minor.

R   Collins, Murray, Kenny, Langridge, Lloyd, Aldeburgh Festival/Bedford, recorded 1992
EMI 436 850-2 (2 CDs)

The Little Sweep, op. 45 **   1949

Mary Poppins did wonders for the reputation of chimney sweeps. But Britten's concept went back further, to the 'little black thing' in Blake's 'The Chimney Sweeper' and maybe to the brutish stereotype in *The Water Babies* by Charles Kingsley. Britten had after all played the part of its central character Tom at the age of six (and Tom's master, who beat him regularly, was called Grimes . . . funny, that). It gave him a fresh idea for the second Aldeburgh Festival – a short children's opera about a chimney-boy set in the local Suffolk community. The 'little sweep' Sammy – press-ganged into child labour by his unscrupulous employers – would be rescued by other children, and set free. Not only that, the opera would be preceded by a short play about its preparations, and the audience would have to take part by learning some of the songs themselves. The whole 'entertainment' was called *Let's Make an Opera!*

The result is at times a little twee for contemporary ears. Yet the piece is one of the best travelled of all Britten's stage works. It's been recorded in French and Czech, and performances abound in Budapest, Darmstadt or Tenerife. Britten tossed the score off in about ten days, but it is as well to remember this was not the composer of *Simple Symphony* or *Friday Afternoons*. He had already written *Peter Grimes* and *The Rape of Lucretia*, was in the middle of his *Spring Symphony*, and embarking on *Billy Budd*. So *The Little Sweep* is not just a *jeu d'esprit*, but part of his mature output. It derives from his passionate belief that 'music should be useful – and to the living', and that the composer should serve his community. Some Britten loyalists protest too much that this work is a commentary on the victimisation of children: of course, he needed to engage the audience's sympathy for his child-hero, but his priority was to show there was a different way to write an opera, and to put some of the stuffed shirts on their mettle. He had his audience singing along in five beats to a bar, for instance, and joining in a waltz in alternating simple and compound time – not to mention squawking like herons, tweeting like chaffinches, or hooting like owls. But just then he was scoring similar twittering for three professional singers in the third number of his *Spring Symphony*, so who were the audience to complain?

Britten's economy of means is, as ever, conspicuous. His orchestra is simply a string quartet, four hands on the piano, and nine instruments to hit or shake (how resourceful he is in finding colour in percussion). There are delicious moments in the score: the lament 'O why do you weep?', the passacaglia for 'Help, help, she's collapsed', and the galop as the children tidy the room – which sounds as if a full orchestra is giving chase. The upward key shifts for each stanza in 'O Sammy is whiter' must have kindled memories of the boy Britten playing for assembly at Gresham's School, and pushing 'Praise, my soul, the King of heaven' up a semitone every verse.

Modern performances usually rewrite the spoken drama (as was always intended), and some of Eric Crozier's lyrics in the opera itself may grate a little today. 'Chimbley-sweepers must 'ave boys', 'He'll be a black boy', 'He's aching for it, ain't you, Sam?' ... These things can be tweaked a little, though it's hard to get round Sammy's famous song, 'Please don't send me up again', which has often been sung at Britten's expense. His own recording has a very 1950s approach to the spoken dialogue (more elocution lesson than drama), and also points up the danger inherent in Britten's plan of casting Juliet, the eldest of the seven children in the opera, as an adult rather than a child singer. But it does boast David Hemmings as Sammy.

R Monck, Begg, Wells, Tear, Lloyd, Finchley Children's Music Group, Medici String Quartet/Ledger, recorded 1977 EMI 565 111-2 (2 CDs, with *Rejoice in the Lamb*)

R Hemmings, Thomas, Vyvyan, Cantelo, Pears, Anthony, Alleyn's Choir, EOG/Britten, recorded 1955 London 436 393-2 (2 CDs, with *Gemini Variations* and *Children's Crusade*)

Billy Budd, op. 50 ****   1950–1; revised 1960

After five years writing chamber operas, Britten returned to
the big stage with *Billy Budd*. It is an even greater achievement than *Peter Grimes* in many ways, though enjoyment of
its many thrills and delights is harder-won.

All the action is aboard ship in the Napoleonic Wars –
and one apparent difficulty is that there is no action. Nothing happens. The warship HMS *Indomitable* is becalmed in
a mist for most of the opera, and while its one sighting of a
French ship creates some excitement – indeed a shot is fired
– the French are out of range and the mist returns. But there
is a tense, knotted internal drama over a handsome young
sailor, Billy Budd, pressed willingly into the King's service,
who despite being the most fervent and popular loyalist in
the crew is falsely accused of mutiny. His accuser is the bul-
lying Master-at-Arms, Claggart, in whom Billy (nicknamed
'Beauty') excites both jealousy and desire. But Claggart has
failed to allow for Billy's one flaw – a speech impediment at
moments of stress which can turn him violent. The charge of
insurrection in front of Captain Vere, whom Billy worships,
provokes the stammer, and Billy lashes out with his fist and
strikes Claggart dead at the Captain's feet. Vere summons a
court martial, and the officers find Billy guilty of murder, and
sentence him to be hanged. Vere too has shown signs of an
attraction to Billy, but (maybe because of that) declines the
sailor's four confident appeals to save him. At the moment of
execution, the rest of the crew threaten a mutiny – but, like
the chase of the French ship, it just fizzles out. The whole
drama is framed by Vere's continuing torment in old age that
he had been weak and had allowed a good man to die.

For this adaptation of the original story by Herman Melville
(based loosely on historical events), Britten chose E. M.
Forster, who had never written an opera libretto before. Unusually, he opted to write it mostly in prose. He was assisted by
one of Britten's lieutenants, Eric Crozier, who also researched
in some depth the formalities of naval life a century and a half

earlier. Unlike *Grimes*, which is built from a series of land-mark numbers, *Budd* is continuous and complex. From the start Britten was determined to turn Crozier's research into convincing shipboard bustle and commotion, so that, by half-way through the first Act, we are completely drawn into the naval milieu. Only then does the contrast of the marooning mist have its impact, paralysing the crew's desire for action. It matches the moral dilemma in which Vere is becalmed, to which he responds with similar inaction.

Amid the superficial (though effective) clatter of bugle calls and naval protocol, one of the most fascinating aspects of *Budd* is its sonority. It is of course rare for an opera to have no female voices – as is necessarily the case with this story – but this has no fewer than seventeen solo male roles, plus a multi-layered male chorus which produces a fabulously rich sound in the sea shanties. Britten basks in the challenge of creating sufficient textures to delineate the characters, and we find bass solos, for instance, being partnered surprisingly by the bass instruments of the orchestra in a feast of deeply dug sound. It is almost the exact opposite of the soprano glitter of *The Turn of the Screw* three years later.

This is in many respects a true grand opera, with thrilling set-piece moments such as the rising excitement of the crew as they prepare to do battle with the French. The chorus, to the thunder of the orchestral and stage drums, sing of 'the moment we've been waiting for' and call for action – 'Now for deeds!' But in the end there are no deeds – not from the ship's cannon, not from Vere, not from the potentially mutinous crew – except of course for Billy Budd's inadvertent killing of Claggart.

However, Britten also contrives intimate scenes of equal power, but less volume – the near-confrontation between Vere and Claggart, the first interview between Vere and Budd, and the tender, almost eucharistic, encounter between the young condemned sailor and the veteran seaman, Dansker, in the hour before his execution.

Early on, Britten assigned Pears's tenor to the philosopher-captain Vere (perhaps rather unsuited, as Pears would have been, to the nitty-gritty of naval battle), and decided on an heroic baritone for the title role, with as dark a bass as he could find for Claggart. The original opera was in four Acts, but Britten later rejigged it into two: this necessitated the loss of the Captain's Muster at the end of Act I, when the crew devotedly hailed 'starry Vere'. This powerful crowd scene, which resonates later on as Vere's weakness becomes clear, is preserved on the few recordings of the original version.

Unchanged is the defining scene of *Billy Budd*, when Vere breaks the news to Billy that he must hang from the yard-arm in the morning. But it is not actually a scene, as it happens offstage, while the full orchestra plays no fewer than thirty-four major and minor chords, each one different in its scoring and character. It is an unconventional way to handle a dramatic climax, but in the theatre it is a transcendent moment – redemptive for both Billy and his Captain, who becomes convinced that he himself has been saved by the young man he failed.

R   Keenlyside, Langridge, Tomlinson, LSO and Chorus/ Hickox, recorded 1999
Chandos CHAN 9826 (3 CDs)

R   Glossop, Pears, Langdon, LSO/Britten, recorded 1967
Decca 417428-2 (3 CDs, with *The Holy Sonnets of John Donne* and *Songs and Proverbs of William Blake*)

R   Hampson, Rolfe Johnson, Halfvarson, Hallé/Nagano (four-Act version), recorded 1997
Erato 3984 216312 (2 CDs)

Gloriana, op. 53 ****   1952–3; revised 1966

This opera has had a chequered history. It began with a Royal Gala at Covent Garden, six days after the Coronation, when the assembled bigwigs (or 'stuck pigs' as a resentful Britten called them later) could muster little more than polite applause. Despite considerable public success for the rest of the run, the opera disappeared from view for almost ten years. People spoke of its unsuitability for a coronation, as though it was either satirical or pornographic. Cooler assessment today reveals a work well tailored to the occasion (as always with Britten), containing as it does moments of genuine splendour and national rejoicing. But it also explores the conflict between a queen's public duty and private emotions, and in this was remarkably modern – which is presumably what made the begloved and bemedalled audience on the first night so uncomfortable (if they were still awake).

The story tells of the ageing Tudor Queen Elizabeth, known at the time as Gloriana, and her love for the headstrong Earl of Essex, many years her junior. She is jealous of his beautiful wife, but also wary of Essex's impatience, which will lead him to insubordination. His arrogant thirst for military glory leads to a failed military escapade in Ireland: on his sudden return home, he presumptuously charges in unannounced to the Queen's bedroom, to find her revealed as an unadorned old woman. Her courtiers warn her against him: he is arrested and found guilty of treason. The Queen hesitates to sign his death warrant, swayed for a moment by the pleading of his wife, but eventually takes up her pen. The opera ends with a spoken monologue by the Queen, reflecting (in the actual words she used) on her duty and purpose as sovereign, isolated and alone.

Britten often looked to Verdi as his operatic model. Certainly he absorbed from him an immaculate sense of timing and pace. But no other Britten opera has such a Verdian setting, involving politics at court and treachery in high places. Daggers are never drawn, but such is the power and drama of Britten's score that they seem to tremble in their sheaths.

The list of highlights is long. Some have been issued as separate concert pieces, like Essex's Second Lute Song or the Choral Dances. Deserving of special mention is the moment unique in opera when the lead soprano – the Queen – is accompanied by the tuba. She has already been escorted by trombones, to suggest her majesty, but Britten surpasses himself

with the way he represents her grotesque and spiteful humili-
ation of Essex's wife. She appropriates Lady Essex's elaborate
gown and wears it herself, even though it is far too small for
her. The absurd and embarrassing duet between soprano and
tuba is followed immediately by a trio of unbearable tenderness, as Essex, his sister and her husband Mountjoy console
Lady Essex in her distress. Essex's rising resentment is cunningly quenched by the Queen as she appoints him to the military command he so covets in Ireland. They dance together
in one of the many Elizabethan dances Britten incorporates
into the work, but the thunder clouds reassemble above them
in a torrent of A minor that ends the Act. This sequence is a
marvel of dramatic contrast and tension.

In the third Act, Britten surprises us in the way he demonstrates the political instability that Essex poses: he uses a
ballad singer in the streets of London to move the story on
(picking up the trick from *Paul Bunyan* twelve years before).
The Queen redeems herself in Britten's brilliantly conceived
penultimate scene, when she treats Essex's wife with gentle-
ness. But his sister (who matches him in arrogance) enrages
her, and she signs the death warrant with the strains of Essex's
lute song, 'Happy were he', ironically echoing around her.

Some have criticised Britten's handling of the opera's epilogue, because he resorts to melodrama (in its technical sense
of accompanying spoken words with music). Recordings of
this can indeed be disappointing. But it was written for the
stage, and that is where it should be judged.

So often ceremonial music for great occasions is best forgotten. But there is nothing cheesy about this piece, and
nothing 'occasional' either. It has moments of grandeur and
spectacle, certainly. Yet, with the anguish of the Queen, there
is as much grit in the magnificent *Gloriana* oyster as in any
other of his stage works.

R   Barstow, Langridge, Opie, Kenny, Jones, Summers,
Welsh National Opera/Mackerras, recorded 1992
Argo 440 2132 (2 CDs)

The Turn of the Screw, op. 54 *******   1954

This is one of the wonders of twentieth-century opera, with a strong claim to be Britten's greatest. Not a note is wasted, not a note needs changing. So precise and ingenious was he in crafting it that, if performers do what he indicates, it is almost impossible for them to fail.

Britten was first attracted to Henry James's ghost story in the 1930s. He heard a dramatisation on the radio, and then read the book. It was 'eerie', he said, 'an incredible masterpiece'. But it was only in the early 1950s that he decided to fashion it into his fifth chamber opera. The story revolves round two orphans, Flora and her younger brother Miles, growing up in what we come to realise is a haunted house. Their absent and anonymous guardian entrusts them to a new governess, with the ominous stipulation that she must never contact him about them. The Governess is enchanted by the children, but soon becomes aware that, apart from the dimwitted housekeeper Mrs Grose, the mansion is also populated by two ghosts. One is of her predecessor, Miss Jessel; the other is of the former manservant, Peter Quint. Both have a sinister hold over the children, who turn out to be not as innocent as they seem. The Governess resolves to save Miles and Flora from the ghosts' clutches but she is frequently thwarted by the children themselves. She fails in the case of Flora, but sends her away, while the battle to rescue Miles from Peter Quint lasts until the final page of the opera (as it does until the last word of the book). In the book, the ghosts never speak, and could well be merely the figments of the Governess's fevered imagination. In the opera, they are full participants in the psychological drama.

As the story unfolds, our perception of the children changes. At the start we see them singing nursery rhymes in all innocence: 'Tom, Tom, the piper's son' was surely an in-joke by Britten in tribute to his librettist, Myfanwy Piper. By the time Miles sings his haunting aria '*Malo*' with unearthly sounds from cor anglais, viola and harp, we become disturbed. This knowing moment ♫ is the pivot of the opera, suggesting

374   THE MUSIC OF BRITTEN

temptation and evil. The focus of contemporary productions on the sexual innuendo in the story is fully justified: Britten himself admitted this was part of his original thinking. It was also in Henry James's mind. (Britten's encounter with the original book came shortly after he had been so impressed by the film *Emil and the Detectives*, another story about children which was given a disturbing sexual undertow.) Miles's nocturnal attraction to Peter Quint in the final scene of Act I is scored with ravishing, yet almost repellent, beauty. The seductive melismas of Quint's tenor remind us that he is the first man in the drama. They form a clear contrast with the strained brilliance of the soprano tessitura thus far. It is no wonder that Miles responds to the romance and adventure that Quint offers: he can at last break free from domination by the women who surround him. He is not frightened by Quint, because he has known him (well?) in life so recently: Flora feels similarly comfortable with Miss Jessel. The children may well prefer their company to that of their overbearing new Governess, whose arrogant belief in her 'saving power' is ultimately destructive.

Britten opens with a Prologue (accompanied only by piano), in which a narrator sets the scene. Then comes a simple six-bar theme, fifteen variations of which comprise the rest of the opera. In the first Act, the key of each variation rises stepwise: in the second, it falls in the same way. Thus does Britten turn the screw. With this crafty device, Britten builds an unmistakable musical tension, and weaves a psychological web of great complexity. The result is an intensely claustrophobic score, with a range of colour, texture and power that, once again, is scarcely credible from only thirteen players.

R   Vyvyan, Pears, Cross, Hemmings, Dyer, Mandikian, EOG/Britten, recorded 1955
Decca 425 6722 (2 CDs)

R   Lott, Langridge, Pay, Hulse, Cannan, Secunde, Aldeburgh Festival Ensemble/Bedford, recorded 1993
Naxos 8.660109-10 (2 CDs)

The Prince of the Pagodas, op. 57 *** 1955–6

Britten is so identified with opera that it's easy to overlook his interest in dance. In the 1930s he went to the ballet frequently, and was enchanted by Stravinsky's *Pulcinella* and *Petrushka* and Tchaikovsky's *Swan Lake*, which he thought was 'perhaps the loveliest ballet music ever'. He also wrote a short ballet of his own, *Plymouth Town*, orchestrated Chopin's *Les Sylphides* for a ballet company during his American years, and wrote dance episodes in both *Gloriana* and *Death in Venice*.

The Prince of the Pagodas is his sole full-length ballet. Its three Acts contain two hours of music, which make it his longest orchestral score – full of energy, incident and colour. It gave him great trouble, perhaps because of the difficulty of sustaining such a long dramatic span without any words, when the drama (in the nature of ballet) was fragmented into so many short episodes. He kept missing his deadlines, and the first night was postponed for three months. But these delays worked to his advantage: they enabled him to include the gamelan techniques from Bali which so excited him during his visit to Indonesia in early 1956. 'The music is *fantastically* rich', he wrote home, 'melodically, rhythmically, texture (such *orchestration*!!) and above all *formally*'. He ingested the gamelan sound-world, and reproduced it with western instruments – the seven percussion players in Britten's large orchestra handle a total of twenty-four different instruments between them. The effect, halfway through the ballet, is coruscatingly exotic, a foretaste of the gamelan music that accompanies the dancers in *Death in Venice* nearly two decades later.

The choreographer John Cranko devised the ballet's scenario, which is set in the old Emperor's palace in the 'middle kingdom', where kings from around the world come to court his wicked daughter, Princess Belle Epine, who is about to become Empress. Her sister, the virtuous Princess Belle Rose, is captivated by the Prince of the Pagodas, who transports her to Pagoda-land, where the gamelan music catches her and our breath. There she dances with him in his salamander disguise.

They return to overthrow Belle Epine, and the Prince and Belle Rose live happily ever after in Pagoda-land.

This peculiar plot does not allow much room for dramatic manoeuvre, but Britten, through his startlingly vivid musical motifs, at least gives it both coherence and continuity. The old Emperor is wonderfully evoked on the alto saxophone, Belle Epine on prickly strings, Belle Rose on a plaintive oboe, and the Prince on leaping trumpets. The chances of seeing this ballet on stage are rare indeed (although it was re-choreographed twenty years ago by Kenneth MacMillan), and for a long time the only available recording was a cut-down version conducted by Britten, who never again returned to what he regarded as a troublesome work, despite an enthusiastic reception when he conducted it at La Scala in Milan. Fortunately the complete score has now been recorded in its full inventive glory.

R London Sinfonietta/Knussen, recorded 1989
EMI 3 52274 2 (2 CDs, with *Symphonic Suite* from '*Gloriana*')

A Midsummer Night's Dream, op. 64 *****   1959–60

So much of Britten's music has the snap-crackle nervous zip of the athlete that he was that this magisterial representation of Shakespeare's comedy may come as a surprise. Seldom was he so leisurely or relaxed – the very first bars with their barely audible sliding chords on the strings transport us into the domain of dreams and sleep that Britten loved more than any other. It is somniferous music, but not somnolent or self-indulgent: time seems suspended, and yet in reality the spell has been cast in a matter of seconds.

This was the sole Britten opera for which he himself (with Pears's help) crafted the libretto. With great pride in his faithfulness to Shakespeare, all but six words come from the original play. Through a cast of nineteen characters, Britten helps us navigate the story by conceiving the music in three planes: the fairies, the lovers and the rustics. The fairies have a bright, sometimes brittle sonority: Tytania is a high color-atura soprano, Oberon is a counter-tenor, and the other fair-ies are treble voices. Apart from the speaking voice of Puck, who is strikingly characterised by an athletically virtuoso, high-register C trumpet and drums (shades of Britten's 1938 radio score *Lines on the Map*), the fairies' instrumentation fea-tures two harps, harpsichord, celeste and tuned percussion, in which the vibraphone plays an ambivalent role. This is Brit-ten the shaman conjuring a magical, glittering sound, but not a comfortable one: he believed, after all, that dreams could release many things which 'had better not be released' and 'do colour your next day very darkly'. This explains why his Oberon is always a sinister figure, whose trickery with potions is largely for his own selfish pleasure and risks serious harm. The music for the rustics is dominated by low wind instru-ments, bassoon and trombone in particular, and at times we feel Shostakovich is not far away, while the lovers' music relies more on 'conventional' strings and woodwind, and is often reassuringly diatonic, in contrast with the unsettling chromaticism of the fairies.

The story, set in a wood outside Athens, is both elaborate and simple. After a quarrel between Oberon and Tytania, the king and queen of the fairies, Oberon plans to thwart Tytania by sprinkling her with a magic herbal juice, which will make her fall in love with the first living creature she sees after wak-ing up. This turns out to be Bottom, one of a group of rustics rehearsing a play in the wood, whose head has been changed by Oberon's messenger Puck into that of a donkey. The wood is also populated by two lovers, Lysander and Hermia, who are eloping to escape Hermia's arranged marriage with Demetrius, and by Demetrius, who is chasing them, and by his ex-girl-friend Helena, who is chasing him. Oberon decides to help things along by getting Puck to sprinkle the magic juice on Demetrius, so that he falls in love again with Helena. (Oberon's alluring aria 'I know a bank where the wild thyme blows' is a key moment in the opera, and captures the strange yet seductive nature of his embrace.) But Puck gets mixed up, and

sprinkles the juice on Lysander instead, who then falls in love
with Helena. All four lovers therefore end up in a bad temper,
which is only aggravated when Puck tries to make amends by
applying a few more drops. Eventually Oberon rectifies things,
and also frees his wife from her asinine infatuation. The inter-
twined quartet of lovers singing 'And I have found Demetrius
[or whomever] like a jewel' on a simple rising scale feels both
ingenuous and inevitable, and is one of the most enchanting
highlights of the opera – with the ensemble ending on one of
the longest leading-notes in music. The rustics then perform
their hilarious play, 'Pyramus and Thisby', and all ends happily
– but not before the fairies' recessional 'Now until the break of
day' has bewitched us again, leaving Puck to round things off
as Shakespeare intended.

This is unlike any other Britten opera. The lightness of
touch, the absence of obsession, the gentle (and at its best
wickedly funny) comedy – all are a perfect match for Shakespeare, and Britten's music enhances the play.

R   Bowman, Watson, Graham Hall, Herford, Jones, Gomez,
Maxwell, City of London Sinfonia/Hickox, recorded 1990
Virgin Classics VCD 7 59305 2 (2 CDs)

The Golden Vanity, op. 78*   1966

This 'vaudeville' for boys' voices and piano is an eighteen-
minute piece of theatre for the concert platform. The boys
wear costume and use a few props, but there is normally no
set. It tells the story of a battle at sea, and a cabin-boy who
ensures victory for the crew of the *Golden Vanity* by drill-
ing holes in the pirate ship they are fighting, and sinking it.
His captain reneges on his promised reward (the hand of his
daughter), and leaves the boy to drown. But the spirit of the
boy returns at the end of the piece, just as in *Curlew River* two
years before.

Since his student days, Britten had been captivated by the
Vienna Boys' Choir, and he wrote this at their request. They

were fed up with having to play girls' parts in the mini-operas they performed, so Britten obliged with a sprightly boys-only piece – a miniature *Billy Budd*, the words of which it occasionally replicates.

R Choristers of Christ Church and Worcester College (Oxford), Driskill-Smith/Darlington, recorded 2002
Lammas LAMM 146D (with *Children's Crusade, Missa Brevis*)

Owen Wingrave, op. 85   1969–70

I keep trying to enjoy *Owen Wingrave*, but fail almost every time. Most of the characters are cardboard caricatures, and both libretto and score preach at the audience – a turn-off that precludes any emotional engagement in the scenario. It would be easy to blame this on the influence of television (which commissioned it), but I fear it goes deeper than that.

Owen is the youngest scion of the Wingrave family, steeped in military glory. The ancestral home, Paramore, is plastered with portraits of soldier-heroes of earlier generations. But Owen is kicking over the traces. After enrolling at a military cramming school run by Spencer Coyle, he suddenly rebels against the military career his family have charted for him. They promise to 'straighten him out' at Paramore, but after a week's wrangling fail to change his mind. His grandfather disinherits him. His girlfriend Kate calls him a coward, and challenges him to prove himself by sleeping in a room haunted by his ancestors. The experience kills him.

To be honest, Owen is a prig and a weakling, who talks the talk about standing up to his family, but then, at the first flick of their fingers, meekly goes home to be bullied. Kate Julian, a dependant of the family, lives there and is lined up to be his fiancée, which he has apparently accepted without demur. She never shows him any tenderness, and he simply laps up her venom. His aunt, Miss Wingrave, is an absurd figure, with horribly jagged musical lines (vicious sevenths and ninths), while his grandfather, Sir Philip, is no better.

No wonder Pears (who sang the role) pleaded with Britten at least to allow the old man two words of regret when Owen dies at the end.

The only characters of any complexity are Coyle and his wife, who belong to the military world, yet sympathise with Owen in dealing with his family. How much more interesting the opera would have been if Kate or Owen's aunt had shown some feminine subtlety and understanding. Instead there is no moral dilemma, no grit in the oyster – just grit.

When he decided to use this Henry James ghost story, Britten naturally turned to the librettist who had adapted James so successfully in *The Turn of the Screw*, Myfanwy Piper. But this facile libretto is a turkey – largely, one suspects, because of the interventions of the strongly pacifist composer with Points to Make. In the very first scene, Owen's friend Lechmere brandishes a sword and whoops: 'Ah! you beauty, how many vile foreign heads have you rolled into the dust? Chop! chop! chop!' Oh dear. It is at least an early warning of what's to come.

There are fortunately many redeeming moments in the music. Owen's arrival at Paramore is one (though why, in such a servant-heavy household, he expects his relatives to open the front door is a mystery). The ensemble's reaction to Owen's 'scruples' at dinner is a masterly bit of musical mockery. The smart device of a ballad-singer with trumpet and boys' choir to recount Wingrave family history reminds us of *Gloriana* nearly twenty years earlier, but is in fact lifted from his then unknown first opera *Paul Bunyan*. Owen's 'peace' monologue with the portraits has moments of transcendence like those of Billy Budd in the darbies. The use of bugle calls may be routine, and some of his percussion (woodblock for the clip-clop of horses, or xylophone for the click-click of antlers) would with justice have irritated Stravinsky. But it's a pity that Britten was in such a hurry to move on to *Death in Venice* that he made no concert suite from *Wingrave*. The prelude and short interludes could still be turned into an attractive orchestral piece, to draw people towards the opera as a whole, preferably without surtitles and in a language they don't understand – Serbo-Croat perhaps? Then the music might not shout so loud.

R Coleman-Wright, Opie, Leggate, Stephen, Watson, Fox, Connell, CLS/Hickox, recorded 2007
Chandos CHAN 10473 (2 CDs)

Death in Venice, op. 88 ****   1971–3; revised 1973–4

For years Britten's final opera suffered from being too tangled up with his own life – his love for its lead singer Peter Pears, his feelings for good-looking boys, his concerns about his own creative inspiration, his worries about his health. No wonder Pears at one point said, 'Ben is writing an evil opera, and it's killing him'.

Today's singers have moved out of Britten's and Pears's shadows, and given the work fresh momentum. Based on Thomas Mann's story (as was Visconti's feature film starring Dirk Bogarde), the opera describes the breakdown of an ageing, widowed writer, Gustav von Aschenbach: he has writer's block, and travels to Venice in search of inspiration. There he becomes infatuated with the beauty of a young boy on holiday with his family. When he discovers that Venice is undergoing an outbreak of cholera, he tries to leave, but fails. At first content to observe the youth with Apollonian detachment, he surrenders himself (egged on by a variety of tempters – all sung by the same bass-baritone) to a Dionysian passion, although he and the boy never properly meet. Humiliated by his own lack of self-control, Aschenbach finally succumbs to cholera.

As sung and acted by Philip Langridge, in particular, Aschenbach emerges as a straight man (not a pederast), who is at first almost amused by his reaction to the youth, Tadzio, and rationalises his feelings about beauty. As he becomes more besotted with him, the amusement turns to torment. This is a very different approach from the furtive lust that Pears portrayed, and serves the opera much better.

In much of the book, Aschenbach observes Tadzio from a distance. This is hard to manage on stage. Britten cast Tadzio as a dancer, not a singer, which entails a more developed physique for the boy than the story imagines. Some recent concert performances have suggested that the opera works better unstaged (or semi-staged), where the boy becomes a creature of Aschenbach's imagination rather than a physical presence.

It certainly works well on disc, where the full richness of this extraordinary score strikes home. The harp, one of his favourite instruments, produces pellucid textures. His beloved Venice is evoked with bells, gondoliers' cries and lapping waves in the canals. The baleful tuba represents the plague enveloping the city. It is indeed almost a symphonic poem for tenor and orchestra, with Aschenbach involved in all the work's multiple cinematic scenes. The oriental flavour of the gamelan is present once again, in Tadzio's music for xylophone and vibraphone – at once childlike and cloying, which gives a dangerous knowingness to 'the little Polish god' who notices when he's noticed. Several recent stage productions have surmounted the work's inherent problems and occasional longueurs, and it is now – in its fourth decade – winning acceptance as one of Britten's finest conceptions, rather than just an impressive piece of self-exculpation.

R   Langridge, Opie, Chance, BBC Singers, City of London Sinfonia/Hickox, recorded 2004
Chandos CHAN 10280 (2CDs)

Phaedra, op. 93 ***   1975

This must count as Britten's final work for the theatre, even though it was devised as a Handelian cantata for the concert platform: indeed it has recently been staged. Years before, Eric Crozier had suggested to him that the mythological story of Phaedra's incestuous love for her stepson Hippolytus was a ripe operatic subject, and advocated the French play *Phèdre* by Jean Racine. Britten was immediately keen, but tellingly said that, from his pen, the opera's title would have to be 'Hippolytus'. He had reckoned without Janet Baker.

After her performance of Berlioz songs at the 1975 Aldeburgh Festival, Britten set to work on the Phaedra story immediately, writing it straight into full score (by then he was too weak to go through his normal intermediate stages). The anguish of the wife of Theseus was the perfect vehicle for Baker's voice, and Britten devised a monodrama based on the loose translation of the Racine play by the American poet Robert Lowell. So *Phaedra* it was. In her three dialogues with stepson, servant, and husband, we seem to hear their reproaches, but all refracted through Phaedra's mind.

Britten intersperses these arias with two recitatives, accompanied (in homage to Handel) by a continuo of cello and harpsichord. The arias themselves and the interludes feature a string orchestra and an array of percussion, which Britten uses ingeniously to point up key moments in this psychodrama – whether the timpani at the opening, the redemptive tubular bell near the close, or the brushed cymbal which enriches the stately processional of almost grotesque majesty as Phaedra confesses her guilty secret. This work (with the Third String Quartet) demonstrated conclusively that Britten's creativity and originality were unimpaired by his debilitating heart surgery.

R   Baker, ECO/Bedford, recorded 1977
Decca 425 666-2 (2 CDs, with Baker/Britten recording of *The Rape of Lucretia*)

R   Hunt Lieberson, Hallé/Nagano, recorded 1995
Elatus 09274 90102 (with *The Rescue of Penelope*)

R   Connolly, BBCSO/Gardner, recorded 2010
Chandos CHAN 10671 (with *A Charm of Lullabies*, *Two Portraits*, *Lachrymae* etc.)

35

Incidental music

If there was one musical form that launched Britten's career before he ever tackled opera, it was not orchestral music, not choral music, not solo song – important though these all were to his identity. It was film music. He wrote scores for some thirty-two films in all. The most famous was *Instruments of the Orchestra*, which he turned into his celebrated concert piece *The Young Person's Guide to the Orchestra*. But a decade earlier he had been pitched without warning or preparation into the new GPO (General Post Office) Film Unit, where he had to write music to order for short documentaries, and on a shoe-string. He had to work fast, record his own sound effects (making his own *musique concrète*, in effect), and adjust his score in the cutting-room to fit the pictures and the commentary. He was ideally suited to the job, because he had a quick mind, and could hear the music so clearly in his head that he never needed a piano to compose.

Nearly all the film scores date from an eighteen-month period in 1935–6, but the skills he acquired stayed with him throughout his life. He went on to write incidental music for seventeen theatre productions and thirty-seven radio programmes. But even his operas *The Turn of the Screw* and *Death in Venice* are 'filmic' in their construction: indeed, when various production problems were pointed out to him after he saw *Death in Venice* for the first time (some four decades after his film apprenticeship), he worked out the necessary changes then and there – extending one scene, and re-ordering another – just as if he were sitting with W. H. Auden and John Grierson in a Soho cutting room, tweaking the score of *Night Mail* in 1936.

Rarely has necessity been a better mother of invention. Pressures of both budget and time put Britten's acute musical ear on its mettle. Ten years later, faced with post-war austerity, he drew on his film experience to devise a fresh sound-world for his chamber operas, in which, with just a few players, he conjured what is almost a symphonic illusion. It must count as one of the Post Office's most successful deliveries.

The King's Stamp	1935
Coal Face*	1935
The Way to the Sea*	1936
Night Mail*	1935–6
The Tocher** (also known as *Rossini Suite*)	1935
6d. Telegram	1935
Peace of Britain	1936
God's Chillun	1935

Despite the importance of this film music, it has remained largely unknown even among some of Britten's most fervent admirers. This is partly because it was never designed to stand on its own: it was married to particular images or words, and those have been hard or impossible to retrieve. The music was, in any case, only ever intended to be ephemeral, because films in those days came and then went: retrospective seasons had not been invented. So some of Britten's scores have simply vanished, despite his being by nature a hoarder. But part of what survives has now been issued complete on disc, so we can better understand the way he deepened his creative impulses. This is only an interim phase, however: we still lack the essential visual element. Next must come a DVD of the original films, with a freshly recorded soundtrack.

Immediately after his first film score (for flute, clarinet, piano duo and percussion), for a short documentary about the Silver Jubilee stamps for King George V, Britten was hired for *Coal Face*, a film about the mining industry. Nine years after the General Strike, this was still a hot political subject (the connection with the GPO was tenuous at best), and Britten responded with an inventive score for chorus, piano and percussion, plus some specially created sound effects (a technique he developed further in *Night Mail*). Some years earlier he had attended the British premiere of Mossolov's *Music of the Machines*: he found it interesting and 'fiendishly clever'. But, he asked, 'is it music?' Now Britten had a go of his own, though he never intended his for the concert hall or the stage. *Coal Face* also marks his first collaboration with Auden, who wrote some of the verse, including 'O lurcher-loving collier', a song of the miners' wives which Britten sets for female chorus and piano – a gleaming moment amid the subterranean gloom.

Cinema in the 1930s was a powerful democratising force, similar to that of the internet more recently, and Auden's contribution to these films was geared to 'people like you and me'. So *The Way to the Sea*, which had once been about a royal progress to Portsmouth, switched its focus to the hunger of the masses for the sea, the sun and the sand. This was built round a railway journey, which, after his pastiche Tudor music for wind band and percussion, brings out the best in Britten. But then he had a thing about trains. Earlier that year he had recorded the soundtrack of *Night Mail*, which celebrated the overnight postal train's journey from London to Scotland. This is the most revered of his film scores, and only partly because of the evocative, catchy tumble of words that Auden crafted for the end sequence, to encapsulate the universal experience of receiving a letter in the post. The first choice as composer was not Britten, but Walter Leigh, who fortunately was unavailable. Britten set to work on his twenty-second birthday, and the range of timbres he delivers with only ten players (wind trio, string quartet, trumpet, percussion and harp) is astonishing. It took him only four days to write: he devised many striking new percussion sounds, such as a recorded cymbal stroke played backwards at high speed to accompany a steam engine emerging from a tunnel.

During these eighteen months, Britten also scored *The Tocher* with titbits of Rossini (now separately issued as the *Rossini Suite*); a short piece with boys' speaking voices for a film about telegrams; and an even shorter orchestral number for the overtly anti-rearmament film *Peace of Britain*. He wrote a more extended score with the working title of 'Negroes'. Most of this was later issued as *God's Chillun*, an educational film about the slave trade and the economic development of the Caribbean. Britten worked West Indian tunes into his score, which, instead of spoken commentary, used sung recitative interspersed with chorus – perhaps a foretaste of *Billy Budd*. It was a completely new technique which, heard without the pictures, feels a touch laborious.

R Beale, Carewe, Auchincloss, Green, Birmingham Contemporary Music Group/Brabbins, recorded 2006 NMC NMCD 112: 'Britten on Film'

Love from a Stranger *   1936

William Walton was shabbily treated over his music for the film *The Battle of Britain*. Four weeks before the premiere, most of his score was dropped, and another composer drafted in to replace it. Walton was in his mid-sixties and a veteran of the cinema. Britten only ever wrote one feature film score, when he was just twenty-three; he vowed never to write another after much of it was cut or dropped – and he never did. (Welcome to the film world – but the odd thing is, he knew it well.) The manuscript was lost, but Colin Matthews has rescued the music by transcribing it from the original soundtrack (which is groggy at the best of times, and often obscured by dialogue), and by referring to Britten's rough sketches.

What emerges is a vibrant suite of six movements (ideal, in fact, for a short ballet). They cover the opening and closing titles, traffic music, love music, a scene in Brighton and a Channel crossing – each sharply characterised with full orchestra (though no horns). Particularly striking is his use of alto saxophone (which he had first used orchestrally in *Our Hunting Fathers* a few months earlier). Two good things emerged from this murder mystery based on an Agatha Christie story, known in the USA as *A Night of Terror*. Its musical director, Boyd Neel, was so impressed by Britten's speed and facility that he commissioned the Frank Bridge Variations from him the following year – which became the foundation-stone of his international reputation. And the other? A fat cheque for £200.

R   BBC Symphony Orchestra/van Steen, recorded 1999 NMC NMCD073: 'Four British Film Scores' (Britten, Gerhard, Lutyens, Bennett)

King Arthur *   1937
The Sword in the Stone   1939

Incidental music in broadcasting today is all too often synthesised, with live instruments quite a rarity. For his 1937 BBC commission (the first of twenty-eight for radio), Britten could call on a full symphony orchestra (the LSO), complete with E flat clarinet, contrabassoon and three trombones, not to mention the professional BBC Chorus. This was for a dramatisation of Arthur's life and times directed by Val Gielgud: with Britten's thirty numbers, it is a substantial score. Most of it was worked into a four-movement suite by Paul Hindmarsh in 1995 – the first hearing since 1937 for music which, according to Britten, 'certainly comes off like hell'. He was right. The 'Wedding March' grimly foretastes the *Sinfonia da Requiem* of three years later, the 'Wild Dance' is driven with demonic energy, while the 'Death Music' floats eerily in suspended animation – perhaps uneasily capturing Britten's own state of mind at the time, six weeks after the loss of his beloved mother. Apart from the second movement, the suite often fails to hang together, and there are one or two heraldic fanfares too many. But the score's individual moments of excitement are well worth exploring: Britten was fond enough of it, after all, to pinch bits for his Piano Concerto and his *Ballad of Heroes*.

Camelot held the prospect of being a money-spinner for Britten a year or two later, when he nearly landed the score for a Hollywood film about King Arthur. The project foundered, but not before he'd returned to the subject for another radio programme, this time a six-part BBC serial of *The Sword in the Stone*, T. H. White's novel about Arthur's boyhood. It was the first music Britten wrote after crossing to North America in spring 1939, where he dashed off some fifteen cues, with echoes of his own boyhood heroes Wagner and Beethoven, as well as Donald Duck at one point! These have been condensed by Colin Matthews and Oliver Knussen into a short concert suite which, like so much of this incidental music, is now limited to curiosity value.

R   *The Sword in the Stone* (suite): Nash Ensemble/Friend, recorded 1995
Hyperion CDA 66845 (with *Phaedra*, *Sinfonietta* etc.)

On the Frontier   1938
The Ascent of F6   1937

Auden and Isherwood wrote a three-act melodrama *On the Frontier* for the Arts Theatre in Cambridge, and dedicated it to Britten, who provided incidental music from two trumpets, an accordion, various drums, a cymbal and a gong – plus a seven-part choir and himself on the piano (with Wulff Scherchen turning the pages). Peter Pears took several solo roles. This followed on from the first Auden–Isherwood–Britten collaboration in February the previous year, *The Ascent of F6*. That substantial score was for eight percussion instruments, ukulele and two pianos, with three solo singers and small mixed chorus. Britten wrote it with iron self-discipline while he was reeling from the sudden death of his mother at the end of January. The primitive television service on the BBC broadcast the play in 1938, a month after it had carried the premiere of his Piano Concerto with sound only. It still treated Britten gingerly: this time it carried just three of his music cues.

An American in England	1942
Britain to America	1942
The Rescue of Penelope **	1943
Men of Goodwill	1947

Britten came home from the USA in 1942 with a cheque for a thousand dollars in his pocket to write *Peter Grimes*. But he still needed some bread-and-butter work to help finance the three years he was to spend planning and writing the opera. Two propaganda series on the BBC, designed to cement the transatlantic wartime alliance, fitted the bill, and also strengthened his claim for exemption from military service. But, of his sixteen wartime commissions from the BBC, the most substantial and worthwhile was the incidental music for Edward Sackville-West's drama about the return home of Odysseus from the Trojan War, *The Rescue*.

Scored for narrator, four singers and full orchestra, it has now been adapted into a half-hour concert suite, entitled *The Rescue of Penelope*. Those who complain that Britten short-changed us with orchestral music should add this largely instrumental piece to the scales. It is vividly coloured, as in his unorthodox choice of the alto saxophone for the heroine Penelope. In Britten's hands the instrument sounds aching rather than sinister, while his high-pitched trumpet in D ensures the dominance of the goddess Athene. There are foretastes here of *Grimes*, of *A Midsummer Night's Dream*, even of the footfalls in *The Prodigal Son*. But some of his orchestral effects – such as Odysseus' slaughter of the suitors with twelve arrows from his bow – are unique to this score, which has a sustained complexity uncommon in incidental music.

Britten had a lifelong love of a traditional Christmas – indeed one work he was contemplating just before his death was a Christmas opera for children. His last incidental music for the BBC was for an international sequence of festive messages, *Men of Goodwill*, consisting of orchestral variations on 'God rest ye merry, gentlemen'.

R   *The Rescue of Penelope*: Baker, Hagley, Ainsley, Hallé/
Nagano, recorded 1995
Elatus 09274 90102 (with *Phaedra*)

Stratton	1949
This Way to the Tomb	1944–5
The Dark Tower	1945
Johnson over Jordan	1939

The last incidental music Britten wrote was for a Ronald
Duncan play, *Stratton*. Although he had in effect dropped
him as an opera librettist after *The Rape of Lucretia* in 1946,
Britten remained in touch with him through his son Roger.
The score for the *Stratton* music has long been lost, but the
original discs (recorded under Britten's own baton for the
production in Brighton) recently turned up – a fascinating
archaeological find. The sixteen minutes of music have an
almost relentlessly grim tread, to match the dark nature of
the play. It is dominated by a persistent dotted figure, with
the ominous rhythms reinforced by timpani, side drum, and
pizzicato cello and double bass. Only one cue suggests any
shafts of sunlight – a faster, lighter mood akin to his music
for *The Way to the Sea*.

He had earlier written music for Duncan's masque *This
Way to the Tomb* for four solo singers, small chorus, percussion and piano duet. This consists mainly of an anthem, *Deus
in adjutorium meum* (see chapter 30, 'Church music'), three
songs (see chapter 33, 'Songs') and a boogie-woogie number,
which has now been arranged for cabaret ensemble. For
Louis MacNeice's radio play *The Dark Tower*, Britten used a
trumpet, strings and percussion, but for J. B. Priestley's play
Johnson over Jordan he had a much larger theatre orchestra
available. Some ideas he reused in his piano work for the left
hand, *Diversions*. There have been several new productions
of the play on BBC Radio, but using only a small part of
Britten's original score.

R   *Stratton*: EOG Orchestra/Britten, recorded 1949
Pearl GEMS 0231 (with 1946 broadcast of *The Rape of
Lucretia*, featuring Kathleen Ferrier)

Round Britten Quiz VI

ANSWERS ON PAGE 411

1 When Britten first lived in London, where did he usually
   get his hair cut?
2 Which opera was sometimes unkindly referred to as 'The
   Stern of the Crew'?
3 How much money did Britten's father, a dentist, leave in
   his will?
4 What was the fourth recreation Britten listed in his 1975
   Who's Who entry, after 'tennis, swimming, walking'?
5 What was the telephone number of the Britten family at
   12 Kirkley Cliff Road?
6 What was Prince Philip heard to say at a concert when
   Britten's *Serenade* was being performed, and the horn soloist left the platform to play the final movement offstage?

36

Folksongs

Much to the irritation of some folksong purists, Britten rein-
vented the concept of arranging traditional songs. Instead of
simple accompaniment bound to the vocal line, Britten paint-
ed pictures and wove textures on the piano (and later on the
guitar and harp), which illustrated the mood and meaning of
each song, in language of his own.

He began his tampering in 1940, during his self-imposed
exile in the United States. Perhaps it was the first symptom
of the homesickness that developed a year or so later with his
discovery of the East Anglian poetry of George Crabbe. In
essence he preserved the tune as an unaccompanied melody,
with a commentary (usually on the piano) that amplified the
tune, but did not overcome it. This comfortably satisfied the
demand Vaughan Williams made of any folksong arranger:
'Do these settings spring from a love of the tune?' As a cham-
pion of the great folksong revival at the turn of the twentieth
century, he welcomed these arrangements by 'a fiery young
steed', as he called Britten.

Britten arranged more than sixty folksongs in all, most of
them grouped in seven separate collections. I have singled out
my favourites in groups below. Pears and Britten recorded
some twenty-five of them, and singers today often use them
as encores in song recitals, as well as recording individual
numbers. But the excellent omnibus recordings on Naxos
(including the orchestral versions) are well worth seeking out.

R 'Folk Song Arrangements', vols 1–6, with unpublished
songs: Lott, Langridge, Bonell, Johnson, recorded 1995
Naxos 8.557220-21 (2 CDs)

R 'Folk Song Arrangements 2', for voice and harp; orchestral
arrangements, and miscellaneous folksongs: Langridge,

Allen, Ellis, Northern Sinfonia/Bedford, recorded 1995
Naxos 8.557222

'The Salley Gardens'	by 1940
'Little Sir William'	by 1940
'The Ash Grove'	by 1941
'The Bonny Earl o' Moray'	by 1940
'O can ye sew cushions?'	by 1942
'I wonder as I wander' – Niles	1940–1?
'The trees they grow so high'	by 1942
'Dink's Song'	?
'The Crocodile'	by 1941
'Oliver Cromwell'	by 1940

The bitter-sweet character of English folksongs is captured nowhere better than in one of the first of Britten's arrangements, 'The Salley Gardens'. He chooses the melting key of G flat major for this pentatonic tune, which means that the melody lies entirely on the piano's black notes, apart from one F natural in each verse – which is in contrast to the yearning flattened seventh (F flat) and sixth (E double flat) in the piano's opening bars. This 'flat' sonority is Britten's inspired method of making the music itself 'full of tears': the more conventional choice of G major would have been far too cheerful.

Each of these songs has its own special magic. 'Little Sir William' begins blithely enough with the schoolboys fooling around on the green, but the mood darkens as a mother finds the body of her missing son, stabbed with a penknife. His assailant, in the traditional words from Somerset, was 'the Jew's wife', but Britten altered this after publication to 'the School wife', which is the wording used in reprints of the vocal score. The melody never changes, but Britten's piano part moves deftly from playfulness to poignancy.

'The Ash Grove' has the simplest canonic accompaniment, mostly in tenths, with a lovely touch of birdsong as 'warbles the blackbird his note from the tree'. Two Scottish folksongs, 'The Bonny Earl o' Moray' and 'O can ye sew cushions?', contain the seeds of his Burns cycle *A Birthday Hansel* more than thirty years later. The familiar 'I wonder as I wander' is unaccompanied, apart from five interludes on the piano, and 'The trees they grow so high' starts the same way, but, as the sad story unfolds of a boy and girl marrying too young, the piano builds a haunting commentary. The gentle love song, 'Dink's Song', comes from a collection of American ballads Britten picked up in the USA, but it's unclear whether he arranged it then or later.

The two fast songs in this collection were ideal for Britten and Pears to round off a recital. 'The Crocodile' is a long ballad which Britten sets in four different keys – a fantastic song; while 'Oliver Cromwell' by contrast is a nursery rhyme which he rattles through in forty seconds – guaranteed to bring the house down. Along with four other songs in the group, Britten later arranged it for orchestral accompaniment.

'*La Noël passée*'	1942
'*Voici le printemps*'	1942
'*Fileuse*'	1942
'*Le roi s'en va-t'en chasse*'	1942
'*La belle est au jardin d'amour*'	1942
'*Il est quelqu'un sur terre*'	1942
'*Eho! Eho!*'	1942
'*Quand j'étais chez mon père*'	1942

These eight French folk-songs were published as a collection – a present for the Swiss soprano Sophie Wyss, who was the first interpreter of Britten's vocal music before the war. By the time he returned from the United States earlier in 1942, he had chosen to work with his partner Peter Pears instead. So these charming songs were a kind of 'thank you and goodbye'. She gave the first complete performance at a wartime recital with Gerald Moore at the National Gallery, but shortly afterwards did record five of them with Britten accompanying. Again, most of them have been orchestrated.

'The Plough Boy' – Shield	by 1943
'The Foggy, Foggy Dew'	by 1942
'Sweet Polly Oliver'	by 1945
'The Miller of Dee'	by 1946
'O Waly, Waly'	by 1946
'Come you not from Newcastle?'	by 1946
'Pray Goody'	1945–6?
'The Stream in the Valley'	1946

The third set of folksongs (four of them also arranged with orchestra) contains the two best-known of Britten's arrangements. 'The Plough Boy' is not a folksong at all, but was composed by William Shield in 1787. The ambitions of the merry-ploughboy-turned-saucy-footman belong to the pen of an eighteenth-century W. S. Gilbert, with cynical comments on the great and good of both Commons and Lords. Britten summons up the whistling ploughboy on the piano, by reproducing Shield's piccolo in the piano right hand – one of those Jack-the-lad characters of whom he was so fond.

'The Foggy, Foggy Dew' is a gloriously ingenuous setting of ingenuous words, which tell a Suffolk weaver's story about his long pursuit of a 'fair young maid', who managed to inveigle herself into his bed, had his child and then apparently disappeared, leaving him a single parent. The teasing piano part is a perfect match for the insouciance of the words. It has rightly become famous – but not without upsetting the spluttering classes. Peter Pears's uncle caught a broadcast of the song, and immediately wrote to him:

> I heard last night a recorded song of yours which made me
> distinctly sorry. You will probably know which one I mean
> without my describing it in detail. I cannot help writing
> to ask whether on serious consideration you do not agree
> with me that it would be much better stopped if possible,
> by destroying the record or otherwise. Now that the
> record is bound to reach hundreds or thousands of places
> where it will be heard by innocent and susceptible boys

and girls, there can hardly be two opinions but that it must do immense harm.

Britten was outraged. 'Dirty old man!', he said.

The uncle's blushes were not spared either with 'Sweet Polly Oliver', and its tale of cross-dressing and love, told with Britten's delight in canon. The Scrooge-like figure of 'The Miller of Dee' (in which Britten cleverly conjures up the mill mechanism) might have been more to his taste, or the high-minded love touchingly created in 'O Waly, Waly': here once again Britten contrives to write an unaccompanied song with piano. The high jinks of 'Pray Goody' (unpublished in Britten's lifetime) make a good encore.

One of the rarest delights here is 'The Stream in the Valley', a setting of a German folksong with piano and cello accompaniment, which Britten seems to have written specially for a radio recital he and Pears were giving with the French cellist, Maurice Gendron, in November 1946. Britten could perhaps have tossed it off as just a device to bring the three of them together at the end of the recital. But, although it sounds simple, it is clearly the fruit of the utmost care and resource, and the result is bewitching. It was never published (and perhaps never performed again) in Britten's lifetime, but certainly holds another key ☞ to understanding him.

'Sally in our Alley' – Carey	by 1959
'The Brisk Young Widow'	by 1954
'Soldier, won't you marry me?'	1952
'The Deaf Woman's Courtship'	1952
'Ca' the yowes'	by 1951
'The Lincolnshire Poacher'	by 1959
'Early One Morning'	by 1957
'Tom Bowling' – Dibdin	by 1959

It's often hard to be precise about when Britten made his folksong arrangements, because so many first appeared as encore items, and were therefore not listed on any printed recital programme. Furthermore, some of the early versions of the manuscripts show that Pears would write out the tune and the words, and Britten would sketch in a few thoughts for the accompaniment, which he probably elaborated in performance, with some further improvisation on the day. For instance, his enchanting setting of Henry Carey's eighteenth-century song 'Sally in our Alley' has an unrecognised, and unrecorded, precursor: in the Britten archives, there is a much earlier pencil sketch – with sparse and quite different piano accompaniment – which shows that he and Pears included it in a recital in New York on 12 November 1940. The fact that the manuscript is worn suggests they did so several times thereafter, but this gets no mention in any of the Britten literature.

'The Brisk Young Widow' is a song of terrific vitality, while the duets 'Soldier, won't you marry me?' and 'The Deaf Woman's Courtship' delight with their teasing wit. Britten remembered how, as an encore on their fundraising recital tour of 1952, Kathleen Ferrier used to sing the part of the Deaf Woman in 'a feeble, cracked voice, the perfect reply to Peter [Pears]'s magisterial roar. A masterpiece of humour, which had the audience rocking, but never broke the style of the rest of the concert.'

The brilliance of 'The Lincolnshire Poacher' owes much to Britten's artfulness in keeping the piano in the tonic key the whole way through, whatever happens in the melody. But there are moments of touching sensitivity too – as in the spell Britten casts at the opening of 'Early One Morning' or the simple way he honours Charles Dibdin's original melody, harmonies and words for 'Tom Bowling' (more famously preserved by the cello solo in Henry Wood's *Fantasia on British Sea Songs*). Its maritime lament for the doppelgänger of Billy Budd ('his form was of the manliest beauty, his heart was kind and soft') no doubt appealed to Britten in equal measure with the music, for this must surely be the finest song in the English language.

'The Last Rose of Summer'	1957
The Minstrel Boy'	1957
'O the sight entrancing'	1957
'I will give my love an apple'	1956

Britten also published ten folksongs from Ireland, but these are seldom heard now, and no wonder. Most of them sound routine, and lack interest as they ramble on, slow and purposeless. He does no favours, for instance, to the wonderful tune for 'The Last Rose of Summer'. You can't win all the time. But the next two listed songs do recapture some of the spirit of the earlier sets. The fourth is from a separate group for voice and guitar: it has simple appeal, unlike its companions, which often seem to lose their rhythmic drive.

| 'King Herod and the Cock' | 1962 |
| 'The Twelve Apostles' | 1962 |

Two settings for unison boys' choir and piano were written for the London Boy Singers to perform at the 1962 Aldeburgh Festival, when it became clear that the projected work *The Bitter Withy* was too difficult for them (see chapter 29, 'Choral music'). A tenor soloist joins them for 'The Twelve Apostles' (which is a variant of 'Green grow the rushes, oh!'). This is one of those songs that is perhaps more fun to sing than to listen to, though Britten does his best to hold our attention with the opening piano flourishes: each of the twelve verses begins on a different note of the twelve-note chromatic scale.

'Lord! I married me a wife'   1976
'She's like the swallow'   1976
'Bonny at Morn'   1976
'Lemady'   1976
'Bugeilio'r Gwenith Gwyn'   1976
'Dafydd y Garreg Wen' – Owen   1976
'The False Knight upon the Road'   1976
'Bird Scarer's Song'   1976

These eight folksongs were among the last things Britten did. He wrote them for voice and harp, so that Pears could use them (as encores) in his recitals with the Welsh harpist Osian Ellis. They recapture some of the spirit of his earlier settings for voice and piano. The two lilting Welsh songs, written presumably to honour Ellis, mark the seventh foreign language in Britten's vocal tally (after Latin, French, Italian, German, Russian and Scots – the eighth if you include Old English!). The exasperation in the first song, about a wife 'who gave me trouble all my life', is bound to amuse the audience, the ballad about the false knight is engaging despite its length, and 'Bird Scarer's Song' is simply wacky. 'Bonny at Morn' had been arranged differently nearly twenty years earlier for voice and guitar.

37
What might have been

Every composer has a quiverful of arrows that never found their mark. Some works get started, but run out of creative steam. Some are toyed with out of duty or loyalty to people or places, but the composer's heart isn't in them. Some are overtaken by events. Others never get beyond the drawing-board.

In Britten's case there are plenty of references in his voluminous correspondence to works that he intended to write, but never did. Some reached the sketching stage (and have since been completed or edited), others are known of only as a name. Even with a composer who was so prolific across such a relatively short working life, it is intriguing to ponder the pieces he never wrote . . .

Symphonies and concertos

The Bewitched Violin

Boosey & Hawkes prematurely announced a symphonic poem under this title (based on a folk story) in 1941. A performance was advertised for March by the NBC Symphony Orchestra, conducted by George Szell, but the work never developed beyond some extensive sketches.

Cello Concerto

Britten said in a newspaper interview in March 1941 that he was writing a concerto for Emanuel Feuermann, who had premiered Schoenberg's Cello Concerto. No sketches survive.

Clarinet Concerto

Britten began this work, intended for the jazz clarinettist
Benny Goodman, shortly before his return to England in
1942. The surviving sketch has been performed, and other
material added to make *Movements for a Clarinet Concerto* (see
chapter 27, 'Symphonies and concertos').

Harp Concerto

An American harpist requested a concerto just before Britten
left the USA for England in 1942. A contract was signed with
fee and deadlines specified, but no sketches survive.

Saxophone Concerto

As well as the cello concerto he spoke of in a 1941 interview in
New York, Britten said a work for saxophone was in progress.
It was intended for the German-American saxophonist Sigurd
Rascher, whom Britten had got to know in America after first
encountering him in Tuscany in 1934 in the company of
Wulff Scherchen. No sketches of the concerto are extant.

Concerto for String Quartet and Orchestra

This was first planned in 1948 for his favourite quartet, the
Amadeus. He mentioned it to Norman Del Mar, his assist-
ant conductor in the English Opera Group, who reminded
Britten of the idea eight years later. But it was never written.
He would perhaps have had in mind Elgar's *Introduction and
Allegro*, which he admired for its sonorities in contrasting and
combining the string quartet with the full string orchestra.

Organ Concerto

A concerto was planned for the organist Ralph Downes at the
inauguration of the Royal Festival Hall organ in 1954. Britten
developed bursitis in his right shoulder, which impeded his
work, and the project was never revived.

Other orchestral works

Sonata [or Partita] for Orchestra

This was planned as a four-movement piece in 1942–3, and Britten contemplated it as a new work for the 1944 Proms season. An orchestral sketch for the *Sonata* has recently been turned by Colin Matthews into one of the *Movements for a Clarinet Concerto*.

Choral music

For the Time Being

This large Christmas oratorio had words by Auden. He and Britten first started talking about it in 1942, but Britten never quite got round to the music. It was probably symbolic of their failing friendship.

Mea Culpa

Britten contemplated an oratorio in response to the H-bombing of Hiroshima and Nagasaki, and discussed it extensively with the BBC in early 1946. The text was drafted by Ronald Duncan, who had suggested the idea: according to him it came to nothing because of contractual difficulties.

Sea Symphony

After his heart operation, Britten began making notes for a companion piece for his *Spring Symphony*, based on English poems about the sea. He mapped them out in an old school exercise book. He'd had Vaughan Williams's *Sea Symphony* performed at the Aldeburgh Festival in 1972, perhaps to check up, as he did with Strauss, 'how the old fox worked his tricks'.

Church music

Life of Christ

Following the success of *Saint Nicolas*, Britten thought of tackling the lives of other saints. But then he decided on a Life of Christ. In summer 1953 his plan was that he and Pears would prepare a libretto from the non-canonical gospels. He wanted to concentrate on the humanity of Christ. (In the same way, Elgar had himself scoured the Bible to create the librettos for his oratorios *The Apostles* and *The Kingdom* – and his interest was in the ordinariness of Christ's disciples.)

St Peter

An oratorio intended for York Minster was first discussed in February 1955 with Ronald Duncan. Musical synopses and a draft libretto were written, with the interspersion of hymns for the congregation, and Britten was highly enthusiastic. Finally, two years later, he cried off, saying he wasn't in the right frame of mind, but was sure it would happen one day. It never did. But Duncan's libretto was still in his desk when he died.

Mass

Britten wrote one proper Mass, the *Missa Brevis* for boys' voices and organ. He intended to write a bigger setting for chorus and orchestra for the Leeds Festival, and there were extensive discussions about it in 1957. But he wrote the *Nocturne* instead, and some of the Mass was subsumed into the *War Requiem* for Coventry Cathedral.

Chamber music

Piano Quintet

He suggested this to Elizabeth Sprague Coolidge, the American musical patron, as a successor to his first String Quartet.

He envisaged himself playing the piano part – but the piece never went further.

Vocal work for Dieskau Consort

In the early 1960s Britten planned a piece for Fischer-Dieskau's baritone, with a cello part for his first wife Irmgard Poppen. After her death in childbirth in 1963, Britten dropped the idea.

Instrumental music

Piano work

This was promised to Sviatoslav Richter but not written.

Songs

Work for three voices and string orchestra

It was intended in 1938–9 for Sophie Wyss and her two sisters (two sopranos and an alto) to sing with string orchestra and percussion.

Stage works

Ballet on a Basque theme

After completing *Plymouth Town*, Britten worked on a second ballet scenario provided by Violet Alford, associate of Cecil Sharp and a collector of folk dances. But he never finished it.

The Canterbury Tales

In 1944 Britten discussed with Ronald Duncan the idea of a Chaucer opera, and reckoned on starting it with 'The Nun's Tale'. When Glyndebourne asked for a chamber opera, Britten realised this wouldn't work.

Abelard and Heloise

After composing *The Rape of Lucretia*, Britten discussed with
Duncan an opera based on the famous twelfth-century story
of doomed love. But it hit the buffers when Glyndebourne
said they wanted a comedy. Two years later Eric Crozier started to draft the text for a concert piece on the same subject,
with the two lovers played by Peter Pears and Nancy Evans.

Letters to William

This opera, based on Jane Austen's *Mansfield Park*, was
designed to feature Kathleen Ferrier and Joan Cross, who
suggested the idea to Britten. Ronald Duncan began work on
a libretto after the staging of *Lucretia* in 1946. But he was then
dumbfounded to discover by chance that Britten was already
working with Crozier on *Albert Herring*, and indeed Britten
never did use Duncan as a librettist again.

Civil War

Britten contemplated a grand opera for the 1949 season at
Covent Garden, about a family with split loyalties during the
English Civil War. He wanted a big role for Joan Cross as the
matriarch of the family, prompted by seeing Bertolt Brecht's
Mother Courage.

The Tale of Mr Tod

A children's opera based on the darkest Beatrix Potter tale
was under discussion with the librettist William Plomer in
1951-2, but foundered on copyright issues.

Tyco the Vegan

Britten discussed a science-fiction opera about space travel
with the librettist William Plomer in 1952. He envisaged it as
a children's opera with audience participation, as in *The Little
Sweep*. It was displaced by the commission to write *Gloriana*
for the Coronation.

Greek mythology opera

Once *Gloriana* was finished, Britten resumed discussions with William Plomer about a children's opera. He was keen to take a cautionary tale from Greek mythology and bring it up to date. He was most taken with the myths of Phaeton and Icarus.

Nonsense of Edward Lear

Yet another children's operatic idea, based around the non-sense verse of Edward Lear, was discussed in 1955.

King Lear

Britten first read the Shakespeare play in 1943, and annotated his copy. He seriously contemplated adapting it into an opera in the 1960s, with Dietrich Fischer-Dieskau in the title role, and Pears as the Fool.

Anna Karenina

Britten commissioned a draft libretto in 1965 from the pro-ducer Colin Graham, based on Tolstoy's original. Britten said he couldn't think of anything more important than 'finding another medium (the operatic) for this wonderful story'. He wanted the Russian soprano Galina Vishnevskaya to sing the part of Anna and her husband Rostropovich to conduct it, with Pears as Anna's cold-hearted husband, Karenin. He was hoping for a commission from the Bolshoi Opera, but this was kiboshed by the Soviet invasion of Czechoslovakia in 1968. Plans to do it on a smaller scale at Aldeburgh leaked out in the press, which put Britten right off his stride.

David Copperfield

Britten asked the novelist Angus Wilson to write a libretto based on the Steerforth/Little Emily/Lowestoft plot of *David Copperfield*.

Ballet on an aboriginal theme

This was discussed during his tour of Australia in 1970 as a collaboration with the painter Sidney Nolan.

Christmas opera

He promised this for Pimlico comprehensive school, where his friend Kathleen Mitchell (wife of his publisher Donald) was headmistress. He mapped out the scenario in some old notebooks in 1974–5, based on a Chester miracle play. He retained a child's love of Christmas all his life, so he would probably have completed this if his health had allowed.

Incidental music

The Tempest

From 1950 on, the actor John Gielgud repeatedly tried to persuade Britten to write music for *The Tempest*, either as an opera or as incidental music. Britten apparently agreed to the idea of a film, shot on Bali, with gamelan music for Ariel: this was in 1961, after Gielgud had produced his *A Midsummer Night's Dream* at Covent Garden.

Akenfield

The director Peter Hall says he won Britten's agreement in 1972 to write a score for a film of Ronald Blythe's book *Akenfield*. It was to be an all-Suffolk venture, with author, composer and director all hailing from there. It would also have been Britten's first film score since *Love from a Stranger* in 1936. But Britten must have known by then that his worsening health would preclude anything happening for quite a while. Indeed Hall went ahead with the film in 1974 and used Tippett's Corelli Fantasia instead.

Even for a composer who never threw anything away, there are works we know about, but have simply got lost. Bach's manuscripts were supposed to have vanished because they'd been used as butter-papers, but Britten's scores never suffered to that extent. All the same, chunks of his incidental music have disappeared, doubtless because of the hurried manner of their composition and the ephemeral nature of the work. Five of his GPO film scores have gone this way (along with the films presumably), and so have three BBC radio scores: *The Chartists' March* for male-voice choir and percussion; *The Four Freedoms*, a score for two flutes, piccolo and viola, to accompany words by Louis MacNeice; and *Hadrian's Wall*, an Auden feature, for male-voice choir, percussion and string quartet. Several scores for the theatre await rediscovery: *The Duchess of Malfi* (Webster/Auden), *Easter 1916* and *Spain* (both by Montagu Slater). One day Britten's orchestration of pieces by Chopin for a new ballet of *Les Sylphides* may turn up. So may his music to accompany Hardy's poem *The Dynasts*, two cabaret songs for Hedli Anderson, *Give up love* and *I'm a jam tart*, and a Stephen Spender song *Not to you I sighed: no, not a word*.

The search continues.

Round Britten Quiz answers

ANSWERS TO QUIZ I

1 May 1937, for dangerous driving. (He was acquitted.)
2 Malaysia. His work on the United Kingdom national anthem was an arrangement.
3 Football (he played right half in the South Lodge XI).
4 Six.
5 He played the celesta in Louis Durey's *Images à Crusoe* at the Wigmore Hall in 1942.
6 The family spaniel (otherwise spelt Caesar).

ANSWERS TO QUIZ II

1 Reykjavik.
2 August 1938, playing his Piano Concerto (which was being premiered at the Proms): the live TV relay carried sound only.
3 Two: *Six Little Piano Pieces*, op. 19, in July 1934, and the ballad *Jane Grey* at the 1957 Aldeburgh Festival.
4 A performance of *The Sea* by Frank Bridge.
5 Fresh herrings.
6 Their housekeeper, Miss Hudson.

ANSWERS TO QUIZ III

1 *The Little Sweep.*
2 Catch a cricket ball.
3 Third Cello Suite.
4 Vaughan Williams.
5 The train service provided by the rail company LNER.
6 *El amor brujo* by Falla.

ANSWERS TO QUIZ IV

1 Sherry trifle, always covered with hundreds-and-thousands.
2 *Paul Bunyan* and *Owen Wingrave*.
3 *Treasure Island* by Robert Louis Stevenson.
4 The photocopies of the orchestral score arrived late, and he couldn't read them.
5 Brahms.
6 A sailor suit.

ANSWERS TO QUIZ V

1 Three: counter-tenor (*Death in Venice*), piano and strings (*Young Apollo*), bass (*The Rescue*).
2 Copland.
3 Johnnie the parrot.
4 The whip.
5 The incidental music to the Auden–Isherwood play *The Ascent of F6*.
6 Attend church.

ANSWERS TO QUIZ VI

1 Whiteley's.
2 *Billy Budd*.
3 £15,000 (around £750,000 in today's money).
4 Bird-watching.
5 Lowestoft 112.
6 'Well, *he's* obviously had enough, then!'

Acknowledgements

Enjoyable as it has been to rummage through the nooks and crannies of Britten's life and music, it was also daunting to follow the footsteps of Nicholas Kenyon's Mozart, Richard Wigmore's Haydn, Edward Blakeman's Handel, and Michael Tanner's Wagner in Faber's series of Pocket Guides. Edith Britten would be proud, but not surprised, that her son comes so hard on their heels (though perhaps not as hard as my ever-patient publishers would have liked). In commissioning this Guide for Faber and Faber with her infectious enthusiasm, Belinda Matthews encouraged me both to follow the route they had set and to go off piste as necessary for the first twentieth century composer in the series. The result is a somewhat irregular format, with typographical and stylistic challenges which my project editor, Kate Ward, has tackled with remarkable initiative and composure. I also thank my copyeditor Michael Downes and the eagle eyes of Donald Sommerville at proof stage.

A miscellany such as this draws heavily on the labour and scholarship of the biographers, musicians and commentators who have trodden the path before me, and who are acknowledged in chapter 8. But I am particularly grateful to those who have given advice on the manuscript, Colin Matthews and Paul Kildea, as well as Anne Surfling and Pam Wheeler, whose uncommonly sciurine memories at the Britten-Pears Library are a rich resource. Its Librarian, Nicholas Clark, and Philip Reed have also been good enough to answer particularly recondite questions. Many of their combined insights are reflected here, but all errors, omissions or misjudgments must be laid at my door. Research by Julian Spencer of the Rolls-Royce Enthusiasts' Club has also shed valuable light on Britten's penchant for luxury transport.

The Trustees of the Britten-Pears Foundation have kindly allowed me to quote extensively from the letters, diaries and other documents of Benjamin Britten and Peter Pears in Aldeburgh. Her Majesty The Queen has graciously agreed to the publication of extracts from the correspondence of the late Queen Elizabeth The Queen Mother. I am also indebted to those who administer the Estates of the following for permission to reproduce copyright material: W. H. Auden, Sir Lennox Berkeley, Eric Crozier, Ronald Duncan, E. M. Forster,* Sir John Gielgud,† Imogen Holst, John Ireland, Christopher Isherwood, Hans Keller, Elisabeth Lutyens and Beth Welford. I am grateful to Alan Garner for letting me use an unpublished letter to Britten, and to the relevant publishers and producers for agreeing to the repetition of *aperçus* by the following: Theodor Adorno, Dame Janet Baker, Beverley Baxter, Leonard Bernstein, John Drummond, Osian Ellis, Dietrich Fischer-Dieskau, Joyce Grenfell, Sir Peter Hall, Robin Holloway, Anita Lasker-Wallfisch, Gerald Moore, Mstislav Rostropovich, Peter Shaffer, Dame Edith Sitwell, Igor Stravinsky, Galina Vishnevskaya and Lady Walton. In some cases it has not proved possible to trace the appropriate people for permission but, if they make themselves known, future editions of this book can be amended accordingly. I apologise in advance for any inadvertent omissions.

My family and my day-job colleagues have been long-suffering as this book, like all the best stories, has grown in the telling, and I thank them for their forbearance. I should also mention two trusty foot-soldiers who between them have marched every step of the journey. Towards the end I reluctantly demobilised my veteran Sony VAIO laptop, because its exhausted characters (in Haydnesque fashion) were literally leaving the keyboard one by one. But Pippin, my young Apple Macbook Pro, was quick to earn his spurs, managing effortlessly to retrieve snippets of information I thought I had safely stored, if only I knew where.

John Bridcut
Liss, August 2010

* The Society of Authors as agent for the Provost and Scholars of King's College, Cambridge
† The Sir John Gielgud Charitable Trust

General Index

Index of Britten's Music